SHADOW LINES

SHADOW LINES

Austrian Literature from Freud to Kafka

Lorna Martens

UNIVERSITY OF NEBRASKA PRESS   Lincoln and London

Publication of this book was assisted by a grant
from The Andrew W. Mellon Foundation.

Acknowledgments for previously published material
appear on pages ix–x.

Library of Congress Cataloging-in-Publication Data

Martens, Lorna, 1946–
    Shadow lines : Austrian literature from Freud to Kafka /
Lorna Martens.
        p.   cm.
    Includes bibliographical references and index.
    ISBN 0-8032-3186-5 (alk. paper)
        1. Austrian literature—20th century—History and criticism.
    2. Duality (Logic) in literature.   3. Polarity in literature.
    I. Title.
    PT3818.M37   1996
    830.9'9436'0904—dc20   95-39266 CIP

031997—3520XII

To Christine Natasha

CONTENTS

ACKNOWLEDGMENTS

I AM GRATEFUL TO A number of institutions and individuals for their support with the preparation of this work. A Yale Senior Faculty Fellowship and a Guggenheim Fellowship provided two free years without which the book would not have been written. Summer grants from Yale University, the Austrian Institute, and the University of Virginia enabled me to travel to collections in Vienna, Cambridge, and Freiburg and to continue work on the project over several summers.

Peter Michael Braunwarth of the Österreichische Akademie der Wissenschaften graciously facilitated access to transcriptions of unpublished Schnitzler manuscripts in Vienna.

I would particularly like to thank Walter H. Sokel, who read the entire manuscript, for his suggestions and encouragement. I am also grateful to my colleagues Benjamin Bennett, Beth Bjorklund, Peter Demetz, Rob Leventhal, George Schoolfield, Howard Stern, and Renate Voris, who read drafts. Finally, I would like to thank my readers for the University of Nebraska Press, Judith Ryan and Wolfgang Natter, for their useful comments.

Various parts of the book appeared previously as articles. A slightly longer version of chapter 2, part 1, appeared as "The Theme of the Repressed Memory in Hofmannsthal's *Elektra*," *German Quarterly* 67 (Winter 1987): 38–51. A more detailed version of chapter 2, part 3, was published as "Musil and Freud: The 'Foreign Body' in *Die Versuchung der stillen Veronika*," *Euphorion* 81 (1987): 100–18. Chapter 3 is a revised and expanded version of my article "Irreversible Processes, Proliferating Middles, and Invisible Barriers: Spatial Metaphors in Freud, Schnitzler, Musil, and Kafka," *Focus on Vienna 1900*, ed. Erika Nielsen (München: Fink, 1982), pp. 46–57. The first three sections of chapter 4 are a slightly revised version of my article "Mirrors and Mirroring: 'Fort/da' Devices in Texts by Rilke, Hofmannsthal, and

Kafka," *Deutsche Vierteljahrsschrift für Literaturwissenschaft und Geistesgeschichte* 58 (1984): 139–55. Chapter 5, part 4, appeared in a longer version as "A Dream Narrative: Schnitzler's 'Der Sekundant,'" *Modern Austrian Literature* 23, no. 1 (1990): 1–17. Chapter 6, part 3, is a revised and slightly expanded version of "Art, Freedom, and Deception in Kafka's *Ein Bericht für eine Akademie*," in *Deutsche Vierteljahrsschrift für Literaturwissenschaft und Geistesgeschichte* 61 (1987): 720–32.

The photograph of Kolo Moser's buffet "Der reiche Fischzug" appears courtesy of Österreichisches Museum für angewandte Kunst, Vienna, where the buffet is located.

ABBREVIATIONS

TG   Beer-Hofmann, Richard. *Der Tod Georgs.* Stuttgart: Reclam,
      1980.
SE   Freud, Sigmund. *Standard Edition of the Complete
      Psychological Works of Sigmund Freud.* Translated by James
      Strachey. 24 vols. London: Hogarth Press, 1953–74.
BI   Hofmannsthal, Hugo von. *Briefe 1890–1901.* Berlin: S. Fischer,
      1935.
BII   ———. *Briefe 1900–1909.* Wien: Bermann Fischer Verlag, 1937.
PL   ———. *Plays and Libretti.* Edited by Michael Hamburger.
      New York: Pantheon, 1963.
PVP   ———. *Poems and Verse Plays.* Edited by Michael Hamburger.
      London: Routledge & Kegan Paul, 1961.
SP   ———. *Selected Prose.* Translated by Mary Hottinger, Tania
      Stern, and James Stern. New York: Pantheon, 1952.
CS   Kafka, Franz. *The Complete Stories.* Edited by Nahum N.
      Glatzer. New York: Schocken Books, 1976.
K   ———. *Gesammelte Werke.* Taschenbuchausgabe in 7 Bänden.
      Frankfurt a.M.: Fischer, 1976.
FW   Musil, Robert. *Five Women.* Translated by Eithne Wilkins and
      Ernst Kaiser. New York: Delacorte, 1966.
M   ———. *Gesammelte Werke in neun Bänden.* Edited by Adolf
      Frisé. Reinbek bei Hamburg: Rowohlt, 1978.
MWQ   ———. *The Man without Qualities.* Translated by Eithne
      Wilkins and Ernst Kaiser. 3 vols. London: Pan Books, 1988.
YT   ———. *Young Törless.* New York: Pocket Books, 1978.
AD   Nietzsche, Friedrich. *On the Advantage and Disadvantage of
      History for Life.* Translated by Peter Preuss. Indianapolis:
      Hackett, 1980.

R   Rilke, Rainer Maria. *Sämtliche Werke.* 12 vols. Frankfurt a.M.:
           Insel, 1976.

OAP   Schnitzler, Arthur. *Anatol: Living Hours; The Green
           Cockatoo.* Translated by Grace Isabel Colbron. Great Neck
           NY: Core Collection Books, 1977.

EW   ———. *Das erzählerische Werk.* 7 vols. In *Gesammelte Werke
           in Einzelausgaben.* Frankfurt a.M.: Fischer, 1977–79.

DW   ———. *Das dramatische Werk.* 8 vols. In *Gesammelte Werke
           in Einzelausgaben.* Frankfurt a.M.: Fischer, 1977–79.

IR   ———. *Illusion and Reality. Plays and Stories of Arthur
           Schnitzler.* Translated by Paul F. Dvorak. New York: Lang,
           1986.

SHADOW LINES

INTRODUCTION

THE PURPOSE OF THIS BOOK is to show how a reorientation in epistemological concerns took place specifically in Austrian culture around 1900, and in what ways Austrian literature from about 1890 to 1924 participates in this reorientation. It manifests itself most dramatically, though not exclusively, in the theories of Sigmund Freud, with *The Interpretation of Dreams* (1900) as the decisive turning point. "Flectere si nequeo superos, Acheronta movebo" ("If I cannot bend the powers above, I shall stir up Acheron"): the Virgil quotation with which Freud heralds the discovery of the unconscious indicates what direction the refocusing of interest most generally takes. With his epigraph, Freud echoes Friedrich Nietzsche's more dispassionate observation in *On the Advantage and Disadvantage of History for Life* that "cheerfulness, clear conscience, the carefree deed, faith in the future—all this depends . . . on there being a line which distinguishes what is clear and in full view from the dark and unilluminable." Austrian writers around 1900 are interested precisely in the other side of this line. They are intrigued by what may be metaphorically designated "the dark area." They are intent on what Rainer Maria Rilke calls "Raumgewinn," the winning of space—on the possibility of gaining access to the dark area, as well as on the need to deny or limit access to it.

The "dark area" is variously defined. Despite the new interest in psychology, definition is not just a matter of displacing a traditional dualism onto the human psyche. The idea of a dark region within the self can be found as early as Augustine, and particularly in the last decades of the nineteenth century, with the popularity of Arthur Schopenhauer's conception of "the world as representation" and the corresponding notion of a fusion of outer with inner reality, the split tended to be relocated within. Yet inasmuch as it is psychological, the new concern takes a step away from the typical late nineteenth-century dualism which accords value to the unreflected life instincts, to the ability to "feel" or "live," and deplores hyperconsciousness and self-analysis, which threaten these instincts. The pose of the late nineteenth-century "decadent" hero was that he was being cheated out of something he was entitled to by birthright. The writers I am concerned with here are interested in something barely known—its composition, its accessibility. The dark area, moreover, is no longer seen as a delicate thing, a fragile and elusive unity susceptible to disintegration. Instead, it is increasingly reevaluated, whether it is defined in terms of psychology or not, as a seat of power. It is often accorded the status of a temporal "origin," for example by Freud, or a spatial "ground" in poetic metaphor. It comes to be viewed as the point of reference for everything that goes on in the light area. It emerges variously, around 1900, as the unconscious (Freud), the sexual drive (Freud, Arthur Schnitzler, Robert Musil), the death instinct (Freud, Schnitzler), the dangerous chaos below the surface of things (Rilke), the inaccessible totality (Hugo von Hofmannsthal), or the unsayable (Fritz Mauthner, Hofmannsthal, Musil, Ludwig Wittgenstein). These seemingly anomalous entities all perform the same structural function within a dualistic scheme, and, despite local differences above all in their evaluation as something valuable versus something terrible, they are accorded similar attributes: they are unassimilable to the place where we are, to the rational, everyday world; they are the object of our quest; they are fundamentally inaccessible; and they are powerful.

How does the dark area relate to the world of cognition and language? How can it be experienced, known, kept, recovered? The writers are concerned to establish that what we know, or the place where we are, is indeed grounded in something outside itself (the unknown); and yet at the same time, they hope to obtain a kind of certainty about or knowledge of this excluded region. They devise strategies both for defending it against too easy acquisition, and for gaining insight into it. These strategies, as interesting as the new fascinations themselves, posit the ideas of inaccessibility or discontinuity, or serve as heuristic devices to shed light on the dark area, or play with the ambivalence inherent in inclusion and exclusion to evoke the illusion of absence and presence at once.

In the following chapters we will encounter a family of constructs that have the same structure as the Freudian unconscious, in that their essential features are inaccessibility and unknowability. While the content of each construct is by definition shadowy, its antithetical relation to the known and accessible is all the more clearly defined. These constructs represent themselves above all as the *other* of the place to which we do have access, namely, consciousness, language, reason, the self, the present, the apparent, life, and so on. And it is precisely from this place, the place where we are, that the dark other appears inaccessible and unknowable; for as we shall see in more detail in the course of the following chapters, motion in the opposite direction, from it to us, *is* possible; in short, we cannot get to the dark area, but it can get to us. Thus we will encounter dualities on the model of consciousness versus the unconscious: rational versus irrational, present versus past, self versus other, life versus death, and language versus the unsayable. In each case the name, the specific content of a pair is less important than the structural relation between the two terms. Roland Barthes's commentary on the figure of antithesis describes this relation:

> Far from differing merely by the presence or lack of a simple relationship (as is ordinarily the case with paradigmatic opposites), the two terms of an antithesis are each *marked*: their difference does not arise out of a complementary, dialectical movement (empty as opposed to full): the antithesis is the battle between two plenitudes set ritually face to face like two fully armed warriors; the Antithesis is the figure of the *given* opposition, eternal, eternally recurrent: the figure of the inexpiable. Every joining of two antithetical terms, every mixture, every conciliation—in short, every passage through the wall of the Antithesis—thus constitutes a transgression.[1]

The antithetical relation between the pairs of terms—their polarization as "inexpiable" opposites—is, of course, made, not given in the nature of things. Where the writers adopt pairs of opposites that they found ready-made in the cultural tradition, they play up the antithetical nature of the terms. Thus the Freudian unconscious is a plenitude, whereas the pre-Freudian unconscious—the "unconscious of the philosophers" and of Theodor Lipps, as Freud points out (SE 5:614), indicated merely a contrast to consciousness. Even where an oppositional relationship between two concepts is questionable, as is perhaps most patent in the opposition present versus past, the authors energetically *antithesize* the concepts.

The new paradigm may be brought into focus by comparing it to the Romantic use of dualities. In the Romantic trope of division between nature and culture, self and world, prominent since Jean-Jacques Rousseau, disunity is represented as a current, actual, painful state of affairs, but one that is neither original, nor permanent, nor essential. Dissociation is our fallen state, not an absolute state. For William Wordsworth and Samuel T. Coleridge the human imagination accords with the vital, creative principle in nature; its process parallels the generation of the universe in God. If Ralph Waldo Emerson finds that "the axis of vision is not coincident with the axis of things,"[2] this alienation of the "me" from the "not me" must nevertheless be seen relative to his conviction that man partakes of God the creator and thus is essentially at one with the world. In German letters around 1800 reenactments of a tripartite eschatological scheme, of a three-part account of human history, emerge. It is characteristic of such schemes to conclude on a triumphant note of synthesis. Thus Friedrich von Schiller in "Über naive und sentimentalische Dichtung" ("On Naive and Sentimental Poetry") synthesizes the two typological phases of civilization "nature" (exemplified by the ancient Greeks) and "culture" (the modern condition) into "the divine" or "the ideal"; Friedrich Schlegel defines the romantic as the universal and unifying (albeit with the historicizing addition of the "progressive"); Novalis figures the future Golden Age as a mystical atopia where differentiations and time are abolished; Friedrich Hölderlin envisions a future "Day of the Gods" involving the return of Christ and also of Dionysus; Heinrich von Kleist in "Über das Marionettentheater" ("About the Marionette Theater") resolves original "charm" ("Anmut") and "grace" ("Grazie"), and secondary "consciousness," into a third stage of "grace" ("Grazie") or return to original innocence, possible when infinite consciousness has been attained. The turn-of-the-century literature under consideration recurs to duality as an explanatory principle. But the interest in resolving the opposites into an ultimate harmony fades. In place of the Romantic fashion of privileging wholeness and integrity as natural and originary, and to induce, out of an apparent present disunity, an underlying or final unity, we find irreducible duality posited both as the starting point and end of any given process. Duality is evaluated not as a regrettable and temporary condition meriting dissolution or sublation but, rather, as the inevitable groundwork of human existence.

The turn-of-the-century dislocation of the Romantic *épistémè* also fundamentally changes the character of the side of the duality that we are not on, the "not me." In the same measure as it becomes remote and inaccessible, it *deepens* into something mysterious, untheorizable. The same contrast holds between the turn-of-the-century dark area and the demonic dark area posited by such Romantic writers as Ludwig Tieck and E. T. A. Hoffmann. Turn-of-the-century writers like Hofmannsthal

and Schnitzler plainly owe much to their Romantic predecessors in fig-
uring the dark area as dangerous and powerful. But this region's disappearing trick into the shadows; its inscrutability; its way of demanding
to be quested after and then denying access; its withholding of its supposed plenitude from the inquiring consciousness; its erection of a mysterious line between it and us that itself becomes an object of fascination—these are the new attributes of the dark area that appear at the
turn of the century and share the central focus.

This epistemic shift may, undoubtedly, be related to developments in
later nineteenth-century European intellectual history. It reflects the interest in the burgeoning science of psychology and the increased interest
in psychopathology, in the explanatory power of an irrational part of the
self, which that science, in particular the French school, brought with it.
It is also linked to the much-commented-on sense of the inauthenticity
of the given, and hence belief in the hidden nature of the real, that has
been attributed to the hegemony of capitalism in Europe as a whole.
Particularly with the eclipse of transcendence since Nietzsche, a quest
for that elusive real became an issue. Philosophies of depth, which attempted to find the key to confusing, changing, inauthentic-seeming,
opaque surface phenomena in some, preferably one, ulterior truth, appeared attractive, particularly where that truth was identified with
something irrational. The popularity of Schopenhauer's philosophy,
with its distinction between the world as "will" and as "representation," where the Will, a reformulation of Immanuel Kant's *Ding an sich*,
is the primal generative force, is symptomatic of the tendency.

While the impact of these trends was felt on the continent generally,
the social and political configuration in the Austro-Hungarian Empire,
according to various accounts, provided a climate that was particularly
favorable to their reception. Retrospectives on the empire by Stefan
Zweig (*Die Welt von Gestern* [*The World of Yesterday*]), Josef Roth
(*Radetskymarsch* [*Radetzky March*]), and Robert Musil (*Der Mann ohne
Eigenschaften* [*The Man without Qualities*]) emphasize the sense of extreme stability evoked, particularly in the upper middle class, by a seemingly unshakable social order, sustained peace, general prosperity, and
the longevity of Emperor Franz Josef; and at the same time, strong intimations of incipient instability, brought on by the restiveness of the nationalities governed by the Dual Monarchy, irreducible social hetero-
geneity, which was on the increase in Vienna, and widening conflicts
between social and religious groups within that society. Deep cleavages

yawned between a rigid and hierarchical social structure and the multifarious forces of change, between official discourse and political actuality, between accepted moral standards and sexual practice—in short between appearance and reality. While extreme caution must be exercised in making connections between art and the social conditions in which art arises, turn-of-the-century Austrian culture is an area in which, as a result of the conjunction of volatile social and political circumstances and an efflorescence of the arts, such connections are persistently made. From the standpoint of this study, it is not surprising that Austrian authors at the turn of the century, given the society in which they grew up, should have been particularly receptive to dual schemes, the analysis of boundaries, and a preoccupation with the underlying.[3]

For the Austrian fin de siècle the opening moment of the new fascination with dualities may be seen in the reception of early Nietzschean philosophy. For Nietzsche, in his influential early work *The Birth of Tragedy*, polarized the apollonian and the dionysian; the world of individuation, appearance, and light, and the world of unity, depth, and irrationality; and the Socratic thirst for knowledge and artistic creativity; and it was precisely the latter term of each duality, which Nietzsche represented as more fundamental, that captured the imagination of his readers. In the early essay *On the Advantage and Disadvantage of History for Life* Nietzsche also rejects the Hegelian idea of progress in history and replaces it with a duality of past versus present that subordinates history and the past to the interest of the living subject. No reconciliation, no sublation is envisaged here: the emphasis is on conflict. The historical past, with its infinite clutter, as an object of mediated knowledge for the subject, must be made to foster life and action in the present, or be forgotten.

At the turn of the century, duality becomes useful. Freud is well known for his persistent adherence to duality, throughout all the modifications in his theories, as an explanatory principle. In *The Interpretation of Dreams* he mapped the field of inquiry by dividing it into two areas divided by the "line" of censorship, the conscious systems and the repressed unconscious. A decade later he extended his dualistic mode of thought by opposing the libidinal instincts and the ego instincts; and a decade after that, in *Beyond the Pleasure Principle*, where he posited a new duality consisting of the life versus the death instincts, he declared, "Our views have from the very first been *dualistic*, and to-day they are even more definitely dualistic than before—now that we describe the opposition as being, not between ego-instincts and sexual instincts but between the life instincts and death instincts" (SE 18:53). In each case he capitalizes on the notion of conflict between the two terms, which he exploits for its energetic, generative potential. Thus in *The Interpretation of Dreams* Freud makes the conflict between the unacceptable desires generated by the unconscious and the subject's perception-consciousness system, which must shield itself from knowledge of these desires, responsible for the unintelligible outward appearance of dreams. As we shall see in chapter 1, his discovery of the unconscious (that is, his positing of a hidden entity that exists in perpetual and inevitable conflict with the conscious psyche) may be seen as a hermeneutic strategy: it allows him to interpret dreams.

In literary texts by Schnitzler, Hofmannsthal, Musil, and Kafka, the dark area becomes, much as the unconscious in Freud's theory, the elusive object of a quest or else it intrudes to disturb the peace. Invoking it thus becomes a strategy for producing texts, for generating plot in narrative and conflict in drama. In chapters 2, 3, 4, and 5 we shall see, through a series of interpretations of texts, some of these uses of the dualistic model. Taking examples by Hofmannsthal, Schnitzler, Musil, and Kafka, but also Freud, Rilke, and Richard Beer-Hofmann, these chapters focus on recurrent figures and devices whose purpose is to assert, elaborate, suspend, and reinstate duality.

Chapter 2 discusses the temporal figure of past versus present. The theme of the pathological memory at the turn of the century suggests that a rift yawns between past and present. The past is a version of the dark unknown and as such, it is relegated to the other side of the line. Where Nietzsche in *On the Advantage and Disadvantage of History for Life* deems a fascination with the past unhealthy, Josef Breuer and Freud in *Studies on Hysteria* brand the intrusion of the past into the present in the form of the traumatic memory pathological. Later, in *The Interpretation of Dreams* and in keeping with his institutionalization of conflict, Freud regards such intrusion as inevitable, though problematic. The three literary texts under discussion in chapter 2, Hofmannsthal's *Elektra* (*Electra*), Schnitzler's "Blumen" ("Flowers"), and Musil's "Die Versuchung der stillen Veronika" ("The Temptation of Quiet Veronica") treat the subject of the repressed memory in ways that approximate the spectrum of positions taken by Nietzsche, Breuer and Freud, and Freud in *The Interpretation of Dreams*.

Chapter 3 discusses the spatial figures of irreversible process, proliferating middles, and invisible barriers. Death and sex in Schnitzler and the irrational and unsayable in Musil have the same attributes as the Freudian unconscious: inaccessibility, mystery, power. All three writers use the same spatial figures to illustrate how the dark other is inaccessible to us when we reach for it with our reason and our language, yet is capable of revealing itself to us. Kafka uses the same figures, but parodistically, in a way that questions the existence of the goal independent of the perceiving subject.

Chapters 4 and 5 focus on the related devices of mirroring and the dream, respectively. In turn-of-the-century literary texts both the mirror and the dream function as boundary-crossing devices, whose nature, however, ultimately underscores the existence of the boundary. Mirroring, which represents the narcissistic expansion or wishful thinking of the self, and the world of the dream magically lift the barrier between ourselves and what is beyond our reach. Yet this achievement is temporary and illusory; it is undercut by the unreal nature of the mirror image and the dream.

Finally, the structure of antithesis provides the groundwork for an act of power: for crossing the boundary to the mythicized dark area, for rendering accessible what has been declared essentially inaccessible. This notion of boundary crossing has legitimized several important projects. Besides Freud's influential theory of interpretation, the modernist self-legitimation of art involves the idea of crossing the boundary posited by antithesis. In chapter 6 I discuss how art is conceived as the triumph of the artistic imagination over reality in the production of the real. Chapter 7 addresses the question of language skepticism at the turn of the century and shows how art is elevated to a privileged means of crossing the barrier that an inadequately referential language erects between us and the truth. The final section of that chapter circles back to Freud's *Interpretation of Dreams* in order to show how contemporary assumptions about language inscribe themselves in his hermeneutics and his metapsychology, creating a kind of "language crisis" between these two aspects of his endeavor.

The closing moment of the fascination with duality is marked by the emergence of a new epistemological model. This second, later tendency, of which we see the beginnings in the period under consideration, involves a denial of the quest for meaning in an ulterior source and a debunking of the dual structure generally. Instead, convention—the formation and imitation of codes—comes to be posited as an explanation of how things work. The clearest example is Wittgenstein of the *Philosoph-*

ical Investigations, where he rejects his own earlier view, propounded in the *Tractatus logico-philosophicus,* that language is reference and declares instead that language is usage. In the *Tractatus* the "picture theory" of language is based on the vertical relation of surface and depth: language represents a substratum of thought, which in turn represents a substratum of things. Two sharp boundaries divide three discrete realms, which in Wittgenstein's argument are coextensive and also homologous. Wittgenstein limits his conclusions about the representational adequacy of language by drawing, in Kantian fashion, yet another sharp boundary. He states in the Preface, "What can be said at all can be said clearly, and what we cannot talk about we must consign to silence. Thus the aim of the book is to set a limit to thought, or rather—not to thought, but to the expression of thoughts."[4] The sayable has its limits: beyond them lies the realm of the transcendent, the mystical, the ethical, and the aesthetic, which is inexpressible.

In the *Philosophical Investigations* Wittgenstein replaces the vertical relation between signs and referents by a horizontal relation between speakers of the language at any given time. Intersubjective meaning, which inheres in language conceived as usage, replaces referential meaning. Words are clarified by the contexts in which they are used: their meaning is conventional, anchored in forms of life, and subject to historical change. Through the book runs a polemic against the hallowed concepts of philosophies of depth: depth, the hidden, the prior, essences. Wittgenstein repeatedly advises against looking for an explanatory beyond. Biased now in favor of the manifest, the commonsensical, and the normal, Wittgenstein reduces and dismisses the hidden, suggesting that it is a concept that language has imposed on thought: "A *picture* held us captive. And we could not get outside it, for it lay in our language and language seemed to repeat it to us inexorably" (para 115).

The suspicion Wittgenstein directs at the order language has imposed upon our thought, and his demand for a clear view, has its precedents in the work of such late nineteenth-century thinkers as Hippolyte Taine, Nietzsche, and Ernst Mach, theoreticians who formed the immediate intellectual background for turn-of-the-century Austrian writers. Each of these writers energetically polemicized against the traps language sets for our understanding (our "grammatical habits," as Nietzsche said in *Beyond Good and Evil*),[5] as a prelude to replacing them with his own more scientific, more rational theory of how things work. Mach's theory amounted to a decrying of the dual in favor of his own celebrated "monism," whereby he dissolved the veteran subject/object split into a cosmos consisting of "elements" ("colors, sounds, pressures, temperatures, smells, spaces, times") that "depend both on external and internal circumstances," or as he sometimes called them, "sensations."[6] Mach thus approximates a counterpole to the dualistic thinking of the turn of the century. And Mach's thought is not without parallels in turn-of-the-century literature: the literary themes of appearance versus reality and permanence versus change, which are the topics of chapter 6, dissolve traditional boundaries without instituting new ones.

Thus by the time Wittgenstein wrote the *Philosophical Investigations*, conventional thought, represented by language, was a scapegoat that had been sacrificed at many different altars. But Wittgenstein, unlike Mach, actually exploits convention as a positive explanatory principle. In this he was preceded by Robert Musil in the work that occupied the last twenty years of his life, the novel *The Man without Qualities* (1930–42). In his youth Musil had been an ardent reader of Nietzsche, and he wrote his dissertation on Mach; more pertinently, however, this postwar novel, set on the eve of World War I, takes an ironic look at the seeming stability of prewar society, which, the reader is invited to reflect, is on the verge of being disrupted. A recurrent theme in the novel is to show how convention dominates life and thought. At the same time Musil is at pains to debunk the workings of convention as contingent and its orderings as specious. One of the hero Ulrich's main insights, upheld by the novel, is that there is no necessity or reason in history. Rather, history takes place like a whispered saying passed from ear to ear. The "course of history" is not like that of a billiard ball, but like that of clouds. "World history," to his mind, is equivalent to "muddling through" (MWQ 2:70). It is the anti-hero Arnheim who believes in reason in history. Historical change takes place according to the "Principle of the Insufficient Cause" (MWQ 1:155), which Ulrich applies specifically to the Parallel Action, a seventy-year jubilee for Emperor Franz Josef that is planned with immense to-do and that is so called because it is designed to outdo a similar thirty-year jubilee planned for Emperor Wilhelm. Yet at the origin of the Parallel Action and the resulting furor is not a trace of a central idea.

The Parallel Action functions as a microcosm for society and history, in which system and chaos are wondrously mixed. Social change is frequently effected by seemingly superficial surface phenomena. Hence in Musil's persiflage the lack of a word for an Austro-Hungarian foments social unrest. The catalyst for the Parallel Action, as for so many other historical events, is the indefinable word "wahr" ("true").

Ultimately, Ulrich believes, beneath all existing orders is chaos, or an inexhaustible potential for other possibilities. *Everything could be different.* "This order of things is not as solid as it pretends to be; nothing, no ego, no form, no principle, is safe, everything is in a process of invisible but never-ceasing transformation" (MWQ 1:296). This insight does not prevent him from questing for an ultimate, valid order, which crystallizes, in the latter part of the novel, into a characteristic Musilian duality, here named "love" (mysticism) versus "power" or "violence" ("Gewalt") (intellectualism or competitive activity of any sort).

In my reading Kafka is a pivotal figure in the switch to the second paradigm. For Kafka's work may be seen to represent the vanishing point of the dualistic tendencies we see in Freud, Hofmannsthal, Musil, and others. The extreme allusiveness of his stories can be traced to his use and amplification of the devices of his predecessors. Particularly in his works written from 1917 until his death in 1924, he parodistically mimics their strategies, employing them not as explanatory devices but as devices that themselves merit explanation. He thus takes these strategies to their logical dead end. He adopts his predecessors' expedients without their heuristic implications; he flattens them, using them merely as methods for creating and expanding texts, and thus achieves narrative expanse without depth (that is, the revelation of hidden meaning). If Kafka's stories disorient the reader, it is because despite their overt emphasis on seeking and finding, they do not attempt to show the reader anything. As the narrator in "On Parables" says, "All these parables really set out to say merely that the incomprehensible is incomprehensible, and we know that already" (CS 457). Returning to a Kantian sobriety concerning the accessibility of the absolute, and supplementing it with an ironic sense that belief in its accessibility is inevitable, Kafka shows how the quest for an ultimate principle does not yield the principle; instead, the assumption of such a principle generates the quest. Kafka shows the shaping power of an ulterior fiction on human behavior.

The structures I find in turn-of-the-century Austrian literature are, to be sure, neither exclusively limited to it nor universally present within it. An interest in dualities is observable in turn-of-the-century European literature generally, although, I would argue, in Austria it is present to a more intense and obsessive degree. A strain of the European literature of the 1890s, typified by Maurice Maeterlinck's "transcendental psychology," glorified a "cult of the soul" that attributed mystical value to an unfathomable, unconscious region of the psyche.[7] This literature was not without influence on Austrian writers: Musil, for example, uses a passage about the mysterious depths from Maeterlinck's *Le Trésor des humbles* (*Treasure of the Humble*) as the epigraph to *Die Verwirrungen des Zöglings Törleß* (*Young Törless*).[8] Thomas Mann, a non-Austrian contemporary of Hofmannsthal and Rilke, persistently structures his work around dualities similar to those found in turn-of-the-century Austrian literature: the rational, bourgeois, Northern, everyday world opposes the realm of the irrational, Southern, dionysian. Joseph Conrad's "heart of darkness," where "darkness" designates wilderness, prehistory, the darkness at the center of man's soul, evil, and death, is, with its attributes of mystery, power, and silence, strikingly similar to the dark other invoked by Schnitzler and Musil. In Marcel Proust, Paul Valéry, and André Gide one also sees variations on dualistic schemes.

Finally, the patterns that interest me are by no means universal in Austrian literature in the period under consideration. They have only marginal relevance to the work of Karl Kraus, for example. As Nike Wagner shows, Karl Kraus has a Weininger-like penchant for antithesis when characterizing the sexes: *Geist* (the male) opposes *Geschlecht* (the female).[9] Nevertheless, one of Kraus's dominant preoccupations, his critique of language, is quite different from the language skepticism that will be one of the concerns of this book (in chapter 7). Kraus is mainly interested in the relationship of language to power, in the fact that public opinion can be manipulated by a distorting use of language, and not in the notion of an ineffable region beyond the reach of language that justifies his contemporaries' skepticism. Kraus's critique implies that there is a true state of affairs to be learned, and correspondingly, he tirelessly directed his efforts toward trying to clean up language usage.

The literary writers who are most important for this study, Schnitzler, Hofmannsthal, Musil, and Kafka, favored different genres, are remembered in literary histories for different kinds of accomplishments, had different habits of writing, and cultivated different relations with the public. The chapters that follow stress their similarities. Yet it should be understood that each author had his own emphases and his own particular brand of preoccupation with dual schemes. Before turning to a discussion of the figures and strategies that the authors have in common, therefore, let us locate these emphases and preoccupations in the work of each.

Arthur Schnitzler (1862–1931), a writer of psychological fiction and the leading Austrian dramatist of his day, was the oldest of the group of friends that composed the inner clique of the Jung Wien circle. A medical doctor, his strongest interest was in psychiatry and psychopathology. Freud, impressed by the perspicacity of the psychological insights in his fiction, wrote to him in 1906, "I often asked myself in astonishment where you could have got this or that secret insight, which I acquired through painstaking research, and finally I reached the point of envying the poet whom I had otherwise admired." In a letter of 1922, trying to explain why he had for years avoided meeting him, Freud spoke of "a kind of fear of a doppelgänger."[10] The prominent Schnitzlerian themes of love and death, his depictions of conflict and unconscious motivations, and his interest in dreams do manifest an uncanny similarity to Freud's concerns. Schnitzler followed Freud's work from his 1886 translation of Jean-Martin Charcot's *New Lectures* on and tried especially after 1912 to come to terms with his theories, though not uncritically. But it is generally acknowledged that Schnitzler arrived at his themes independently of Freud.

Any reader of Schnitzler's day-to-day personal diary will quickly ascertain that he took the plots for his stories from life.[11] Yet for all its closeness to the details of his life, Schnitzler's work does not lack consistency in theme and form. A fascination with opposites, with incompatible realities, and with lines of division runs through his texts. The dramatically minded Schnitzler, who imports his sense of theatrical effect into his fiction as well, repeatedly builds his plots around a clash that depends on the existence of boundaries: the clash between reality and fantasy (e.g., in "Leutnant Gustl," "Andreas Thameyers letzter Brief" ["Andreas Thameyer's Last Letter"], "Flucht in die Finsternis" ["Flight into Darkness"], and "Fräulein Else"); between lovers' views of each other (e.g., *Das Märchen* [The fairy tale], *Liebelei* [*Playing with Love*], "Die überspannte Person" [The overexcitable person], "Frau Berta Garlan"); between forbidden desires and the dictates of morality (e.g., "Die Toten schweigen" ["The Dead Are Silent"], *Der Schleier der Beatrice* [The veil of Beatrice], "Der Sekundant" ["The Second"]); and between states of mind in a single protagonist (*Der Weg ins Freie* [*Road into the Open*], "Der Mörder" ["The Murderer"], *Der junge Medardus* [The young Medardus], "Flucht in die Finsternis"). Beyond his preference for plots based on conflict, Schnitzler is interested in probing the validity of traditional boundaries. In particular, he loves to unsettle the hierarchical relation between conventional pairs of opposites—notably life and art (e.g., "Mein Freund Ypsilon" [My friend Ypsilon], *Die Frau mit dem Dolche* [*The Lady with the Dagger*], *Der grüne Kakadu* [*The Green Cockatoo*], *Zum großen Wurstel* [At the big Punch and Judy show], *Große Szene* [*The Big Scene*], "Der letzte Brief eines Literaten" ["The Last Letter of a Writer"]) and reality and dream (e.g., *Alkandi's Lied* [Alkandi's song], *Paracelsus*, "Der Sekundant" ["The Second"], *Traumnovelle* [*Rhapsody: A Dream Novel*])—by showing the transgressive power of the second, subjective term.

While underscoring, exploring, and dissolving boundaries characterizes Schnitzler's work, in his fiction of the 1890s in particular one finds a steady emphasis on the irrational and the unknown—the "dark area." In one story after the other Schnitzler affirms the power of the unconscious, of sexuality, of the repressed, of death. The finality of death, in his work of this decade, exercises a power over the minds of the living equal to or greater than erotic fascination ("Blumen" ["Flowers"], "Die Toten schweigen," "Die Nächste" [The next woman], and *Der Schleier der Beatrice*). The stories that demonstrate the disruptive energies of sex and death often have eye-catching plots. Schnitzler is attracted to the flashier aspects of psychology, such as trauma ("Die Toten schweigen"), compulsion ("Die Braut" [The bride], "Erbschaft" [Riches], "Die Nächste"), the return of the repressed ("Die Toten schweigen," "Blumen"), or the infant memory trace ("Der Sohn" ["The Son"]). With these plots he employs a stock of equally eye-catching formal devices, including uncanny repetition ("Die Frau des Weisen" ["The Sage's Wife"], *Der Schleier der Beatrice*), sudden reversals ("Reichtum" ["Riches"], *Der grüne Kakadu*), and symmetry (*Alkandi's Lied*, "Die kleine Komödie" ["The Little Comedy"], "Die Toten schweigen"), including circular form in *Reigen* (*Merry-go-round*).[12] After the turn of the century he becomes more interested in portraying character—for example, Sala in *Der einsame Weg* (*The Lonely Way*), Georg von Wergenthin in *Der Weg ins Freie*, Medardus in *Der junge Medardus*, Hofreiter in *Das weite Land* (*Undiscovered Country*), Herbot in *Große Szene*, Gräsler in *Dr. Gräsler, Badearzt* (*Dr. Graesler*). Issues also occupy him: the Jewish question in *Der Weg ins Freie*, antisemitism and medical ethics in *Professor Bernhardi*, journalism in *Fink und Fliederbusch*, the life of working-class women in *Therese*. In certain works written after 1917, however, including "Casanovas Heimfahrt" ("Casanova's Homecoming"), *Die Schwestern oder Casanova in Spa* (*The Sisters, or Casa-*

nova in Spa), *Traumnovelle*, and "Der Sekundant," he returns to his old themes and to techniques of the 1890s, such as symmetry, doubling, and reversal. Schnitzler's early and his late works, that is, those most committed to affirming the power of the irrational, will consequently be of greatest interest to us here.

Hugo von Hofmannsthal (1874–1929), the descendant of a patrician Viennese family, won fame early. By the time he was seventeen he was celebrated as a boy genius who had written and published, under the pseudonym Loris, lyric poetry and critical essays of extraordinary high quality. Around the turn of the century he abandoned poetry, complaining that his lyric vein had dried up. By 1903, however, he had found a new voice as a dramatist, and after 1906 he collaborated as a librettist with Richard Strauss.[13]

The young Hugo von Hofmannsthal was already an accomplished man of letters, who had devoured world literature by the time he was eighteen. Within the next decade he had completed a dissertation in Romance philology on the Pleiade poets and a *Habilitationsschrift* on Victor Hugo. The essays and fictive dialogues he wrote in his twenties sparkle with literary allusions. His sensitivity to and recall and command of what he had read formed his own creative method, and the breadth of his reading fueled his own production. Adaptation turned into a preferred mode of composition. Schnitzler remarked ungenerously in a diary entry of 12 December 1902 that his friend showed an "almost incomprehensible taste for literary borrowing." Frequently these adaptations were quite exact. Hofmannsthal remained a great literary borrower throughout his life. In marked contrast to Schnitzler, his sources of inspiration for specific pieces were primarily not his concrete experiences but, rather, literary.[14]

While Hofmannsthal indubitably borrowed, he was an author who increasingly came to have his own set of special themes: being/becoming, fidelity, the social, existence. These themes are already in place in one form or another in his poetry and lyric drama of the 1890s, and by the time Hofmannsthal turned to drama after the turn of the century, we find these principal concerns in nearly every work, persistently connected to new plots. This use of literature as a vehicle for abstract ideas, for "concealing depth on the surface," in Hofmannsthal's own words, correlates with his penchant for allegory. In particular, his characters embody abstract ideas and make no pretense at being realistic psychological figures. As Hermann Broch remarks critically in *Hofmannsthal*

und seine Zeit (*Hugo von Hofmannsthal and his Time*), Hofmannsthal's
dramatic figures are mere "stock types."[15]

Thoughout his entire production Hofmannsthal's habits of thought
were dualistic. His poems are typically structured around thesis and antithesis: many begin with a statement that is then followed by a second
contrary or qualifying statement, introduced by a *doch* (yet), *und den-
noch* (and nevertheless), or *jedoch* (however). In his analytic pieces, notably *Ad me ipsum*, he organizes his ideas into antithetical pairs, such as
preexistence/existence, being/becoming, transitoriness/lastingness, and
solitude/community. Many critics have remarked how he constructs his
dramas around character pairs, playing out his ideas through two contrasting characters.

Hofmannsthal's compulsion to work with antithesis is stronger than
any lasting commitment to preferring one term of a given duality over
the other. His values change over the years. For example, the concept
"life" (always positive) undergoes slippage. His early work, such as *Der
Tor und der Tod* (*Death and the Fool*), celebrates a Nietzschean "life"
over rationality and consciousness, in complete conformity with the
fashion of the day. In the mid-1890s, mystical unity and magical mirroring become the desirable states, but they are attainable only in deficient
forms, temporarily or in retrospect; they are undercut by such inescapable verities as the otherness of the world, the necessity for choosing a path in life, and the inescapability of death. The pleasure and the
pain together are called "life." Finally, "life" becomes the mature, realistic solution to the givens of the human condition, the choice of a mode
of life or decision to commit oneself, as opposed to "preexistence," or
youthful floating in a state of suspended possibility.

Even in a given work, or in sequential works, a balancing of alternatives is more characteristic of Hofmannsthal's thought than a commitment to one over the other, so that preference may fall now on one term,
now on the other, of a given duality. His dualistic propensities coexist
strangely yet compatibly with his persistent idealization of unity and
wholeness. This idealization, as exemplified by his 1905 notebook entry,
"Does this not become more and more our mission: to overcome duality
completely and everywhere," places him closest of all our authors to
Romanticism and justifies the application of the term "neo-Romantic"
to him.[16]

Robert Musil (1880–1942) grew up in provincial Austria. After attend-
ing military academies as an adolescent, he was trained as an engineer

and then studied philosophy and experimental psychology from 1903–1911 in Berlin, writing his dissertation on Ernst Mach. From 1911 until the *Anschluß* he made his home primarily, though reluctantly, in Vienna.

Of all the writers that concern us, Musil was the most deeply and tenaciously committed to a dualistic mode of thought. Duality remained his overriding preoccupation and major theme, albeit with various refinements in the definition of the terms, from his first novel *Young Törless* to his mammoth, unfinished *Man without Qualities.* He became convinced that the coexistence of irreconcilable opposites was a fundamental given of human existence, whose exploration constituted a philosophical problem of the highest order and whose articulation merited the artist's fullest effort. As he put it in an essay of 1925,

> It seems, however, that a bifurcation runs throughout the whole of human history, dividing it into two spiritual conditions, which, even though they have influenced each other in many ways and entered into compromises, have nonetheless never properly mixed with each other. One of the two is familiar as the normal condition of our relationship to the world, to people, and to ourselves. We have evolved . . . by means of the *sharpness* of our mind to what we are: lords of an earth on which we were originally a nothing among monsters. Activity, boldness, cunning, deceit, restlessness, evil, a talent for the hunt, lust for war, and the like are the moral qualities to which we owe this ascent. . . . In contrast to this spiritual condition stands another, no less demonstrable historically even if it has left a less powerful imprint on our past. It has been characterized by many names. . . . It has been called the condition of love, of goodness, of renunciation of the world, of contemplation, of vision, of approach to God, of entrancement, of will-lessness, of meditation.[17]

The duality formulated here corresponds to the one Musil articulates in *The Man without Qualities:* "violence" versus "love." I will be more concerned with Musil's earlier work, with *Törless* and the two novellas that comprise the volume *Unions (Vereinigungen,* 1911), "The Temptation of Quiet Veronica" and "Die Vollendung der Liebe" ("The Perfecting of a Love").

Young Törless (1906) tells the story of an adolescent boy's attempt to come to terms with the dark ground of the irrational, with sexuality and violence, which seems simple and self-explanatory when it comes over

us, yet unfathomable and remote when we regard it with the eyes of reason or try to represent it in words. That is, when one is in the irrational
state, reflection does not take place and one perceives no conflict; but
when one looks at the irrational from the vantage point of the rational,
the duality is complete and irreducible. Törless's attempt to "understand" the irrational leads to a study of the mechanisms that govern
the relation of rational and irrational, in particular the—equally inscrutable—point of transition between them.

The dualities involved in *Unions* are similar, except that Musil modifies the terms of the opposition, which figured in *Törless* as rational and
irrational, to asexual and sexual—no doubt because both stories have female protagonists and Musil thought it inappropriate to attribute rationality to women. Whereas in *Törless* duality is absolute and uncontami-
nated, here Musil is intent to demonstrate how a trace of the opposite
always inheres in a phenomenon, especially in a state of conciousness.
His purpose is to show that things contain their opposites or that opposites contain each other. Hence in "The Temptation of Quiet Veronica"
the heroine is divided between two men, between animal and spiritual.
But they prove not to be truly opposite: the one is contained within the
other. Veronica's "rebirth" or self-finding involves the unification of all
opposites. In "The Perfecting of a Love" a monistic universe (Claudine's
life with her husband) falls apart into dualities: here/there, present/past,
surface/depth, and so on. However, these dualities prove to be merely
surface aspects of a single, basic, unified depth where all oppositions are
resolved. The line or turning point between two superficial opposites is
at the same time the void, the ground below all consciousness, where fidelity and infidelity are one, where Claudine's finding of her true self is
at once the most profound form of unity with her husband.

In *Törless* to a degree, but in the *Unions* stories to a much greater degree, Musil is concerned with what will become a major preoccupation
in all his future fiction, such as *Drei Frauen* (*Three Women*) and *The
Man without Qualities*: the artistic representation of the opposites that
constitute the dualities and of the subtle relations between them. The
stories of *Unions* are experiments in style: tempests in a restricted space,
these densely constructed stories attempt to render, principally through
the technique of simile, psychological phenomena that are too delicate
for ordinary language. Typical of Musil, especially in *Unions* and *The
Man without Qualities*, is a rhythmic approach to the problem of the
line. His worrying of the question of duality translates into a temporal

rhythm, a rapprochement or momentary unification that *must*, then, ebb into dissolution once again. The back-and-forth, seasick, nonprogressive rhythm of a Musil story—proliferating length without an advance of the story line, fascination with a barrier rather than linear directness or progress—gives a temporal dimension to his modeling of transition that must be considered alongside his predilection for formulating antithesis in spatial metaphors.

Franz Kafka, born in 1883 and hence three years younger than Musil, spent most of his life in his native Prague. Like his compatriot Rilke, who left the cultural island of Prague for good when he went to study at the University of Munich at age twenty-one, Kafka did not find in Prague an adequate indigenous literary tradition on which to found his own style. The biographer of his youth, Klaus Wagenbach, has demonstrated that Kafka's puristic German has little in common with the Prague German literature of his day, where "linguistic chaos," dominated by a melodramatic, precious, adjective-laden style, ruled.[18] Kafka's fiction had its roots elsewhere. It has been asserted with justice that his style, seemingly so unique and homogeneous, quotes from a variety of different literary styles.[19] Many studies juxtapose Kafka to some earlier writer to whom he is perceived to be similar: Miguel de Cervantes, Charles Dickens, Gustave Flaubert, Søren Kierkegaard, Nietzsche, August Strindberg. Kafka's relation to his immediate German-language predecessors in the political unit of which he was a part—Austria—has, however, not received much attention.[20]

There can be no doubt that Kafka knew the work of Schnitzler, Freud, Hofmannsthal, and Musil, not to mention Nietzsche, whose philosophies suffused their intellectual milieu. He read Nietzsche while he was still in *Gymnasium*; in 1902 he defended him against Max Brod's attacks.[21] Hofmannsthal was an early formative influence. Wagenbach writes that Kafka knew his work through the journal *Der Kunstwart*, to which Kafka subscribed from 1900–1901 to 1904, and in which Hofmannsthal was a favored author. Kafka's reception of Hofmannsthal was positive.[22] His knowledge of Freud dates from summer 1912 at the latest.[23] While he never discusses Freud in his letters or diary, his diary entry of 23 September 1912, in which he describes the genesis of the just completed "The Judgment," contains the telling phrase "thoughts of Freud, of course." His reaction to Schnitzler was mixed. In a letter of 14–15 February 1913 to Felice Bauer, he praised some of his early work, including *Anatol*, *Reigen*, and "Leutnant Gustl," but rejected his later "great plays" and "great prose" as "full of a truly staggering mass of the most sickening drivel." As for Musil, who favorably reviewed his *Betrachtung* (*Meditation*) and *Heizer* (*The Stoker*) in 1914, Kafka followed his literary progress with interest.[24]

Kafka's fiction combines two modes prevalent in these Austrian writers: psychological fiction and allegory. As a psychological narrator Kafka's distinctive innovation vis-à-vis Schnitzler and Musil, and the tradition of psychological fiction generally, is that he confines himself rigorously to the perspective of the main character, abstaining from commentary and keeping interpolations by an independent narrator to a minimum. He thus effectively reduces the focus of a third-person text to that of the first person. This technique, which Friedrich Beißner in his essays "Der Erzähler Franz Kafka" (1952) and "Kafka als Dichter" (1958) termed "Einsinnigkeit" ("monoperspectivity"), lends his stories an unprecedented obscurity. Whereas traditional psychological fiction, whose objective is to reveal, not to conceal, frequently introduces an authoritative voice that reports reliably on the characters' psychic depths, in Kafka's works the main character's perspective engulfs the reader. In *The Trial* and even more so in *The Castle*, where the principal characters' perspectives are relativized only by a sequence of contradictory and doubtful secondary testimonies, the question of authority, of which voice we are to believe, is relegated to constant abeyance.

Kafka nevertheless shares some techniques with the technical innovator Schnitzler. Schnitzler, who introduced the interior monologue into German with his 1900 novella "Leutnant Gustl," is the probable source of Kafka's use of the same technique in "The Burrow." In some of his first-person narratives, for example "A Report to an Academy" and "Investigations of a Dog," and arguably also in other stories such as "A Little Woman," "The Burrow," and "Josephine the Singer," Kafka avails himself of the device of the unreliable first-person narrator, a device frequently found in Schnitzler. Unreliable first-person narratives are, of course, not "einsinnig": a second implied voice questions the narrator's. Beißner's theory of the omnipresence of "Einsinnigkeit" in Kafka's fiction in fact holds best for his third-person works.[25]

Kafka's texts abound in parallels to Freud. There is ample evidence that Kafka's thematization of the father-son relationship ("The Judgment," "The Metamorphosis") and his frequent representation of conflicted characters (such as Georg Bendemann in "The Judgment," Gregor Samsa in "The Metamorphosis," Josef K. in *The Trial*) are autobiographically motivated. Yet these themes markedly resemble Freud's central theories of the Oedipus complex and the repressed unconscious. Kafka also uses various techniques that closely resemble the mechanisms of the dream as Freud described them. His descriptions of the outside world frequently reflect or concretize his protagonist's fears, desires, and fantasies. Thus in *Amerika* the hugeness, confusingness, and darkness of Pollunder's country house reflect Karl Rossman's confusion, and where the description veers into the fantastic, it approximates Freudian dream distortion. Similarly, the surreal scene in "The Judgment" where Georg Bendemann's father leaps terrifyingly on the bed and thunders his fatal judgment enacts Georg's repressed subservience to his father; Josef K.'s repeated discovery of his two guards being whipped in a storage room in *The Trial* enacts his desire for revenge on them and what they represent; the doctor's supernatural adventure in "A Country Doctor" appears to play out his conflicting sexual desires.[26] The sequentiality of Kafka's narrative resembles in places the associative illogic of a dream, for instance in the second chapter of *The Trial*, where Josef K. seeks and finds the court in an obscure tenement. Finally, Günther Anders's idea that Kafka constructs narratives around "extended metaphors," the literalization of common German figures of speech, which has found widespread acceptance among critics, is, as we shall see in chapter 7, a technique that Freud ascribes to the dream work.[27]

By "allegory" in Kafka I mean the implication of an ulterior meaning. His stories are well known for their resistance to being read at face value. Persistently pointing beyond themselves, they suggest a hidden significance, although precisely what this significance is, they persistently refuse to yield up. His narratives support multiple allegorical interpretations: critics have read his works as religious, psychoanalytic, social, and existential allegories, as allegories of Judaism and of the artist. Kafka thus takes allegory far beyond Hofmannsthal's relatively straightforward allegorizing. Yet one sees Hofmannsthal-like techniques particularly in Kafka's early works. In *Beschreibung eines Kampfes* (*Description of a Struggle*), in Hofmannsthal's manner, characters represent abstract ideas. Frequently, like Hofmannsthal, Kafka splits characters into two, using two characters to represent what might be seen as different aspects of a single character. Thus the child in "Unglücklichsein" ("Unhappiness") in *Meditation* is another aspect of the narrator; Georg Bendemann and his Petersburg friend in "The Judgment," in Kate Flores's interpretation, represent different sides of a single (Kafka's own) personality.[28]

But Kafka's most important point of contact with the turn-of-the-century Austrian writers is his parodistic use of dualities—dualities that his predecessors, and to an even greater degree his contemporary Musil, took extremely seriously. Where they see the world as governed by two terms both of which are real, Kafka affirms only the term occupied by the subject, setting up the unknown or "dark" term merely as an elusive, infinitely receding, unattainable goal. Its nature remains undefined, except through the (by definition unreliable) subject.[29]

Starting with *The Trial*, but particularly with his work of 1917 and beyond, in such texts as "The Great Wall of China," "The Next Village," "A Common Confusion," "Advocates," "Give It Up!," "On Parables," *The Castle*, and "The Burrow," Kafka favors the plot of the frustrated quest. As we shall see in detail in chapter 3, he bases this type of plot on the structural principle of the infinite regress. These stories of nonarrival exemplify Kafka's habit of employing an ostensible code—in this case the quest plot—without proffering the message that was traditionally attached to the code, of employing a strategy without adopting its implications but, rather, subtly debunking them.

The favorite plot of the frustrated quest suggests that Kafka is hinting at a general psychological law: that the subject is unwittingly so invested in maintaining the possibility of a meaning that is *beyond* apprehension, that is, in maintaining an object to quest after, that it unremittingly *manufactures*, again unconsciously, the unattainability of the object of its desire, of its quest, of its fear, and so on, at the same time as it ostensibly and consciously strives to attain or vanquish it. Lack of fulfillment, as well as the obsessive pursuit of the goal, are thus foregone conclusions. This psychological interpretation is best demonstrated not through the enigmatic parables and novels where human beings quest in vain—where Josef K. seeks the law or where K. strives to attain the Castle—but in the parodistic and uniquely transparent animal tale "Investigations of a Dog." In this story, unlike in any other, Kafka hints broadly to the reader that the dog-narrator's quest is motivated by a psychological blind spot. The blind spot is that the dog refuses to acknowledge the existence of human beings. He blanks them out of the lives of dogs.[30] If we human readers add the missing human element to the story, what strikes the dog as mysterious and worthy of investigation becomes ordinary. The mysterious seven dogs he sees dancing on their hind legs can be understood as circus dogs; the "Lufthunde" who float in the air are lap dogs; food, which seems to come "from above," comes from human beings. The dog's blindness to the presence of humans turns his queries into obsessions. But why this singular blindness? Evidently, the dog has an unconscious interest in maintaining it, in prolonging his pursuit of these interesting questions, rather than finding a conclusive and thereby disappointing answer.

In the stories where human beings quest in vain one frequently finds the complication that the goal of the search seems to be generated by, or even mirrors, the hero.[31] In the parable "Before the Law" the man from the country is informed that the gate before which he waited a lifetime in vain was "meant for him." In *The Trial* Josef K. himself infuses the court proceeding against him with energy. Indeed, the contradictory court, at once lofty and sleazy, reflects the two sides of Josef K. himself, his façade of respectability versus his inner, sexual self. In *The Castle*, likewise, the castle's principal move in the game to which K. challenges it is to echo him. Like the court in *The Trial*, it is at once sublime and disreputable, and mirrors a similar enigma in K., who appears now as a shining hero, now as a wily adventurer. In these works, not only does the unattainability of the object of the quest appear to be a function of the hero; inextricably involved with this question is to what extent the subject makes or determines its own object. Is Kafka commenting on the nature of knowledge: all a man can know is his own face?[32] Or, and this would be by far the stronger statement, is he propounding a general law of human psychology: that the quest, or affectively charged relation of a subject to an object, is the fundamental expression of man's vital instinct, such that the subject *manufactures* not merely the unattainability of the object of desire but the object itself? This latter reading is not upheld by "Investigations of a Dog": the dog does not invent the existence of humans, but merely fails to register it. This animal story is of uncertain status, however: like the story of an ape in "A Report to an Academy," it may be read as a parodic variation on Kafka's more serious stories about human beings, so that the interpretation it overtly proffers, that the mysterious "other" is a full and not an empty term, must not necessarily be applied retrospectively to them.

The chapters that follow do not focus on authors but, instead, pursue lines that are common to more than one author. Collectively, these chapters aim to identify and elucidate what I take to be the central epistemological model of the Austrian *Jahrhundertwende*. As is to be expected of a construct that possesses high strategic value, whether as the foundation of a theory (in the case of Freud) or for the emplotment and also the self-legitimation of literary texts, it is rarely articulated overtly, in a straightforward expository fashion. Rather, it articulates itself in recurrent figures, themes, and devices, which, in turn, reveal the model's logic and its uses. With an end to investigating this logic and these uses, the following chapters are organized around these figures, themes, and devices, juxtaposing in each case analyses of texts by several authors in order to demonstrate the diversity as well as the continuity of a given pattern.

1 FIGURES OF DUALITY

THE DECADENT MOVEMENT in fin-de-siècle art eschewed the vital: the decadent hero par excellence, Des Esseintes of Huysmans's 1884 novel *A rebours* (*Against the Grain*), abhors anything that resembles life or health and pursues his taste for the artificial, the exotic, and the perverse in perfectly enclosed chambers, in an inverted paradise where he can isolate himself completely from the real world. But a nostalgia for naturalness, spontaneity, simplicity, community, and health preceded and also ran parallel to this relish for decadence. Throughout the second half of the nineteenth century the habits of mind that led to a solitary, unproductive, vicarious existence such as Des Esseintes's were widely castigated as conducing to misery.

The personality thus fated to create its own unhappiness was given to an excess of reflection. Reflection was seen to inhibit action and undermine happiness; always divided against themselves, these anti-heroes were incapable of the kind of unambiguous feeling that inspires deeds and makes contentment possible. They were incapable of seeing things in terms of black and white, of beginnings and endings. For them all concepts (such as "love") dissolved, on reflection, into nuances. The type of the overconscious anti-hero, of the decadent hero *malgré soi*, recurs in literature before and during the 1890s. We find versions of it in Henri-Frédéric Amiel's *Fragments d'un journal intime*, written in the 1850s but published in this abridged version in 1882–84; in Fëdor Dostoevskij's *Notes from Underground* (1864); in Edouard Rod's *La Course à la mort* (1885; The race to death); in Arne Garborg's *Traette Maend* (1891; Tired men); in Paul Bourget's *Physiologie de l'amour moderne* (1891; Physiology of modern love); and, to name some Viennese examples, in Hofmannsthal's *Death and the Fool* (1893) and Schnitzler's *Anatol* (1893).

These works thus do not uphold the decadent values, but rather vitalistic ones. Health is equated with living, with feeling, with the unreflected life instincts, with the ability to experience passion and fuse with the moment in experience. But these life instincts were considered delicate: they were the prey of forces within the self, of reflection and self-consciousness. The decadent anti-hero is someone who would like to live, who would like to be natural, but who cannot embrace life.

Within the field of the opposing tendencies of vitalism and decadence, certain epistemic figures, figures that impose a way of knowing on the world, dominate. We see here versions, as in Des Esseintes's "paradise" and in the essential *dividedness* of the overconscious anti-hero, of the key figures that will persist, albeit appropriated for a variety of new interests and invested with different values, throughout the work of Hofmannsthal, Schnitzler, Musil, Freud, Kafka, and others. The first figure is the line, conceived as a boundary or a horizon: a dividing or enclosing line. The second figure declares the areas divided by the line to be opposites, such as light versus dark or figure versus ground. The third figure, which frequently involves an organic or otherwise natural image, such as a plant or flower or flowing water, invokes continuity, and as such is a boundary-crossing device.

My initial purpose in this chapter will be to examine these figures in three different contexts: in a philosophical text that was seminal for fin-de-siècle letters, Nietzsche's *On the Advantage and Disadvantage of History for Life* (1874); in a literary text, Hofmannsthal's famous lyrical drama *Death and the Fool* (1893); and finally in Freud's earliest psychological work, *Studies on Hysteria* (1895), which he coauthored with Josef Breuer. I hope thereby to show that these figures were firmly entrenched in the fin de siècle, that they were employed in the service of a single model or value system, and that they, along with the model, were readily transferrable from discipline to discipline. The three texts under discussion all operate with dualities, which occur in spatial and temporal versions: as light versus dark (betokening known versus the unknown, consciousness versus the unconscious), and as the past versus the present. They operate with images of the enclosure (signifying the integrity of the subject) and the dividing line (signifying the self versus the other). In all three texts, health and happiness are identified with remaining firmly within one's own space or time. At the same time, without acknowledging any discrepancy, the three texts all affirm the value of continuity.

I shall then trace the shift in Freud's work from a monistic conception of the psyche, already put into question by the end of *Studies on Hysteria* with the introduction of the concept of repression, to a dualistic conception in *The Interpretation of Dreams*. It will be seen that the three figures continued to be used, but in the service of a new model. Freud institutionalized the dangerous area on the other side of the line within the psyche as the unconscious. The section on *The Interpretation of Dreams* discusses the logic of that construct, both as the foundation for Freud's metapsychology and as an interpretative strategy.

Nietzsche's *On the Advantage and Disadvantage of History for Life*

Nietzsche's second Untimely Meditation, *On the Advantage and Disadvantage of History for Life*, was one of his most influential philosophical texts for the fin de siècle. Immensely appealing and persuasive, reasonably consistent in its argument, and a stylistic tour de force, Nietzsche's famous polemic against historical studies and the historical consciousness of the Germans was widely read as soon as it appeared and remained enormously popular. Mauthner, considering what works influenced his own language skepticism, singles out this essay for particular mention and recalls that in his student days "the second untimely meditation . . . struck into our midst like a bolt of lightning," and adds, "for myself, I confess that no work by Nietzsche ever again made such a tremendous impression on me."[1] For the young Hofmannsthal, Nietzsche was a revelation. In a letter of 1892 to Felix Salten he wrote, "We experience in 3 pages of Nietzsche much more than in all the adventures, episodes, and agonies of our lives" (BI:57, my translation). He knew *On the Advantage and Disadvantage of History for Life* by age sixteen at the latest, for he cites it as the epigraph for his poem "Gedankenspuk" (1890). Nietzsche's piece not only is a principal source of the vitalistic values that captured the imaginations of our authors, but it contains most of the figures that we will see repeated and permuted in their works of the 1890s and beyond. Nietzsche's superb rhetoric spins out images that are based on these figures, one suggesting the next. The essay's flamboyant beginning chapter and declamatory final chapter, where Nietzsche stresses the disadvantages rather than the advantages of history for life, will serve as a useful starting point for our investigation of turn-of-the-century Austrian writers. I am interested, therefore, in one position taken by the text, namely the polemic against historical study, where the relevant figures occur, and shall not discuss the rest of the essay, where Nietzsche speaks of monumental, antiquarian, and critical history.

Nietzsche begins section 1 of the essay with a proclamation on the nature of happiness. He conjures up the spectacle of the blissful animal, contrasted with miserable man. The characteristic of animals he singles out as conducive to bliss is not, as one might expect, their lack of reason or self-consciousness or language—though by implication these are among their virtues too, since all these human attributes will come under fire as problematical in the final chapter—but, rather, their lack of memory. If the animal frolics about, happily eating and digesting, it is because it knows no past, but only an eternal present moment. Ironically, man, not the animal, is tied to a chain: the past. Past time always comes fluttering back:

> He cannot learn to forget but always remains attached to the past: however far and fast he runs, the chain runs with him. It is astonishing: the moment, here in a wink, gone in a wink, nothing before and nothing after, returns nevertheless as a spectre to disturb the calm of a later moment. Again and again a page loosens in the scroll of time, drops out, and flutters away—and suddenly flutters back again into man's lap. Then man says "I remember" and envies the animal which immediately forgets and sees each moment really die, sink back into deep night extinguished for ever. . . . This is why he is moved, as though he remembered a lost paradise, when he sees a grazing herd. (AD 8–9)

As Nietzsche's final reference to paradise underscores, the animal is happy because, a being undivided, it is never at one remove from itself. Nothing prevents it from fusing with the present moment, the present experience. In this passage Nietzsche establishes presence and unity as paramount values, equivalent to happiness.

This showy, pathetic, rhetorical opening is a false façade for Nietzsche's principal purpose in the essay, which is to criticize the contemporary state of affairs in German culture and to try to trace its causes. The real target of his ire is nineteenth-century historicism, together with Hegel's idea that history is a process. Nietzsche dislikes the prevalence of foreign influences in German life, which create an uncertain, imitative, weak culture instead of a natural, indigenous, original one. This state of affairs is exacerbated by the value placed on knowledge, learning, and absorbing the legacy of the past, which cripple all action. In the polemical final section Nietzsche places great confidence in youth and its energy, and exhorts youth to shake off its shackles. He suggests that young people are being ruined by their present form of education: instead of stuffing their heads full of other people's ideas, they should trust their own experiences, their own unmediated perceptions, and their natural inclination to act. Words, especially concepts, are the handmaidens of false, mediated knowledge: his generation is "sown with concepts as with dragon's teeth, engendering concept-dragons, in addition suffering from the sickness of words and without trust in any feeling of our own which has not yet been rubber-stamped with words" (AD 61). The essential value, for Nietzsche, is life. He opposes life to thought. People generally think too much and do not live enough. They are "cogitals" instead of "animals." The antidotes for the historical malady, Nietzsche asserts, are the unhistorical and the "superhistorical," the "superhistorical" being a view that puts no faith in progress but, rather, recognizes that static structures, imperishable types, and, ultimately, egocentric motivations underlie all historical events.

The opening paragraphs with their polemic against memory thus have little to do with the main contention of the essay, the urgent message that excessive reverence for history is nefarious. They do not lead into it, nor, if we consider things in reverse, do they strictly follow from it. True, if people had no memory, past time could not enter their consciousness. But the historical past is not remembered—it is taught. Moreover, if we abolished memory we would abolish the continuity of self-awareness in the subject himself, the organic continuity that Nietzsche will later insist must be maintained, where he speaks of man feeling "a coherent living system of his own experiences grow within" (AD 60), and of culture growing out of life like a flower. Memory is a false foe.

But Nietzsche wants to make a radical beginning, to show that the past is unnecessary for life, to ground life in the present. The optimal climate for fostering genius and heroism is at the center of his concerns. The great deed, he surmises, is born of an untutored vitality, a forgetful exuberance, an ability to concentrate ruthlessly on the project at hand. Hence not merely inattention to history, but a personal ability to block out all thoughts extraneous to the deed itself, are desirable. In *The Genealogy of Morals*, where Nietzsche will accord positive value to memory as a precondition of promising and hence as an expression of man's strength, he speaks more plausibly than in *On the Advantage and Disadvantage of History* of the necessity of "forgetfulness" ("Vergeßlichkeit").[2]

Let us return to the opening argument. After presenting us with the spectacle of the animal frolicking in its paradise of forgetfulness, Nietzsche introduces a number of metaphors that figure past and present (or remembering and forgetting) visually. The effect is to loosen "present" and "past" from the conceptual framework of a temporal continuum and to give the impression that they may be polarized, indeed placed in a relation of opposition to each other. The first is a metaphor of light and dark: "All acting requires forgetting, as not only light but also darkness is required for life by all organisms" (AD 10). Nietzsche goes on to speak of the necessity of sleep. Dark as well as light, sleep as well as wakefulness are necessary for life. Where the alternation of dark and light still implies a temporal process, Nietzsche continues with a frankly spatial image, that of the horizon:

> And this is a general law: every living thing can become healthy, strong, and fruitful only within a horizon; if it is incapable of drawing a horizon around itself or, on the other hand, too selfish to restrict its vision to the limits of a horizon drawn by another, it will wither away feebly or overhastily to its early demise. (AD 10)

In this passage Nietzsche calls for an inside and an outside, a here and a there, and a boundary separating the two. The image of the horizon is ingenious. For the horizon is truly a boundary that polarizes: what is on our side of it is visible, what is on the other side is invisible. A primary division, Nietzsche claims, must take place whereby man limits himself to a certain defined area and stops looking beyond it. Yet the drawing of the horizon is dependent on the position of the subject; the subject can to some degree (and must, says Nietzsche) control his own horizon. The horizon is also a circle and thus recalls the notion of paradise Nietzsche invoked when talking about animals.

Nietzsche continues:

> Cheerfulness, clear conscience, the carefree deed, faith in the future, all this depends, in the case of an individual as well as of a people, on there being a line which distinguishes what is clear and in full view from the dark and unilluminable. (AD 10)

In this passage the metaphor of the horizon—here termed a "line"—is fused with the metaphor of light versus dark, where light and dark have become metaphors no longer for activity and rest, or wakefulness and sleep, as previously, but for the known and the unknown, for things clear and things obscure. With this last metaphorical displacement Nietzsche recalls Kant's figure of delimitation in the *Critique of Pure Reason*, the strict boundary that Kant erected between objects of possible experience, to which the categories of our understanding apply and of which knowledge is possible, and "things in themselves," or noumena. Wittgenstein in the *Tractatus* would take up the same figure in drawing a sharp boundary between the sayable and the ineffable. Nietzsche, however, is not interested in describing the limits of what is possible, but in prescribing what is healthy. According to him, the health, strength, and fruitfulness of all living things consists in their ability to stay within the illuminated area and to shut out the dark, to be on *one* side of the line and ignore what lies beyond.

Thus in these paragraphs, Nietzsche establishes a chain of equivalent dualities: present/past, light/dark, inside/outside, known/unknown, health/sickness.

Nietzsche then brings forth new images: the unhistorical figures as a cloud of mist and man's intellect as a flash of light within it. The flash of light is an old metaphor for the imagination or intellect. In Wordsworth's *Prelude* 6.13, in the sections on crossing the Alps and the ascent of Mt. Snowdon, the poet evokes an access of the imagination as flashes of light arising out of a vapor or above a sea of mist. Emerson describes moments of transparency or ecstasy, that is, a feeling of oneness with the universe, as flashes of light. Nietzsche will recur to the notion that all living creatures need a protective, womblike or nestlike enveloping haze (AD 41, 57). In another of Nietzsche's images, man's intellect is a living whirlpool within a dead sea. What is essential in these metaphors of Nietzsche's is a division of things into background and foreground. In Nietzsche's argument the foreground of life, the positive pattern, is impossible without a background of forgetting.

Once he has created this basic opposition, once he has drawn the essential dividing line, Nietzsche can shift gears and put his ostensible affirmation of duality into its correct perspective. For in the further course of the text Nietzsche introduces a different and contradictory ideal model, one that undercuts the polemic against memory or what Philippe Lacoue-Labarthe terms Nietzsche's "onto-zoology."[3] This new model is organic continuity. An initial division between the terrain proper to the self, where the self can healthfully reside and where subdivision is no longer possible, and alterity, which must be ignored, is merely a precaution, a practical measure to prevent further, repeated dividings. In the final section (10) Nietzsche sums up his positive program for German culture. It is built on an organic metaphor ("like a flower"). Nietzsche maintains that once one has life, culture can blossom out of it, instead of being "tacked on like a paper flower" (AD 59). Culture should be natural and organic, not tacked on and artificial. In the process of developing this organic metaphor, Nietzsche disconcertingly reverses the value that his inside/outside duality had when the life-fostering horizon was under discussion. There positive, here it is assimilated to a dichotomy between being and seeming and takes on pejorative connotations. The present-day Germans are "crumbled and fallen apart, on the whole half mechanically divided into an inside and an outside" (AD 61). Previously, in section 3 of the essay, he had already allowed the inside/outside figure to metamorphose into an object of his dislike: namely, the dichotomy between German "Innerlichkeit," the Germans' so-called content, and their false façade of conventionality, their outward form. German "Innerlichkeit," Nietzsche insists, today consists only of stuffed-in extraneous fare and hence brings only indigestion, or the lethargy of a snake who has swallowed a rabbit (AD 24).

According to the organic view of culture, all divisions are anathema. A young man should feel "a coherent living system of his own experiences grow within" (AD 60). At this stage, there will be continuity and no more "inside" and "outside": "Thus the Greek concept of culture . . . will be unveiled to him, the concept of culture as a new and improved nature, without inside and outside, without dissimulation and convention, of culture as the accord of life, thought, appearing and willing" (AD 64).

Nietzsche's ambivalence between affirming continuity and upholding duality nevertheless persists into the final chapter. This chapter is a hymn to life, the mystical ultimate value that he counterposes to "thought." The word "life" sounds insistently: "above all men must learn to live" (AD 58), "full and green 'life'" (AD 61), "First give me life and I will make you a culture from it!" (AD 61). Yet the dualistic mode of argumentation has by no means been abandoned. Nietzsche chooses to stress a duality that was already present in the opening chapter: health/sickness. The individual firmly rooted in *life* is healthy, while the individual without a horizon, without the ability to forget, thrust into an "endless-unlimited light-wave-sea of known becoming" (AD 62), is sick with "the historical malady" (AD 62). This final duality is astutely chosen, for it ostensibly harmonizes with the value of "life" and the organic metaphor, and hence it purports to reconcile the vocabulary of continuity with the vocabulary of division that has been indispensable to Nietzsche's argument.

The tension between insisting on duality and according value to continuity is one we will encounter repeatedly in turn-of-the-century Austrian texts. This tension will recur as one between psychic conflict and psychic integration, between an interest in hidden meaning and a desire for interpretive accessibility, and as a nostalgia for a realm of enduring values versus a perception of the reality of social change and the necessity for personal transformation. Regardless of the content with which the terms are infused, the authors we shall consider typically hesitate between affirming transition and evaluating transition as transgression.

Hofmannsthal's *Death and the Fool*

Nietzsche's influence on Hofmannsthal's most famous lyrical drama, *Death and the Fool*, is obvious, not only because the Death figure refers to *The Birth of Tragedy*, calling himself one of Dionysus's kin, but because the Fool, Claudio, embodies Nietzsche's historical type who is incapable of living in the present. Just as in *On the Advantage and Disadvantage of History for Life*, the mystical value *life* is placed in an antithetical relationship to the past, the intellect, conceptual language, art and artificiality, and knowledge generally. Claudio calls it "old, all too confused knowledge."[4]

The play is an allegorical critique of aestheticism. Claudio is a static character, the type of the aesthete, drawn without nuances so that Hofmannsthal can condemn him. The stage decoration is significant: the curtain opens on the overly intellectual Claudio in his study at sunset, where he is surrounded by various antiques—"Altertümer"—and art objects. In the opening soliloquy Claudio presents his self-portrait. It might seem odd that a dramatic character should state his problems so forthrightly, yet it is appropriate that this overly conscious character should be overly conscious of his problems.[5] We find Claudio looking out of the window at a natural scene. The first thing that becomes apparent is that all his perceptions are mediated by art. Claudio begins:

Now the last mountains lie in gleaming shrouds,
Clothed in the moistened glow of sun-steeped air.

> There hangs a wreath of alabaster clouds
> Above, here rimmed with gold, grey shadows there:
> So once did Masters of past centuries
> Paint clouds which bear Our Lady through the skies.
> (PVP 95)

Claudio sees the clouds as alabaster wreaths. They have a gold border like a dish or a book. He looks on the scene as if it were a *picture*, framed by the window. The clouds remind him further of clouds painted by early masters.

Claudio starts imagining a mythical people living in the mountains— interesting to him because he conceives of them in contrast to himself. They are simple, while he is complicated; they live, and he does not; they feel, he does not; they live in a community, while he is isolated; they are natural, but he is surrounded by artifice.

Claudio's problem is that he lives mediately, in other words, not at all. He complains that he has had no experiences, neither positive nor nega- tive—no passions, no extremes of joy or suffering. Instead of living his life, he thinks about it. He describes his joys as "lost," his tears as "un- shed," his sufferings as "petty," his joys as "gone stale." If he lives, he lives vicariously. The ornaments in his room—the cups, the lutes, the objets d'art—are symbols of the experiences others have had. He studies life instead of living it. Overconscious, he is incapable of forgetting, of losing himself in the moment of experience. Instead, he compulsively compares everything to something else, thus depriving the experience of its immediacy and reducing the unknown to the known:

> If ever I felt a feeble breath or stir
> Of natural emotion or desire,
> At once my conscious mind, which never yet
> Has learnt to sleep or to forget,
> Would leap awake to meddle in the game
> And kill the urge by giving it a name.
> When thousands of comparisons occurred,
> Then faith was gone and bliss an empty word.
> (PVP 99)

He kills things by naming them. In a further passage, Claudio says:

> I turned about and contemplated life:
> In which the runner does not gain by speed,

Nor courage help the fighter in his strife,
Misfortune need not sadden, nor luck lead
To happiness.
(PVP 103)

Concepts ("speed," "courage," "misfortune," "luck") are, we infer, at odds with life: with running, fighting, feeling sorrow, and feeling joy.[6] Claudio's house is situated in an enclosed garden. Hofmannsthal remarks in *Ad me ipsum* that "claudere" means "to close." Like Huysmans's Des Esseintes, Claudio closes himself off from life, but here such aestheticistic estrangement is pejorative. Claudio's problem is not merely that he closes himself off, however, but that he does so imperfectly. Here the play approaches most closely Nietzsche's metaphorical illustration, through the metaphors of the line and the horizon, of the right and the wrong way to live. Claudio perpetually desires what is beyond his enclosure, what is far away. He scorns what is within his reach, which seems empty and uninteresting: "But when my gaze approaches what is near / All things grow bleak, offensive, dull, and dim" (PVP 97). It is indicative that he sits at the window of his room, at the border between inside and outside, and longs for what is outside. He idolizes the mountain people for their distance from him. The more he imagines they are not like him and have what he does not, the more they fascinate him. In short, Claudio is not happy with his enclosure. He does not block out what is beyond. He does not follow Nietzsche's precept of defining the enclosure as the totality. Here, as in *On the Advantage and Disadvantage of History for Life*, drawing a line is useful only if one ignores what is on the other side.

The spatial state of being neither here nor there is restated in Claudio's relation to time. Like Nietzsche's historical man, he cannot forget, cannot live in the present:

Not wholly conscious, nor free from consciousness,
My sufferings petty and my joys gone stale,
Always I dragged along that awful curse
Which made my life a book, some twice-told tale
Partly not yet intelligible, partly no longer so.
(PVP 103)

Intelligibility divides itself into past and future. Claudio lives his life in a blank present, in an absence between memory and anticipation. The same image occurs two more times (PVP 115, 133–34). In one instance the temporal caesura in Claudio's life is, as in Nietzsche's text, reexpressed in the spatial terms of inside and outside. Claudio is condemned to live without knowing or to know without living. Hence he is permanently on the opposite side of the gateway to life:

> As meadow flowers, uprooted, flow
> In dark flood water, driven on,
> So my young days have passed and gone;
> If that was really life, I never called it so.
> Then . . . then I stood behind the gate of life,
> Awed by its wonders, full of deep desire
> That mighty storms should blast it with lightning's
>   fire,
> Cut every bar as with a marvellous knife.
> It would not happen . . . but I stood inside,
> Bereft of grace, and could not recollect
> Even myself or my most fervent wishes,
> Bound by a spell that froze and petrified.
> (PVP 115–17)

Nietzsche's equivalences past/present, inside/outside, health/sickness are thus also inscribed in Hofmannsthal's text. The mystical thing called "life" is implicitly characterized, through Claudio's failure to attain it, by unity, by spatial and temporal presence.

The figure of paradox characterizes Claudio. Claudio is perpetually in two places at once and hence in neither. He is neither alive nor dead. He is *death in life*. During his lifetime he was as if dead: "I saw the very sun with eyes long dead" (PVP 103), he laments, where the sun functions as the eloquent symbol of nature and life. He lives only in the few moments before death, when his whole life comes back to him with extraordinary vividness and when a sense of being alive rises in him with unparalleled intensity. His final speech adds paradox to paradox: "Dying, at last I feel that I exist. . . . / So from the dream of life I now may wake, / Cloyed with emotion, to death's wakefulness" (PVP 135). His pregnant death stands in chiastic relation with his empty life.

"Death is the mother of beauty," writes Wallace Stevens.[7] This is precisely Death's function here. Only when a barrier is imposed from the outside, when the horizon is drawn, can Claudio live. Death is *life in death*. He introduces himself as "to Dionysos, Venus most akin" (PVP

113).[8] In Nietzsche's *Birth of Tragedy* Dionysus is associated with music; the Death figure here plays the violin.

Death scolds the Fool after the manner of Nietzsche in *On the Advantage and Disadvantage of History for Life*, for having had the chance to live, to infuse the rubble of history with his own independent spirit, and for having failed:

> What all men have, you, too, were given:
> An earthly life, to be lived in earthly fashion.
> Inside you all a faithful spirit dwells
> Who to this chaos of dead matter
> Can lend significance and tells
> Each one to make his garden so
> That, in it, joys and cares and work may grow.
> (PVP 117)

Death parades before Claudio the people he hurt during his life: his mother, his girlfriend, his friend—people who *really* lived. Whereas the emptying figure of paradox characterizes Claudio's life, the inclusive figure of oxymoron is a recurrent theme of their experiences: they speak of "sweet sorrows" (PVP 121), "tender gloom" (PVP 131; "süße Schwermut"), and so on. Genuine life, it is implied, includes suffering as well as joy, the depths as well as the heights of human experience.

In the last minutes before his death, Claudio finally feels the genuine pain he should have felt during his lifetime. Death puts Claudio in contact with his past: ironically, Claudio *never* lives in the present. This return to the past engages the same ideal of continuity that we encountered in Nietzsche. Indeed, this play affirms continuity more forthrightly and emphatically than *On the Advantage and Disadvantage of History for Life*, and also more globally. Hofmannsthal celebrates not only the continuity of an individual's past with his present, as does Nietzsche, but also a mystical interconnectedness of the individual with the rest of the universe. The positive images in the play have to do with transitions and with integration. They are mainly expressed in terms of liquid: streaming, flooding, surging, melting; of air: floating into, blowing through; and of weaving. Thus when Claudio hears Death's violin, he exclaims,

> In shuddering and long-awaited gusts
> Most mightily this music thrusts

At me; unending hope it seems
And infinite regret, that streams
As if from all these ancient, silent walls
My life, transformed, were flowing back to me.
(PVP 109)

Death brings his youth back to him, which he reexperiences as "a youth-ful sea" in which he felt "that I could float and melt in air." "How over-joyed I was, how rapt to find / Myself a link in life's encircling chain!" Claudio exclaims, "And, guided by the heart, I soon divined / The stream of love that nourishes all hearts" (PVP 111).

The system of values this play upholds is ostensibly more coherent and less patently fraught with tension than Nietzsche's, where the use-fulness of duality and the value accorded to continuity coexisted in un-declared disharmony. Hofmannsthal's ideal is unity, that is, the individ-ual's mystical sense of oneness with all of creation. Hence enclosure per se is pejorative. But given the practical condition of limitation, it is bet-ter to be content with one's enclosure, better to be at one with what is within it, than perpetually desirous of what one cannot have. Never-theless, it comes as no surprise that in *Death and the Fool* too, an unre-solved tension exists between the ideal of unity and the expedient of the enclosure. Unity remains a purely hypothetical ideal. For the character Claudio it is realizable only with extinction in death.

The subordinate figures, the Mother, the Young Girl, and the Man, are designed as a collective counterexample: they present a model of how to live that ostensibly reconciles limitation with unity. But Hofmannsthal accomplishes this reconciliation only by sleight of hand. It is implied that by leading the lives proper to them, that is, within their respective enclosures, by having normal, irreversible human experiences, they mys-teriously partake of the totality, of that mysterious thing called Life. In the case of the Mother the opposition between human limitation and universal boundlessness is explicitly lifted and replaced by the comfort-ing suggestion of analogy: her restricted household environment is, it is suggested, related to the frame within which the whole world weaves, the human cycle to universal temporality. The Mother says,

This hand: it waters flowers, beats the dust
From cushions, rubs brass handles bright and clean—
So the day passes; but the head has nothing
To do: all day a padded wheel revolves,

With premonitions, nightmare anxieties,
Mysterious feelings of unwarranted pain,
Connected, I suppose, with the obscure,
Unfathomable sacrament of motherhood
Which is akin to all the deepest workings
Of this world.
(PVP 123)

With the expedient of the enclosure, in which happiness is theoretically possible if one does not look beyond, the issue of desire portends trouble. Like Claudio, the subordinate figures desire. Hence the replete, tautological images of contentment have no more place in their biographies than they do in Claudio's. Hofmannsthal is obliged, using another sleight of hand, to substitute for them the figure of oxymoron. Attaining the object of desire is sweet, losing it is bitter; hence life is bittersweet. Hofmannsthal implies (assuming that we are willing to make do with oxymora as the product of our enclosure) that there is a right kind of desire. The Young Girl and the Man, unlike Claudio, desire truly, not just compulsively. If Claudio attains what he wants, he ceases to want it. If these figures attain the objects of their desires, it is implied, they are happy; when they do not they are genuinely disappointed; in either case they partake of life, of its ephemeral joys and its sorrows.

Breuer and Freud's *Studies on Hysteria*

In the "Preliminary Communication" or first essay in *Studies on Hysteria*, which Breuer and Freud coauthored in 1892, we see a model for sickness and health remarkably similar to that in Nietzsche's *On the Advantage and Disadvantage of History for Life* and in Hofmannsthal's *Death and the Fool*. Moreover, these authors unroll precisely the same chain of metaphoric equivalences we saw in Nietzsche's essay, and which Hofmannsthal to a large extent duplicated: present/past, light/dark, inside/outside, known/unknown, health/sickness.

The essential elements of the theory of hysteria proposed in the "Preliminary Communication" are the idea that the psyche can be split; the idea that the split has an external cause; and the notion that the split signifies mental illness.

The idea of the split consciousness or *double conscience* was in itself nothing new; Freud and Breuer refer to the work of Alfred Binet and

Pierre Janet. Freud's later innovation, in *The Interpretation of Dreams*, would be to declare the split in consciousness a fundamental feature of every healthy psyche. The split becomes nonpathological, in fact necessary; conflict becomes an intrinsic part of the psyche and psychic development. In *Studies on Hysteria*, however, it is taken for granted that a split consciousness is a sign of illness. The "other consciousness" manifests itself in hysterical symptoms.

According to Breuer and Freud, the cause of the split psyche is not itself psychic. Rather, the original, healthy wholeness of the psyche is disturbed by something foreign to it, something introduced from the outside. This "foreign body," as Breuer and Freud call it, is the memory of the trauma. Often the trauma took place far in the past, but its repressed memory nevertheless sits in the psyche, remarkably fresh. The underlying analogy in this conception of illness and health is that of body for mind. Just as the integrity of a physical organism is disturbed when a "foreign body," say a splinter, invades it, the psyche is made ill by an external trauma that lodges itself in the mind in the form of a memory. Breuer and Freud conclude: "Hysterics suffer mainly from reminiscences" (SE 2:7).

The authors thus propose a monistic conception of psychic health. The healthy psyche is perceived to be whole and unitary. "Illness" means that a boundary that should be inviolable, that between inside and outside, is transgressed. A similar boundary is presumed to exist between present and past. The pathogenic element is a piece of the outside and a piece of the past, which interrupts the autonomy and also the presentness of the self.

Breuer and Freud's model of health and illness is thus identical to Nietzsche's in *On the Advantage and Disadvantage of History for Life*. Both the temporal and the spatial versions of Nietzsche's line are implicit in Freud and Breuer's formulation of a "remembered trauma" as the cause of hysteria.

According to Breuer and Freud, the psyche's natural defense against unpleasant stimuli from the outside is *abreaction*. The organism reacts to the outside stimulus by producing an excess of affective excitation. In the normal healthy pattern, this excess excitation is got rid of through the normal affective reaction, for example revenge or shouting. The memory to which the excitation is attached is expelled in the same process. Alternately, we integrate memories through association with other memories. The implicit ideal, then, as in Nietzsche's text, is continuity: provided the past is not expelled outright, it should gradually fade, be imperceptibly absorbed into the present.

When the subject is in a state of shock resulting from a trauma, abreaction fails to take place, so that the memory enters the psyche, causing a psychic split. The split-off part of the psyche where the memory of the trauma resides is inaccessible to the subject's normal consciousness. The cure then takes place when this dark area is "brought to light," in Breuer and Freud's metaphor, or made conscious in the psychoanalytic cure and expelled in words. "Consciousness" here, one notes, has a different value from that in *On the Advantage and Disadvantage of History for Life* and *Death and the Fool*. It is no longer memory's partner in iniquity, striving to destroy "life." Instead, the ally of health, it stands in opposition to memory.

Studies on Hysteria is a book with a drift in its argument. Freud, who writes all the case studies but one, drifts away, in the course of these studies, from the monistic conception of health he proposed along with Breuer in the "Preliminary Communication," so that by the end of the book, when he writes his separate theoretical conclusion, he has moved close to the theory of the dualistic psyche that he will announce in *The Interpretation of Dreams* and that will be fundamental to his thinking from that work onward. In his concluding remarks in "The Psychotherapy of Hysteria" he comes to see the trauma (coming from the outside) as less and less important in the etiology of hysteria; its place is taken by an affect coming from within, which is incompatible with other conscious ideas. The trauma is retained primarily as a way of explaining the onset of the symptom. At the same time, he plays down the idea of mental illness. For if the psyche generates its own conflicts, conflict can no longer be thought of as unhealthy in itself.

Let us take as an example the case of Elisabeth von R., Freud's patient. In this case study, the trauma consists merely of the moment when the conflict between Elisabeth's erotic feelings and her moral ideas becomes apparent. Standing at her dead sister's bedside, she thinks, "Now I can become his wife." Freud designates this moment, and other comparable moments of Elisabeth's awareness of her love for her brother-in-law, as the onset of hysterical conversion. Thenceforth, Elisabeth experiences hysterical pains in the leg—pains that revive a preexisting somatic condition, but which the patient also associates symbolically with her unmarried state (she "stands alone," "cannot take a single step forward," etc.). There is no question of serious mental illness: Freud writes, "What she had in her consciousness was only a secret and not a foreign body" (SE 2:139).

The key concept in the shift in Freud's ideas is repression. Freud comes to the conclusion that repression is the sine qua non of hysteria. The earliest Freudian idea, repression is a fascinating notion, which by its own logic leads to the idea of a dual psyche. Repression is allegedly the psyche's defense mechanism. The subject represses the incident to which the conflicting emotion attaches in order to protect itself from an unpleasant stimulus. But repression is an ambiguous defense. Let us compare it to abreaction, the forthright defense mentioned in the "Preliminary Communication." Abreaction allows the psyche to expel excitation along with the troublesome memory trace. Repression, in contrast, tucks the memory of the trauma away into the psyche. Consequently, it itself is the mechanism that creates the hysteria: it is simultaneously a defense and a capitulation, a wall and a gate. It protects the organism and at the same time makes it susceptible to mental illness.

As Freud's own strategy, repression may be seen as a device that enables him to explain why the unpleasant incident is retained and preserved as a pathogenic source. Repression is the psyche's built-in mechanism for creating its own split. Repression functions as a temporal as well as an axiological concept: some bit of the past is preserved, along with the desire that is deemed unacceptable. It brings with it a change in the notion of forgetting: forgetting is no longer straightforwardly healthy but might be a sign that repression has taken place.

Freud will never drop the idea of repression. In *The Interpretation of Dreams* repression is instrumental in filling out the unconscious, or one might even say in creating it, for infantile wishes, produced by the primary process, become unpleasant at the onset of the secondary process and are *repressed* into the unconscious. Throughout Freud's writing repression will retain its dual function of defense and preservation. In Freud's dynamic model of the psyche, repressed ideas demand to be discharged, in a converted form because they cannot be acknowledged, either as symptoms (*Studies on Hysteria*), dreams (*The Interpretation of Dreams*), or sublimated creative activity (*Leonardo da Vinci and a Memory of His Childhood*). This need for discharge leads to the idea of the "return of the repressed," an idea first explicitly formulated in the 1896 essay "Further Remarks on the Neuro-Psychoses of Defence." At the same time repression retains its second function of preservation. Thus in *The Interpretation of Dreams*, unconscious ideas are "indestructible." In the "Leonardo" essay, no matter to what extent Leonardo sublimates and converts his repressed love for his mother into latent homosexuality, the erotic attachment is preserved. Even in Freud's theoretical statement at the end of *Studies on Hysteria*, it becomes clear that the idea of repression conflicts with the ostensible aim of curing the patient: "The cathartic method . . . cannot affect the underlying causes of hysteria: thus it cannot prevent fresh symptoms from taking the place of the ones which had been got rid of" (SE 2:261). The cathartic method can cure the symptoms but not the cause of hysteria, for the propensity to repress is always present.

It is useful to contrast Freud's concluding remarks with Breuer's extensive final essay, which remains faithful to the theories of the "Preliminary Communication." Breuer sees the key to hysteria in hypnoid states. The implication is that two completely different systems are operating in the psyche of the afflicted patient: the conscious system and the hypnoid system. Each system is accessible from the outside, in a different manner, to stimuli and to the analyst. The hypnoid system is prone to attack from the outside by the trauma and open to accepting and harboring pathological material; the analyst can also gain access to it by hypnosis. Breuer's model for health is monistic: he sees the hypnoid system as abnormal. Healthy persons do not have a hypnoid system, and the physician's task is to try to get rid of it in the hysterical patient.

For Freud, the key to hysteria is not the hypnoid state, but repression and defense. Freud's system is dualistic: the mechanism for creating illness, repression, is contained in the psyche. The psyche thus becomes the site of permanent conflict. In his concluding remarks, Freud moves the split and the idea of conflict into the psyche. At the same time, the absoluteness of the split is undermined. Freud continues to believe that a boundary separates repressed (pathological) material from the rest of the psyche, but he begins to be interested in making the dividing line less strict:

> A foreign body does not enter into any relation with the layers of tissue that surround it, although it modifies them and necessitates a reactive inflammation in them. Our pathogenic psychical group, on the other hand, does not admit of being cleanly extirpated from the ego. Its external strata pass over in every direction into portions of

the normal ego. . . . Nor does the treatment consist in extirpating something . . . but in causing the resistance to melt and in thus enabling the circulation to make its way into a region that has hitherto been cut off. (SE 2:290–91)

Why does Freud see things this way? I would suggest that he does so because his model opens the door to an exploration of the unknown, with its attendant fascination. It enables him to recast the task and the role of the analyst and to turn him into a yet more powerful figure. A "foreign body" in the psyche demands a surgeon. The hypnotist—the figure behind Breuer's "hypnoid states" and his belief in hypnosis—is a magician who can open the door to the second, closed-off consciousness. The Freudian analyst is a detective-hero. On the one hand he is a clever, enormously patient sifter of clues, one who puts the pieces of the puzzle together—an investigator or interpreter. On the other, he is someone constantly struggling against resistances, an overcomer of defenses, a hero.

Freud's refashioning of the role of the analyst emerges in the metaphors he uses to describe the organization of pathological material in the psyche, metaphors that, he tells us, are not necessarily compatible with one another. Two crucial metaphors for the mind are the labyrinth and the archaeological site. Freud presents a threefold description of the psyche, as a temporal (chronological), a spatial, and a dynamic construct—a threefold description that he will retain and elaborate in the metapsychology in *The Interpretation of Dreams*. In the context of this discussion he speaks of the "logical thread" that the analyst must follow—along an "irregular and twisting path" (SE 2:289), in "a zig-zag, twisted line" (SE 2:290). These images, implicitly, cast the mind as a labyrinth, the analyst as Theseus, the pathological material as the Minotaur. Concurrently, Freud repeatedly uses the word "stratum" ("Schicht") to refer to the mind. The patient finds "disconnected" things when she or he "clears up material lying within the same stratum" (SE 2:292). The analyst may "bury" ("verschütten") things by accident (SE 2:292). This is the vocabulary of archaeology. The archaeological metaphor engages the ideas of outer/inner, light/dark, and surface/depth, and it also captures the temporal opposition present/past. Yet the earth is *penetrable* by the archaeologist—as the psyche is by the analyst. Like the labyrinth, it essentially provides an impediment that the analyst has to struggle through.

Both metaphors institute a dual relation of the pathological kernel to the rest of the psyche: it is incompatible with it, yet potentially accessible. The archaeological metaphor subtly changes the evaluation of the "pathogenic kernel," for unlike the monster at the center of the labyrinth, there is nothing unnatural about something being buried below the earth. Hence this metaphor will prove compatible with Freud's insight in the years following the publication of *Studies on Hysteria* that the normal psyche is dual, and it will prove more durable than the labyrinth metaphor. The analogy between archaeology and psychoanalysis is one that will continue to fascinate Freud. It dominates his interpretation of Wilhelm Jensen's novel *Gradiva* (1907), where the burial and excavation of Pompeii give a model for the repression and unearthing of childhood memories.

Thus with Freud's introduction of the concept of repression we see an important shift in value in the way the antithetical configuration familiar from Nietzsche and Hofmannsthal is regarded. The antithetical structure itself is retained. But unity is no longer privileged; humankind is no longer exhorted to stay in the light (the present, the known) and shun the dark (the past, the forgotten). No longer is conflict, wishing to be in two places at once, equated with being nowhere, with nonlife. Instead, duality is elevated to the very explanatory mechanism that makes the psychic system work, and it therefore, despite the attachment of repression to the topic of mental illness in *Studies on Hysteria*, already takes on the appearance of the normal state of affairs.

The Institutionalization of Conflict as an Interpretative
Strategy in Freud's *The Interpretation of Dreams*

In the years between the publication of *Studies on Hysteria* and *The Interpretation of Dreams*, Freud recognized that the traumas his patients related were not real but imaginary, concretizations of the patients' own unacknowledged childhood desires. This insight was the basis for positing the unconscious. Psychological conflict thus does not have an external cause, but is purely internal and normal. Where in *Studies on Hysteria* duality is a sign of ill health, in *The Interpretation of Dreams* the antithetical structure is seen as inevitable. "We must recognize," Freud insists, "that the psychical mechanism employed by neuroses is not created by the impact of a pathological disturbance upon the mind but is present already in the normal structure of the mental apparatus" (SE 5:607).

In *The Interpretation of Dreams* psychic duality is firmly instituted. Freud establishes it, in the progressive stages of his argument, in hermeneutic, topographic, temporal, and dynamic modes.

Ostensibly, the antithetical structure is ill-suited to a hermeneutics. By virtue of their very endeavor, hermeneuts assume the existence of motivated signs. The supposition that sign and meaning inhabit irreconcilable regions scarcely lightens the task of interpretation. Freud too aims to motivate the sign whenever possible. In *Studies on Hysteria* he motivates the patient's symptom through the trauma, and in *The Interpretation of Dreams* he motivates the manifest content of the dream through the dream work and, even more so, through the symbol, which resembles what it signifies (stick: penis). Yet the antithetical structure, in a way that will presently become clear, will make it possible for Freud to insist on the certainty of interpretations based on extremely indirect, unapparent, or tenuous motivations.

In *Studies on Hysteria*, the formulation of repression afforded Freud a way out of an interpretive quandary. With it he found both a simpler and a more plausible motivation for hysteria than the trauma. Once he could posit repression, he no longer had to search for external traumas that motivated his patients' elaborate complaints—traumas that, once found, may well have struck him as disappointingly trivial compared to what he presumed to be their effects. In *Studies on Hysteria* Freud stood before the perplexing symptom. Instead of focusing his efforts on finding an event in the patient's biography that corresponded to and hence explained it, he displaced the barrier between himself and it, between himself and the symptom's resistance to interpretation, into the patient herself, in the form of a conflict between her conscious organization and the unacceptable affect.

In *The Interpretation of Dreams* Freud employs the same strategy with the dream. He introduces his investigation with the following premise about the interpretability of dreams: "The aim which I have set before myself is to show that dreams are capable of being interpreted. . . . 'Interpreting' a dream implies assigning a 'meaning' to it—that is, replacing it by something which fits into the chain of our mental acts as a link having a validity and importance equal to the rest" (se 4:96). By positing that every dream has a "latent content," he proposes that the incoherent material of the dream can be replaced by significant sentences, sentences that contain important revelations about the dreaming subject. Just as in *Studies on Hysteria*, but with greater confidence and more daringly,

Freud starts with two things (the interpreter and the dream), and out of them fabricates three: the interpreter, the manifest content, and the latent content. His hermeneutic strategy, again, consists in relocating the barrier of incomprehension that exists between the interpreter and the phenomenon to be interpreted (interpreter//dream) to a new place within the phenomenon itself, between the dream and its hidden meaning (interpreter/manifest content of the dream//latent content). He thus displaces the inaccessibility of the dream to the place the dream comes from, which he names in his final chapter (7) the "unconscious."

In *Studies on Hysteria*, Freud, having posited repression as the cause of hysteria, still had to account for the specificity of the symptom. His solution was to retain the trauma precisely as an explanatory agent for the symptom (e.g., the patient's symptom is smelling burned pudding because pudding happened to be burning at a moment when the conflict in her feelings became apparent to her). In *The Interpretation of Dreams* he confronts a similar problem. How is the particularity of the manifest content explained? How may the interpreter link a particular dream with a particular meaning or latent content? His first step toward a solution is the ingenious notion of censorship. This barrier between the patient's unconscious (the site of latent meanings) and preconscious (whence the dream can proceed unproblematically into consciousness) does not merely divide antithetical psychic areas. The censorship inevitably distorts anything that passes it. Passage is, to Freud's mind, an exigency of the system viewed as dynamic. The presumption of distortion enables Freud greatly to simplify the task of interpretation. He narrows down the interpretive possibilities by making a generalization about dreams. Every dream, Freud claims, originates as a wish. In adults, the wishes are censored, distorted beyond recognition, so that the dream's manifest content bears little resemblance to what it represents.

Compared with *Studies on Hysteria*, his strategy in *The Interpretation of Dreams* is more daring because the conclusions he comes to cannot be objectively verified. In *Studies on Hysteria* the success of therapy appears to validate his theory. Thus the last time he glimpses Elisabeth von R., a patient he cured of hysterical lameness, she is at a ball, and he sees her "whirl past in a lively dance" (SE 2:160).[9]

Freud's theory of interpretation opens out into a theory of the human psyche. This theory is in turn grounded in a theory of the psychic development of human beings, which in its turn is grounded in their actual biological development. Freud will reiterate in later works what is implicit in *The Interpretation of Dreams*: the unconscious, consisting of wishful impulses, is present in infants from the start; the preconscious comes into being with language acquisition.[10] This ultimate grounding in what Freud sees as the uniform empirical human mode of being allows him to claim universality for his theory of interpretation: it is a theory that holds true for all cases.

In his chapter 7 Freud institutionalizes the irreconcilable duality that informs his theory of interpretation in a mapping of the human psyche. The interpretive duality between the latent and the manifest content of the dream is reinforced by the metapsychology, such that the "latent" or hidden meaning in the hermeneutics becomes the "unconscious" of the metapsychology. The "unconscious" comprises two systems, the Unconscious (Ucs.) and the Preconscious (Pcs.): the Ucs. is designated as the source of the dream wish, while the Pcs. supplies the rational and verbal form of the "dream thoughts," which allows us to conceive of the hermeneutic object as consisting of significant sentences. Our task here will be to examine the process, purposes, and implications of this institutionalization.

In his description of the psyche, Freud asks us to think of the psyche in three ways: as topographic, dynamic, and temporal. The topography, which he discusses in the section "Regression," is the simplest and also most trivial representation. It may be seen as the last vestige of Freud's attempt to talk about brain anatomy in the *Project*. Here, however, it is wholly metaphoric. As a spatial representation, it is the system that connects most obviously with Freud's archaeological and labyrinth metaphors in *Studies on Hysteria*. Freud posits his "discovery," the Ucs.—the substantive, and not merely adjectival, unconscious—nonchalantly in this first mention, as a region or "system" in the mind. He observes briefly that it is the place that supplies "the motive force for producing dreams" (SE 5:541) and refers the reader to his section on the dynamic representation of the psyche (entitled "Wish-Fulfilment") for an explanation. "Wish-Fulfilment" and the following sections, where Freud presents his argument for the Ucs. conceived as dynamic, bear close scrutiny.

The most essential and serious representation of the psyche is the dynamic. Without energy, the psychic system would not be set in motion to begin with, and there would be no transitions from one so-called locality to the next. Hence in the first section on the dynamic, "Wish-Fulfilment," Freud emphatically equates the dream wish with energy: "Nothing but a wish can set our mental apparatus at work" (SE 5:567).

The dynamic involves three operative notions: excitation, energy, and quality. Excitation has to do with the body: the term presupposes that the mind operates at the service of the organism. Energy is another term for excitation, but energy leads Freud away from purely physical metaphors into economic ones: energy can be saved, squandered, budgeted, and so on. Quality, finally, is entirely psychic; it implies pleasure or unpleasure. The equation is as follows: excitation implies a buildup of energy; qualitatively, this buildup of quantity implies unpleasure. Conversely, the discharge of energy, initiated by wishing with an end to achieving satisfaction, is pleasurable. Freud retains the notion of the "Constancy Principle" or "Principle of Inertia" from his *Project* and contemporaneous letters to Wilhelm Fliess: the primitive psychic apparatus tries to keep itself so far as possible free from stimuli. Such stimuli may impinge on it from the outside, but they also arise internally, as somatic needs (SE 5:565). The notion of internal needs allows Freud to introduce an economic argument. In the case of a somatic need, the organism can no longer merely try to get rid of excess excitation as quickly as possible. It has to regard the exitation created by the need as *energy* with which to satisfy the need.

Freud formulates the primary and secondary processes as two different ways of budgeting energy. The primary process—where primary implies both chronologically prior and more primitive—tries to discharge the excitation arising from the stimulus as quickly as possible. Freud gives as an example a hungry baby: "A hungry baby screams or kicks helplessly" (SE 5:565). The infant discharges in motor activity the excitation aroused by its somatic need. Freud's second example is the hallucination, which, he asserts, is a close cousin of the dream. From the purely dynamic example of the baby, he moves to one that engages the psychic concept of wishing. Once the individual has had the "experience of satisfaction," with the need is born a "psychical impulse" (SE 5:565–66) that seeks to "recathect the mnemic image of the perception [of satisfaction] and to re-evoke the perception itself." Freud calls such an impulse a "wish." The hallucination is its fulfillment.

The primary process, which Freud will eventually designate as the mode of operation of the unconscious (SE 5:599), follows what Freud calls the "unpleasure principle" (equivalent to the Constancy or Inertia Principle from the *Project* and letters to Fliess; later Freud would call it the pleasure principle). In short, the unconscious can do nothing but wish. Freud states, "As a result of the unpleasure principle, . . . the first ψ-system [i.e., the unconscious] is totally incapable of bringing anything disagreeable into the context of its thoughts. It is unable to do anything but wish" (SE 5:600). Consequently, the primary process squanders the energy derived from the stimulus by hallucinating an image of the satisfaction. But hallucinating is no real solution at all, for it does not remove the need. The primary process sacrifices true fulfillment to the pleasure of discharge.

The secondary process, which, as its name suggests, comes into being later (it will be identified as the mode of operation of the preconscious, SE 5:599), involves a more efficient expenditure of energy. The secondary process inhibits the discharge of excitation; energy is converted to thought; and thought brings about the real fulfillment of the wish or removal of the need.

Freud's argument in chapter 7 inscribes a hermeneutic circle: his investigation of dreams beckons toward the grander project of formulating a metapsychology, while the metapsychology in turn promises to shed additional light on the mysteries of dreams. At the beginning of the "Wish-Fulfilment" section Freud hypothesizes that adult dreams always involve an unconscious wish. He surrounds this hypothesis with many disclaimers: "I cannot offer any proof" (SE 5:552); "My supposition is . . ." (SE 5:553); "I am aware that this assertion cannot be proved to hold universally; but it can be proved to hold frequently, even in unsuspected cases, and it cannot be *contradicted* as a general proposition" (SE 5:554). Freud then moves from dreams to a discussion of the primary process. We are evidently meant, in turn, to apply the argument he presents in this discussion to dreams. Dreams, Freud implies, behave like hallucinations. By the end of the "Wish-Fulfilment" section Freud believes that he has accumulated evidence to support his hypothesis that dreams always emanate from the unconscious, even though he will reiterate later that the unconscious genesis of dreams is unprovable. He states confidently, "The reason why dreams are invariably wish-fulfilments is that they are products of the system Ucs., whose activity knows no other aim than the fulfilment of wishes and which has at its command no other forces than wishful impulses" (SE 5:568).

In formulating the dynamic Ucs., Freud takes a leap. For dreams cannot be assimilated unproblematically to the model of hallucinations. Yet more disturbing, the primary process does not logically imply or "prove" the unconscious. We do not need the Ucs. to explain hallucinations, Freud's example of a manifestation of the primary process conceived as wishing. Three dislocations are necessary to move from the discussion of the primary process and the example of hallucinations to the case of dreams. Each one involves abandoning commonsensical ground—for Freud's argument about the primary and the secondary processes thus far, and the examples of the baby and the hallucination, are eminently plausible—and embarking into speculation.

First, unlike in the case of hallucinations, the "wishful impulses" that trigger dreams do not, for the most part, originate in somatic needs. Freud has covertly introduced the idea of *purely psychic* (and hence less provable) desires.

Second, Freud needs to account for the fact that the dream, like the hallucination, takes place in the medium of visual images. In the case of the hallucination he asserts that the primary process recathects the visual memory of the fulfillment of the need. But in the case of adult dreams, the infantile desires that motivate these dreams include "sexual wishful impulses from infancy" that were, we assume, never fulfilled in reality. Thus, despite Freud's references to unconscious memories, for example, to "the memories on the basis of which the unconscious wish brings about the release of affect" (SE 5:604), there is no mnemic image of such wishes' fulfillment; or rather, there could only be a mnemic image of an *imagined* fulfillment. Paul Ricoeur in *Freud and Philosophy* explains this basing of dreams in the hallucinatory revival of perception, which he sees as a discrepancy, as a relic of Freud's belief in the reality of the childhood seduction scene.[11] Thus in the case of an unconscious wish, we are dealing with something that was never either an objective need or, in many cases, attained real satisfaction—something, in short, for which there is no evidence, which Freud introduces a priori, yet something that ultimately will bear the weight of grounding his theory.[12]

Third, the psychic wishes harbored by the Ucs. are completely out of date. Fulfilling them today, as Freud states explicitly (SE 5:604), would create unpleasure. Freud's theory finds a way of dealing with this problem: these wishes, he contends, are unconscious, repressed, precisely because they are unacceptable to the adult consciousness. Yet the question remains, if one adopts a questioning attitude toward Freud's reasoning, why the organism bothers to preserve this archaic baggage.

In sum, the unconscious desires that give rise to dreams are purely psychic as opposed to somatic, archaic rather than contemporary, and they were never fulfilled in reality.

Hence the dream does not relate to the generating wish the way a hallucination relates to a somatic need. It is not a perceptual re-creation of a past fulfillment in response to a present need, but the distorted expression of an unfulfilled desire, distorted because the wish is unacceptable. Dreams are intrinsically different from hallucinations.

Consequently, the unconscious, the hypothesized repository of the desires that engender dreams, is not derivable from the dynamic description of the metapsychology. It is an addition to Freud's system of the primary and secondary processes. These processes would work perfectly well without the hypothesis of the Ucs. Indeed, the primary process alone expresses the idea of the primacy of desire in the organism; the unconscious is not needed for that.

At this point we might do well to scrutinize why the Ucs., whose hermeneutic variant and precusor in the text, the *latent content*, appeared to be an imaginative construct, is necessary in this system. Why not cross out the Ucs.? Why not reject the notion of infantile desires that, according to Freud, form the substance of the Ucs.? Why does Freud retain them and find a place for them in the psyche and then label it the most important place of all?

Let us consider what function the Ucs. performs in the context of Freud's theories. Freud first advanced a hermeneutic of dreams, whereby interpretation was facilitated by the assumption of hidden meanings, hidden meanings that, moreover, possess a significant degree of uniformity in all cases: every dream is a wish. Freud then offered a dynamic description of the mind that posited desire as the organism's original motivating force. The Ucs. may be seen as a rapprochement of these projects, of Freud's hermeneutic enterprise and his dynamics. The dream's resistance to interpretation, and Freud's consequent assumption of dream distortion and a latent meaning, is compatible with the notion of a region harboring unacceptable wishes, wishes that live and demand discharge although we are not aware of them, wishes whose fulfillment today would be unpleasurable. The energy of the primary process may conveniently be located precisely in the same region, the Ucs. Indeed, Freud writes that the Ucs. is in possession of "the instinctual force which is at the disposal of the repressed wish" (se 5:564).

In this fusion of the hermeneutic and the dynamic into a concept uniting both, the Ucs., the temporal plays a critical role. The dream wish must be unacceptable, hidden, yet alive: all these conditions are met, to Freud's mind, if the desire is conceived as an *infantile* sexual desire. The sexual nature of the desire fulfills the criterion of unacceptability. The genesis of the desire in the prehistoric period of early childhood, which is subject to amnesia, guarantees its hiddenness. The continued existence of the wish—indeed, its undiminished energy—remains to be explained. It is an article of faith for Freud that what is chronologically prior cannot be obliterated by what comes later. His belief in the importance and in-destructibility of what is past is already evident in *Studies on Hysteria*, not so much in his theory of the pathogenic kernel as in his revision of that theory, by which pathogenic strata are perceived as being entangled with the normal mind. It was implicit in his archaeological metaphor for the mind, where the analyst must carefully remove layers of sediment to discover relics of the past. Decades later, in *Civilization and Its Discontents* (1930), Freud would affirm, again in the context of a lengthy archaeological analogy, "We are inclined to take the . . . view [neigen zu der Annahme: my translation] that in mental life nothing which has once been formed can perish" (SE 21:69).

What then is the significance of the Ucs.? Freud says that the Ucs. is "indestructible" (SE 5:577). It provides the absolute grounding of Freud's system—both the hermeneutics and the energetics. As we have already seen, Freud needed the Ucs.—supplemented by the Pcs. as the supplier of rational and verbal form—as a source of hidden meanings in his theory of interpretation. In his energetics, he needs it as an inexhaustible source of energy. In economic terms, it is a capitalist who cannot go broke. Its needs—unfulfillable because fulfilling them would contradict the plea-sure principle—are permanent, not intermittent and fulfillable like phys-ical needs. The Ucs. is a symbol for unfulfilled desire as the basis of all energy and therefore of all life. Of the secondary process, Freud says, "Thought is after all nothing but a substitute for a hallucinatory wish" (SE 5:567). Devising an analogy to the mythical Titans, Freud stresses both the power and the immortality of unconscious wishes: "These wishes in our unconscious, ever on the alert and, so to say, immortal, re-mind one of the legendary Titans, weighed down since primaeval ages by the massive bulk of the mountains which were once hurled upon them by the victorious gods and which are still shaken from time to time by the convulsion of their limbs" (SE 5:553). The status of the Ucs. as ground is made explicit by Freud: it is the "core of our being" (SE 5:603). Speaking of our unconscious as opposed to our conscious psychic life, Freud states, "The unconscious is the true psychical reality; in its innermost nature it is as much unknown to us as the reality of the external world" (SE 5:613).

While the Ucs. as a source of energy makes the system work, it also endangers it from the inside with its elemental, titanic force. Freud describes the psyche as a "citadel" that is constantly threatened by unconscious forces (SE 5:568). Given the status of the Ucs. as the unknown and as an indestructible source, what role does therapy play? Supposedly, its task is to extinguish the unconscious processes and bring the Ucs. under the domination of the Pcs.: The task of psychotherapy "is to make it possible for the unconscious processes to be dealt with finally and be forgotten. . . . What performs this work is the preconscious, and *psychotherapy can pursue no other course than to bring the Ucs. under the domination of the Pcs.*" (Freud's italics; SE 5:578). Freud's celebrated statement that *"the interpretation of dreams is the royal road to a knowledge of the unconscious activities of the mind"* (Freud's italics; SE 5:608) also suggests that the Ucs. is accessible. But in fact, the analyst can only hold a candle into the darkness; it would undermine Freud's entire metapsychology if therapy could be complete. As Freud stresses, the structure of the mental apparatus as he has described it is normal, not pathological (SE 5:607–8).

Freud finally circles back to the dream and writes it into this scenario of dangerous unconscious energy. The dream serves, precisely, as a safety valve for the organism (SE 5:579), which allows excitation to be got rid of in a harmless fashion, for at night, the door to motility is closed.

Let us recapitulate how the Ucs. comes into being. The hermeneutic endeavor imposes a hiddenness on wishes that, in the dynamic view, trigger the system. "Hidden" implies in dynamic terms an energy that cannot be leashed by the preconscious and is otherwise inaccessible. This energy obtains in desires that existed prior to the preconscious, namely earliest, or infantile, desires. Then, in a move back from the dynamic to the hermeneutic, Freud explains the existence of dreams as a "safety valve" for the discharge of this energy. Freud's argument makes a neat circle. His initial, perplexing insistence in chapter 2 that every dream is a wish—an assertion that flies in the face of common sense and makes the reader wonder why Freud is so intent on it—proves retrospectively to have its purpose: if *every* dream is a wish, dreams *may* be seen as safety valves for unconscious energy. And if one has such energy and such safety valves, the notion of an "indestructible" unconscious is validated.

At this point it will be useful to compare Freud's system in *The Interpretation of Dreams* with the model we have derived from Nietzsche's

On the Advantage and Disadvantage of History for Life, Hofmanns-thal's *Death and the Fool*, and Freud and Breuer's "Preliminary Com-munication," namely, with the equivalencies present/past, light/dark, inside/outside, known/unknown, health/sickness. Three principal dif-ferences stand out. All will be significant for the literature discussed in the following chapters.

First, in a significant reversal of values, Freud attributes the source of life to the dark rather than, as Nietzsche in the passage discussed and in Freud and Breuer's work, to the light area. The ground for Freud in *The Interpretation of Dreams* is more important than the figure; the uniform Ucs. is more important than character; the irrational is more fundamen-tal than thought and reason; the past is more important than the present; the unknown is more interesting than the known.

In his perceptive interpretation of Freud's Virgil epigram "If I cannot bend the powers above, I shall stir up Acheron," Carl Schorske observes that Freud, in conferring "titanic" strength on unconscious wishes, as-cribes power to something that he, as scientist and psychoanalyst, has power over.[13] Freud thereby compensates through his theory for his powerlessness as a Jew in Viennese political life. If Freud cannot bend the powers above, he will stir up the depths. Appropriating power for himself through such roundabout means may well contribute to Freud's motivation for "discovering" the unconscious. However, it should not be forgotten that Schopenhauer preceded him in according power to the Will, and that Nietzsche accorded similar priority to the dionysian. In his later works Nietzsche also grounded human life in an irrational force, the will to power. Literary works also dramatized the power of the irrational before the appearance of *The Interpretation of Dreams*; chap-ters 2 and 3 of this book discuss some examples among Schnitzler's works of the 1890s. Freud's discovery of the unconscious was an inge-nious move, but at the same time it accorded with a more general ten-dency of his time. The reversal of values alone does not constitute the revolutionary nature of his theory.

Second, it is essential for Freud that the two conflicting terms coexist simultaneously. Gone is the identification of health with existence in the here and now. For Freud, to be human means to be where one is not, to be divided. In according priority to the "dark" Freud chooses to emphasize a disruptive force rather than advocating the suppression of whatever might threaten self-contained plenitude. Nietzsche, Hofmannsthal, and Freud and Breuer had put the chain of metaphors at the service of a system that was essentially static. Freud's system in *The Interpretation of Dreams* is dynamic. If desire triggers the system, conflict is its generative device, the mechanism that produces dreams and neurotic symptoms. This dynamism, the interplay of force and resistance, is also admirably suited to the construction of literary plots. Unsurprisingly, therefore, conflict will be a universal characteristic of the dualities employed by Schnitzler, Hofmannsthal, Musil, and Kafka. The conflict between the two terms generates the story.

Third, for Nietzsche, Hofmannsthal, and Freud and Breuer, the terms of the duality are firmly antithetical. Continuity is affirmed, ostensibly at least, within the context of a different topic than that to which the antithetical structure is applied. The tension between duality and continuity is not overt but rather obscured. Nietzsche, Hofmannsthal, and Freud and Breuer make no attempt to investigate the possibility of transition between the terms of their dualities; indeed, precisely the lack of such transition is imperative; it confirms the antithetical nature of the terms. For Freud in *The Interpretation of Dreams*, however, the very topics to which the dual structure is applied, the quest for meaning and the topic of energy/desire, imply transition between the terms. The hermeneutic endeavor necessarily posits that the relation between sign and meaning is motivated. Desire and energy, likewise, imply a processual movement between impulse and outcome. Thus while one can still speak, in *The Interpretation of Dreams*, of the dualities present/past, light/dark, inside/outside, and known/unknown, the terms of these dualities are subject to more complex demands than Nietzsche's, Hofmannsthal's, or Freud and Breuer's. They must be antithetical—yet mutually accessible. The Ucs. must be hidden and yet not hidden. What this means for Freud is that he must forever balance two contradictory characteristics of the Ucs., allied to two different purposes of his theory: he must maintain both the penetrability and the impenetrability of the Ucs. Freud thereby introduces the issue of interaction between the two terms themselves. Inasmuch as his goal is interpretation, Freud is particularly interested in strategies of transition; to this end he devises the complex theory of the dream work, to which we shall return in chapter 7. The literary authors, who have no comparable hermeneutic ambitions, will, as we shall see in chapter 3, deal with the question of transition more schematically. Among them, Musil is the most interested in methods. Yet all the authors invest in the model of accessibility and inaccessibility, which comes as part of the bargain with a dark and elusive unknown: precisely the possibility of access gives it its allure.

Nowhere more than in Freud's work is duality so richly exploited. Vis-à-vis earlier philosophical celebrations of the irrational, namely, Schopenhauer's and Nietzsche's, Freud's decisive innovation is his insistence on *conflict* as the basis of life. The Freudian libido bears a remarkable and often-commented-on resemblance to Schopenhauer's Will and to Nietzsche's will to power. All of them are the key to life. With the Will, Schopenhauer, who precedes Freud in overthrowing the Cartesian primacy of reason, makes desire the primary motivating cosmic force. The Will, insatiable, is characterized by constant striving. True, "appearances" of the Will are forever coming into conflict with one another; true, one's intellect may sometimes tame one's Will; but for Schopenhauer, nothing systematically opposes the Will. For Nietzsche likewise, the will to power is not systematically and permanently opposed by another force. On the contrary, Nietzsche is at pains to show how thorny problems of history—why the weak have prevailed over the strong, and why the ascetic ideal has seemingly won out over the will to power—are in fact reducible to the sole agency of the will to power.[14] Freud, by reading an exigency of the hermeneutic enterprise (hidden meanings) into the energetic enterprise (human energy needs an outlet, a mode of passage), produces remarkably fruitful results. The ingenious notion of a barrier that distorts allows him to turn duality into *conflict*. Unconscious desire must be discharged, but it is opposed by the powerful censorship. While this desire is the primal motivating force, it does not motivate straightforwardly but, rather, always in a distorted or sublimated form. Its products, therefore, do not resemble itself. Hence Freud can relate not only dreams and pathological symptoms to a far-flung latent content: in such later works as *Leonardo da Vinci and a Memory of His Childhood* the genesis of art is explained according to the same model, as sublimated libido, and in *Totem and Taboo* and *Moses and Monotheism* Freud extends the model to the collective and accounts for the origin of religion in the same fashion, where taboo or morality takes the place of the censorship. Unconscious energy, libido, that *must* be discharged, yet *must* discharge itself through a powerful, distorting barrier, becomes responsible for the major products of human creativity.

Leafed through old diaries tonight. What an uncanny power the past has. It even pulls the present along with it, so that the present seems like something past. You don't believe in the present any more. —Arthur Schnitzler, diary entry of 24 July 1891

IT HAS BECOME A commonplace of popular psychology to discredit memory. Provided it is not a question of studying for exams, *having memories* provokes a variety of associations ranging from mildly negative to metaphysically suspect. The person who is "in touch with himself" lives in the present and cheerfully orients himself toward the future. Reliving the past counts as morbid, un-Californian. Merely *having* memories is a sign of old age, a sign that the most important and exciting events of life are past. Dwelling on past happiness testifies to a dearth in the present, to not enough happening, while recollecting past misfortune spoils a present that might better be enjoyed. In the wake of Henri Bergson and Marcel Proust genuine memory has been mysticized as "spontaneous" or "involuntary." Ordinary, conscious recollection, which as Bergson postulated operates uniquely in the interest of present action, is considered an exercise in self-deception: it falsifies, confers value retrospectively, imposes a discourse, even a plot, on the elusive events themselves.

Our contemporary negative evaluation of memory can be traced to late nineteenth-century *Lebensphilosophie* and its celebration of the present moment, and also to the pervasive influence of the work of Sigmund Freud. My topic in this chapter is memory as it figures in works by three of Freud's literary contemporaries. I shall discuss Hofmannsthal's *Electra*, a play of 1903; Schnitzler's short story "Flowers," published in 1894; and Musil's novella "The Temptation of Quiet Veronica" of 1911. In all of these works the past figures as a trauma, whose memory brings with it severe pathological consequences. Hence temporality, which might normally be thought of as a continuum, is artificially hypostatized into a radical polarization of past and present. Past and present thus become a duality whose boundaries can be inspected, whose relationship to one another can be probed, whose respective values can be assessed. Both the fact that these questions are posed and the way in which they are answered in these three texts situate the texts on the threshold between traditional vitalistic values, which as we saw in the last chapter stressed a monistic resolution to the problem of duality, and the new position exemplified by Freud's *Interpretation of Dreams*, which capitalized on the inevitability and permanence of conflict.

In all three texts, the basic paradigm is this: the persistence of the past, through the unlucky propensity of the human mind to remember, spells illness, while its reabsorption into the present, through a process of forgetting, is heralded as the return of health.

There are few precedents for such a negative evaluation of human memory. The most obvious parallel occurs in Breuer and Freud's *Studies on Hysteria*. As we saw in the preceding chapter, Breuer and Freud's central thesis is that hysteria is caused by the memory of a trauma. Two of the three works under consideration, Hofmannsthal's *Electra* and Musil's "The Temptation of Quiet Veronica," clearly borrowed the idea of the traumatic memory from *Studies on Hysteria*. Where Freud and Breuer themselves got the idea of the pathogenic memory is not so clear. There is nothing remotely similar to it in contemporaneous or earlier psychological or psychopathological theory, even though memory research was currently in vogue. The closest parallel is found in a work discussed in detail in chapter 1, Nietzsche's *On the Advantage and Disadvantage of History for Life*. In contrast to Nietzsche, none of the three literary texts extend the notion of the troublesome past to the historical past; they are exclusively concerned with individual psychology. Yet Hofmannsthal's drama contains a reference to Nietzsche's opening paragraphs, to the catchy dictum about the happy animal and the polemic against memory. Besides Nietzsche, *Studies on Hysteria* calls possible literary ancestors to mind: the idea of the repressed memory and its eerie return reminds one of ghost stories, and, given the indebtedness of Breuer and Freud's proposed cure, the "cathartic method," to Aristotle's *Poetics* and to Greek tragedy, one thinks of the Furies as well.

If Breuer and Freud's theories held an appeal for their literary contemporaries, it is no doubt because *Studies on Hysteria* itself is heavily indebted to a variety of classical and other literary models. Freud himself apologized to his readers that his case studies resembled short stories more than serious scientific work. The theory of hysteria that Breuer and Freud propose in their "Preliminary Communication," the theoretical essay that begins the volume, is itself suggestively literary. Their story of illness and cure is homologous to the traditional three-part structure of initial (naive or false) order—disorder—final, enhanced order on which innumerable literary plots, particularly comedies, are based. Act 1: the memory of a trauma lodges itself in the psyche like a foreign body, which is inaccessible to normal consciousness. Act 2: hysteria results. Act 3: the patient is cured when the analyst brings the memory to light.

In *The Interpretation of Dreams*, where psychic duality is seen as normal and inevitable, the conceptual and topographic antithesis preconscious/unconscious is ingeniously imprinted on the temporality of the human life span: it is grounded in a continuous temporality that is marked by a caesura, namely, the formation of the preconscious or secondary process. As a result our earliest past, our infancy, is cut off from our rational processes. "The core of our being," in Freud's formulation, "consisting of unconscious wishful impulses, remains inaccessible to the understanding and inhibition of the preconscious" (SE 5:603). Moreover, many memories are similarly inaccessible (in Freud's formulation, "a wide sphere of mnemic material is inaccessible to preconscious cathexis" [SE 5:604]). The wishful impulses, according to Freud, which attach to "a store of infantile memories" (SE 5:604), "can neither be destroyed nor inhibited" (SE 5:604); they are "ever on the alert and, so to say, immortal" (SE 5:553). Thus the past and the present persist in an antithetical relationship, as in *Studies on Hysteria*, but one that is incapable of being dissolved. The temporal unconscious is an indestructible repository of infantile desires and infantile scenes. With the dualistic psyche comes a parting from Freud's earlier view of the past, which sees it as something that must either be integrated or expelled. Instead, the past becomes something that can neither be successfully integrated, nor eliminated: it is a perpetual source of potential trouble.

The theory of the repressed memory, with its radical polarization of past and present, is thus the germ of a train of thought that leads Freud to formulate his conception of the dualistic psyche. In the three literary texts I shall consider, the theme of the pathological memory situates

these texts near the same point of transition from a suspicious constata-
tion of duality to a positive insistence on it. In all of them, the past is
horrible—and fascinating. But in each, horror and fascination are mixed
in different proportions. The rift between past and present and the grip of
the past over the present appear as more or less absolute, and the ideal of
living wholly in the present is more or less ambiguously affirmed. As we
shall see, Hofmannsthal's drama is the most conservative, closest to the
spirit of Breuer and Freud's "Preliminary Communication." Schnitzler's
short story resembles more Freud's position in his concluding essay to
Studies on Hysteria, where, as we saw in the preceding chapter, he inscribes conflict into the psyche with the notion of repression. And
Musil's novella already shows some similarity to the theory in *The
Interpretation of Dreams*.

Hofmannsthal's *Electra*

Hofmannsthal's *Electra* is a brilliant, allusive literary adaptation of the
theory of the pathological memory and the psychoanalytic cure.

Critics have long assumed the influence of Josef Breuer and Sigmund
Freud's *Studies on Hysteria* on *Electra*.[1] It is known that Hofmannsthal
had the first edition of *Studies on Hysteria* (as well as Freud's *Interpretation of Dreams*) in his personal library.[2] Since Bernd Urban's 1978
study *Hofmannsthal, Freud und die Psychoanalyse*, we even know what
passages in these works are marked. We do not know exactly when Hofmannsthal read *Studies on Hysteria*; however, he asked his friend
Hermann Bahr, in a letter that critics believe was written in 1903 while
he was working on *Electra*, if he could borrow the work: "Could you perhaps loan me (send me) just for a few days the book by Freud and Breuer
about curing hysteria by freeing a suppressed memory?"[3] And Hofmannsthal himself later stated, in response to a critic's inquiry, that *Studies on
Hysteria* was one of two works he "leafed" through while working on
Electra (BII 384).

The catalyst for Hofmannsthal's interest in psychopathology seems to
have been Bahr. The *Electra* plan first crystallized, Hofmannsthal said in
a letter to Otto Brahm, in May 1903, during a conversation he had with
Bahr and the actress who later played Electra, Gertrud Eysoldt. Previously, his plan had only been vague (BII 125). In the same period in
which Hofmannsthal was working on *Electra*, 1902 and 1903, Bahr himself wrote his *Dialog vom Tragischen*, a study in which he spoke of the

"hysteria" of the Greeks and referred explicitly to "those two doctors" Breuer and Freud. Bahr began working on the Freudian-Aristotelian part of *Dialog vom Tragischen* in 1902. In the back of his "Merkbuch" for 1902, summarizing what he did during the year, he writes, "Worked on my dialogue on tragedy: Aristotle, Freud."[4] He notes further that he read Sophocles' and Euripides' *Electra*. A 1902 notebook, "Credo II," contains notes for the part of the *Dialog* involving Freud—Bahr speaks of "the 're-venge' of the suppressed affects"—while a diary entry of 8–9 April mentions his "occupation with the catharsis questions." In the same period, he was a frequent visitor of Hofmannsthal's in Rodaun. Bahr finished the entire dialogue in the spring of 1903, and, as we know from a letter Bahr wrote to Hofmannsthal on 19 July 1903 thanking him for his comments, Hofmannsthal had read *Dialog vom Tragischen* by that date, that is, just before his period of intensive work on *Electra*.

There are several striking parallels between *Dialog vom Tragischen* and *Electra*: (1) Bahr applies Breuer and Freud's main ideas, on repression as the cause of hysteria and abreaction as its cure, to Greek tragedy. (I shall argue that Hofmannsthal applies the same ideas to *Electra*.) (2) Bahr connects Breuer and Freud's idea that the repression of a traumatic memory is pathogenic to Nietzsche's celebration of the dionysian and his denunciation of repressive *Bildung*. (The influence of *The Birth of Tragedy* on *Electra* is obvious.) (3) Bahr speaks peripherally of the untragic nature of Goethe. (This was Hofmannsthal's own idea; since 1901 he had carried around with him the notion that Goethe was incapable of writing tragedy, and the first inspiration for *Electra*, which came in September 1901, involved writing something contrary to *Iphigenie*, "something of which it cannot be said: 'this Greekish product seemed to me upon rereading devilishly humane.'")[5] These parallels between *Electra* and *Dialog vom Tragischen*, Hofmannsthal's frequent contact with Bahr, and last but not least his enthusiastic response to *Dialog vom Tragischen*, which he finds has a personal application to himself (BII 128–29), all speak for the hypothesis that Hofmannsthal read *Studies on Hysteria* and discussed with Bahr *all* of the ideas about Greek tragedy listed above between spring 1902 and summer 1903, so that the first idea, namely Bahr's application of Breuer and Freud's ideas to Greek tragedy, has, like the second and third, its parallel in *Electra*.

The evidence thus supports the claim that Hofmannsthal drew on *Studies on Hysteria* for *Electra*; it draws a fairly tight circle without, however, affording definitive information about the nature and extent of the borrowing. The question remains in what way and to what degree Breuer and Freud's work left its mark on the play. Here we have no page of Hofmannsthal's own notes, such as Alewyn found linking the novel *Andreas* to Morton Prince's *The Disassociation of a Personality*, to document exactly what Hofmannsthal borrowed.[6]

Critics who have written on the influence of *Studies on Hysteria* on *Electra* have perceived this influence to lie in the hysterical behavior of the female figures. Indeed, a remark of Bahr's confirms that Electra was meant to suggest a hysteric: he wrote to Hofmannsthal in 1904, referring to Gertrud Eysoldt, "One of her notes—the hysterical one—you brought it out wonderfully for her in Electra." Heinz Politzer, who goes furthest with this line of interpretation, finds that Electra, Clytemnestra, and Chrysothemis are all hysterics.[7] Michael Worbs believes that the play is a monodrama centered around the figure of Electra and that Hofmannsthal modeled Electra on Breuer's patient Anna O.[8] I find this interpretation plausible, as will become evident in my discussion later. I am not, however, convinced by Worbs's defense of Electra against Urban's argument that she is an imperfect hysteric. Urban makes the point that Electra, unlike Breuer and Freud's hysterics, *remembers* the trauma instead of repressing it. Worbs's response naturalizes Electra precariously as an Anna O.–style hysteric with a split personality at the expense of her most striking characteristic: her precise, vivid, obsessive recall of her father's murder.

While both Electra and Clytemnestra exhibit hysterical behavior patterns, as I shall discuss in more detail later, it seems to me that the parallels between Hofmannsthal's play and Breuer and Freud's work are neither exhausted by nor even most significantly located in this type of resemblance. Rather, one of the central themes in *Electra* is memory, and Hofmannsthal develops this theme in peculiar conformity to Breuer and Freud's conception of the pathogenic memory. I shall argue that Hofmannsthal ingeniously constructs his play around Breuer and Freud's theory of the repressed memory and the psychoanalytic cure.

To judge from the textual evidence in *Electra*, Hofmannsthal perceived parallels between the theory of the repressed memory and the psychoanalytic cure and the ancient theme of guilt and retribution in his Greek source. Breuer and Freud's theory varies a structure on which a primitive conception of justice, the conception of justice that informs the Electra legend, is based. According to this conception, a misdeed causes a wrong that can be righted, effaced from the memory of the injured party, only when the criminal has been adequately punished. Breuer himself noted the parallel and ascribed the human "instinct of revenge" to what he saw as a fundamental psychological law, the need to "abreact" excess excitation (SE 2:205–6). In the blood-for-blood system of justice as in Breuer and Freud's theory of trauma and abreaction, an original order is unsettled by an act of violence, and order is restored only when a similar act of violence is performed against the "foreign body" or criminal.

There are exact parallels in *Electra* to Breuer and Freud's theories of the pathogenic memory and the psychoanalytic cure as well as numerous less precise, more impressionistic parallels between the two works. Not surprisingly, the clearest allusions to these theories occur in the parts of the dialogue where Hofmannsthal diverges most decisively from his Greek source: in the characterization of Clytemnestra; in Clytemnestra's dream, which Electra recounts and claims credit for having sent her; in the long interview between mother and daughter that is the dramatic high point of the play; and in the finale where Electra dances and dies. I shall begin by pointing out these parallels and then go on to discuss Hofmannsthal's specifically literary *mise en scène* of the psychological theories.

Electra gives the impression of an economy, even a poverty of means. In this compressed one-act play, where the atmosphere of hostility and nervous tension present at the outset boils up rapidly into open conflict before resolving in a brief catharsis, we find an obsessive, pounding repetition of a few motifs, which virtually saturate the dialogue: the motifs of the animal, of blood, of the eye, the gaze, hands, water. Yet these few motifs ripple off into associations whose borders are nowhere fixed. The omnipresent animal motif, for example, which sets the play in sharp contrast to Goethe's "humane" *Iphigenie*, is on everyone's tongue—allusions to wildcats, snakes, flies, dogs pervade the dialogue and the stage directions. No character is spared the comparison with animals, and animals, in turn, suggest every conceivable association: thus the dog cluster within the animal motif suggests fidelity, mistreatment, and hunting when applied to Electra, servility or degraded behavior when applied to the servants, Clytemnestra, or Chrysothemis.

The principal characters are even more densely and diversely constructed. Under one optic they seem barely able to hold together over the psychological undertow. Under another, they appear as complex, overdetermined symbolic entities with which Hofmannsthal engages various fields of reference. This symbolic, multidimensional use of character may be understood as Hofmannsthal's answer to an intellectual climate dominated by Nietzsche, Mach, and French psychology, in which the self appeared *démodé*. Hofmannsthal himself in an essay of 1903 pronounced the self a "metaphor."[9] Thus the characters in *Electra* are not "characters"—a concept that Bahr too disgustedly rejects as out of date in his *Dialog vom Tragischen*[10]—but symbolic figures with more than one referent, vehicles charged with a diverse freight of meanings. Clytemnestra, for example, at once incorporates the nervous behavior of a hysteric and the sophistic poses of a fin-de-siècle aesthete—an identification that provides almost a comical touch in this otherwise dark, brooding play.

Supported by Hofmannsthal's own commentaries on the play, critics have tended to interpret the principal characters as contrasting pairs. Thus Electra and Clytemnestra are seen to represent the past versus the present, Electra and Chrysothemis being versus becoming, and Electra and Orestes words versus deeds.[11] The themes that link the play to Breuer and Freud's work, those of the traumatic memory, hysteria, and the cure, also lend themselves to discussion in terms of complementary character pairs.

One of the most intriguing aspects of Hofmannsthal's play is the interdependence of the Electra and Clytemnestra figures, an interdependence not present in the Greek source. This interdependence is alluded to several times in the dialogue. Electra says to her mother, "What weighs heavy on your heart also / touches mine" (PL 25; "Mir geht zu Herzen, was auch dir zu Herzen geht"); "Then you will never dream again, then I need / dream no longer" (PL 40); and most notably, "I know not how I should ever perish— / except of this, that you should perish too" (PL 25). Their interdependence is then demonstrated by the fact that Electra mysteriously dies after Clytemnestra is killed, as if her function had thereby somehow been fulfilled. The two women resemble interlocking circles: each one seems to be a part of the other as well as an entity in her own right. I shall argue that each woman represents a part of the other's psyche. Specifically, each personifies the memory of the trauma, the murder of Agamemnon, for the other.

Clytemnestra resembles a hysteric who has repressed the memory of her deed and is now in a somnambulistic state. Her behavior bears striking resemblance to that of Breuer and Freud's most dramatic patient, Anna O., in her "second condition." She comes on stage barely able to keep her eyes open, complaining of confusion, dizziness, hallucinations, and evil dreams. Like the classic hysteric, she cannot remember the traumatic incident that caused her illness. She has completely repressed the fact that she murdered Agamemnon. "First it was beforehand, then it was over—in between, I did nothing," she wails.[12]

As the repudiated, maltreated daughter, Electra embodies Clytemnestra's repressed memory, the portion of her psyche that she refuses to acknowledge. Electra is memory incarnate. Critics have pointed out that in her imagination, time has contracted into two points: the moment of her father's murder, which she constantly recalls, and a future moment when the murder will be avenged, which she persistently anticipates. The sole purpose of her existence is to keep alive the memory of the murder and to agitate for revenge.[13] Thus her death at the end of the play is easily explained: once Orestes has killed Clytemnestra, the living memory of Agamemnon's murder has no further function. Electra's specific role as the "foreign body" or pathogenic kernel lodged in Clytemnestra's mind becomes evident in the dramatic climax of the play, the interview between mother and daughter. Confronted with her daughter, Clytemnestra starts to babble unmotivatedly about the deed, as if the repressed had returned, even though Electra did not provoke her by alluding to "the deed":

> Deeds! We and deeds! What odd words!
> For am I still the same who has done the deed?
> And if so! Done, done! done! What a word
> to throw in my teeth!
> (PL 33)

It is characteristic of a repressed memory that it does not fade gradually but, rather, preserves its original freshness until it is expelled. Electra recalls her father's murder with all the freshness of an event that just occurred and with undiminished affect because, to use Breuer and Freud's terms, the trauma was never "abreacted," that is, the murder was not avenged. Critics have often commented on Electra's peculiar inability to act, to perform the act of revenge herself. They concur that her role exhausts itself in talking. Electra's role as a repressed memory explains both her inability to act and her loquaciousness. The very definition of a repressed memory, according to Breuer and Freud, is that action, or abreaction, is denied to it. Instead, the memory festers and causes psychic disturbance (thus Electra claims credit for sending Clytemnestra an evil dream), and above all, it "speaks," or returns, through the symptom. Electra's outbursts cannot be seen as the cathartic speech of the patient, for they do not relieve her; they are not at all the equivalent of the deed. Rather, her speeches are the perpetual crying out and reminding of the symptom.

If Electra embodies Clytemnestra's repressed memory, Clytemnestra herself, as the murderess of Agamemnon, quite literally personifies the memory of the trauma for Electra. This memory must be extirpated— that is, Clytemnestra must be killed—for Electra to rest. E. M. Butler has remarked that in their interview, mother and daughter appear like a hysterical patient and a Viennese analyst.[14] This interpretation, which is suggested by the dialogue itself ("She talks like a doctor," says Clytemnestra of Electra) is not incompatible with the interpretation of Electra as Clytemnestra's repressed memory, given the hermeneutic complicity of the memory with the doctor that Freud's text suggests. Electra appears as the caricature of the domineering psychoanalyst who tries to goad the resisting patient into admitting what the analyst knows and the patient is reluctant to speak out. She maneuvers her mother, who beseeches her for a cure, toward speaking of the repressed memory and—her main objective—naming the secret sacrificial animal, who is of course Clytemnestra herself. But the most significant parallel between Electra and the doctors who invented psychoanalysis occurs in Electra's vision of the "cure." Electra articulates this vision twice, once when she describes the dream she sent Clytemnestra and once at the end and climax of their face-to-face interview. Let us here look only at the briefer dream version. (The interview version, in accordance with its purpose of terrorizing Clytemnestra psychologically, is swollen with details of how Clytemnestra will suffer before meeting her bloody fate, which are not relevant to our present purpose.) Electra says:

I lie
and hear the steps of him who looks for her.
I hear him walk through the rooms, I hear him
raise the curtain from the bed: screaming
she escapes, but he is after her:
the hunt is on, down the stairs
through vaults, vaults upon vaults.
It is much darker than night, much quieter
and darker than the grave, she pants and staggers

in the darkness, but he is after her:
he waves the torch in his left, in his right the axe.
And I am like a dog upon her heels:
If she tries to run into a cave, I leap
at her from the side, thus we drive her on
until a wall blocks everything, and there,
in the deepest darkness, yet I see him well,
a shade, and yet limbs and yet the white
of one eye, there sits our father:
he does not heed it and yet it must be done:
in front of his feet we press her down,
and the axe falls!

(PL 20–21)

What inspires Electra to fantasize this particular scenario of revenge? It has no parallel in Sophocles' *Electra*. Rather, Hofmannsthal uses it to replace Clytemnestra's premonitory dream in Sophocles' tragedy, which is entirely different in content and is not sent by Electra. But the central elements of the psychoanalytic cure as described by Breuer and Freud are here. One of their fundamental metaphors is inside versus outside, or dark versus light: the analyst, in search of the memory of the trauma, must penetrate into "the dark," into the second, split-off consciousness, or region of the mind that contains the pathogenic kernel, and bring it "to light." Thus in Electra's vision Clytemnestra must be pursued *into* the palace and killed *inside*; Aegisthus will also be killed inside. In Electra's vision Orestes will illuminate the dark interior with a torch, and in the action itself Electra will similarly want to light Aegisthus's way into the palace. In his concluding essay to the *Studies on Hysteria*, Freud introduces a number of implicit metaphors whose general effect is to cast the analyst as a hero and the analyst's task as an adventure. One such implicit metaphor describes the mind as a labyrinth. Freud speaks of the zigzagging path and the logical thread the analyst must follow. Theseus-like, the analyst follows "the most roundabout paths" "from the surface to the deepest layers and back, and yet . . . in general . . . from the periphery to the central nucleus" (SE 2:289). He penetrates into ever-darker areas. In Hofmannsthal's text we find similar images: Orestes the avenger, wielding his torch, pursues Clytemnestra through dark subterranean passages in the palace, as if into the inner recesses of the mind. If Clytemnestra tries to duck off to one side, Electra, doglike, jumps at her sideways (the zigzag path). Finally, what should be at the end of the chase? In "deepest darkness," where one can go no further, is dead Agamemnon—that is, the repressed memory in person. Just as the analyst would want to return to the precise cause of the hysteria, Electra wants the action to come full circle: she wants Clytemnestra to be slaughtered at the feet of dead Agamemnon.

Electra's relation to Chrysothemis has often been described as one of being to becoming, not least by Hofmannsthal himself.[15] Chrysothemis wishes to live in the present, to lead a woman's life, to marry and have children, unburdened by memories of the past. Electra is as if her negative image on all of these counts: she is fixated on the past; revolted by sexuality, she perceives in her surroundings only an endless reproduction of the bloodshed; and her only version of the female cycle is a daily period at sunset that she devotes to mourning for her dead father. It is principally in contrast to Chrysothemis that Electra herself takes on the aspect of a hysteric. Electra too recalls certain features of Anna O.'s story, which must have left a deep impression on Hofmannsthal: Anna O., also traumatized by the death of her beloved father, appeared asexual to Breuer, spent a certain phase of her illness reliving the past, and had periodic attacks of hysteria for a few hours daily around sunset. But Electra and Chrysothemis are related primarily through their reference to Nietzsche rather than to Freud. "Can't you forget?" demands Chrysothemis of Electra. Electra retorts, "Forget? What? Am I an animal? forget? . . . I'm not an animal, I can't forget."[16] This interchange echoes the famous opening of Nietzsche's On the Advantage and Disadvantage of History, "Consider the herd," with which Nietzsche initiates a comparison between the happy animal, which forgets, and his less fortunate fellow creature, man, who remembers: "Man says 'I remember' and envies the animal which immediately forgets" (AD 9). The purpose of this polemic against memory is, ultimately, to encourage German youth not to orient itself on the learning of bygone days and emulate foreign cultures but, rather, to develop its own immediate relationship to life. Chrysothemis, who unlike Sophocles' Chrysothemis represents a serious philosophical position, approximates a young person according to Nietzsche's prescription. In Electra, despite her illness, Hofmannsthal gives voice to an equally serious counterposition, namely, the position of the human being who, unlike the "happy animal," cannot forget a heinous crime.[17]

Hofmannsthal's achievement in *Electra* is to bring several fields of reference into suggestive association: the system of retributive justice from Greek tragedy; Breuer and Freud's conception that memory causes illness, familiar also from Nietzsche; and the existential and ethical issue of our proper relationship to temporality, the past, and change. As we have seen, Breuer and Freud's theory of the traumatic memory and the psychoanalytic cure has the same underlying structure as the primitive conception of justice that informs the Electra legend. By juxtaposing two topics that have the same tripartite, circular structure, Hofmannsthal displays the analogy between a system of justice that demands blood for blood and the extirpation of the pathological memory in the psychoanalytic cure. He also creates an ideal space in which to air a philosophical and ethical issue dear to his own heart, or, as one critic puts it, "What is to him life's deepest moral dilemma: the problem of reconciling the need to remember with the need to forget."[18] He stages a confrontation between memory seen as a defining characteristic of humanness, as one of the bases of our ethical system, and memory seen as a faculty that undermines our happiness and health.

This philosophical issue is ultimately left unresolved. It is obvious that Chrysothemis's standpoint, that "Bleiben ist nirgends," to speak with Rilke, is inescapably correct and that Hofmannsthal endorses it here as he does more explicitly in other works. We cannot cling to the past, embodied by filthy, degraded Electra. Hofmannsthal duplicates the polarization of past and present in *Studies on Hysteria* and, like Breuer and Freud, condemns this polarization inasmuch as the retention of the past obstructs becoming. As in Breuer and Freud, the past is subordinated to the present as the area of highest concern, and the underlying ideal is continuity, a fading of the past into the present. Yet Hofmannsthal assigns humanness to Electra's point of view, remembrance. For despite Hofmannsthal's flirtation with memory as a psychopathological phenomenon, he is also concerned with memory as an ethical category, as a faculty that helps guarantee morality and justice. The memory of an old evil must be got rid of properly, by righting the wrong that caused it. As we know, Hofmannsthal conceived his play, whose imagery is drenched with sexuality and violence, and which takes place at night, as a counterpart to Goethe's light-flooded *Iphigenie*. In contrast to Goethe, Hofmannsthal insists on closing the circle of retribution, on punishing the evildoers, before life can blossom once again.

The principal wit in the drama lies in the way Hofmannsthal combines far-flung subjects, the ancient with the ultramodern, and subjects that lie against each other's grain, in the sense that Greek tragedy accords a positive, Breuer and Freud a negative value to remembrance. Ingenious, too, is the way in which Hofmannsthal artfully links the fields of reference in a carefully constructed symbolic structure. We have seen how he uses the technique of overdetermination in creating the main female characters. He also links blood-for-blood justice with modern notions of psychopathology by emphasizing homologous images. One such image, which makes its presence felt chiefly between the lines, is the circle. Revenge-obsessed Electra is determined to "close the circle" [den Kreis schließen] of crime and retribution. Hofmannsthal stresses the idea: in her perfectionistic fanaticism, Electra wants the crime against her father to be reversed exactly, to the point that Clytemnestra and Aegisthus should be killed with the same axe they used to kill Agamemnon. This perfect circle corresponds to the circle of the psychoanalytic cure, where the analyst strives to return to and extirpate the precise cause of the hysteria, the memory of the trauma. Justice can be done, health can be restored, catharsis can be achieved only if the act that created the imbalance is annuled by another, similar act. Hofmannsthal's indebtedness to Breuer and Freud in his adaptation of Greek tragedy is less surprising when one considers these authors' indebtedness to Aristotle's Poetics. The analogy between the conception of justice that informs Greek tragedy and the psychoanalytic conception of health is written between the lines of their "Preliminary Communication," in the introduction of the term "cathartic": "the injured person's reaction to the trauma only exercises a completely 'cathartic' effect if it is an adequate reaction—as, for instance, revenge" (SE 2:8). In Hofmannsthal's drama the "perfect circle" of revenge has its counterpart in the cycle of becoming, the animal cycle of birth, procreation, and death in which Chrysothemis is so anxious to participate and which Electra judges despicable.

Female sexuality links the circle-cycle motifs with another image Hofmannsthal uses to suggest parallels between his various fields of reference: the image of the dark, enclosed space. We have seen that Hofmannsthal gives concrete spatial form to the notion of the split-off second consciousness in the subterranean regions of the palace, where Electra envisions Orestes chasing Clytemnestra back to the darkest recesses where dead Agamemnon sits. These subterranean regions also suggest a tomb or grave; Hofmannsthal exploits an analogy that exists as a potential extension of Freud's archaeological metaphor in his concluding essay to the *Studies*. But Hofmannsthal's most ingenious idea is to equate, in Electra's words about Clytemnestra, the womb and the grave. Electra cries, "Why, then I crept out of my father's grave / and played in swaddling clothes upon / my father's scaffold!" (PL 25). With this final permutation of the dark enclosed space, with the womb, Hofmannsthal takes us back to the etymological origin of the word "hysteria," and thus back to the topic of psychoanalysis.

Schnitzler's "Flowers"

In the 1890s Schnitzler wrote a number of pieces that engage the theme of memory—the psychologically intrusive memory, the obsessional memory, the repressed memory that returns. These pieces—the stories "Flowers," "Die Frau des Weisen," "The Dead Are Silent," and "Die Nächste," and the plays *Das Märchen, Der Schleier der Beatrice,* and *Der Schleier der Pierrette* (*The Veil of Pierrette*, published in 1910 but based on a sketch of 1892)—propose that one remembers in spite of a conscious determination to forget. Schnitzler's point seems to be to demonstrate that our unconscious psychic forces are more powerful than our conscious volition and that our memories are not under our conscious control. They return particularly when we would like to suppress them. In most of the stories the obsessional memory is caused by a traumatic shock involving the death of a loved one, in which the afflicted character is somehow implicated by guilt.

The parallel to the ideas of Breuer and Freud is striking. It would be a mistake to accord too much weight to putative influence, however. The story that is most centrally concerned with memory, and that most similar to *Studies on Hysteria*, is "Flowers," and it was published before *Studies on Hysteria* appeared. Schnitzler's interest in memory had personal causes. In the period from 1890–92 he was tortured by memories of his girlfriend Mizi Glümer's past (he couldn't reconcile himself to the fact that she had had two previous lovers), and after her death in 1893 her memory haunted him. He based the plot of "Flowers" on experiences he had with Mizi Glümer and another girlfriend.

"Flowers" is about the repression of a guilty memory and how that memory takes on an ominous power. In *Studies on Hysteria*, repression is an ambiguous defense against unpleasant ideas—ambiguous in the sense that the repressed returns in the form of hysterical symptoms. In "Flowers" the narrator represses his feelings about his unfaithful girl-friend, a repression symbolized by his casting her out of his house. He thereby deepens a rift that was initially created by her. He refuses to forgive her and tries to think of her as "dead." But then she actually dies. The rift between them becomes absolute. A focal point of Schnitzler's interest in dualities in the 1890s is the irreconcilable antithesis life versus death. It is death that commands fascination: again and again Schnitzler creates situations where death figures as the site of a mysterious and inexorable power, which it exercises over the living.

In "Flowers" the narrator not only killed his girlfriend in his imagination; by rejecting her so cruelly, he is possibly actually responsible for her death. By dying, the girlfriend acquires a strange power over him. When she was alive, he had the power to keep her at a distance or summon her at will. But when she dies, she moves beyond his reach. By the same token, he becomes accessible to her: she begins to haunt him. His girlfriend had been in the habit of sending him flowers every month to commemorate one of their happiest days. Now the flowers arrive after her death, just as if nothing had changed. There is a rational explanation, which we are meant to disregard, since it does not soften the impact of the eerie incident on the narrator's psyche. The flowers arrive, as fresh as Breuer and Freud's repressed memories, and enclosed in a coffinlike box. They are plainly meant to represent the *living* dead. They also represent the past. They invade the present of the narrator's room—the room he shut his girlfriend out of. They behave like a hysterical symptom. He imagines that the flowers speak, complain; they appear to him a message from the dead.

The narrator keeps the flowers even though they wither and die. They make him sick. As the days go by, the real events that happen around him lose their clear contours and take on the character of an unclear dream. When his present girlfriend Gretel is with him, he finds her words too loud and the colors too strident. The narrator finally admits, "More powerful than I is the memory, it comes when it wants."[19] The past proves more alive than the present: we are obviously meant to compare the power the dead woman exercises over the narrator's mind with Gretel's ineffectual efforts to capture his attention.

The flowers represent the dead woman, and thus the narrator's guilt feelings, but they have another function as well. Schnitzler chose to have the dead woman send an organic gift. The flowers go through a natural process of blooming, fading, and dying. Schnitzler seems to be suggesting that in the healthy pattern, memories should be processed in the same way. As the flowers fade, they perform for the narrator the process that he should have gone through with the woman herself—a process of gradual forgetting. The narrator is fortunate that he does not throw the flowers out, as he did the woman. In fact this afflicted "patient" is not capable of throwing them out; in the end Gretel—in whom it is tempting to see an analyst figure—casts them out of the window.

This story, which reads like a literary rendition of the theory of the pathogenic memory from *Studies on Hysteria*, is founded on the same values that we already encountered in both *Studies on Hysteria* and *Electra*. Here too, the past is an embarrassment. Especially where it is bound up with trauma, death, and guilt, it cannot simply be repressed, for the repressed returns. Here too, the ideal for the past is a continuous absorption or fading into the present. But compared with *Electra*, there is a shift in emphasis. Hofmannsthal assimilates fashionable psychopathological ideas, but the play remains relatively conservative in its philosophical values, which are anchored in vitalism. The play builds up toward its dionysian finale, where a blaze of torches and spontaneous rejoicing greet the news that Clytemnestra and Aegisthus are dead and Electra herself dances and dies. The illumination is not the light of reason, but the flame of life. Hofmannsthal emphasizes forgetting the traumatic past and allowing life to resume its normal course, which means living in the present. Schnitzler is much more interested in the phenomenon of duality. The fascination in this story is centered not on the cure and the underlying ideal of continuity, but on the polarization of present and past, of life and death, and on the past's eerie ability to return, to invade and overpower the present. The trauma involves a death, but what is important is the internalization of this event by the protagonist and his resulting psychological conflict.

Musil's "The Temptation of Quiet Veronica"

Musil, as we shall see, moves more than a step further in the direction of a fascination with dualities and conflict. "The Temptation of Quiet Veronica" is the dense, tangled, difficult, strictly speaking *unreadable* product of a long and agonized process of composition. As he complained later, for "2½ years, and one can say: nearly day and night,"[20] Musil struggled with writer's block to render psychological experiences too elusive for ordinary language. "The error of this book is to be a book," Musil wrote of the novella and its companion piece "The Perfecting of a Love," which he published together under the title *Vereinigungen* (*Unions*). "One should spread out a few pages of it under glass plates and change them from time to time."[21] Barely accessible except through the analysis and comparison of the four earlier versions of the story that have survived, "The Temptation of Quiet Veronica" has inspired the least commentary of all of Musil's major prose. In discussing Musil's borrowings from Freud and Breuer and the theme of the repressed memory, I will be disengaging one relatively simple filament from an extremely complex fictional web.

"The Temptation of Quiet Veronica" is an expansion of a story that Musil published in 1908, "Das verzauberte Haus" (The enchanted house). "Das verzauberte Haus" is a straightforward and quite readable story about the incompatibility of fantasy and reality. It happens to be constructed according to the "aba'" pattern of Breuer and Freud's hysterical comedy, although it does not involve the theme of repressed memory and otherwise betrays no influence of *Studies on Hysteria*. The plot mechanism is activated by the doings of the heroine's lover. The heroine is a dull, sleepy, unreceptive girl who can only achieve spiritual liberation when no man is around to interpose his reality between her and her fantasies. When she refuses her lover he leaves, presumably to kill himself. The expulsion of the lover results in her experiencing a solipsistic self-finding alone in her own house and an afflatus that, paradoxically, involves a "mysterious spiritual unification" with her lover. The story ends on the negative term of the antithesis: when a letter from the lover arrives, testifying that he is alive, the heroine relapses into her former state of dim and muffled consciousness.

Karl Corino has conjectured that Musil expanded this story into "The Temptation of Quiet Veronica" in order to create a suitable companion piece for the much longer, more sophisticated, and more complex novella "The Perfecting of a Love." In "The Perfecting of a Love" Musil takes up again the central problematic of his first novel, *Young Törless*. Throughout his life Musil was fascinated by psychological conflict and by the concomitant philosophical theme of irreconcilable duality. The theme of reason versus mysticism, of language versus the unsayable, persists from *Törless*, published in 1906, to the monumental *Man without Qualities*, on which Musil was still working when he died in 1942. Törless's "confusion" consists in his inability to find a middle ground between a rational view of things and the irrational. In "The Perfecting of a Love" Musil goes beyond *Törless* inasmuch as he does not simply present an irreconcilable opposition but examines how two seemingly antithetical terms impinge on and infect each other. He investigates modes of transition between the terms and the notion of their unification.[22] The heroine at the beginning is a happily married woman who is faithful to her husband. At the end she commits adultery with a stranger. The intervening narrative shows the sequence of tiny modifications in consciousness by which her initial attitude changes into its opposite.

By way of expanding "Das verzauberte Haus" into something similarly complex, Musil Freudianizes the story.[23] The heroine takes on hysterical overtones, and Musil substitutes a repressed memory for the lover as the source of her oppression. The parallels to Breuer and Freud are too obvious to be overlooked.[24] The memory itself involves an episode with a sexually aroused and arousing Saint Bernard dog that Veronica was both attracted to and frightened by when she was fifteen years old. This trauma is a purely psychological nonevent, during which the heroine principally becomes aware of her conflicting emotions. The idiosyncratic bestial element aside, the memory, which involves sexuality and occurs in puberty, conforms to the typical hysterogenic trauma as Breuer describes it in his concluding essay to *Studies on Hysteria*. Musil embeds the memory of the Saint Bernard in descriptive language that emphasizes that it is a repressed memory precisely in Freud and Breuer's sense. When Veronica's memory comes back, we are told that it is "all at once, across an expanse of many years, there again . . . unexpected, hot, and alive," "out of all context, hot, and still alive" (M 6:204, my translation). The expressions "unexpected," "out of all context," "hot," and "alive" underscore that the memory was isolated from the associative chain of normal recollection and was also particularly alive or vivid, all of which corresponds to Breuer and Freud's theories. We know from the "Preliminary Communication" that repressed traumatic memories have no connection with normal memories, that "there is no extensive associative connection between the normal state of consciousness and the pathological ones in which the ideas made their appearance" (SE 2:11). These memories also persist with remarkable freshness. The authors assert, "The memories which have become the determinants of hysterical phenomena persist for a long time with astonishing freshness and with the whole of their affective coloring" (SE 2:9). Musil adds a whole passage that emphasizes these and other "Freudian" qualities of the memory:

> But then she looked at him, and she herself hardly knew what she was thinking, except for an inkling that the only thing she did know about it all—this sudden memory that was there now, lying in her all shining, solitary—was very far from being anything that had a meaning in itself: *it was something that some great fear had once prevented from coming to perfection, and since then it had lain within her, hardened and encapsulated, blocking the way for something that might have developed in her, and it must fall out of her like a foreign body.* (FW 202, my italics)

> [Aber da sah sie ihn an und wußte kaum, was sie dachte, und ahnte, daß das, was sie einzig davon wußte, vielleicht—diese plötzliche Erinnerung, die blank und allein in ihr lag—überhaupt nichts war, das man aus sich selbst begreifen konnte, sondern nur dadurch etwas, daß es—*irgendeinmal durch eine große Angst an einer Vollendung gehindert—seither verhärtet und verschlossen sich in ihr verbarg und einem andern, das es hätte werden können, den Weg versperrte und aus ihr herausfallen mußte wie ein fremder Körper.* (M 6:210; my italics)]

Again, we learn that the memory is isolated from normal consciousness and normal associative chains. It is connected to a *fright* or *fear* (trauma). It blocks Veronica's natural development. Finally, Musil also applies Breuer and Freud's exact terminology, the metaphor of the foreign body ("Fremdkörper"), to the memory. In "The Temptation of Quiet Veronica" Musil makes clear that the trauma is directly responsible for the onset of Veronica's dull, unresponsive state. Recovering the memory, in turn, brings about a spiritual liberation. When the repressed memory is expelled, Veronica experiences an extraordinary epiphany and blossoms forth.

The repressed memory story allows Musil to retain the plot structure of "Das verzauberte Haus," which, like that of "The Perfecting of a Love," involves successive antithetical states. But Musil introduces a radical revision—which is at the same time a typical Musilism—into Breuer and Freud's concept of the hysterogenic memory. The seemingly straightforward situation of correlation between the "Veronica" plot and Breuer and Freud's story of hysteria and cure is complicated by a new theme that is at cross-purposes with the theme of the repressed memory: the theme of doubleness, of the double optic or two different ways of seeing things. The theme of the double optic is familiar from *Young Törless*, and Musil also adopted it as the basic problematic of "The Perfecting of a Love." In "The Temptation of Quiet Veronica" the theme is centered on the topic of animal sexuality. Animals appear to Veronica under two radically different aspects, as aggressive, frightening, repugnant beasts, and as mild, impersonal, warm, seductive presences. She sees these two aspects of animals reproduced in the two men in her life: the aggressive Demeter resembles a ferocious animal, the mild Johannes resembles a gentle one.[25] Similar ambivalence characterizes virtually all of Veronica's perceptions. Thus Johannes himself represents for Veronica at once the male principle of rationality and order (as in "Das verzauberte Haus") and this gentle animal. His departure elicits in her the conflicting reactions of revulsion against his living presence, which seems to her like a dead body blocking her way, and animalistic attraction.

The "double" theme is a powerful formula in its own right. But it is based on premise that is entirely at variance with the presuppositions underlying the theme of the repressed memory. It assumes that not wholeness and integrity, but duality and conflict are the basic state of psychic being. The "double" theme engages a different plot mechanism from the theme of the repressed memory. Psychic duality yields a story of perpetual oscillation between two conflicting alternatives. Törless, for example, sees things alternately under the aspect of rationality and irrationality. The heroine of "The Perfecting of a Love" alternates between the optic of a faithful married woman and that of a woman about to commit adultery with a stranger. Veronica alternates between an attraction to and a revulsion against animals and anything that reminds her of animals. This oscillating, repeating paradigm is quite different from the linear progression of antithetical states that characterizes the plot structure of hysterical comedy as Breuer and Freud devised it.

Musil's second-to-last draft of "Veronica," which he wrote in August 1910, is most useful in helping us understand his intentions in the final published version, for this draft, written in diary form, closely approximates the final story and is comparatively clear. In the diary version it is evident that the new theme of the double optic does not just create a case of conflict between two independent paradigms. Rather, the "double" theme, the theme of Veronica's conflicted psychology, is, bizarrely, *anchored* in the theme of the repressed memory. Musil ascribes Veronica's psychic conflict to an episode involving animal sexuality, in which Demeter wordlessly grabs her head and presses it down while she is reflecting on her rooster memories: "She never again forgot the moment: *from then on there were two things in her*, where there had formerly been only one; reality as well as ideas could appear as if on two levels. On the one, normal level everything was impossible, as if on account of a great fright; there, she immediately felt disgust and fear, as if something slimy and strange threatened her. But on the second, everything was as if plunged into a hot fog, which loosened what happened from you personally."[26]

In the course of the case studies, Freud comes increasingly to the conviction that the hysterogenic "trauma" is a moment when a conflict in the patient's feelings impresses itself on her consciousness. According to this revised theory of the trauma, the patient represses the conflict along with the incident to which her awareness of it was attached, and it manifests itself thenceforth through conversion, in the symptom. Did Musil orient himself in his presentation of Veronica's psychology on this theory of Freud's? Plainly not, for nowhere in Freud's theory is found the notion, fundamental in the passage from "The Temptation of Quiet Veronica" just cited, that the traumatic episode imprints an ambivalent attitude on the subject, so that the traumatic conflict reproduces itself in her future perceptions. It matters little that Musil technically avoids a clash with Freudian theory by ascribing the genesis of the conflict to an unrepressed, unforgotten memory, instead of to the memory of the Saint Bernard. The point is that Veronica's "double" view of things, her ambivalence, originated in a traumatic episode that inspired excitement and fear in her and instilled the same dual reaction in her in perpetuity. "*From then on* there were two things in her. . . ." The Saint Bernard and the rooster memories are functionally equivalent: both involve animal sexuality, and both provoked the same affective reaction in Veronica.

Thus Musil clearly uses (and abuses) psychological theory in order to create a thoroughly Musilian antithesis. This antithesis, whereby "reality as well as ideas could appear as if on two levels," is familiar from *Törless* as Törless's "simple" versus "confused" perspective. It will reappear in *The Man without Qualities* as the antithesis mysticism versus rationality. Here and in "The Perfecting of a Love" Musil tailors the same duality to fit female protagonists, conceived according to the cliché of his day: Veronica and Claudine alternate between an interest in sexuality and—in lieu of "reason"—sexual indifference or a revulsion against sex.

Musil's innovation vis-à-vis Freud and Breuer's theory consists in his having his heroine reproduce rather than repress the situation and the conflict that characterized the trauma. Veronica persistently projects the animal context of the trauma and her ambivalent reaction to animal sexuality onto her experiences. Most strikingly, her relationship to Johannes plays out again her relationship with the Saint Bernard. Numerous hints let us know that Veronica makes an unconscious association between Johannes and this dog, the "kindly animal" who nevertheless made a sexual advance. When Johannes proposes to her she reacts exactly as she did to the dog, with "hot fright and a refusal." Furthermore, Veronica's propensity to see things in terms of animal sexuality and of her conflict is not even restricted to the period before she recovers the repressed memory, to her "ill" state. After she recovers the memory, her immediate reaction is to respond to Johannes as though he were an animal, and in a double fashion: first he seems to her like a dead body ("I bumped into his aliveness everywhere the way you bump into a dead body"), and then he attracts her ("Then a raging desire seized me, as if two swarms intermingled, reeling").[27] The expulsion of the memory thus leads only to further conflict.

Extraordinarily, even Veronica's spiritual rebirth, which begins after she recovers the memory and Johannes leaves, is trapped in the terms of the memory. The ethereal narcissism of the epiphany in "Das verzauberte Haus" becomes animalistic in its tone. The mysticism and the beauty of the epiphany from "Das verzauberte Haus" quickly fade. When Veronica enters her room, which is like her own body, the room's peculiar, squalid smell excites her. She is tempted to wallow in it in a thoroughly bestial manner. In short, the "cured" Veronica experiences well-being, yet a well-being precisely in the terms of the memory, animal sexuality. And her conflict persists: Musil explicitly states that the room has a double effect on her, frightening as well as reassuring:

> This room was, like an animal, so hugely horrible and full of faceless vices that mutilated me, and yet putting itself protectively around me in such a dumb and kindly and lifeless way, no matter what it forced me to do in it.
>
> And my breathing, as I felt this doubleness, became faster and faster, and I sat there all confused and frightened. . . .[28]

Musil constructs a paradoxical situation where the expulsion of the memory both liberates the heroine and frees her to indulge in fantasies involving aberrant sexual predilections that correspond to the very fabric of the memory. The memory thus does not so much obstruct the self's normal course of development as it—whether because it corresponds to preexisting proclivities or because it leaves an indelible imprint on the psyche—conditions the self in its own direction. There is no real getting rid of it. Veronica's psychic conflict runs so deep that a pathogenic memory merely intensifies it, whether the memory is repressed or recovered.

In the final version Musil suppresses both the overt plot line and the narrator's explanatory remarks, so that the text itself gives us no hints on how to read it. He also introduces a peculiar tentativeness in his statements, for a reason we shall return to. Moreover, Musil revises the story in the direction of a confusing all-inclusiveness, combining elements that in their tendencies are quite antithetical. Throughout the period of composition of "The Temptation of Quiet Veronica" Musil's observable strategy was to include as much as possible from the earlier version or versions in each successive revision. Thus here he appends, in an unlikely match, a modified version of the ending of "Das verzauberte Haus" to a modified version of the diary narrative. The final version cannot by any means be seen as the product of a definite and spontaneous intention, and it is even tempting to regard it as a kind of jackdaw's nest, the uncertain product of a hoarding of ideas and of hesitation. It is indeed difficult to say whether the final shape of the story, in its complexity and supreme lack of clarity, is the product of Musil's own psychological ambivalence, his typical inability to decide between alternatives, or of his fascination with the notion that phenomena have a dual effect on the psyche, corresponding to the psyche's inherent conflict, and his determination to render this idea artistically.[29]

In the final version Musil takes care to resolve discrepancies, polish details, and tie together loose ends. He works on the mechanics of the plot, making precise anything that was formerly present only in a slapdash fashion. Thus he painstakingly concocts a fusion of the Johannes story and the repressed memory story, making clear what was left vague in the diary version, namely that Johannes's departure and the recovery of the memory are essentially equivalent actions, so that while finding the repressed memory triggers Veronica's psychological rebirth, the arrival of Johannes's letter is nevertheless able to put a stop to it. What of the theme of psychic conflict we saw in the diary version? Musil modifies his innovations and his revisionist use of the theme of the repressed memory considerably, but he does not forsake his basic commitment to conflict psychology or to the idea that memories are formative and not "foreign bodies" in the psyche.

Musil's changes in the theme of the repressed memory must be seen against the background of another major change in the novella, which Annie Reniers-Servranckx aptly calls, using Musil's own words, the "change for the dreamlike." She writes, "The utopian is a match for the real; everything perceptible is referred to some indefinite, absent, unknown, possibly future thing, of which there is 'already' a presentiment but that can 'not yet' be drawn into the horizon of consciousness and spoken."[30] Most of what Johannes and Veronica say and what Veronica thinks, including references to animals, now appear as metaphors for the unsayable, for some ultimate truth about the self that cannot be expressed directly in words.[31] As Veronica says to Johannes, "So it's not just animals: this thing is yourself and a solitude, it's you and once again you" (FW 186). Musil also makes the direction of phenomena—for example, whether something is a cause or an effect, whether something originates in a barely remembered past or lies ahead in an indistinct future—thoroughly ambiguous. We can apply Johannes's remark to the images of Musil's story themselves: "They are things beyond the horizon of consciousness . . . , things that can be seen gliding past, along the horizon of our consciousness—or rather, it is only a new horizon, tense with strangeness, inscrutable, no more than a possibility, a sudden intimation, and there is nothing on it yet" (FW 181).

Thus while Musil works out the mechanisms of the plot and the details of the story with a high degree of precision, at the same time he suppresses explicit explanations. The surface or "real" level of the narrative becomes more tentative in its tone and tends to cloud over, and elements of this surface level seem to point beyond themselves without it being clear to what they point. The theme of Veronica's conflicted psychology before she recovers the repressed memory is definitely present, but we are not told in so many words, as we are in the diary version, that it originates in one particular past incident. Rather we are told, "All her sombre life long Veronica had been in dread of one kind of love and had yearned for another kind. . . . So she wavered between Johannes und Demeter" (FW 210). Did this conflict originate with the traumatic episodes, or did the traumatic episodes reinforce and give specific direction to a preexisting conflict? In the time span covered by the narrative before the return of the Saint Bernard memory, Veronica is preoccupied by animals and their dual aspect of aggression and servility. As in the diary version, half of her pulls toward Johannes, half toward Demeter; each man represents a different aspect of animality, while Johannes represents both passive animality and rational order. In addition, Veronica is fascinated by the story of a farmer lady who keeps dogs instead of lovers. But it is unclear to what extent these preoccupations are the result of the traumatic memory and to what extent they simply come into being as part of the process of recovering it.

As in the diary version, finding the memory in the final version leads Veronica both to a repulsion against Johannes, who reminds her of an exhausted animal, and to an attraction to Johannes in landscape and animal terms. The theme of conflict does not then persist into Veronica's epiphany in her room. Musil reverts to an ethereal epiphany: he drops the animalistic finale of the diary version and replaces it with a modified version of the ending of "Das verzauberte Haus." Yet traces of animality do persist into Veronica's uplifted state: "Surely an animal would be like that other dimension" (FW 212), thinks Veronica, for example. On the whole, however, animality fades into the background, while another theme becomes prominent and takes on the burden of aesthetic interest, namely, the theme of the unification of opposites. Musil constructs an aesthetically pleasing complement to the theme of the duality of phenomena that dominates Veronica's depressed state with the theme of the double-in-one. Alone in her house, Veronica feels that the boundary between herself and things—her room, events, Johannes—is eliminated. She has a series of mystical, paradoxical experiences of oneness with the other. Thus "the space between herself and the objects around her ceased to be emptiness; instead there was a strange network of relations" (FW 208–9); "nowhere herself; and yet she felt nothing but herself" (FW 215); "It was as if she were gazing at herself out of his eyes and with every movement feeling not only herself being touched by him [Johannes] but also in some indescribable way his sense of touching her" (FW 217). Musil will later attribute the same kind of experience to Moosbrugger in *The Man without Qualities*.

In summary, then, while the repressed memory story in the final version is not as obviously awkward as in the diary version—the aesthetic center of gravity having been shifted onto the depth-psychological, mystical "behind the horizon of consciousness" theme and also onto the conflict-and-unification-of-opposites theme—the difficulties are nonetheless still there. Musil remains committed to the idea that conflict is the basic state of Veronica's psyche. This conflict is present both before and after the repressed memory is recovered, except during Veronica's actual epiphany in her room. The epiphany is still colored by the terms of the memory (bestiality). Finally, Musil expresses his skepticism at the idea of a cure: Veronica's fragile afflatus dissipates on its first contact with reality. Musil repeatedly puts the reality of the spiritual rebirth and Veronica's belief in its reality into question: "Her waking life, that creeping life of hers by day, would once more founder. She knew that" (FW 212–13). This is one of several remarks with which Musil undermines the solidity of her spiritual breakthrough. Indeed, precisely what Veronica envisions actually happens: the arrival of Johannes's letter destroys her illusory solipsistic paradise, and she falls back into her former state of dulled consciousness.

Musil thus deforms Breuer and Freud's theory of the repressed memory and the psychoanalytic cure. For whatever reason he may have borrowed the theory, he plainly had no use for the monistic concept of the psyche that it entailed. In the novella he thus sets the pathogenic traumatic episode against a background not of psychic integrity but of psychic conflict. In effect, he combines two opposing kinds of conflict: a conflict between past and present (borrowed from *Studies on Hysteria*), and conflict, nominally originating in a past incident, as a basic state of being, whose perpetuation is guaranteed by the temporal continuity of human experience. He thereby presents a much more problematic view of the past and of past experience than that suggested by Breuer and Freud's theory of the pathogenic memory. An intuitive conception of the past puts it in a relationship of continuity with the present: through the faculty of memory, past experience carries over into and influences present experience. The theory of the repressed memory, stemming as it does out of a historical context of vitalism in which happiness is identified with an unreflecting immediacy, puts the past in an adversative relation with the present. Musil does not wholeheartedly embrace either view, however. He is plainly suspicious of a conception of the past as something that can be repudiated or expelled, but he is also disinclined to believe that past experience can always be successfully integrated, made to fade into a dominant present.

Musil's view of the past manifests a coincidental similarity to that of Freud in *The Interpretation of Dreams*. To be sure, there is no theory of the unconscious and infantile desire in Musil's novella. Musil returns to the more intuitive and conventional idea that the past exerts a formative influence on the present. Musil does not advance an original conception of the past, as does Freud with his image of infantile scenes and in his work on screen memories and *Nachträglichkeit*. After borrowing one image of the past, that of the pathogenic memory, Musil backs away from its consequences, and he also avoids making any clear alternative statement about the past and memory.[32] Yet as in *The Interpretation of Dreams* the past in "The Temptation of Quiet Veronica" stands in a similarly awkward relation to the present: it is in conflict with present interests, yet it remains unassimilable and ineradicable.

We therefore see that where Hofmannsthal's attitude toward duality could be described as negative and Schnitzler's as intrigued, Musil's commitment to duality is much more pronounced. As a consequence, his treatment of the past and of memory is more troubled than that of his predecessors. Like them, Musil works with constructs. But the neatly stylized—and hence easily excised—antagonism between past and present is gone, replaced by a mixture of conflict and continuity. Musil does not offer new solutions as much as he introduces confusion into existing ones. But his confusion is finally more commensurate with the complexity of the problems involved in the past and in memory than the lucid oppositions concocted by his predecessors.

IN THE FICTIONAL works I plan to discuss in this chapter, the writers all play with the idea of bringing a "dark area," or mysterious unknown, "to light." Just as Freud in *The Interpretation of Dreams* chose to illustrate his theory of the mental processes first with a topography, in terms of the interaction between spaces, the literary authors choose space as the appropriate dimension for such play. The texts thus manifest certain homologous spatial configurations. A number of assumptions underlie all the homologies. First, it is assumed that the "dark" area exists in antithetical relation to an area that is in fact often referred to as "light." Second, the dark area is seen to be primary. For example, it may be accorded the status of a spatial ground (in Musil) or a temporal origin (in Freud). Third, the idea of spatial continuity (or temporal continuum) between the two places, and the possibility of spatial progression (or temporal process) from one place to another, are examined carefully.

Sometimes continuity is denied, and progression is shown to be impossible. A convenient way to prove lack of continuity, that "you can't get there from here," is to posit some form of the infinite regress, to follow the example Zeno set in his paradoxes, such as the Paradox of Achilles and the Tortoise. Achilles never catches up with the tortoise because space is privileged over time and then segmented in such a way as to yield infinite time. In the examples I shall discuss, this kind of procedure results in figures I shall call the "proliferating middle," the "receding origin," and the "invisible barrier."

On the other hand, the writers examine closely the circumstances under which the dark area is accessible. In other words, they are concerned not only with mediation, which implies trying to relate two discrete, discontinuous terms, but also with transformation, that is, a continuous process by which one entity turns into another. The possibility of transformation results in the figure of the "irreversible process." It should become clear that these figures are all linked and all proceed logically from the idea of trying to understand the unknown (or rather, what is known to be unknown). As examples I have chosen some of Schnitzler's works, in particular the story "The Dead Are Silent" (1897), Musil's *Young Törless* (1906), and Kafka's "An Imperial Message" (1919). We shall also return to Freud and *The Interpretation of Dreams* (1900) by way of comparison. I discuss the examples by Schnitzler first. They show the basic pattern of transformation versus mediation and irreversible process, and they precede and therefore cannot be derivative of Freud's mental topography.

Schnitzler's "The Dead Are Silent" and Other Works

It is well known that the psychological effects of shock and death are a main theme in Schnitzler's work. Typically, the afflicted character seeks unsuccessfully to come to terms with a traumatic experience, that is, to establish rational control over the irrational. In several early stories the power and the wholly alien otherness of the irrational is dramatized by the introduction of a third thing, which might be described as an obsessional image. The image presents itself to the subject with the force of a message from the other world. In the ordinary course of events, the subject would assimilate the experience of the loved one's death, and the split would heal in the course of time; mental integration would eventually be restored. The appearance of the third thing blocks this possibility. Its effect is to transform the original traumatic event into a mysterious source, into a kind of abyss that casts forth questions to which there are no answers. It thus polarizes the subject's relationship to the experience into an irreconcilable opposition between the self and the abyssal other.[1] There are obvious parallels in such phenomena to Freud's theory of the symbolic substitution of the hysterical symptom for the repressed traumatic confict outlined in *Studies on Hysteria* (1895), although several of the stories were written before *Studies on Hysteria* was published. In the story "Der Andere" (The other man), written in 1889, the "third thing" is a strange man whom the narrator sees kneeling at his wife's grave. Was he her lover? Tormented by this insoluble question, the narrator, who had been on his way toward recovering from his grief, becomes reobsessed with the dead woman. As an enigma, a possible source of a mysterious message, she "comes to life" for him again. In the story "Flowers" (1894), a bouquet that arrives from a recently deceased former mistress similarly causes the narrator to become obsessed with her memory.

It is part of the logic of this type of triadic structure that apparent progress away from the obsessional image or mysterious other—what appears to be the victory of conscious volition—is in fact regression toward it. Once its priority has been established, it exercises an unrelenting pull. In "Die Nächste" (written in 1899) the main character, by making love to another woman, seemingly overcomes the guilt and sexual inhibition that a recurrent mental image of his dead wife has called into being. She looks like his wife and thus rivals the image in its attractive force. But the pull of the *dead* woman's image is stronger. Overcome with horror, the protagonist transfers his guilt onto the woman for *mimicking his wife* and *restores* the condition of death (and thus of guilt and sexual inhibition): he *repeats*, so to speak, the death of his wife, by stabbing his new lover with a hatpin.

An excellent example of the unidirectional motion toward the unknown other despite the apparent movement of the subject in the opposite direction is the plot of "The Dead Are Silent" (1897). Schnitzler adopted the plot of this story from an unpublished pantomime of 1892. He was extraordinarily fond of this plot, for he subsequently reused it twice, in the historical drama *Der Schleier der Beatrice* (1899) and in the ballet pantomime *Der Schleier der Pierrette* (1910).[2] All of these works take place in two antithetical spaces, a space representing respectability and order and an "outside" space of eros and death. In all of them, the heroine capriciously leaves the domain of order and has an erotic adventure that ends with the loved one's death. When she tries to turn and flee, she finds that her step into the dark region was irreversible—she is inexorably pulled back by death. A token of the dark and terrible region pursues her back into the safe world of the living to reclaim her. In different proportions, each work invites a psychological or an allegorical interpretation. In the psychological reading, to which "The Dead Are Silent" best lends itself, guilt exercises a terrible power over the mind: our guilty secrets lay traps for our rational consciousness and betray us. In the allegorical reading, which is more appropriate in the case of the two dramas, Death's long arm punishes the foolish mortal who dares toy with his finality.

In "The Dead Are Silent" the opposites are initially established in the form of geographical locations. On the one hand there is Vienna, the city, with its lights and crowds. On the other there is the dark, empty region outside the city limits. The topos of the city and the region beyond are too familiar to require explanation: what is interesting is that here the two locations, Vienna and non-Vienna, are separated by a river (the Danube) and connected by a bridge. The story is about a woman who desires the illicit pleasures of having a lover, yet does not want to forgo the security and respectability of her bourgeois marriage. She meets her lover secretly one night. They go driving in a coach and suddenly find themselves on the bridge, where they step outside and linger. On the bridge, her lover presses her to make a decision: either to run away with him (to leave Vienna) or to forget him and go back to her husband. Neither idea is compatible with the woman's policy of brinkmanship (or bridgemanship); but not wanting to lose her lover, she agrees to go "a little ways" into the "darkness" (also referred to as "Abgründe," abysses [EW 2: 29]) beyond the bridge.

The event that follows reminds one of Freud's explanation in *Totem and Taboo* of the origin of the expressions "Diesseits" and "Jenseits": it was a primitive custom to isolate the potentially dangerous dead by taking their bodies to the other side of the river (SE 13:59). The lovers have scarcely crossed the bridge when the coach overturns. The man appears to have been killed. It conforms to the nature of the region of enigmas that we do not know whether he is actually dead or not. The woman experiences a number of reactions in rapid succession. Finally "she had the sensation of waking up" (IR 147); clarity prevails, and she fears for her reputation. She hastily imposes an interpretation on the event that she later comes to distrust: her lover is dead; nothing can be done about it; in any event, she must disappear from the scene of the accident and pretend that, as far as she is concerned, the whole incident never took place. She rushes back to the city, *retracing her steps exactly*. But by crossing the river the first time she committed an irreversible act. Although she seemingly succeeds in reaching her home and concealing the horrible adventure from her husband, the "return" is in fact a return to the forbidden thing she is trying to suppress. She involuntarily blurts out the information to her husband in the form of the telling and ironic sentence, "The dead are silent" (IR 154). The more she has apparently succeeded in mastering the experience in the enigmatic region, the more it has in fact become *her* master. The conclusion we can draw is that the bridge is of a peculiar type: it can be crossed repeatedly in one direction, but never in the other.

Let us compare with this Schnitzler's rendering of the same plot in *Der Schleier der Beatrice*. The childlike femme fatale Beatrice, a woman of the people who manages to convince a duke to make her his bride, leaves her wedding, seemingly on a whim, to seek out her former lover, the poet Filippo Loschi. She proposes a suicide pact. He, in despair over his own weakness of will in once again being drawn to Beatrice after having broken with her, drinks from a poisoned chalice and dies. She hestitates; then, terrified at seeing her lover dead, flees the spot. But although Beatrice flees back to life, she leaves her veil near Filippo's corpse, so to speak in the realm of the dead. Schnitzler makes the idea of the "pull of death" explicit by having Beatrice feel something like a tugging on her dress when she wants to leave:

No one knows! I can go back!
Truly—can go back! Why do I tarry?
Are you holding me there? As if something were pulling
at my dress.
(DW 3:133, my translation)

Even though she runs away from the scene, she is as if cornered by death. When she returns to the wedding party the duke notices she has lost her veil (which symbolizes, among other things, the—lost—virginity of the bride). He demands that she fetch it. Beatrice consents to do so only when she is told that the penalty for refusing is immediate death. But the penalty for complying turns out to be death as well: although the duke himself promises her forgiveness and a safe return, her brother Francesco stabs her. By having once promised herself to death, she remains death's property.

Where Freud, in *Beyond the Pleasure Principle*, will declare the sexual instinct (Eros) and the death instinct opposites, Schnitzler consistently identifies the realms of sex and death. For him, sex and death form the Janus face of the mysterious power that pulls the strings of human life. In "The Dead Are Silent" non-Vienna is the site of both sex and death. In *Beatrice*, likewise, Schnitzler cannot resist adding a macabre twist that bespeaks the same identification. When the duke enters the house where, unbeknownst to him, Loschi's corpse lies, he wants to make it the scene of his wedding night. He says to the recoiling Beatrice,

Oh, does shame stir for the last time?
So imagine it's a grave, so black and silent,

In which we chastely bury our sighs.

(DW 3:163, my translation)

Schnitzler reuses the same motif in *Der Schleier der Pierrette*: when Arlecchino, the groom figure, enters the room of the dead lover figure Pierrot, he "wird zärtlicher" ("becomes more tender") toward Pierrette (DW 6:125).

The underlying structure of all these Schnitzler plots, and that which all of the following examples will presuppose, involves two distinct antithetical terms. In the various examples these antithetical sites are occupied by what in the traditional codification of narrative are thought of as different levels of narration: by the plot structure, by metaphoric imagery, or by abstract concepts. I shall therefore use neutral terminology to refer to the two terms: Let us call the first term A and the second term B. The only relationship this form of designation is meant to suggest is that A is primary and more important, while B is secondary.

In terms of concepts, it could be said that the first term, A, signifies, in the most general sense, the unknown: the unexplicable, the inaccessible, the unassimilable. It can be seen to correspond to the unconscious, the life instinct or the death instinct, or the sexual drive—in short, to any incomprehensible force (in "The Dead Are Silent," to non-Vienna). The second term, B, involves either the knower or the known: it relates to consciousness, understanding, thought, conscious volition, and their instrument, language. It is not my object here to show that the texts are connected by a concern with similar concepts, however, but rather to demonstrate how the two terms occur in all of them and how they relate to each other by certain mechanisms.

Several generalizations can be made about the relation of A and B in all the examples. A is invariably more powerful than B. B, the "knowing" part, has no control over A. When B attempts to comprehend A—in either sense of comprehend, to understand or to encompass—it merely creates inadequate representations of A, which are in fact just extensions of B. We could call them B_1 B_2, B_3, and so forth. These variations on B are futile attempts at mediation between A and B, which A by its very definition eludes. The relationship of B to A is the relationship of Psyche to Eros: when it comes with a lamp, the object of inquiry runs away.

Under these circumstances, how does B even know A exists? Periodically, A manifests itself to B, in a form which I shall call A_1 (Schnitzler's third thing or obsessive image). A_1 is the product of, and presumably a symbol or *pars pro toto* of A—but in the sense of a continuous transformation, rather than a mediation between discontinuous terms. A only appears in the guise of A_I when B is as if asleep, however: A_I overwhelms B and cancels it out. One could say, in the psychological metaphor, that A_I becomes "the state of consciousness," so that B cannot examine it. (This is the case in "The Dead Are Silent" during the presumptive death and the "return" of the death when the woman lets down her defenses). One could also say—in the topographical metaphor—that any distance separating A and B suddenly disappears, or that it takes no time whatsoever to traverse that distance. Thus there are two possible states of things: either A_I [A_I: $\cancel{B}$], *or* A and B, where there is no means of access from B to A [B B_I ∞ A].

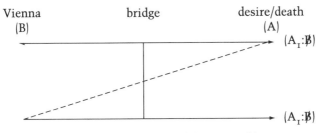

Vienna   bridge   desire/death
(B)   (A)

$(A_I:\cancel{B})$

$(A_I:\cancel{B})$

"The Dead Are Silent": Figure of the irreversible process.

We now arrive at two new questions: What is the relation of A_I to A, and what is its relation to B?

Freud's *The Interpretation of Dreams*

Freud devotes most of *The Interpretation of Dreams* to discussing the relation of A_I to A. A_I in this text is of course the hitherto unfathomed phenomenon of the dream, which Freud has set out to interpret. To explain it, he assigns to it a mysterious origin A; that is, he "discovers the unconscious." As we saw in chapter 1, instead of a phenomenon that is difficult to explain, we suddenly have a mysterious source and its product: two things instead of one. A is a *mysterious* source because it is the source of wishing in general, rather than of any given A_I. A, the unconscious, is of course inaccessible to B, the consciousness. The dream, however, a product of the unconscious, gains access to B in the form of

A$_{1}$, thus presenting a version of A to B. In other words, Freud suggests that movement from one pole to the other is unidirectionally possible. The idea is quite similar to the structure of irreversible process in "The Dead Are Silent." Either the subject is dreaming, and the representative of the unconscious floods consciousness, or the subject is awake, and A and B are mutually inaccessible.

How can what was originally perceived as "other," the dream, suddenly be seen to be a messenger from or representation of another source? How, in other words, can the inaccessibility of the dream meaning be displaced onto the unconscious?[3] Quite simply: by transforming the perceived barrier between the interpreter and the dream text into the metaphor of an *invisible barrier* separating consciousness from the unconscious. This barrier is the powerful "censorship," which guards the route of access from consciousness to the unconscious and vice versa. In chapter 7 of *The Interpretation of Dreams* Freud employs a spatial metaphor—his topography of the mind—to show how the unconscious wish penetrates through to consciousness. The wish cannot take the direct, forward, daytime route to B, any more than consciousness can look directly into the unconscious, because it runs up against the "censorship." The wish can take what Freud calls "the regressive direction," however—the regressive route of the "primary process" or primitive hallucinatory wish fulfillment. Taking this path causes the unconscious product to undergo a number of modifications. The wish first collides with the "censorship" in its attempt to proceed in a progressive direction; and then, regressing, it goes through the memory traces. In the course of this roundabout movement, what Freud calls the "dream work" occurs. By the time the unconscious wish (now the "dream") reaches consciousness, it has become a "manifest content," a transformation of the original "latent content" through the work of condensation, displacement, dissolution into visual images, and secondary revision. Freud thus defines the "regressive route" or relation of A to A$_{1}$ as a number of *formal* alterations. The manifest content *is* the latent content—but in a different, unrecognizable *form*. Freud emphasizes the idea of the "dream work" as a formal change by asking us to abandon temporarily the idea of the psychic systems as localities and to think of them as "processes" ("Vorgänge"), "like the lenses of the telescope, which cast the image." He redefines the censorship by comparing it to "the refraction which takes place when a ray of light passes into a new medium" (SE 5:611).

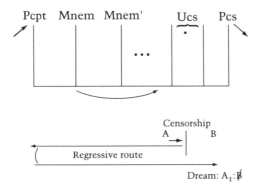

The upper diagram is taken from *The Interpretation of Dreams*. The lower diagram shows the process by which the unconscious wish (A) becomes the dream (A$_I$) and the relation of both to the dreamer's consciousness (B). Pcpt = perception; Mnem, Mnem' = the memory traces.

By creating the ideas of a mysterious source, an irreversible process, and an invisible barrier, Freud finds that he is able to explain completely the relation between A$_I$ and A, the dream and the unconscious. In doing so, however, he neglects a thorough investigation of the relation of B (the analytic or analyst's consciousness) to A$_I$. In fact, A, the wish-generating source, can in a certain sense be seen as an invention of B, a B$_I$, a hermeneutic strategy by which B can understand A$_I$. Consciousness defines the unconscious as the source of wishes, and knowing that one is looking for a wish greatly facilitates the reconstruction of the actual latent content. Freud does not say that A mediates between A$_I$ and B; but it is this predefining of the mysterious source as wishing that makes dream interpretation possible, and this allows Freud optimistically to make the irreversible process inherent in the logic of his system *reversible by interpretation*. Reversibility also brings with it a surprising degree of parallelism between the process by which the dream-to-be-interpreted is constituted and the analyst's work. As Paul Ricoeur notes in his study on Freud's hermeneutics, condensation and displacement, the processes that turn latent content into manifest content, are meaningful operations comparable to rhetorical procedures. "The dream-work," Ricoeur writes, "is the inverse of the analyst's work of deciphering and is homogeneous therefore with the mental operations of interpretation which trace it back."[4]

Freud already anticipates such objections in *The Interpretation of Dreams*, where he admits near the beginning of chapter 7 that not every dream can be interpreted completely: "The question whether it is possible to interpret *every* dream must be answered in the negative. It must not be forgotten that in interpreting a dream we are opposed by the psychical forces which were responsible for its distortion. . . . There is often a passage in even the most thoroughly interpreted dream which has to be left obscure" (SE 5:524–25). In the metapsychological writings of 1915, where it is no longer primarily a question of the interpretation of dreams, he formalizes the implications of this disclaimer by revising the topography and the definitions of the functions of the various psychic systems so that the unconscious becomes more logically accessible to the analyst. Although Freud reaffirms its antithetical quality, asserting that its processes are timeless and that it knows no contradictions, he explicitly devalues the unconscious as an absolute origin; it becomes merely the first psychic place. What was formerly "Acheron," the dark area, is partially domesticated. In the essay "The Unconscious," the unconscious wish is seen to be an "instinctual *representative*" (SE 14:186; "Trieb*repräsentanz*;" my emphasis), secondary to the instincts ("Triebe") themselves. The transformational or representational operations of the psyche are now initiated in the unconscious itself, and its "thing-presentations" (SE 14:202; "Sachvorstellungen"), subject to condensation and displacement in that system, transform themselves in an orderly fashion into conscious material by acquiring "word-presentations" ("Wortvorstellungen") in the preconscious.

Musil's *Young Törless*

The concept of two states or "two different ways of seeing things" is the main theme of Robert Musil's *Young Törless*. The possibility of Freudian influence on this early novel has been much debated, but the debate has always centered around the theme of sexuality in the novel and its possible relation to Freud's theories in *Three Essays on the Theory of Sexuality*.[5] The similarities between the theme of the two states and the related spatial imagery that runs through the novel, and Freud's topography of the mind in *The Interpretation of Dreams*, have not been discussed, although the parallels are overwhelming. One finds in *Törless* the same idea of two places, the irreversible process, and the invisible barrier.

In *Törless* place B is clearly labeled as reason, thought, and language. Images of light are used to refer to it: it is called "The bright diurnal world" (YT 56). The other place, place A, is related to sensuality and is evoked mainly in images: the image of *the other place across the river*, darkness, the ocean, a bottomless hole or abyss, a gap, and, of course, the irrational and imaginary numbers and infinity. The character Törless is in quest of "a gate" ("ein Tor," M 6:46) or "a bridge" ("eine Brücke," M 6:65) by which he can get from one place to the other. There indeed exists such a gate, but it can be entered only in one direction; that is, the region beyond, A, can enter into consciousness, B. The resulting unity— which corresponds to our A_I—is called the "simple" view of things. Musil writes, "What looks grand and remote so long as our words are still reaching out towards it from a long way off, later, once it has entered the sphere of our everyday activities, becomes quite simple and loses all its disturbing quality" (YT 79). But when Törless tries to go through the gate in the other direction, he fails.

$$A_I : \cancel{B} \longleftarrow A$$

The simple state.

What he is trying to reach seems to him "far away" or confused. The gate closes, or an "invisible frontier" forces Törless to stop, or the gate becomes a kind of nonbridge which is already part of the incomprehensible other region itself. Musil writes, "What originates outside and approaches from a long way off is like a misty sea full of gigantic, everchanging forms. . . . And between the life one lives and the life one feels, the life one only has inklings and glimpses of, seeing it only from afar, there lies that invisible frontier, and in it the narrow gateway, where all that ever happens, the images of things, must throng together and shrink so that they can enter into a man" (YT 130).

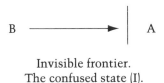

Invisible frontier.
The confused state (I).

Alternately, when Törless—whose very name reflects his lack of success in finding a gate—tries to approach the object of his desire, it recedes like a horizon, maintaining its distance from him: A_I immediately deepens into A, the mysterious source. Or, worse, it seems to retreat before him while he withdraws from it: the distance between increases, the middle proliferates. Musil writes of Törless, "Between events and himself, indeed between his own feelings and some inmost self that craved understanding of them, there always remained a dividing-line, which receded before his desire, like a horizon, the closer he tried to come to it. Indeed, the more accurately he circumscribed his feelings with his thoughts, and the more familiar they became to him, the stranger and more incomprehensible did they seem to become, in equal measure; so that it no longer even seemed as though they were retreating before him, but as though he himself were withdrawing from them" (YT 30).

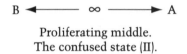

Proliferating middle.
The confused state (II).

The irrational numbers are Musil's central figure for the proliferating middle. According to Törless they function, in the context of an equation, as a nonbridge (YT 90). One uses them to get from here to there, to solve a mathematical problem, but when one tries to retrace one's steps, one stares into the abyss of the infinite regress that these numbers represent.

All consciousness can do is create inadequate representations, that is, transform the receding mystery (A_I) into an unsatisfactory image of itself (B_I). Musil is much more pessimistic than Freud about the possibility of successfully penetrating the unknown through interpretation. The unsuccessful effort of consciousness to seize its object is usually represented by a small light object emerging momentarily from and falling back into an immense dark background or depth: as a lit leaf against the darkness beyond the window (YT 29); as a tiny, bright figure (Basini's) against a dark background (YT 64); as illuminated drops of water that are sprayed up and fall back into a dark sea (YT 111). Musil explicitly labels the last image as a figure for an attempt at interpretation and thereby reveals interpretation to be a form of unsuccessful mediation. He writes of Törless,

> All he had to help him in interpreting this tide of emotion that would flood through his whole being was the images it cast up into his consciousness—as if all that could be seen of a swell stretching endlessly far away into the darkness were single, separate droplets of foam [nur einzelne losgelöste Teilchen] flung high against the cliffs

of some lighted shore and, all force spent, immediately falling away again, out of the circle of light. . . . Törless could never hold on to them; and when he looked more closely, he could feel that these incidents [Repräsentanten] on the surface were in no proportion to the force of the dark mass, deep down, of which they seemed to be the manifestations [die zu vertreten sie vorgaben]. (YT 111)

Musil is particularly interested in the process by which the simple state of things, A_1, becomes the confused state of things, A and B. Since the two states are successive in the same subject, one would suppose that some kind of perceptible gradation beween them exists. But the two states are entirely antithetical; there is no gradation between them. They have the alternating relation of Wittgenstein's duck-rabbit; that is, one sees things either one way or the other way.[6]

Wittgenstein, Duck-Rabbit.

In certain Jugendstil counterchange designs in which the "background" is the negative form of the pattern, similarly, the viewer can alternately see the light shapes on a dark ground and the dark shapes on a light ground, but cannot focus on both readings simultaneously. Some of Kolo Moser's designs are good examples of the interchangeable pattern-background relation, for example, the stylized fish on the vertical intarsia strips on his buffet "Der reiche Fischzug" (The rich catch) of 1900.

It is said of Törless, "His attention was wholly concentrated on this straining to rediscover the point in himself where the change of inner perspective had suddenly occurred" (YT 130). But between A and B (when observed from B), there is a barrier ("Grenze") which has no extension or breadth in space; and when Törless considers it as a temporal alternation, he finds that the moment of change has no duration in time: it is described as a "jerk" ("Ruck"), a "split" ("Riß"), and the like. There is simply nothing there to examine. The moment or place of change bears a strong resemblance to Freud's censorship. As we recall, Freud described it as a kind of lens or process of refraction—something that changes the form of that which is trying to pass from A to B. Musil likewise describes the moment of change as something like a "click" ("Knacks") that corresponds to the "scarcely perceptible muscular sensation which

Kolo Moser, buffet, "Der reiche Fischzug." Courtesy of Österreichisches Museum für angewandte Kunst, Wien, where the buffet is located.

is associated with the focusing of the gaze" (YT 130).[7] When B, therefore, tries to comprehend the *substantial* transformation that is evidently taking place, B fails. The attention is instead transferred to the *mechanism* of change, the "click." Like Freud, then, Musil examines the problem of how things can be the same, yet different. It is to be assumed that some process of transformation takes place; but in Musil's version, when one tries to retrace that process, one reaches an impasse. The assumed "process" of transformation, the medium, shrinks into a hypothetical imperceptible line of division, comparable to a blank where a presumptive original text has been obliterated by a censor's mark.

Kafka's "An Imperial Message"

Inaccessible places, proliferating distances, and invisible barriers are so common in Kafka's stories that a list of examples would be long. I would like only to point out a few things about one parable, "An Imperial Message," the structure of which presents an interesting variation on the related schemata I have discussed in the works of Schnitzler, Freud, and Musil. In this parable as elsewhere in Kafka's fiction, the spatial relations are much more precisely articulated than in the previous examples. Kafka is interested not only in the idea of irreversible process, like his predecessors, but in the infinite series itself, in the successive stages of mediation by which B attempts to get to A. Furthermore, the implications of Kafka's dualistic schema are different.

The parable is about a nonarriving message from the emperor. First, it is apparent that no human failing is responsible for the nonarrival of the message; for it is stressed that the emperor's faithful messenger gets the message absolutely straight. The message fails to arrive because space (and thus time) increases as the messenger begins to run in the direction of the intended recipient of the message. As the messenger rushes forward, he is actually getting farther and farther away from his goal. We learn of more and more places the messenger has to traverse—rooms, stairs, courtyards, palaces, the city mushrooms between the palace and the recipient. As a result, the *origin* or palace and its mediating element, the messenger, seem to recede. It is interesting to compare to this the process described in "A Common Confusion" which Kafka wrote a few months after "An Imperial Message," in which "A" (our B) is always missing "B" (our A) either because time is increasing over constant distance, or because distance increases at simultaneity; the upshot, that the elusive "B" stamps off furiously "impossible to tell whether at a great distance or quite near him" (CS 430), indicates that the proliferating middle and the invisible barrier are simply versions of the same thing.

Second, the origin (the palace or emperor) is clothed with a mystique of importance, mystery, and forbiddenness similar to that of the A in all our previous examples. The mystique of the origin is enhanced by the fact that the emperor *dies* immediately after he whispers the message to the messenger.

Third, it is noteworthy that the recipient of the message is entirely passive. For example, he makes no effort to go to the palace or meet the messenger. His inaction is clarified by the final sentence of the story. It is said that the recipient *dreams* the message ("Du erträumst . . . sie dir" [κ 4:129]) from the window. The entire idea of the message is thus a creation, a dream, or in other words a *wish* of the recipient. With his wish, the dreamer spans the distance between the window and the palace unproblematically and in an instant.[8] But the process is irreversible. Suddenly a messenger becomes involved, and he cannot get back to the expectant consciousness. In other words, consciousness cannot retrieve the message.

The longed-for arrival of the message might be interpreted as the fulfillment of the wish. One might compare the *idea* of the message (the distance from window to palace) to Freud's idea of the hallucinatory wish-fulfillment image that quickly flashes into consciousness by way of the regressive route, and the hoped-for *arrival* of the message (the reverse distance from palace to window) to the slower reality principle, which involves thought processes moving in the progressive direction toward motility. This interpretation is not entirely satisfactory, however. It leaves unanswered the question that, though it is never explicitly posed, dominates the story, namely: *what is the content of the message?* The recipient dreams the *idea* of the message, but its *content* eludes him. B at the window imagines the message (A_I) to be coming from a distant source. But when he tries to focus on it, his attention is immediately transferred to the *mechanism (or medium) bringing it, the messenger.* In this story A_I is thus curiously interrupted or amputated. Such interruptions are characteristic of Kafka's versions of the infinite regress: the object of desire is subject to repeated division, such that each term in the series splits into two parts, one that remains entirely unknowable, and another that leads by contiguity or metonymic substitution in a hopelessly wrong direction, along a different vector, farther and farther away from the original goal. Thus in *The Castle,* the attention of the hapless "land-surveyor" K., who ironically starts his investigations from the hotel Zur Brücke (At the Bridge) is diverted from the castle itself to a series of lesser goals that have an increasingly tenuous relation to the castle but are equally unattainable and thus assimilable to the unknown "castle" region. In "An Imperial Message," similarly, the dreamer's attention shifts from the emperor to the messenger and then to various places along the messenger's route. Attempts at fusing the two irreconcilable areas can produce a blank or "zero," which may be portrayed as a mental lapse: the animal in "The Burrow" (1923/24), who fallaciously wishes to enjoy the security of the burrow and at the same time to police his security from a vantage point outside it, manages to be in both places at once, that is, cross the border from outside to inside, only in a kind of dizzy half sleep. Alternately, such attempts at fusion generate an additional term outside the desired unity, an "eternal third" that, if the experiment is repeated, is capable of proliferating to infinity and thus proves, as Kafka writes in "On Parables" (1922/23), that "the incomprehensible is incomprehensible" (cs 457).[9]

In contrast to Schnitzler, Freud, and Musil, Kafka questions the possibility of any transfer of information from A to B. Consequently, in "An Imperial Message," there is no proof of the existence of A outside of the dreamer's imagination. The message, A_I, is displaced by the messenger. A_I turns out to be nothing more than a medium without a message, a form empty of content. This medium which is apparently failing to transmit a message has the heuristic value of a telephone that fails to ring and that its owner assumes is therefore broken. The malfunctioning medium does not prove that the emperor was trying to contact the subject, but merely that the subject *wished* that this were so. Thus A_I is revealed to be a mere B_I, a construction of B.

Whereas Freud optimistically supposed that the inquiring analyst can see through the distorting form to grasp the latent content of the wish, Kafka seems to be parodying the idea of content. The story suggests that there is no content at all, but merely *forms of thought*. Here the form is wishing. The parable suggests that the entire non-B complex is inauthentic as a thing in itself. It is merely a complicated, far-flung construction of B. The A complex is not the antithesis of B (much less a genuine source of anything), but just an opposite which can easily be shown to orginate in B. In a similar fashion, the apparent reversal of priority in the use of the terms A and B in "A Common Confusion" acquires significance. Kafka's calculation diverges from the logic of his predecessors. Törless's confusions exemplify the pattern of the relations between the antithetical terms in its purest form: unity is possible, but as soon as Törless tries to go in the opposite direction, he finds two, and two proliferates into three and infinity. Freud makes three out of two, but stops at three; his three does not lead to infinite regress. For Kafka one is not even a possibility. One would be the equivalent of zero, or no story of all. One automatically generates two, two produces three, and three becomes infinity.

BY 1900, THE MIRROR metaphor had a long tradition in European literature. It appeared predominantly in connection with mimetic theories of art, but it also, for example, figured as a symbol for self-love and vanity in the reception of Ovid's Narcissus legend.[1] The mirror was first used as an analogy for artistic representation by Plato in the *Republic*; it lost its pejorative connotations in post-Aristotelian poetics and persisted as a metaphor for the ideal of mimetic fidelity to which art should aspire until about the middle of the eighteenth century. Concurrently, it appeared in philosophical discussion as a metaphor for the mind. In the Romantic period the specular model of representation and cognition fell into discredit with the rise of expressive theories of art.[2] The mirror acquired a new function, that of illustrating the problem of self-consciousness. Heinrich von Kleist's celebrated essay "About the Marionette Theatre" (1810) is a central example. In Romantic and post-Romantic autobiographical narrative, the mirror metaphor recurs persistently to suggest an alienated self-image, the self as seen by the other.[3]

With the psychopathological research of Charcot and Janet in the 1880s and the discovery of the split personality or "double conscience," interest in self-consciousness not only began to diminish, but a model that split the self into mirroring halves became untenable. Freud's psyche is antispecular in its conception; it is split, but into conflicting, that is, nonmirroring areas. One could say that his discovery of the unconscious rendered invalid a tradition use of the mirror as a figure for self-consciousness. Concurrently, mirroring began to take on a new function in literary texts written around and after 1900 by authors, who, like Freud, came from the Austro-Hungarian Empire. My purpose here will be to examine this new use of the mirror metaphor in certain texts by Rilke, Hofmannsthal, and Kafka. I shall then return to Freud in order to discuss why the mirror image is absent in his work, as well as, in Jacques Lacan's rewriting of Freud, his postulation of a "mirror stage."

The new use of the mirror metaphor should be seen within the context of the epistemological reorientation that informs both Freud's work and that of his literary contemporaries, the insistence on the coexistence of conflicting terms, whereby, as we have seen, inaccessibility is the fundamental characteristic of the term typically designated as "dark." Yet as we saw in the last chapter, such writers as Schnitzler, Freud, and Musil are intrigued by the possibility of gaining access to the inaccessible place. The two "places" are thus both continuous and discontinuous, antithetical and one; the barrier between them is absolute, yet potentially nonexistent.

Both Freud and the other writers of the period are concerned not only to develop structures that articulate the light/dark problematic, but also to create heuristic strategies that are empowered to lift the barrier, yet at the same time affirm its existence.[4] These devices of inclusion and exclusion simultaneously represent having and not having, knowing and yet not knowing, recovery and the impossibility of recovery. They could be called *fort/da* (gone/there) devices after the child's game in *Beyond the Pleasure Principle*. They involve supplementing the original antithetical duality by a third term, the device itself. While the third term lays no genuine claim to subsuming both original terms, it appears, by sleight of hand, to let the part subsume the whole. It sublates the duality, makes the dark area accessible, and also purports to reverse linear temporality in a process of recovery by which the end proves a return to the origin. In *The Interpretation of Dreams*, the dream itself functions as such a device. When the subject is dreaming, the unconscious becomes accessible to consciousness through its representative, the dream. Moreover, the dream "floods" consciousness, asserting itself, temporarily, as the sole psychic reality. It thereby establishes continuity between repressed and infantile material and the present moment, and it also bridges the gap between the formulation of an unconscious wish and its fulfillment, whereby the fulfillment is, of course, fictitious. The dream and the related hallucinatory image are very frequently used *fort/da* devices in the literature of the period as well. Schnitzler and Hofmannsthal, for example, use fictional dreams and hallucinations much as Freud uses real dreams as a hermeneutic strategy.

The mirror can likewise function as a *fort/da* device. This figure, along with the related phenomena of doubling and repetition, offers the same intrinsic ambiguity as the dream. The mirror image appears to affirm the self by constating its existence, yet it displaces the self to a location where it is not; it replaces the other by the self, in other words, but puts the self into a relation to itself that formally reproduces that of self to other. Repetition, likewise, the temporal equivalent of the mirror image, seems to establish continuity in time by recovering a lost past, yet it does so in a way that renders questionable the "now" of the self's present moment.

The texts I shall consider are Rilke's Sonnet to Orpheus II/3, Hofmannsthal's "Terzinen IV" (Stanzas in terza rima IV) and "Der Kaiser von China spricht" ("The Emperor of China Speaks") and Kafka's "The Burrow." The mirror metaphor in these texts, written as they are by three different authors, does not have a single field of reference. One could say most generally, however, that the mirror is used as a metaphor for a unity that represents the fulfillment of all desire, a construction capable of overcoming the dualism that is seen profoundly to structure existence, yet one that underscores the conflict it purports to overcome. In its affirmative function, the mirror opens up and reveals the "dark area" and creates a unity that is ideal (da). In its negative function, the space it wins and the unity it creates are admitted to be an illusion (fort). Each of the texts marks a moment of insight into the potential and limitations of imaginative mirroring. I discuss them in an order that is intended to show how the fulfillment promised by mirroring can be undermined with increasing insistence as an illusion. At the same time, the heuristic value of mirroring is displaced by the recognition that the mirror's expansion of space is merely a projection of the fulfillment of desire. This progression culminates in Kafka's disillusioned universalizing of the structure of desire as a process, rather than a metaphor, and his emphasis on the self-reflexiveness, or nonexistence, of the goal.

Before discussing the texts written around the turn of the twentieth century, it will be useful to consider the mirror in Kleist's 1810 essay "About the Marionette Theatre," which can serve as a point of contrast. The mirror in Kleist's essay is a dangerous looking-glass. It becomes a figure for pernicious reflection. Kleist plays on the various implications of Ovid's tale of Narcissus, but he stresses the aspect of knowledge, the seer's prediction that the boy will lead a long life only "if he does not come to know himself" ("si se non noverit"). He wishes to demonstrate "what confusion consciousness had made in the natural charm of mankind."[5] The aspect of desire, Narcissus's fatal attraction to his image, the most memorable feature of Ovid's story and also the implication that texts around 1900 tend to adopt, plays only a minor role, as mediated or reflected desire: it pleases the youth to resemble another youth whose beauty, immortalized in sculpture, is publicly acknowledged.[6] A renewed glance in the mirror then sets in motion the fatal process of self-objectification or mediated self-knowledge. By making a conscious effort to copy the statue, the boy splits himself into two, observer and observed, subject and object. Noticing the unflattering discrepancy between his mirror image and the statue, he increases his efforts to imitate the original. The sharpening of consciousness caused by the boy's repeated failure to conform to his ideal leads in turn to a progressive loss of grace. Spirit and body separate into puppet master and marionette.

Kleist's mirror, then, has the following properties: first, it splits an originally unified self into two halves, viewer and viewed; second, it represents a barrier that prevents the halves from rejoining; third, it institutes an irreversible process, a dialectic of diminishment through reflection that culminates in loss of grace.

Readers will recall that Kleist's metaphor is embedded in a tripartite schema of lost origin, inauthentic present, and sublation. Kleist proposes that an original paradisical state of wholeness or innocence is succeeded by a state of reflection or mediated vision, but suggests at the end of the essay that, just as parallel lines cross at infinity, the state of reflection will terminate with infinite consciousness or innocence regained. He assigns the mirror to the middle, fallen state.

The Austrian writers, in contrast, optimistically promote the mirror to an instrument of a sublation that, though admittedly fictitious and temporary, is nonetheless aesthetically beautiful. The mirror's properties remain the same, but the turn-of-the-century authors interpret them in a way diametrically opposed to Kleist. First, instead of splitting what is whole, the mirror doubles space. The "known" or "light" area can even be expanded infinitely, by adding mirrors, as if one were to "enlarge" a room by covering all its walls with mirrors. Second, the barrier of the wall appears to disappear. The other is not introduced, but rather eliminated. One recalls Lacan's "mirror stage" or "Imaginary," the stage of primary narcissism or autoeroticism. Kleist's conception, in constrast, more closely fits Lacan's "Symbolic Stage," the stage of speech, in which the voice of the other controls the angle of inclination of the mirror.[7] Third, the mirror creates an eternal "ahead," by which the goal, the thing that appears to be at the furthest distance, reflects the thing that is in actuality furthest behind. The mirror thereby gives the illusion of turning into a circle what is in fact an irreversible linear process. In *Beyond the Pleasure Principle*, Freud explains the phenomenon of repetition similarly, by asserting that it represents the individual's desire to return to his (or her?) origins, that is, to the inorganic. Freud's name for this drive is of course the "death instinct" ("Todestrieb"). The Austrian mirror likewise has its ominous side. In Kleist's scheme, if the boy could manage to rejoin or reabsorb the specular image, we would judge this restoration of unity a happy turn of events. In the new conception, however, approaching the mirror has the negative implication of restricting the space once gained. If the mirrored subject converges with the mirror image, space is abolished entirely. The mirror reverts to wall; it becomes a barrier, an absolute line or limit. According to the logic of the mirror, we project the objects of our desire. If we actually attain the desired goal, it cancels itself out. The apparent circle shrinks to a line; the hoped for return to the origin is really the end.

Rilke's Sonnet to Orpheus II/3

Rilke's Sonnet to Orpheus II/3, which is about the essence of mirrors, illustrates several aspects of the new concept. It engages the central theme of the *Sonnets*, transformation and the unification of opposites, but I shall discuss it without reference to its place in the cycle here. Rilke emphasizes the mirror's *fort/da* properties, so that the mirror becomes a model for *Raumgewinn*, for the winning of space, and the lifting, yet emphasizing, of barriers.

> Mirrors: never yet has anyone knowingly described
> what you are in your essence.
> You, in-between spaces of time
> filled as it were with lots of sieve holes.
>
> You, still the squanderers of the empty hall—
> At dusk, wide as the woods . . .
> And the chandelier goes like a sixteen-pointer
> Through your impenetrability.
>
> Sometimes you are full of painting.
> Some seem to have gone *into* you—,
> others, you shyly send on their way.

But the loveliest will remain—, till
over there, into her withheld (contained) cheeks,
The clear dissolved Narcissus penetrated.
(My translation)

[Spiegel: noch nie hat man wissend beschrieben,
was ihr in euerem Wesen seid.
Ihr, wie mit lauter Löchern von Sieben
erfüllten Zwischenräume der Zeit.

Ihr, noch des leeren Saales Verschwender—,
wenn es dämmert, wie Wälder weit . . .
Und der Lüster geht wie ein Sechzehn-Ender
durch eure Unbetretbarkeit.

Manchmal seid ihr voll Malerei.
Einige scheinen *in* euch gegangen—,
andere schicket ihr scheu vorbei.

Aber die Schönste wird bleiben—, bis
drüben in ihre enthaltenen Wangen
eindrang der klare gelöste Narziß. (R 2:752)]

Mirrors, in this sonnet, are paradoxical entities. They are both full
("erfüllt") and empty ("Löcher"). They multiply the dimensions of the
empty hall, yet are impenetrable as walls. Imagery with sexual overtones
establishes what will prove their fatal attractiveness for the narcissistic
self-admirer. In their contradictoriness, Rilke suggests, mirrors display
femininity. On the one hand they are capable of reproduction and, accordingly, promiscuous: they are "wide as the woods"; and a "Lüster,"
with the connotation of desire ("Lust"), goes through them like a charg-
ing stag. But they also have such qualities as impenetrability and shy-
ness, and are therefore modest and chaste. In an earlier poem, "Narziss,"
Rilke connects the quest for the self-image to sexual desire even more
explicitly. The self-seeker, regarding his image in the pond, speculates,

What is forming there and surely resembles me
and trembles upwards in tear-stained signs,
that could perhaps have come into being in the same way
inside a woman; I couldn't reach it

no matter how I struggled for it, pressing into her.
(My translation)

[Was sich dort bildet und mir sicher gleicht
und aufwärts zittert in verweinten Zeichen,
das mochte so in einer Frau vielleicht
innen entstehen; es war nicht zu erreichen,

wie ich danach auch drängend in sie rang.
(R 3:57)

Here both the mirror image and the beloved woman with whom
Narcissus identifies his reflection are self-projections that elude possession. In the sonnet, the mirror similarly contains a woman's reflection,
"the loveliest."

The elliptical final stanza is a cluster of double meanings and paradoxes. The sudden, illogical tense change ("will remain, until penetrated") assures the permanence of the superlative love object, for no future event is cited that would destroy it. At the same time, Rilke evokes
anterior time ("penetrated"). A past act of sexual union will destroy the
beauty's existence. In the first stanza Rilke playfully mixed temporal
and spatial attributes to describe the paradoxical essence of mirrors,
their compounding of absence and presence: "You, in-between spaces of
time / filled as it were with lots of sieve holes." In the final stanza, if
"drüben" ("over there"—within the mirror's space) evokes a space that
has no independent existence and thus establishes a spatial differentiation that is meaningless, mirror logic can presumably also annul the normal temporal relations involved in cause and effect. The beauty is permanent, yet her lastingness is also undermined from the start. Rilke
implies, in a compact pun, that only unattainability guarantees permanence: the beauty is "enthalten," "contained" in the mirror, in the same
measure as she is "withheld" from lovers. As an untouchable ideal, untouchable because the self cannot unite with its own mirror image without destroying it, the beauty will remain. But identical with the self as
she is ("Narcissus"), she will never be unpossessed. The final stanza presents an interesting variation on the end of Ovid's Narcissus story. In
Ovid's tale, the inflamed Narcissus finally dissolves ("liquitur") and
thus metamorphoses into the actual substance of the image, the mirroring pond. In the sonnet, the movement of convergence annihilates the
image ("the loveliest will remain, *until*"), and also results in the sexual
dissolution of the admirer ("the clear dissolved Narcissus"). The attempt
to possess the image in the mirror, "the loveliest," or in other words the
self as an idealized love object, fails.

Hofmannsthal's "Terzinen IV" and "The Emperor of China Speaks"

Hugo von Hofmannsthal's earliest *fort/da* device was the dream; it appears in poems as early as 1893,[8] while the mirror is a later conception, appearing most prominently in poems of 1896 and 1897.[9] In a poem of 1894, "Terzinen IV," however, the poet combines the dream motif with the mirror effect. He balances a containing or framing movement, sustained by the idea of the dream and by the comprehensiveness he attributes to the state he later comes to call "Prae-existenz" ("preexistence") against a movement of linear temporal progression, the movement of actual life. In *Ad me Ipsum*, an attempt at a self-explanation which he began in 1916 and which remained a fragment, Hofmannsthal writes that one of the self's attributes in the state of "preexistence" is the ability to mirror itself: "Gift of multiplying oneself," he writes, and adds, "the mirrorings."[10] *Prae-existenz* is "early wisdom," or the gift of comprehending cognitively the whole of life of which one will later be merely a part. The purpose of the dream, the most all-encompassing and yet at the same time least real frame, is to join the present moment to the infinite possibilities which the dreamer imagined in his long-since lost state of *Prae-existenz*. If the dream were actually to succeed in realizing these possibilities, it would genuinely be the fulfillment of a wish.

TERZINEN IV

From time to time never-loved women
Come toward us in dreams as little girls
And are unspeakably moving to look at

As if they had once walked with us
On an evening along distant paths
While the treetops move, breathing

And scent falls down, and night and fearfulness
And along the path, our path, the dark one
The silent ponds are resplendent in the glow of the setting sun

And, mirrors of our longing, sparkle, dream-like,
And to all soft words, all hovering
Of the evening air and the first sparkle of stars

The souls quiver like sisters and deeply

And are sad and full of triumphant display
On account of a deep presentiment, which comprehends

Life's vastness and its splendor and severity.

[Zuweilen kommen niegeliebte Frauen
Im Traum als kleine Mädchen uns entgegen
Und sind unsäglich rührend anzuschauen

Als wären sie mit uns auf fernen Wegen
Einmal an einem Abend lang gegangen,
Indes die Wipfel atmend sich bewegen

Und Duft herunterfällt und Nacht und Bangen,
Und längs des Weges, unsres Wegs, des dunklen,
Im Abendschein die stummen Weiher prangen

Und, Spiegel unsrer Sehnsucht, traumhaft funkeln,
Und allen leisen Worten, allem Schweben
Der Abendluft und erstem Sternefunkeln

Die Seelen schwesterlich und tief erbeben
Und traurig sind und voll Triumphgepränge
Vor tiefer Ahnung, die das große Leben

Begreift und seine Herrlichkeit und Strenge.][11]

The poem weighs the idea of the recovery of hypothetical plural goals of desire ("women"), which actual life and the necessity for choosing a single course of action have preempted.[12] In lines 1–2 the dream proposes to replace the dreamer's present, which is overly concrete and haunted by absences ("never-loved women") by an imaginary fullness, located in the past ("little girls"). The dream begins to formulate the terms by which fulfillment could take place. Substituting a spatial image for a temporal process, the dreamer projects the girls away from himself in space, and the small girls "come toward us." Yet there is no touching and no closure. Thus there is no connection between the dreamer's actual present and the future that his past seemed to promise, except of course through the dream itself. The desired women, creatures of his fantasy, approach him as one approaches one's own mirror image. The dreamer avoids Narcissus's appalling realization that "what I desire, I have" ("quod cupio mecum est"). Instead, the expected, but unachieved contact (implied "touch," *Berührung*) modulates into the adverb "touching" ("rührend") in line 3—the girls of the dream are merely "unsäglich rührend anzu-schauen"—to be looked at, not touched. They are *unspeakably* moving presumably both in the sense of the "Chandos Letter" and because the imaginary image sustains no voice.[13] The dream thus sidesteps the simple fulfillment of a wish; instead, there is an interruption.

The dream resumes its course on a new level of hypothetical (subjunctive) statement. Both dreamer and girls are suddenly relocated in space and time: "As if they had once walked with us / On an evening along distant paths." This new level initiates the unfolding of an image that is very far removed from the dreamer's original wish. Present indicative succeeds the introductory statement in subjunctive past; history displaces fulfillment; and movement is now once again possible, but the dreamer and the girls now move forward and parallel to each other, instead of approaching each other from opposite directions. The original poignant wish of the dreamer disappears, or rather reappears as a much less sharply defined *wishing* ("Sehnsucht") on the part of the dream-content character, the young boy that the dreamer once was. The girls, however, are no longer the objects of desire. They and the dreamer are "sisterly" ("schwesterlich"), undifferentiated, and capable of speech. The time is the time of "preexistence," the "evening" of childhood's "eternal daylight."[14] The children walk gradually forward into the night of "existence," a journey that can be taken in one direction only, the direction they are going. The ponds, in which the first stars begin to shine, mirror like eyes the children's longing for the destiny ("stars") they will all too soon enter. Precisely like the youth in "Der Jüngling und die Spinne" (The youth and the spider) where mirroring is explicit, these children in their state of *Prae-existenz* "comprehend" ("begreift") the whole of life ("das große Leben") cognitively, without having any of it in actuality.

The poem ends on the second breach, that between "preexistence" and "existence," when the connecting forward and backward movement of the terza rima breaks off. The dream pointedly fails to reconstruct the connection between the two incompatible states.[15] Once again the dream has reached its limit: it cannot fulfill the dreamer's wishes, rewrite his autobiography. Nor would there be any point in representing the actual course the dreamer's existence took, for this actuality, after all, is not the object of his wish. But the unreal dream succeeds as well as fails. Chiastic correspondence, which features a negative and a positive term in each clause, connects the children's ambivalent longing with the side of the breach they are not yet on: "sad / full of triumphant display, splendor and severity." "Preexistence" mirrors "existence" in all its possibility. The dream, by recovering the comprehension of "preexistence," mirrors that mirror, capturing and encompassing the lost cognitive totality, the knowledge of all desire and its goals, in the present moment of dreaming.

While Rilke's Sonnet II/3 hints at the limitations of mirroring, in "Terzinen IV" these limitations become evident in the manifest fictionality of the dream, which, moreover, does not fulfill all the dreamer's wishes. In Hofmannsthal's "The Emperor of China Speaks," a poem of 1897, the limitations of mirroring become yet more pronounced.

THE EMPEROR OF CHINA SPEAKS:

In the center of all things
I, the son of heaven, dwell.
My women, my trees
My animals, my ponds
Are enclosed by the first wall.
Down below my ancestors lie:
Lie in state with their weapons,
Their crowns on their heads,
As befits each one,
They dwell in the vaults.
Right down to the heart of the world
The tread of my majesty resounds.
Silently equally divided streams
Go eastwards, westwards, southwards, northwards
From my grassy banks,
Green footstools for my feet,
In order to water my garden,
Which is the wide earth.
Here they mirror the dark eyes
The bright wings of my animals,
Outside they mirror bright cities,
Dark walls, thick woods,
And the faces of many peoples.
My nobles, like stars
Dwell around me. They have
Names that I gave them,
Names in token of the one hour

When one of them approached me,
Women that I gave them
And the throngs of their children;
For all the nobles of this earth
I created eyes, stature, and lips
Like the gardener for the flowers.
But between outer walls
Dwell the peoples of my warriors,
Peoples of my farmers.
New walls and then again
The subjected peoples
Peoples of ever more torpid blood
Down to the sea, the last wall
That surrounds my realm and me.

[DER KAISER VON CHINA SPRICHT:

In der Mitte aller Dinge
Wohne Ich, der Sohn des Himmels.
Meine Frauen, meine Bäume,
Meine Tiere, meine Teiche
Schließt die erste Mauer ein.
Drunten liegen meine Ahnen:
Aufgebahrt mit ihren Waffen,
Ihre Kronen auf den Häuptern,
Wie es einem jeden ziemt,
Wohnen sie in den Gewölben.
Bis ins Herz der Welt hinunter
Dröhnt das Schreiten meiner Hoheit.
Stumm von meinen Rasenbänken,
Grünen Schemeln meiner Füße,
Gehen gleichgeteilte Ströme
Osten-, west- und süd- und nordwärts,
Meinen Garten zu bewässern,
Der die weite Erde ist.
Spiegeln hier die dunkeln Augen,
Bunten Schwingen meiner Tiere,
Spiegeln draußen bunte Städte,
Dunkle Mauern, dichte Wälder
Und Gesichter vieler Völker.

Meine Edlen, wie die Sterne,
Wohnen rings um mich, sie haben
Namen, die ich ihnen gab,
Namen nach der einen Stunde,
Da mir einer näher kam,
Frauen, die ich ihnen schenkte,
Und den Scharen ihrer Kinder;
Allen Edlen dieser Erde
Schuf ich Augen, Wuchs und Lippen,
Wie der Gärtner an den Blumen.
Aber zwischen äußern Mauern
Wohnen Völker meine Krieger,
Völker meine Ackerbauer.
Neue Mauern und dann wieder
Jene unterworfnen Völker,
Völker immer dumpfern Blutes,
Bis ans Meer, die letzte Mauer
Die mein Reich und mich umgibt.][16]

"The Emperor of China Speaks" seems at first glance to be constructed straightforwardly according to the principle of amplification. In fact, it is made up of two simultaneous movements at cross-purposes with each other. The first is an obvious, expansive movement, consisting of the emperor's pronouncements about his importance, power, prestige, and possessions. The second is a reductive movement that at first works covertly, through ambiguity, to undermine the self-aggrandizing statements, and becomes overt only at the end.

In the expansive movement, the emperor tries to amplify the point of the self by enumerating his territories in concentric sequence, that is, from the center out. He emphasizes his centrality: citing both divine and human origins, represented by the heavens and the heart of the world, he tries to give the impression that he is at the center not merely of a circle, but of a sphere. The insistent possessive ("meine") underscores his desire for appropriation, his desire to see the earth in all its diversity and vastness as his garden, to regard each wall as a mirror.[17]

But precisely the word "wall," which occurs for the first time in line 5, jars in his description of his omnipotence. If he is so godlike, "son of heaven," why should there be a wall, an interruption in the vastness of his empire? The emperor is plainly deluding himself: as a mortal, he has no real power above and below the earth; his political power extends only two-dimensionally over the face of the earth. He would like to persuade himself that the walls of ever-increasing circumference mark a potentially infinite expansion of his power. But as his territories expand, his powers seem to decrease. We hear of three concentric walls: the first surrounds the palace and its gardens, the second the estates of his nobles, the third the lands of his warriors and farmers. Though the emperor takes care to emphasize his power over *all* these people, the word "my" occurs less frequently, and he cautiously intimates that those who live farther away from his midpoint are less important, less individuated, and lowlier. The walls begin to look like protective enclosures; after the third (line 34), he hastily mentions an unspecified plurality of them (line 37). Beyond these walls live the people least like him ("peoples of ever more torpid blood"). In the last two lines the reversal that had been implicit throughout occurs. There is a limit to the emperor's territories and powers, an "ultimate wall," the sea. At this limit the emperor is surrounded, rather than surrounding. The spatial, concentric dream was a fallacy; the truth is temporal and linear. The sea, as a symbol of otherness and also of life and death, marks the end of the emperor's life.

Kafka's "The Burrow"

In "Terzinen IV" Hofmannsthal emphasizes the beauty of mirroring as a sustaining fiction. In "The Emperor of China Speaks," mirroring is less beautiful; it becomes a mere imperial fantasy, the dream of a self-aggrandizing emperor. In "The Burrow" Kafka goes a step further. He uses the mirror parodistically. Much like the emperor of China, Kafka's animal narrator expands his space and his narrative by mirroring. But while Hofmannsthal uses mirroring as a metaphor to undermine his narrator's pretensions to grandeur, to contrast reality with illusion, in "The Burrow," the animal's quest for unity is not a metaphor at all, but a process. Kafka demetaphorizes the metaphor, literalizes it, and deprives it of depth. Whereas for the emperor of China, declaring all the world his domain would be a moment of solipsistic triumph, for Kafka's narrator attaining unity would mean merely the premature rupture of the process. The animal's repeated and unsuccessful attempts to arrive at his goal are grotesque, but arrival would be a yet more desolate possibility.

The animal in "The Burrow" is obsessively concerned with the existence of an outside (an "enemy"), and indeed there would be no story if it were not for the existence of that elusive second term. Yet the animal is equally obsessed with knowing or possessing that outside by transforming it into a specular image of himself. The concentric pattern of "The Emperor of China Speaks" is repeated here; the narrator builds (or dreams of building) walls to protect himself, each a kind of duplication or mirror of himself. It is plain from the story that by building the burrow ("the construction" might be a better translation of the German title "Der Bau"), the animal is creating another version of himself. The animal declares, speaking of his burrow, that "at such times it is as if I were not so much looking at my house as at myself" (cs 334). He feels physical well-being at the heart of the burrow, but toward its peripheries he is nervous and has the sensation that his fur is thinning (cs 332). He asserts that any wound to the burrow pains him as if it were himself (cs 355); yet he finds that the burrow "is so essentially mine that I can calmly accept in it even my enemy's mortal stroke at the final hour, for my blood will ebb away here in my own soil and not be lost" (cs 340).[18] If we interpret this compulsive doubling according to Freud's remarks on the *Doppelgänger*, it represents the animal's effort to secure his own immortality. "It is always a mistake to have just one copy of anything," the animal laments (k 5:137, my translation). Thus he does not stop at building his burrow but goes on grotesquely repeating the same doubling actions with his Castle Keep, and so forth.

The animal thus tries to eliminate the outside or other by creating a perfect enclosure or specular boundary. Yet every specular extension has some flaw. For the animal *must* maintain his fear, his assumption of the otherness of the other, in effect the distance created between himself and the illusory object of his fear. In other Kafka stories, for example, "An Imperial Message," a similar distance is created by desire. The character's adventures, the life of his mind (neurotic though it may be), depend on a self-imposed delusion that there exists a goal which he cannot reach, or which cannot reach him. To the reader it is apparent that given the underground setting Kafka chose for "The Burrow," the animal would not create a private paradise, but would rather literally entomb himself if he succeeded in building a perfect enclosure. So the protective walls are, of necessity, penetrable. The animal's ruminations on self-protection, which expand his story, turn into a precarious series of flawed walls (or mirrors) whose real purpose is to allow him to escape convergence with his mirror image.

The animal naturally reads the hole in his wall differently. His exit, he realizes in panic, could very well be his enemy's entrance. He worries obsessively about this imperfection: "There at that one place in the dark moss I am mortal," he reflects (k 5:132, my translation). We realize that if it were not for the hole, the animal, who in effect invents his enemy, would have no story to tell. First-person narrators are ultimately grounded in themselves. In "The Burrow" Kafka plays a game with the absurdity inherent in this situation by translating the notions of figure and ground into the literal spatial relations that constitute the plot. The animal thus attempts not only to extend the limits of his self like the emperor of China, but also to be on the outside as well as the inside of whatever limits he constructs. He is unable to enjoy the comparative security of the burrow (because of its flaw) and is equally incapable of parting from it. He therefore dashes neurotically back and forth, in and out.

In the spatial metaphor, the animal naturally fails to become his own ground. Rather expectedly, he is attracted to the *fort/da* place, the border of the burrow. Yet the border is precisely the most dangerous place for him, for it corresponds to the surface of the mirror. The animal worries at length, for the space of six pages, how he is going to pass that barrier. Faced with self-extinction, he conceives another mirror image displaced back from the border: he wishes he had a "trusted friend" to supervise his descent. Finally he traverses the border in a barely conscious state, the familiar state of Kafka's heroes when the goal actually presents itself.[19] For unbeknownst to the animal, the mirror image is the real object of his fear. At the end of the narrative, his terror crystallizes into the image of an immense animal who will devour him. We know that the narrator himself is huge and that he lives on eating "small fry" or smaller animals. There are other indications as well that the huge beast he visualizes in the infirmity of his old age is his mirror image. For example, the animal interprets a hissing sound he hears as his enemy's intake of breath after he digs away earth with his snout. Since he himself has been digging in precisely this manner, and since the pecularity of the hissing is that he cannot locate the direction it is coming from, it can probably be understood as his own breathing. To give another example, the animal notes that to judge from the noise his opponent seems to be digging incessantly, yet without any evident plan; he has said exactly the same thing of himself. Finally, the animal stylizes his enemy's thoughts and perceptions as a mirror image of his own. He reasons that the enemy cannot have noticed him until he noticed it: "So long as I knew nothing about it, it simply cannot have heard me, for at that time I kept very quiet" (CS 359).[20] The animal is, then, his own real enemy; as he let slip earlier, "by now it is almost as if I were the enemy" (CS 337). The animal's attempt to transcend temporality by mirroring is thus shown to be an illusion. In fact, he too with his serial mirroring is involved, like the emperor of China, in an irreversible process.[21]

In both the Hofmannsthal poems and the Kafka story, mirroring is used as a device to expand the self, or the area under its control, by imaginary identifications. Both writers operate within the framework of a dialectic between what they see as the strict limitations of the self in terms of the concrete realities of its existence, and the fantasy life of the psyche, which expresses itself in a desire to push back these limits. By mirroring, the self appropriates for itself everything it wishes to be but is not, everything it desires but does not possess. By representing this appropriation as a fantasy, or, in the case of Kafka, as the neurotic playing out of a fantasy, however, by asserting that the restrictions of biographical actuality can be transcended only imaginatively, the authors ultimately confirm only the existence of the psychic demand. But Kafka departs from the Romantic presupposition that still informs Hofmannsthal's thought, the assumption that unity would be desirable. Kafka redefines the tension between the possibility of fulfillment and the limitations imposed by reality as a necessary fiction. It is the animal narrator who is distressed to discover that unity is desirable but impossible. Kafka, by permitting a second reading to emerge between the lines, shows us, rather, that the *positing* of the desirability and the impossibility of unity is essential. In his story, the values assigned to *fort* and *da* are implicitly reversed. The attainment of the goal would have the negative value of *fort*, while its nonattainment means a positive, though anguished, *da*.

In Kafka's fiction generally, the "other," inasmuch as it is imagined at all, becomes a purely self-reflexive category, with none of the power, legitimacy, or beauty it had in earlier Austrian texts. The goal and the enemy who interferes with the attainment of the goal—both are necessary constructs of our imagination. Failing to arrive at a goal becomes an existential strategy. Deferring arrival is, likewise, the open secret of art. In another of Kafka's stories, "A Hunger Artist," the title figure achieves fame with his fabulous ability to postpone gratification in the form of eating. At the end of the story, the hunger artist admits he is a fraud:

starvation is easy, for the object that would still his hunger does not exist. The possibility of achieving unity, of converging with the object of fear or obtaining the object of desire, becomes the real enemy, a symbol of death and likewise of the end or impossibility of narrative—a blank.

In conclusion it can be said that the mirror has two equally possible uses as a metaphor. The first is to illustrate representation and cognition, whereby one can emphasize the faithfulness or deceptiveness of the mirror copy. Kleist draws on this tradition in the "Marionette Theatre" essay, but gives it negative implications; mirroring becomes a figure for self-consciousness and, by extension, for the alienating domination of the self by the other. The second use of the mirror, the one we have seen in the Austrian texts, is to illustrate the structure of desire. The mirror image represents a goal of desire, inasmuch as fulfillment is understood as a self-projection, a superimposition of the self on the other, an expansion of the self, and the possibility of recapture. As a goal it is by definition unattainable, for if the subject reaches out to grasp the image, it vanishes. The obdurate reality of the other asserts itself in the surface of the mirror.

Strictly speaking, the two fields of reference engaged by the mirror metaphor, cognition and desire, are present in all the texts we have considered, although one or the other predominates. In Kleist's parable of the youth, the image the youth sees in the mirror is an object of knowledge, but desire initiates and also perpetuates the self-objectification that leads to loss of grace. In the texts written by Freud's contemporaries, the image in the mirror is the object of desire, but the idea of cognition enters into the mirror metaphor inasmuch as all the authors imply that the mirror image is perceptually accessible. The mirror as a visual figure, with its connotations of light and space, engages the epistemological field; so does its temporal equivalent, repetition, when it is conceived as recollection, as in Hofmannsthal's "Terzinen IV." If the mirror figures as a fort/da device, as a heuristic device, it is because the authors propose that we have imaginative access to the fulfillment of our desires (da). They stress, however, that the mirror image represents a self-projection, and hence an illusion; real fulfillment is impossible (fort). The emperor of China and Kafka's animal think that they know, possess, or master what is outside of themselves, but in fact they only project images of themselves onto this outside. Their blindness is corrected by the poet's insight.

In all the texts written by Freud's contemporaries, then, one finds a subordination of questions of cognition to questions of desire. If the texts are able to balance the heuristic implications of mirroring with its connotations of desire, it is because the underlying fields of reference, the epistemological field and the topic of desire, are similarly structured. That is, the mirror acquires its function within a context where a structure that might be seen as proper to desire comes to govern epistemology, where meaning exercises all the power and fascination of an object of desire and is seen to be as difficult of access. The known area and the dark unknown stand in approximately the same relation as desire and its goal. The mirror, as a *fort/da* device, engages both.

Freud, Lacan, and the Mirror

The image of the mirror is conspicuously absent from Freud's work. In his writing on doubling and repetition, in "The Uncanny" (1919) and *Beyond the Pleasure Principle* (1920), Freud does not discuss mirroring; two incidents involving mirrors are relegated to the footnotes and not integrated into the argument.[22] Yet it is striking to what extent the phenomena of doubling and repetition in Freud's work resemble what we have called—borrowing the term from Freud—the *fort/da* function of the mirror in the literary writers. Doubling and repetition interest Freud precisely because they have both an affirmative and a negative significance. In "The Uncanny," citing the work of Otto Rank in *Der Doppelgänger* (1914; *The Double*), whose ideas he follows rather closely, Freud hypothesizes that in the stage of primary narcissism and the corresponding stage of primitive culture, the double expressed a desire to ensure the immortality of the self by creating a second copy of it. Yet at the same time the double has menacing connotations: it represents a repressed or overcome portion of the self that "returns."[23] In *Beyond the Pleasure Principle* Freud finds that the significance of repetition is similarly contradictory. On the one hand, the compulsion to repeat expresses the subject's desire to master new situations and is thus consonant with the pleasure principle. On the other, it expresses the living organism's desire to return to life's origins in the inorganic, its "death instinct."

But not only is the image of the mirror missing from the argument of these works; references to the mirror (or to the Narcissus myth) do not occur in Freud's writings on narcissism. The mirror's connotations of cognition and representation may have suggested an approach and a terminology Freud wished to avoid; presumably, he could find no place in his theory for an image traditionally associated with the discourse of self-consciousness. Seemingly, the mirror image offers an ideal point where a confrontation between a theory of the self based on knowledge and a theory of the self based on desire could be brought about. The contemporary literary use of the mirror metaphor, where, as we have seen, the topic of desire predominates, has implications for a theory of cognition: if the mirror reflects the fulfillment of our desires, and if we tend to project our self-image onto an area that is not properly our own, then what we know might be seen to be conditioned by what we wish. At certain points in his work, for example in the discussion of the opacity of dreams in *The Interpretation of Dreams* and in the theory of the "ideal ego" presented in "On Narcissism: An Introduction" (1914), Freud comes close to implying that such conclusions could be drawn. Yet he does not draw them explicitly, and in fact he never discusses the issue in these terms. If he did, it would necessitate a reformulation of several aspects of his theories, notably his theory of the perception-consciousness system and the hermeneutics. In the seventh chapter of *The Interpretation of Dreams* Freud shows us that the dark area, never fully illuminated, recedes before the analyst's light. But the spaces thus brought to light are not mirrors; the project of psychoanalysis and scientific knowledge are not thus called into question.

If in the literary texts written by Freud's contemporaries the topic of desire predominates over that of cognition, the same is even more true of Freud. Freud's great and original achievement was to establish an ontology of the self and a philosophy of the self's relations to the other that is not based on cognition, but rather on desire. His works thus break radically with the philosophical tradition of René Descartes and classical epistemology, which took it for granted that knowledge of man is knowledge of man's knowing. The very hermeneutics of *The Interpretation of Dreams* could be seen to depend on a mechanism of desire. The sign (the dream) may *represent* meaning for the analyst, but primarily and most importantly, it is *generated* by the patient's desire. The relation between signified and sign becomes the relation between desire and its fulfillment, and the peculiar opacity of the sign results from the collision of conflicting desires.

The cornerstones of Freud's metapsychology are hence not such concepts as "knowledge" and "self-knowledge," but such new concepts as "libido," "pleasure," "identification," and "introjection." It should be stressed that the key idea of identification is not a cognitive concept. Rather, it is a formula for converting affective relations into perceptual qualities and the reverse. Our desire for an object leads us to idealize the object. In the process of identification, the self takes on the object's ideal qualities.

In the essay "On Narcissism" (1914) Freud implicitly raises the question of whether one can speak of an ego libido and narcissism without introducing the ego as a represented object. Freud indeed speaks, for the first time, of an "ideal ego," which confirms to "cultural and ethical ideals" (SE 14:92). The ideal ego exists as a libidinous object in certain individuals and is distinct from the actual ego ("aktuelles Ich"). Both of these egos are observed and compared by a third entity, the "ego ideal." The "ideal ego" and the "actual ego," as represented objects, are manifestly different from the ego as it figures in Freud's previous work, namely, as an organ of perception, an agent of repression, and the representative of the reality principle. By introducing the ideal ego Freud suggests that narcissism, at least secondary narcissism, implies self-representation and, moreover, that it is inextricably bound up with a moment of false or ideal representation.

But the narcissism essay leaves the question of the genesis of the self-image quite unresolved. How does the self come into being as a represented object? When does self-representation start? Freud does not address the question of self-representation in the narcissism essay but merely states that the child is "his own ideal" (SE 14:94).[24]

In the next essay where he addresses the question of primary narcissism, "Instincts and Their Vicissitudes," written a year later, Freud avoids the notion of a self-image entirely. The child, he asserts, is immediately and automatically capable of distinguishing sensations that come from outside ("stimuli"), which the child can react against by activating its muscles, from those that come from within ("drives"), against which the child is powerless. Thus the child has an initial sense of self, which is based on a simple inside/outside distinction: the borderline is implicitly the surface of the body (SE 14:118–19). In the stage of primary narcissism, then, the child continues to conceive of itself as "inside," but considers the distinction between the self and the outside world equivalent to the distinction between "pleasure" and "unpleasure." The "pleasure-ego" ("Lust-Ich") includes everything that is pleasurable, and the outlines of the body are now forgotten (SE 14: 134–36). Thus in this essay Freud advances a purely libidinal theory of primary narcissism, whereby the child accepts everything pleasurable as "I" and redefines the boundaries of the self at the limits of pleasure.

Freud later, in "Mourning and Melancholia" (1917), *Group Psychology and the Analysis of the Ego* (1921), and particularly *The Ego and the Id* (1923), returns to the question of the formation of the ego and the ego ideal. He asserts that the ego takes on its characteristics by identifying with lost and other objects, in a manner dictated by the id, while the superego (the old ego ideal), which comes into being at the end of the Oedipus complex, serves as an organ of perception for it. Simultaneously, the superego functions as the old ideal ego. With the superego, the child internalizes the stern paternal gaze, the complex of rules and prohibitions represented by the father.

How does this identification with the father come about? In *The Ego and the Id* and *Group Psychology and the Analysis of the Ego*, Freud grounds the Oedipus complex in a prior, primary identification of the child with his father. This is a pre-Oedipal identification that precedes the object-cathexis of the mother. In *The Ego and the Id*, Freud writes, "Behind the origin of the ego ideal" (Freud thus renames the old ideal ego) "there lies hidden an individual's first and most important identification, his identification with the father in his own personal prehistory. This is apparently not in the first instance the consequence or outcome of an object-cathexis; it is a direct and immediate identification and takes place earlier than any object-cathexis" (SE 19:31).[25] And in *Group Psychology and the Analysis of the Ego* he affirms, "A little boy . . . takes his father as his ideal" (SE 18:105). If this identification is taken as an account of the genesis of the self-image, then it is clear why the child's initial sense of self, as suggested in the narcissism essay, is situated in a false or ideal direction.

How are we to understand the term "identification" in this context? Does Freud mean that the child identifies with the father by deciding through an act of perception and cognition that he resembles him? In *The Ego and the Id* Freud gives no clarification of the term. In the earlier essay *Group Psychology and the Analysis of the Ego*, however, he pointedly discusses identification in such a way as to exclude a cognitive conception of the idea. Instead, identification is the "earliest expression of an emotional tie with another person" (SE 18:105). In short, the boy is "particularly interested in" his father and wants to be like him. Freud suggests that identification can be considered in terms of a metaphor of eating. He establishes a clear connection between identification and introjection (SE 18:105, 113–14). In this sense, identification could be seen to be a derivative of a sense of self based on the inside/outside distinction and its "pleasure-ego" variation. In the "pleasure-ego" stage, the self senses that an object is pleasurable and redefines its boundaries so as to include the object. In identification, similarly, the self could be seen to assimilate the pleasure object and metaphorically expand its boundaries to include it. Just as the body eats (and changes its outline) the self "eats" the libidinous object (and changes its outline). If one accepts this interpretation and follows it through rigorously, identification would not presuppose a self-image that is cognitive in nature, but merely a sense of self. Neither, however, would it result in a self-image. In the case of the child's primary identification with the father, then, the child would not need to have a prior conception of itself in terms of qualities. But the identification would irrevocably alter its identity; one might justifiably ask what remains of a child that overstuffs itself with the father. Yet the metaphor of eating makes possible a sleight of hand. Remaining within the metaphor, one could argue that the child takes on the qualities rather than the quantity of what he ingests. Thus he can acquire qualities without losing his fundamental quantitative sense of self, and also without having a prior self-image. Identification is a concept that enables Freud to move magically from desire to representation without confronting the issue of perception in itself.

Be this as it may, the child's primary identification with the father seems arbitrary. As we have seen, Freud expressly avoids grounding the identification with the father in an act of perception and cognition. If we overstep him and assert that cognition is implied, the identification is still not especially plausible: the child has slight basis for perceiving himself to be *like* the father, unless this similarity is suggested to him by others, a complex matter that Freud does not bring up. Nor is it plausible in Freud's own libidinal terms, for according to Freud, the mother, not the father, is the desired object. Would it not be more plausible for the child to identify with the mother? There seems to be no reason for the child to perceive the father as an ideal figure, at least before recognizing that he presents an obstruction to the possession of the mother. In other words, where does the child's relation to the father come from before desire for the mother gives that relation a meaning? The genesis of the identification with the father, and the grounding of the first, idealized sense of self in the father, thus seem irreducible to desire, and Freud neither attempts to nor could account for it in terms of cognition.

Freud's treatment of pre-Oedipal self-representation and primary narcissism leave one with a feeling of dissatisfaction. One has the feeling that one is treading on spongy ground, where there is little evidence, conflicting evidence, and the possibility of different interpretations. Freud seems to be skirting an issue rather than confronting it; his remarks seem to be stepping-stones to other arguments and retouchings of rough spots in prior theories rather than a theory in themselves, or even something out of which one could reconstruct a theory. The absent point around which his remarks seem to circle is a self-image, an issue that Freud does not treat, just as he avoids the image of the mirror.

As is well known, Jacques Lacan's rewriting of Freud involves the postulation of a "mirror stage." This innovation, which not only introduces the idea of the mirror into Freudian theory but gives it a central place, seems directly designed to clarify and stabilize Freud's theories of the self-image, to ground the genesis of a self-image in an act of perception, and to show that desire affects self-representation. Lacan's 1949 essay "The Mirror Stage as Formative of the Function of the I" clearly responds to problems left by Freud's narcissism essay. Lacan designates the "mirror stage," the stage in which infants first recognize their image in a mirror, as the onset of primary narcissism or what he terms the psychoanalytic order of the "Imaginary." He concludes that the child's perception of its mirror image gives it a sense of mastery over itself by allowing it to conceive of itself as a coherent entity for the first time. Previously, the child had perceived itself only in a fragmentary fashion. Now it recognizes its bodily unity and is jubilant. The image constitutes an "Urbild," or in the words of Lacan's commentators L. Laplanche and J.-B. Pontalis, "the first outline of what is to become the ego."[26] What this form of the constitution of the self shows, however, is the imaginary nature of the ego. According to Laplanche and Pontalis, the ego is "constituted right from the start as an 'ideal ego'";[27] or to use Lacan's own formulation, "This form situates the agency of the ego, before its social determination, in a fictional direction, which will always remain irreducible for the individual alone, or rather, which will only rejoin the coming-into-being (le devenir) of the subject asymptotically, whatever the success of the dialectical syntheses by which he must resolve as I his discordance with his own reality."[28] The mirror image is an ideal form which only partially conforms to the reality of the child's being. The child's first perception of itself is thus an ideal, distorted, fictional one. The beauty of the mirror image stands in sharp contrast to the child's actual lack of coordination. It suggests to the child, who is still powerless and lacking in motor control, that it possesses a coordination beyond its actual capabilities.

Hence Lacan establishes the self's first identification with itself, rather than with the father. In later essays Lacan would also rewrite Freud's theory of the child's identification with the father, which left the puzzle of the child's attraction to the father, by asserting that the child desires (to be the object of) the mother's desire, that is, desires to be the phallus, which is represented by the "paternal metaphor."[29] Both of Lacan's theories, that of the mirror stage, where the genesis of the sense of self involves desire, and that of the identification with the father, where self-consciousness involves the desire of another desire, are heavily indebted to Alexandre Kojève's reading of Hegel.

Lacan thus provides an account of the genesis of narcissistic self-overevaluation. With the mirror stage, by incorporating Freud's ideas of identification and bodily outline into his theory, but by taking bodily outline literally rather than figuratively, he also supplies psychoanalytic theory with the missing sense of self that, beneath the shifting and swelling boundaries that Freud's narcissism concept brought with it, had threatened to disappear. Starting with the mirror stage, the child conceives of itself as a distinct, separate, bounded entity. The mirror image, Lacan asserts, "symbolizes the mental permanence of the *I*."[30]

Lacan shows what Freud implies, namely, that self-knowledge is undermined by desire, and in doing so, Lacan polemically takes on the Cartesian tradition, refuting "any philosophy directly issuing from the cogito."[31] Desire implies *méconnaissance*: not only does desire idealize or misrepresent its object; it is also true that an object takes on signification, becomes a sign, because it is desired. The child's recognition of the image causes the child to desire it and identify with it, and the child recognizes it because it is *desirable*, not because it is a correct image of the self.

5 THE LITERARY DREAM

There was a time when meadow, grove, and stream,
The earth, and every common sight,
    To me did seem
    Apparelled in celestial light,
The glory and the freshness of a dream.
—Wordsworth, "Ode: Intimations of Immortality from
Recollections of Early Childhood"

To that dreamlike vividness and splendour which invest objects
of sight in childhood, everyone, I believe, if he would look back,
could bear testimony.
—Wordsworth, on the "Intimations" Ode

Life has at last become to me as real as a dream.
—Oscar Wilde, letter from prison, 1895

THE DREAM MOTIF AS IT flourished in Viennese literature of the 1890s stands in a line of descent from Pedro Calderón de la Barca, Shakespeare, and Franz Grillparzer. At the basis of this motif is the fascinating proximity of dream and life: the intense hyperclarity of dreams on the one hand, and the melodramatic, unpredictable, dreamlike quality of life on the other. Dream and life are opposites, for the dream is "only a dream"—it is an illusion, not real. Yet dreams are so lifelike and life is so dreamlike that the two also seem interchangeable.

The Baroque life-is-a-dream topos aims to reveal the ephemeral nature of human life. No work illustrates this point better than Calderón's *La vida es sueño* (1635; *Life Is a Dream*). At the center of the play is a didactic hoax: the hero is led to believe that a real episode is merely a dream. The hoax leads its victim to muse that life and dream are indistinguishable. Consequently, we can dismiss our life, and the goals we had hoped to attain in life, as a transitory dream, in contrast to the eternal, transcendent realm of lasting values.

Grillparzer in *Der Traum ein Leben* (1834; *A Dream Is Life*)—a play that was, like Calderón's *La vida es sueño*, part of the standard repertoire at the Burgtheater in the late nineteenth century—inverts the structure of Calderón's play. The central section is not a real episode, but a dream, which the dreamer believes is real. This inversion proves the same point as the Baroque model, that life and dream are indistinguishable. But Grillparzer's motive in confounding dream and reality is not metaphysical, but psychological. He is not interested in demonstrating that life is as ephemeral as a dream but, rather, that dreams, as psychic creations, testify to the individual's deepest desires. They are thus a reliable indicator of what motivates the waking, as well as the dreaming, subject.

Grillparzer's use of the dream prefigures Freud's central dictum in *The Interpretation of Dreams*, that dreams reveal hidden wishes. Freud's elaboration of his dream theory in all its detail—the central importance of early childhood and sexuality, the notions of repression, censorship, and dream symbolism—has no parallel in Grillparzer's drama, and Grillparzer's moral message that dreams can be taken as a warning seems quaint in a post-Freudian context. Nevertheless, the psychological focus of Grillparzer's work made it an attractive source for fin-de-siècle Viennese writers. The Viennese authors of the 1890s did not hesitate to exploit all of the traditional significances of the life-is-a-dream topos. But they stood closest to Grillparzer. Always maintaining the opposition between life and dream, they focus on the dream's lifelike quality rather than on life's resemblance to a dream, and their interest is primarily psychological.

The dream theme is closely related to the theme of the mirror, with the interesting complication that Freud's research on dreams interrupted and changed the course of the literary motif as it was used in the 1890s. In the 1890s the dream, like the mirror, is often used as a *fort/da* device. Out of the spectrum of *aperçus* to which the dream's lifelike quality can give rise such writers as Hofmannsthal, Beer-Hofmann, and Schnitzler preferred the idea that dreams are *more* real than so-called objective reality. For Hofmannsthal and Beer-Hofmann, the most conservative, that is, neo-Romantic writers, dreams are more real than our waking life because they recreate the vividness of the perceptions of early youth. As Wordsworth's reference to "the glory and the freshness of a dream" in the Intimations Ode would have us believe, dreams, in these writers' perception, restore an original splendor to things. They banish the distance that reflection places between ourselves and the world and dispel the mists that habit lowers over our perception. For Schnitzler, dreams issue from the wellsprings of our being and directly express our truest subjectivity. In either case, they eliminate the boundary between ourselves and reality. If the mirror projects our image onto things, the dream creates a magical unity between subject and object, and it also asserts the primacy of subjectivity over "things as they are." Yet just as the mirror image is an illusion, the dream too is a passing phenomenon, a fantasm of the moment.

Out of a plethora of possible examples for the *fort/da* use of the dream, I shall discuss Hofmannsthal's "Terzinen III," Beer-Hofmann's *Der Tod Georgs* (Georg's death), and Schnitzler's *Alkandi's Lied* (Alkandi's song), *Paracelsus*, and *Der Schleier der Beatrice*. Then I shall go on to discuss the post-Freudian literary dream, as exemplified by Schnitzler's story "The Second."

Hofmannsthal's "Terzinen III"

Hofmannsthal's "Terzinen III" illustrates the *fort/da* use of the dream.

Terzinen III
We are such stuff as dreams are made on,
And dreams open wide their eyes
Like little children under cherry trees

Out of whose crown the full moon
Starts its pale gold course through the great night.
. . . Not differently do our dreams emerge,

Are there and live like a child who laughs,
No less large in floating up and down
Than the full moon, awakened out of treetops.

The innermost is open to their weaving;
Like ghostly hands in a locked room
They are in us and are always alive.

And three are One: a man, a thing, a dream.

[Wir sind aus solchem Zeug wie das zu Träumen,
Und Träume schlagen so die Augen auf
Wie kleine Kinder unter Kirschenbäumen,

Aus deren Krone den blaßgoldnen Lauf

Der Vollmond anhebt durch die große Nacht.

. . . Nicht anders tauchen unsre Träume auf,

Sind da und leben wie ein Kind, das lacht,
Nicht minder groß im Auf- und Niederschweben
Als Vollmond, aus Baumkronen aufgewacht.

Das Innerste ist offen ihrem Weben;
Wie Geisterhände in versperrtem Raum
Sind sie in uns und haben immer Leben.

Und drei sind Eins: ein Mensch, ein Ding, ein Traum.][1]

"We are such stuff as dreams are made on": with this citation from Shakespeare's *Tempest* Hofmannsthal recalls Prospero's meditation on the transitoriness of human life and endeavor. In this first mention the dream figures as a symbol of transitoriness. In the second line there is an unexpected shift in emphasis. "And dreams open wide their eyes": dreams are no longer just a metaphor for human life but come alive and take center stage. The initial, citing voice cedes to a voice, which we can provisionally call a daydreaming voice, that spins out visual images. These images coalesce into a scene and then into a second scene. The poem thus shifts into an associative, visual mode, whose underlying purpose seems to be to define the nature of dreams.

This second, daydreaming voice compares dreams to other things: children and the full moon. The images Hofmannsthal chooses in order to define the essence of dreams are as weighted by poetic tradition as the dream itself. Children connote innocence, the moon the power of the imagination. Hofmannsthal repeats each of the terms: he introduces them in the context of a scene and then reiterates them in another scene that only slightly varies the first one. Dream, children, moon, treetops: lines 6–9 reconfigure, as in a woven pattern, the elements of lines 2–4. A vague mirroring effect is created, reminiscent of the oversaturation of metaphor in Proust's childhood idyll "Combray," where such entities as flowers, girls, and churches occur so profusely and confusingly both in the plot and as metaphors for one another that the reader quickly loses sight of what is figurative and what is fictional reality.

Hofmannsthal seems to have chosen the words in lines 2–9 not least for the value of their sound. The central expressions—"Traum," "Kind," "Mond," "Baumkronen"—are woven into a sonorous tissue. "Kirschen-bäume" alliterates with "kleine Kinder" and gives a rhyme word for

"Träume." "Krone," "Mond," and "groß" create an assonance on long "o," and "golden" and "voll" an assonance on short "o." "Anhebt" and "leben" support a similar pattern on long "e."

A more detailed examination of the first three stanzas shows that the effect of the two scenes is to undercut the equation of dreams with transitoriness with which the poem opens and to establish a second, opposite equation of dreams with eternity. The first scene, lines 2–5, begins with the mild paradox of dreams opening their eyes, albeit, in a quasinaturalistic metonymy, in association with the onset of night. Dreams open their eyes like children under cherry trees, who, we may assume, are looking in wide-eyed absorption at the spectacle of the full moon rising above the trees. Hofmannsthal, typically at his most serious and least playful when his theme is childhood, adopts the concept not merely as a synonym for innocence, but with its full weight of Romantic nostalgia. "The enchanted circle of childhood," as he calls it elsewhere, is a paradise where things seem eternal and transitoriness has not yet been glimpsed.[2] In his poem "Verse auf ein kleines Kind" ("Verses on a Small Child"), for example, the child in question plays near "the eternal woods" and "the eternal ocean," fanned by "the eternal winds." In "Ein Knabe" ("A Boy"), the child lives in an Eden where the subject/object split has not yet taken place: "For a long time he did not know that the shells were beautiful. / He was too much of one world with them. / The scent of the hyacinths was nothing to him, / And nothing, the mirror image of his own expressions."[3] The simile in lines 2–3 of "Terzinen III" can thus be paraphrased as follows: dreams restore our naive, childlike perception of things. This perception is neither distracted, dulled by habit, nor nostalgic, for we have not yet become aware of our fundamental disunity with the world. We have here, of course, the *da* function of the dream.

Vis-à-vis the children is the moon—less the object of their vision, in Hofmannsthal's logic, than their mirror. For Hofmannsthal, the poetic imagination (symbolized by the moon) is capable of magically unifying what the bleak adult gaze puts asunder, of recreating the lost vision of childhood. In another poem of the 1890s that also evidently owes its inspiration to *The Tempest*, "Ein Traum von großer Magie" ("A Dream of Great Magic"), the Prospero-like magician or poet figure of the dream abolishes walls, recovers past time, and puts the dreamer in sympathetic unity with all humankind. Moreover, the full moon, in its roundness a symbol of wholeness or perfection, echoes the implied charmed circle of childhood and also the presumptive roundness of the children's eyes: "runde Augen machen" is a German idiom for wide-eyed astonishment, especially in children.

There remain the cherry trees. Why did Hofmannsthal choose the image?[4] Partly, no doubt, for the sake of the sound: for the rhyme ("Baum"—"Traum"), and for the long, closed "o" in "Krone," which Hofmannsthal repeats in "Mond" and "große." This long, closed "o" is the sound of surprise in German. It is also the sound that an adult might make to a child to suggest to it that a response of surprise and pleasure ("runde Augen") is appropriate. But "cherry trees" is also a strong visual image, and as such it suggests yet another round shape—the cherries. Thus the underlying image in the first scene, the image that conducts the movement of the daydream and is persistently suggested to the reader, is the circle.

At the beginning of the second scene (line 6), where Hofmannsthal will reassemble the images into a new configuration, there is a pause indicated by an ellipsis. The daydreamer appears to reflect, and then to affirm the immediately preceding train of thought where the dream was compared to children, by repeating the comparison: "Not differently do our dreams emerge, / Are there and live like a child who laughs." But whereas in the first scene (lines 2–5) the emphasis is on looking, astonishment, and a largely static, round perfection, here in lines 6–9 movement is introduced. Dreams, it is said, are alive ("leben"). Thereafter everything is in motion. The child laughs: we can interpolate that it is no longer staring in wide-eyed astonishment at a wondrous object, but watching a moving object. Indeed, the moon is now floating up and down, perhaps even bobbing up and down like a balloon (an analogy that would explain the image of the laughing child). The image of the rising and sinking moon may easily be naturalized by ascribing the motion to treetops tossing in the wind, which create the illusion that the moon itself floats up and down. The associations of wind covertly reinsinuate the notion of transitoriness into this scene, as the rising moon did to a lesser extent in the evocation of eternity in lines 2–5, thereby presaging (as we shall see) the turn of events in stanza 4. Meanwhile, however, we have an image of repeated motion. If the circle is perceived as childlike, repetition is also characteristic of children's play. Thus two equally valid images of the dream are given: dreams restore our childlike perception of things; and dreams are in constant lively motion, albeit a repeating motion.

In the fourth stanza the tone changes. We hear the poet's voice again, which makes a direct statement about the role of the dream in adult life. But if one examines the spatial relations in this stanza—dreams are within us, "in a locked room," in our "innermost"—one can easily discern that a transposition of the space of stanzas 1–3 has taken place. The sheltered enclosure of childhood now reappears as the enclosed, innermost psychological space of the adult that the child will eventually become. The back-and-forth motion evoked in stanza 3 reappears in stanza 4 in the motion of the dream. The ghostly hands recall the waving of the treetops. The dream *weaves* within this closed space—much as the poet wove images together in the middle section of the poem, which we may now justifiably identify as dreamlike. In retrospect lines 2–9 take on the status of an example: they are a case in point for the poet's contention in stanza 4. Paradox characterizes this final stanza. The area within is enclosed, yet "open" to dreams. Dreams are like "ghostly" hands, yet they are "always alive." Our very core is dominated by the flickering activity of the dream, which constantly brings to life what is past and changes, rearranges, and embellishes our memories, the stuff of our lives. "We are such stuff as dreams are made on": Our very core is mutable, subject to the perpetually revising activity of dreams. Here in stanza 4 Hofmannsthal transforms the meaning of the Baroque commonplace of line 1, giving it a psychological rather than a metaphysical significance. And once again, with a slight modification, the poet ascribes both eternity and transitoriness to dreams. Dreams (and we) are transitory, mutable; yet our *identity* with dreams, their domination over our subjectivity, is eternal.

The last line brings a new surprise. "And three are One" sounds a religious note. Once again the poet quotes. With "a man, a thing, a dream" Hofmannsthal presents us with a new Trinity. In fitting complementarity with the theme of the entire poem, this citation, which suggests *eternity* in a religious sense, stands in paradoxical contrast to the citation of line 1, which equated the stuff of human life with transitoriness.

Hofmannsthal's equation is enigmatic. In what way are the three one? We could read the line as a confirmation of the association of "dream," "child," and "moon" made in lines 2–9 (man = child, or dreaming adult; thing = moon, dream = dream). Thus *in the dream* the three are one; or in other words, the dream recreates the unselfconscious vision of childhood in which subject and object are as if one (da).

A second reading, which would give the religious parody a cynical ring, involves circling back to the opening line and the idea of transitoriness. In this reading, *in reality* the three are one: "a man, a thing, a dream" are all alike because they are all transitory (*fort*). As Prospero says in the speech containing the line that Hofmannsthal cites: "The cloud-capp'd towers, the gorgeous palaces, / The solemn temples, the great globe itself, / Yea, all which it inherit, shall dissolve / And, like this insubstantial pageant faded, / Leave not a rack behind."[5]

Yet presumably the poet wishes not merely to repeat the idea of line 1, but to comment on the notion proposed in the interim, that dreams recreate the unity of childhood. In the space created by the possibility of two different readings, a third emerges. "A man, a thing, a dream" are all one, that is, all transitory. Therefore their very oneness, the unity that the dream creates between subject and object (*da*), is also transitory (*fort*). In other words, the adult knows that the immediacy he experienced as a child was transitory, and if he reexperiences this unity in his dreams, he knows that dreams too fade and pass away. In this third reading the final line would be about the *psychology* of transitoriness: in an odd doubling, our present knowledge of transitoriness affects our view of our past childish innocence and of our dreams. From the perspective of the transitoriness of human existence, the "eternity" of childhood, an experience that dreams bring back, appears most fleeting.

"Terzinen III" thus shuttles back and forth between two significances of the dream, which we may designate as *fort* and *da*: between an evocation of the Baroque life-is-a-dream topos, where dreams symbolize the transitoriness of human life (*fort*), and Hofmannsthal's own conception of the dream as the medium of an unreflecting immediacy that approximates the lost vision of childhood (*da*). As Hofmannsthal moves from his initial citation of the Baroque topos, with its metaphysical import, to a more properly fin-de-siècle reassessment of the dream as a psychological symbol in stanza 4—hence as we penetrate the complex layers of the dream's multiple connotations and arrive at the kernel of the poem— the dream reappears as a *fort/da* device in its more limited, psychological sense, the sense we encounter in other poems by Hofmannsthal of the same period. Inasmuch as dreams unify self and things, they are most real (*da*). Yet when one is outside that state, in a cognitive, reflective frame of mind, they are unreal (*fort*). Depending on one's perspective, on whether one is inside or outside of the dream, experiencing or reflecting, the dream will appear as real or unreal, fleeting or everlasting.

Beer-Hofmann's *Der Tod Georgs*

In Richard Beer-Hofmann's *Der Tod Georgs* the significance of the dream is the same as that in "Terzinen III." Beer-Hofmann's novella informs us that the dream conjures forth a reality superior to that of ordinary waking life. It is the medium of fullness, significance, presence, intensity. All things "turn their face toward" the novella's hero, the dreamer Paul. Upon awakening, Paul reflects that the dream offered "no empty hours that were merely bridges to hoped-for richer ones; and nothing that stood along the way, valueless, which one passed by indifferently. All things had turned their countenance toward him—he could not walk past them; they were there for his sake" (TG 54, my translation). Like Hofmannsthal's "Terzinen III," Beer-Hofmann's *Der Tod Georgs* uses the dream as a *fort/da* device, shuttling back and forth between the dream as the most vivid experience and as mere illusion. The Baroque dimension of the theme, the idea of transitoriness, is lacking, but the sleight-of-hand technique, the artful confusion of dream and reality, is if anything more pronounced. The presumption of influence and interinfluence is entirely justified, for Beer-Hofmann's novella, which appeared in 1900, was seven years in the making, and Hofmannsthal, a close friend of Beer-Hofmann's, read it in the early stages of its composition.

Der Tod Georgs warrants a brief discussion because it uses the dream not just as a device but as a literary form. That is, the novella contains an actual dream. Thus it supplies one possible answer to the question of how a pre-Freudian writer might write a literary dream, or approximate dream images in language. *Der Tod Georgs* takes Grillparzer's *Der Traum ein Leben* as its structural (although not as its stylistic) model. But Beer-Hofmann creates a supremely fin-de-siècle text, one similar in its theme, content, and moral message to Hofmannsthal's *Death and the Fool*. We will see that Beer-Hofmann, in keeping with the ideology with which the dream is invested, creates an aestheticist dream.

As in *Der Traum ein Leben*, a central portion of this narrative is a long, involved, intensely lifelike dream. But whereas in Grillparzer's drama the onset of the dream is, if not clearly signaled, at least subtly indicated, Beer-Hofmann obscures the transition between waking reality and dream, so that the reader simply believes that a period of several years has elapsed between chapter 1 (waking reality) and chapter 2 (the dream). We do not find out until the protagonist Paul wakes up at the end of chapter 2 that we have been misled by a narrative *trompe l'oeil* and that the entire foregoing forty-page narrative segment was a dream!

Like Grillparzer, Beer-Hofmann uses the dream to make a moral point. But his moral is different. Beer-Hofmann assimilates the dream theme to one of the fashionable preoccupations of the 1890s: a fear of aestheticism with its typical inversion of truth and artifice and a glorification of "life." Beer-Hofmann's Paul is like Hofmannsthal's Fool. Thus the vividness and beauty of the dream, or more precisely the hero's preference for the dream, is—at least on a first estimation—*bad*, for it is a sign that the hero's vital equilibrium is topsy-turvy. It demonstrates that he derives more satisfaction from the illusory pleasures of the imagination than from actual life. Dreams should not be more real than life; we should not allow their splendors to usurp our sense of the real world. Above all, life should not be "like a dream."

Like Grillparzer, Beer-Hofmann proposes that dreams teach us useful things about ourselves. In the dream Paul has been married for seven years to the woman he saw fleetingly in the opening chapter. She is now dying of consumption. The dream is concentrated into the afternoon of her death. It is punctuated by long, associative digressions: Paul thinks about his character, and especially how it has affected his wife. Bookish, imaginative, and doubting, Paul has inflicted the products of his wide erudition and his restless fantasy on her, thereby creating in her a mirror of himself rather than valuing her for her own sake. After Paul awakens he continues this same line of reflection. He comes to the insight that he had been blotting out reality in favor of products of his imagination, avoiding the present in order to absorb himself in the past, preferring books to life, and effacing the particularity of things and other people with his persistent habit of self-projection—in short, creating a narcissistic universe. Thus the dream is a catalyst for these insights in two contradictory ways: first, it gives Paul a negative example of his own aestheticist bent, which prefers fiction to truth, and, second, it initiates the instructive reflections themselves.

By the end of the fourth and final part of the novella, Beer-Hofmann reconciles these two contradictory aspects of the dream in a grand scheme of things, according to which we live in a just universe, where everything fulfills its own law, and where everything is interconnected: past and present, childhood and old age, a single human being with the rest of the human race and with nature, Paul himself with the Jewish people. Schnitzler, in a letter to Beer-Hofmann of 2 March 1900, com-

plained that somewhere in this ending there was "an impudent swin-
dle." Indeed, the end seems to pop rose-colored lenses over the specta-
cles Beer-Hofmann has bidden us look through hitherto. He subsumes
all the dualities he has set forth previously under a new unity, the "just
law" of the universe. What has appeared irreconcilable can now coexist
in harmony, what has appeared pejorative has, in the new interpretation,
its valid place in the new scheme of things as a transitional phase, an unfinished thought, a necessary counterpart to its opposite. The end confers its benediction on all of Paul's old faults: his propensity to live in
books comes into focus as a not fully developed *aspect* of his empathetic
imagination, and the dream too is ultimately validated and given its
place. Paul reflects,

> He who dreamed created a world and placed in it only what held sig-
> nificance for him; the boundaries of its heavens and its earths were
> set by him; he was omniscient in it, and everything knew of him.
> Dreams lived unyoked by time and space, freer than daytime life;
> and they had leave to exercise their dominion more richly and more
> sweetly and more cruelly and with a more ostentatious show of
> power than life, for every bright morning passed judgment like a
> young wise judge on the confusedly interlaced doings and sufferings
> of nightly dreams, disengaging what had been joined together and
> smilingly restoring everything to its previous state. (TG 111, my
> translation)

Dreams—vivid, poetic, and frankly narcissistic—have their place *because* they will end, *because* morning comes, *because* the fictions they
create are only temporary.

What do these intricate shiftings in the evalution of the dream have to
do with the actual dream? How, if at all, do they leave their mark on its
style? Stylistically, the notion of the particularly vivid or lifelike dream
translates into long, polished, adjective-laden sentences, which aim to
reproduce both the intensity and the nuances of the dreamer's experience. Remarkably, however, the dream is written in a style indistinguishable from that in which Paul's waking perceptions are rendered, in
other words, from that of the rest of the narrative. Like *Death and the
Fool*, *Der Tod Georgs* is anti-aestheticist in its message, yet stylistically
wholly indebted to aestheticism. Theodor Reik, in his early analysis of
the story in his monograph *Richard Beer-Hofmann* (1912), aptly writes
of the style, "A stylistic analysis would yield the approximate result that

the Stefan George Circle, the Bible, and the stories from *The Arabian Nights* had had an influence here. The crowding comparisons, which through their profusion often cancel one another out, these painstakingly sought, precious adjectives, the long, heavy periods."[6] The story is largely told in free indirect style and is often singled out as the first novella to use interior monologue in German. Hence one would expect it to have a primarily psychological objective. But it would be a mistake to relativize its unusual style merely as an expression of Paul's aesthete's sensibility. With its heavy freight of imagery, the cadences of its sentences composed for the ear, this work desires to affect us profoundly, to awaken important insights, to be significant. There is no trace of authorial irony.

Beer-Hofmann evidently considered this idiosyncratic style suitable for the dream too. But free indirect style, with its insistently recurring third-person pronoun, is a convention that is hard for post-Freudian readers to accept in narrated dreams. When Freud retells his patients' accounts of their dreams in the third person, the genesis of the form is clear. But in Beer-Hofmann's text, what are we to imagine? That the author is observing the main character dream, where dreaming is in no way different from the normal thought processes?

What of the dream's plot? Like the narrative, the dream involves little action. It is swollen not only with Paul's perceptions, but with his memories, feelings, and extensive reflections (these too strike the post-Freudian reader as bizarre). There is no dream distortion. There is a feature, common to Grillparzer as well, that we have come to identify with Freud as "the day's residues": the dream draws its substance from prior waking reality. The dream starts with the image that ends the "real" part, the heart-shaped form of linden leaves against the window, and constructs its plot around a waking experience Paul had the preceding evening. But Beer-Hofmann's purpose seems less to be to produce a psychologically plausible dream than to emphasize the interconnectedness of dream and waking reality (in the service of his final point). Over and over, Beer-Hofmann repeats phrases and sentences verbatim or nearly verbatim from fictional reality to the dream and from dream to fictional reality. One critic has counted no less than seventy repetitions that occur at least once in the story.[7] Despite these connections with the events of the preceding evening, however, the dream is disconcertingly inventive. Beer-Hofmann gives the dream a free hand to make up long, detailed sequences. Finally, this dream is not in any obvious way generated by desire. The dream in Grillparzer's *Der Traum ein Leben*, which realizes the hero Rustan's desires in their most horrible form, is, despite its greater historical remoteness from us, psychologically more plausible.

In the same measure as the narrative as a whole is fraught with internal contradiction, the pronounced similarity between dream and narrative has its awkwardnesses as well as its uses. While it certainly supports the idea that the dream is lifelike, it undermines the initial pejorative evaluation of the dream as well as the would-be distinction between dream (more vivid) and life (less vivid). The style of the dream in Beer-Hofmann's novella is a product of ideology, of what the author believes the dream represents, rather than of the observation of actual dreams. The dream figures less as a psychological phenomenon (as in Grillparzer) than as a metaphysical concept seen within an ethical framework (dreams render experience more intense, but they should not seem more real than life). Thus instead of distortion, we have scene-painting coherent in all its details; instead of disjointed action, elaborate reflection; instead of a focus on the present, extensive flashbacks and recollections; instead of displacement of affect, nuances of sensibility; instead of overdetermined associations, invention; and instead of hidden desires, metaphysical insights.

The pre-Freudian literary dream motif, as exemplified by Hofmannsthal's "Terzinen III" and Beer Hofmann's *Der Tod Georgs*, thus fuses the Romantic notion that the dream renders experiences more vivid than they are in life with a reminder that dreams are illusory. Precisely this paradoxical quality of the dream attracts the writers, for it enables them to use it as a *fort/da* device capable of providing momentary access to a magical state of presence and thereby prove the existence of something that has been declared to be fundamentally out of reach. "Dream" in these works stands for subjectivity's claim to absoluteness and also for the limitations with which this claim can be countered. The dream is important to these writers less as a phenomenon than as a concept and a device.

Freud and Schnitzler

When Freud's epoch-making *The Interpretation of Dreams* (1900) entered this literary scene, his new dream theory resembled the literary dream motif of his immediate predecessors in one fundamental respect.

Different though his field, aims, and terminology were from those of the literary writers, his use of the dream as a boundary-crossing device within a dualistic model was similar to that of the Viennese authors in the 1890s. Freud designates the boundary differently in *The Interpretation of Dreams*: it is no longer one between ourselves and things, between our normal state of mind and a more intense type of experience, but one between the unconscious and consciousness, between desire and its (hallucinatory) fulfillment. Nevertheless, the dream in Freud's interpretation renders accessible an area that is beyond the reach of normal consciousness. Thus not only was the subject of Freud's magnum opus, the dream, of great interest to his literary contemporaries; his actual treatment of the subject was not wholly at odds with, but rather seemed an ingenious displacement of their own.[8]

The point in which Freud's dream theory departs radically from his literary and philosophical precursors, and indeed is at cross purposes with the entire life-is-a-dream tradition, is his theory of the dream work and his emphasis on dream distortion. The life-is-a-dream tradition is founded on the assumption of a *trompe l'oeil* similarity between dream and life. The dream may be somewhat more excessive and fabulous than real life, but it is otherwise similar to it. Thus in Calderón's *La vida es sueño* Segismundo's day as a prince, which he subsequently believes is a dream, is a fantastic experience. In *Der Traum ein Leben* Grillparzer models his dream on a fast-moving, melodramatic adventure story. Freud's dream transcripts, with their rambling plotlessness, disjointed associations, and nonsense elements, initiate a totally different genre. Literary writers wishing to adapt Freud's theory to their own productions had to come to terms with dream distortion, and indeed, distortion is one of the hallmarks of the post-Freudian literary dream.

Nowhere is the influence of Freudian dream theory seen more clearly than in the work of Arthur Schnitzler.[9] Thanks to Schnitzler's habit of keeping a day-to-day diary, we know that he was reading *The Interpretation of Dreams* by 26 March 1900, or four months after it was published. Schnitzler's production of literary dreams takes two characteristic forms and falls into two successive chronological stages: dreams occurring predominantly in dramas, which, it seems probable, were inspired by the model of Grillparzer; and dreams involving distortion, which occur in fictional narratives. The chronological caesura between the two types falls in 1900, the date when Schnitzler read *The Interpretation of Dreams*.[10]

In his work of the 1890s Schnitzler is fond of showing, through playful paradox, how the terms of generally accepted hard-and-fast distinctions—being and seeming, life and art, reality and dream—blur into each other. The fictional dream is an excellent instrument for this questioning, for the dream (in its pre-Freudian conception) presents an alternative version of the real; as we have seen on the example of Beer-Hofmann's *Der Tod Georgs*, the unsuspecting reader can be temporarily fooled into believing that the dream is fictional reality. Schnitzler, moreover, in contrast to Hofmannsthal and Beer-Hofmann, is also intent on overthrowing the conventional hierarchical relations between the two terms in order to show how the secondary or subjective term of each duality is in fact primary: true reality is subjective reality. Schnitzler thus, before Freud, already edges toward a Freudian position: where the wellsprings of reality are hidden in the individual psyche, dreams give access to the truth.

Schnitzler's early short play *Alkandi's Lied* (1890) is plainly modeled on Grillparzer's *Der Traum ein Leben*.[11] In *Der Traum ein Leben* Rustan's dream fabricates a story that plays out the consequences of his thirst for adventure and glory in their most dire form: lying leads to treason and murder. The dream is in part fantasy, in part darkly transformed reality. The interpretation we are given at the end seems in its central insight to anticipate Freud: the dream expresses the dreamer's wishes. Grillparzer phrases this insight as a warning:

> But do not forget: our dreams,
> They do not create our wishes;
> They awaken the existing ones;
> And what morning now chases away
> Lay hidden in you as a seed.
> Be on your guard, and so will I.[12]

In *Alkandi's Lied*, similarly, the middle portion of the drama is a dream. As in *Der Traum ein Leben*, the dream writes a melodramatic scenario, translating the dreamer's unconscious desires into action. It thereby functions as an oracle of the truth: it teaches the dreamer a lesson, who, when he wakes up, proceeds to act in accordance with what he has learned from the dream. The theme of poetical power versus political power, not present in Grillparzer's play, helps localize *Alkandi's Lied* as a product of 1890s aestheticism. King Assad, who has little feeling for art, falls asleep when Alkandi's song is played. The song, which sounds intermittently throughout the dream, could be seen to take its revenge by sending him a nightmare. Jealous of his wife for worshipping the dead poet Alkandi, Assad wanders through his realm, forbidding and annihilating all traces of Alkandi. But while he is thus vainly occupied—for Alkandi's song sounds ironically in the background even when Assad triumphantly declares that he has managed to silence it—and far from home, his wife betrays him with the living poet Irsil. Is this the triumph of art, the triumph of the dream? Not necessarily, for on awakening, Assad recoups his power and banishes Irsil.

An important difference between *Alkandi's Lied* and *Der Traum ein Leben* is that Schnitzler, unlike Grillparzer, demands that we reflect critically on the distinction between dream and reality. Unlike Grillparzer and like Beer-Hofmann, Schnitzler obscures the transition from waking to dream. Assad does not remain lying down when his dream begins, but rather gets up, so that the spectator has no reason to believe that the dream is not simply a continuation of the action. The effect is to make the play double-bottomed: what on first reading seems like curiously exaggerated or excessive action reveals itself on second reading to be an exceptionally vivid and persuasive dream. By using this trick Schnitzler poses the question: Are dreams necessarily "less real" than life? Do not dreams reflect our experiences, our opinions, our emotions? Are they not, moreover, a direct outlet for our unconscious thoughts and desires? Whereas in Grillparzer's play Rustan is merely not conscious of the possible consequences of his desires until the dream plays them out, in *Alkandi's Lied*, we know nothing of Assad's jealousy of the poet—and probably he doesn't either—until it surfaces in the dream.

The play *Paracelsus* (1898) makes the point more forcefully than anywhere else in Schnitzler's work that psychic reality is the only reality. The hypnotist Paracelsus, a sixteenth-century figure behind whom, as Michaela L. Perlmann argues, we are meant to see modern figures like Charcot, Ambroise-Auguste Liébault, and Hippolyte Bernheim,[13] shows how tenuous the boundary between fiction and reality is by effacing it for his subject Justina and her skeptical husband Cyprian. Although Paracelsus himself keeps a firm grip on the difference between fiction and reality (as he must in order to be able to manipulate them), his point of view, that truth and falsehood, dream and reality melt into each other, and that "meaning" resides in the eye of the beholder, reigns supreme, while that of his foil and victim Cyprian, an unimaginative character who believes that he knows fake from genuine and dream from reality, is not taken seriously. The hypnotist extols the power of dreams in language that eerily anticipates Freud's *Interpretation of Dreams*:

> Just consider this one thing: every night
> Forces us to descend into an alien realm,
> Exempt from our power and our wealth;
> And all the fullness and earnings of life
> Are far less powerful than the dreams
> That meet our will-less sleep.
> (DW 2:223, my translation)

At the end of the play Paracelsus twirls dichotomies like a magic baton:

> A meaning
> Is found only by him who seeks it.
> Dream and waking, truth and lie
> Flow into each other. Certainty is nowhere.
> We know nothing of the other, nothing of ourselves.
> We are always playing, and clever is he who knows it.
> (DW 2:240, my translation)

One of the most remarkable and instructive examples of the dream motif in turn-of-the-century Austrian literature is Schnitzler's five-act drama *Der Schleier der Beatrice*. The play was first performed in 1900, the date of Freud's *Interpretation of Dreams*. It stands out, first of all, for its striking duplication of Freud's central dream theory, the theory that the dream is a wish. When Beatrice, his beloved, tells him that she dreams she married the duke, the poet Filippo Loschi speaks the following words about dreams:

> I wish it were the truth, Beatrice.
> Then I could sooner look at you
> Without pain and disgust; life itself finishes
>   everything off.
> *But dreams are desires without courage,*
> *Impudent wishes that the light of day*
> *Chases back into the corners of our souls*
> Whence they dare creep only by night;
> And such a dream—it leaves you behind
> With outstretched arms, longing, thirsty.
> (My translation and italics)

[Ich wollt', es wäre Wahrheit, Beatrice
So könnt' ich eher ohne Schmerz und Ekel
Dich sehn; das Leben selbst tut alles ab.
Doch Träume sind Begierden ohne Mut,
Sind freche Wünsche, die das Licht des Tags
Zurückjagt in die Winkel unsrer Seele,
Daraus sie erst bei Nacht zu kriechen wagen;
Und solch ein Traum, mit ausgestreckten Armen
Sehnsüchtig läßt er, durstig dich zurück. (DW 3:68)]
(My italics)

This speech is surely one of the passages in Schnitzler's work most destined to fuel the endless speculation about Schnitzler as Freud's *Doppelgänger*, who anticipated his ideas.[14] *The Interpretation of Dreams* appeared in November 1899; Schnitzler sent *Der Schleier der Beatrice* to press somewhat later, on 31 December 1899. But a preliminary prose draft of act 1, dated 23 January [?] 1899, already makes the equation between dream and wish. Thus there can be no question that the central idea that dreams are wishes predated the appearance of *The Interpretation of Dreams*. As we have seen, however, Grillparzer expressed this idea before Schnitzler.[15]

The second point of interest about this play is that it shows that "Freudian" dream theory, the idea that the dream is a wish, does not represent something radically new and different vis-à-vis the dream as a *fort/da* device as it was used in the 1890s, but is rather a compatible extension of it. A study of the play and the profusion of drafts leading up to the final version shows how Schnitzler replaces in a series of gradual steps the idea that the dream symbolizes momentary subjective belief by the idea that the dream is a manifestation of unconscious drives. In this shift, two things remain constant: the value of the dream as *subjective* reality, and its opposition to so-called *objective* reality. The emphasis, then, moves from the subject's *belief* to the subject's *desire*, but the boundary persists: the border between illusion and reality becomes one between desire and its fulfillment.

Der Schleier der Beatrice is Schnitzler's second published reworking of his 1892 pantomime. As we saw in chapter 3, the basic idea of the pantomime is that a woman forgets something—her veil—at the scene of her lover's death and is forced to return for it. As Filippo Loschi in *Der Schleier der Beatrice* will say, this scene of death is a "place that grants no return" (DW 3:126, my translation). The boundary to the realm of the dead, once crossed, is uncrossable in the other direction. In *Beatrice* the bridegroom (or, in the final version, Beatrice's brother) takes his revenge and kills the heroine.

Atypically for Schnitzler's early period, *Der Schleier der Beatrice* is a play with which Schnitzler had a great deal of trouble. His diaries of 1898 and 1899 attest that he was perpetually dissatisfied with it and kept beginning it anew and revising it. Like his later novel *Der Weg ins Freie* and his historical drama *Der junge Medardus*, this play, set in the Renaissance, tends to fall apart into background, or presentation of milieu, and foreground, or intrigue. The psychological focus wanders: first it is directed at Filippo Loschi, the poet-lover, then it settles on Beatrice. The characters are embodiments of abstract ideas rather than psychologically realistic figures. This is particularly true of the principal female figure Beatrice. Schnitzler, who is usually adept at creating psychologically plausible female characters, at least where the women are victims, casts the dangerous Beatrice as the traditional femme fatale type. Finally, whereas in the short and relatively sparse "The Dead Are Silent" and the later ballet *Der Schleier der Pierrette* the mechanism that constitutes the plot is eerie and effective, this same scheme, fleshed out as a five-act Renaissance drama, degenerates into melodrama. *Der Schleier der Beatrice* gives us complication without nuance.

It is perhaps because of its imperfections, because its seams show, that this play is so revealing. Schnitzler plainly labored to transpose the central problematic of the intrigue, the theme of transgression, onto the historical setting. The action takes place in early sixteenth-century Bologna, on the eve of the conquest of Bologna by the Borgias. By the end of the play Bologna's fortifications are completely surrounded by enemy troops; the city is about to fall. Before this, the frenetic quality of life in the city, with its sudden abrupt actions, characterizes the eve of destruction. The breakdown of social conventions in Bologna foreshadows its downfall. The duke, dazzled by the beauty of Beatrice, makes a snap decision to wed this girl from the artisan-shopkeeper milieu, thereby marrying far below his station. At the party following this *mésalliance* (in act 4) the action becomes eerier. The breakdown of order spreads. Loyalties are brutally betrayed: a Borgia traitor is tortured and made to speak, a courtesan stabs a nobleman, the duke has his old deputy killed, the bride's sister Rosina is viciously jealous of Beatrice. All of this action on the political and social scale is in turn anticipated by the circumstances surrounding the intimate intrigue, Beatrice's affair with the poet Filippo Loschi. The walled-in garden in which Loschi lives, and from which he banishes the faithless Beatrice, anticipates the fortifications of Bologna. His decision to heed the appeal of this femme fatale and readmit her leads to his death, which anticipates the fall of the city. Finally, the extravagant party he throws preceding his death parallels the party the duke throws preceding the city's fall.

Beatrice, the femme fatale, is the agent of transgression in the play. She causes the persons who are actually empowered to act—the men in the drama—to indulge in irresponsible and disruptive actions, to forget their obligations, to override conventions against their better judgment, and to disregard their own and others' welfare in pursuit of an illusory happiness with her. As a personality, she is, in Schnitzler's own words, "an unconscious, elemental, highly female creature" who childishly and mischievously behaves as if taking one thing did not mean forgoing another, as if actions were readily reversible, as if she could go from one man to another and back.[16] The duke says, contemplating the body of Filippo Loschi,

> He died for you? And you betrayed him?
> And me for him? And then him again for me?
> What kind of creature are you, Beatrice?
> (DW 3:164–65, my translation)

Schnitzler discussed his pantomime, "The Dead Are Silent," and his new idea for the play with Hofmannsthal on 1 November 1897.[17] Schnitzler was distressed and spurred to get to work on the play by Hofmannsthal's remark "I'll write that too."[18] For whatever reason the idea attracted Hofmannsthal, there are strong connections between the final version of the play and Hofmannsthal's work, so that one could say that *Beatrice*, among Schnitzler's works, is uniquely Hofmannsthalesque.[19] The enclosed garden where the poet Loschi lives is a motif familiar from such early works by Hofmannsthal as *Der Tod des Tizian* (Tizian's death), *Death and the Fool*, and "The Emperor of China Speaks." Beatrice herself is a negative version of Hofmannsthal's "child." Consider the opening lines of Hofmannsthal's poem of 1896, "Ein Knabe":

> For a long time he did not know that the shells were beautiful
> He was too much of one world with them.
> The scent of the hyacinths was nothing to him,
> And nothing, the mirror image of his own expressions.[20]

Loschi says similarly of Beatrice,

> You were not
> Made to marvel. Never did the wonder
> Of existence namelessly startle you;
> Never did you sink in reverence
> Before the bright colors of this world.
> (DW 3:126, my translation)

To judge from the extant drafts of the play, Schnitzler seems to have planned from the beginning to use the dream motif. It appears in these drafts in very different contexts. In the successive manuscripts we see a gradual shift from the dream-versus-reality idea to the dream-as-a-wish idea. In a fragment dated 24 April 1898, where the principal characters are Hans von Traun and Agathe (Schnitzler had not yet decided to cast the fable as a Renaissance drama), the dream is used as a metaphor to stress the absolute disparity, to Agathe's mind, between marriage to a rich man and a love affair with the impoverished soldier Hans: they are as incompatible as dream and reality. Agathe (Beatrice) has an odd experience of "waking up" in the middle of the wedding dance. Upon returning to Hans, she says,

> I am intoxicated
> By sudden wakefulness; I come out of a deep sleep.
> . . .
> How strange! Now I understand all this.
> In the dream I just came out of
> Everything I experienced with you
> Was a dream, and wholly without power.[21]

Here "dream" and "reality" designate opposites, but the allocation of the terms is up to the subject.

In another version, where the lover is a sculptor, the dream motif is again used metaphorically, this time to assert that the dreams of the artist are more real than reality. Asked where he was, the artist (Stefan) replies,

> Where I had no use for anyone—
> By myself. Alone with myself and a block
> Of white marble, which since this morning
> Is a shape in accordance with my mind and will.

> And within me was such a profound radiance
> That around me the whole world sank into darkness.
> Now my day of a thousand suns is gone
> And, as if after an immense wakefulness,
> I enter into a realm of slumber,
> Ready to accept as truth the dreams and shadows
> I encounter, like all the rest of you.

Here again "reality" and "dream" are opposites, but they signify the reverse of what they mean in everyday speech. Schnitzler stresses the subject's power to create an autonomous reality and to disregard what is really there to a much greater extent than in the previous version.

In a version of 22 December 1898, where the protagonist is Filippo Loschi, Filippo emphasizes how our "dreams," our subjectivities, are our reality:

> But as for us, our dreams drink us up
> And the dukedoms of our brief power
> Blossom from the mercies of the moment.

This version is distinctly closer to the dream-as-a-wish idea we see in the final version. Dream is still subjective reality, but the subject is no longer in control; rather, there is something compulsive about the dream, which rules him. The dream appears as a manifestation of a deeper level of the self, not subject to conscious volition.

Finally, in a version of the altercation between Filippo and Beatrice that closely approaches the final one, Filippo expels Beatrice for having dreamed she was the duke's wife.

> All night long I dreamt of being the duchess.
> —And after this dream you go back to me?
> I don't want you that way.
> —You don't understand; I'm not guilty.
> —You aren't guilty, but you *are* sullied.

If we supplement this brief text with the ideas that are more clearly expressed in the final version, Beatrice is, in Filippo's view, sullied by her dream because the dream represents her hidden desires and is therefore an indicator of what she is likely to do next.

In the final published version, Schnitzler allocates two different functions to the dream. First, as Filippo recognizes, the dream is a wish, and desire is the force that governs the subject. In this sense the dream is an agent of transgression, for it effaces the boundary between desire and its fulfillment, between not having and having. Moreover, Beatrice's dream, which by dint of wish elevates her from the lowest social class to the very highest, thereby crossing a firm social boundary, comes true. Thus the dream becomes the symbol of transgression, of uniting fiction and reality, poor girl and duke—a making-one through wish (da). Second, and in contrast, Schnitzler invokes the dream/reality polarity on several occasions (fort). Beatrice cites the standard excuse that dreams are only dreams: "Ein Traum war's doch!" (DW 3:68). Later, pledging to marry Vittorino, a man of her station, she repeats the same idea. Dreams are mere dreams, while reality is waking reality:

No, Vittorino, let's never ask each other
About dreams. Waking alone
Is life, and light is shared.
(DW 3:94, my translation)

The fort and da uses of the dream are thus not in an "and yet" relationship, as they are in Hofmannsthal's poem and Beer-Hofmann's Der Tod Georgs (dreams are real-seeming and yet, in a larger view of things, illusion). Rather, they are in an "and" relationship: dreams are illusion, the illusion/reality duality exists; and dreams transgress this boundary. Where the dream is explicitly the (natural) symbol of desire, the use of the dream to uphold the boundary (dreams are illusion; the illusion/reality polarity exists) appears ironic; for the boundary, which indubitably exists as a de facto, contingent, historical reality (the territorial boundary of the state, the boundary between ruler and subject), breaks down precisely at the point where it is posited as an absolute distinction ("illusion" versus "reality") that governs, rather than is governed by, subjectivity. The plot of the play belies the sharp differentiation between dream and reality, for Beatrice's dream of marrying the duke comes true. When the adoring Vittorino promises her a life where she can rest from her dreams, a dreamless life, we easily read between the lines that this life will fulfill none of her desires.

Thus in the last analysis the fort and da uses of the dream in Der Schleier der Beatrice are in an "and yet" relationship, but one that reverses Hofmannsthal's and Beer-Hofmann's values. In Schnitzler's play, and in Schnitzler's work generally, dreams appear to be an illusion, yet in fact they are the truest reality. Moreover, in its dream-as-wish variation, in its *da* phase, the dream changes its value: it loses the magical, aesthetic quality it had in Hofmannsthal's poem (of uniting what is *unfortunately* separate in real life) and takes on the cynical aspect of a forbidden overstepping of such necessary conventions as law and order.

The dream in *Der Schleier der Beatrice* is a wish-fulfillment dream, but it involves no distortion. The appearance of *The Interpretation of Dreams* marked a change in Schnitzler's literary use of the dream. Schnitzler's extremely early reception of this work testifies to his long-standing fascination with dreams, not just the dream as a literary topos, but with real dreams as a psychic phenomenon. Schnitzler made a practice of recording his own dreams in his diary from 1875 until his death.[22] Reading *The Interpretation of Dreams* intensified his preoccupation with dreams. He himself recalled that reading the book caused him to dream more, and in an unusually vivid fashion, and to interpret while dreaming: "I remember that, when I read Freud's *Interpretation of Dreams* (1900), I dreamed remarkably many and lively dreams and even interpreted during the dreams" (diary entry of 24 March 1912, my translation).[23] After reading *The Interpretation of Dreams* Schnitzler began to record significantly more of his own dreams in his diary, and starting in 1904 he occasionally added interpretations. In a diary entry of 20 May 1904, for example, he writes: "(Taormina. Olga had awakened me on account of a stinging beast, which we couldn't find.) Thereupon I dreamed that a mosquito stings me in Tunis. O. dreams of a helmet of Cesare Borgia's that radiates with a thousand points" (my translation).

In 1908 he began to add what he called "Deutungen" ("interpretations"). As previously, these mainly consist of giving the real-life sources for dream motifs. In isolated instances, he gives classic Freudian interpretations or commentaries on what the Freudian interpretation would be.[24] It is obvious that he was well acquainted with and perfectly capable of giving Freudian interpretations. When Theodor Reik published his book *Arthur Schnitzler als Psycholog* in 1913, which includes a chapter analyzing the literary dreams in *Der Schleier der Beatrice*, "Frau Berta Garlan," and *Der Weg ins Freie*, Schnitzler read it with lively interest.[25] The year before he had interpreted Georg's dream in *Der Weg ins Freie* together with Reik.[26] It is clear that at this point at the very latest, Schnitzler could no longer have written "innocent" literary dreams.

Schnitzler was far from being an uncritical proponent of Freudian dream interpretation. Critics have stressed his disagreements with the

Freudian school.[27] In particular he took issue with Freudian symbolism. He wrote in an undated note:

> Particularly in the interpretation of dreams [psychoanalysis] often proceeds arbitrarily, above all in its overestimation and generalization of the so-called dream symbols. It identified certain things and forms once and for all as dream symbols, and when you ask it for the reasons, it answers that the meaning of these symbols simply followed from the interpretation of dreams. Perfect example of a circulus vituosus. Simple to prove that symbols, as for example stick, tree, etc., suitcase, box, etc., could just as well be interpreted as death symbols, instead of as sexual symbols.[28]

But the obvious traces of the influence of Freudian theory on Schnitzler's own thinking should not be ignored. Thus Schnitzler did not deny that dream symbolism of some kind exists. On 6 March 1919 he wrote of one of his own dreams, "Sometimes the dream god doesn't give himself too much trouble with his symbolism" (my translation). He found his own symbolic interpretations for his dreams. An example:

> Dream: An airship in the room, but still so far away that I ask someone next to me for a telescope. I see how the balloon bumps against the ceiling and regret that it can't get through. (Symbol for problems with work.) (Diary entry of 8 April 1919, my translation)

It should furthermore be stressed that disagreements with the Freudian school would not necessarily prevent Schnitzler from using Freudian insights in constructing his own literary dreams. Correct or not, Freudian theory offered an increasingly widely known set of techniques for dream interpretation. An author who constructs literary dreams according to Freud's precepts has an automatic means for communicating with the reader through Freud's intertext. It seems probable that Schnitzler took advantage of this means of communication. Schnitzler began to include distorted dreams in his literary works only after he had read *The Interpretation of Dreams*,[29] and these dreams certainly all admit of Freudian interpretation.[30] The first one appeared in "Frau Berta Garlan," a novella Schnitzler was working on while he was reading *The Interpretation of Dreams*. Agreeing with Michaela L. Perlmann, I would argue that, here, Schnitzler made a first attempt at constructing an interpretable dream.[31] Reik certainly gives it an extensive Freudian interpretation in his book *Arthur Schnitzler als Psycholog*. Other distorted dreams follow in *Der Weg ins Freie*, "Casanovas Heimfahrt," "Fräulein Else," *Traumnovelle*, "Flucht in die Finsternis," and "The Second." A salient feature of these literary dreams is that they in no way echo or draw on Schnitzler's own dreams, at least not the ones he recorded in his diary, with the possible exception of the dreamlike events in *Traumnovelle*. In contrast, it is striking to what extent Schnitzler's dreams draw on his stories.[32] Many of Schnitzler's "interpretations" consist in identifying the literary sources of his dream. The independence of these literary dreams from Schnitzler's own dreams, where Schnitzler's stories themselves frequently draw on autobiographical sources, supports the hypothesis that Schnitzler constructed them as Freudian or quasi-Freudian dreams, dreams that were meant to invite attempts at interpretation.

Narrative as Dream: Schnitzler's "The Second"

In the three novellas "Casanovas Heimfahrt" (1918), *Traumnovelle* (1925–26) and "The Second" (1932) Schnitzler developed a particularly innovative and interesting technique for incorporating the Freudian dream into narrative. Instead of merely creating Freudian *dreams*, he used the principles of Freudian dream work to construct part of the main plot, so that fictional reality embodies features of the Freudian dream. In each story there is a dream and, in addition, a mirroring dreamlike portion of the plot. The effect is to fuse the new Freudian dream theory with the old life-is-a-dream idea, with a questioning of the boundary between dream and reality. In the renowned *Traumnovelle*, for example, Schnitzler poses the question of what is dream and what is life so effectively that critics disagree as to whether Fridolin's nocturnal adventures are a dream or not.[33] These adventures mirror the orgiastic dream Fridolin's wife has the same night: certain motifs uncannily appear in both the husband's adventures and the wife's dream but nowhere else, and both the dream and the adventures incorporate the same classic Freudian principles of wish fulfillment and reference to events of the previous day. Schnitzler devised a reality, a plot, that is dreamlike, or as Dorrit Cohn aptly puts it in her study of this novella, "the dream invades a realistic fictional world."[34]

Here I shall discuss "The Second," the latest of the three stories. It has been neglected by critics, but it is the work where, in my opinion, Schnitzler perfected the technique of juxtaposing dreamlike fiction with fictional dream.

"The Second" is one of the pieces that Schnitzler worked on slowly and intermittently, with many revisions, in the years before his death. The idea for the plot goes back to 1911, but Schnitzler actually began writing the story in 1927. The posthumously published version is the last completed one. According to his diary we know that he was still dissatisfied with it and was still tinkering with it when he died.[35] The tale hauntingly echoes old themes and techniques. Schnitzler takes us back to the prewar world of the duel, and the themes are Schnitzlerian classics: love, death, and the dream. He uses techniques that go back to his beginnings as a writer, techniques he developed in the 1890s: plots based in an underlying geometrical design, such as opposite spaces (as in "The Dead Are Silent" and the "Schleier" stories); symmetry, often bound up with sudden reversal (as in the "Schleier" stories, *Der tapfere Kassian* [*The Gallant Cassian*]); flashy effects like eerie repetition (e.g., the return of the dead in stories like "Flowers," "The Dead Are Silent," "Die Nächste," the "Schleier" stories); the playful questioning of the boundaries beween art and life, play and reality, dream and waking by using frames, where the distinction between the frame and what is within the frame collapses.

The plot of "The Second," already sketched out in the plan for the novella of 1911, is based, like so many of Schnitzler's other plots, on a clash between two realities. The title figure and narrator Eissler cannot bring himself to carry out his self-imposed task of telling Eduard Loiberger's pretty young wife Agathe the news that her husband died in a duel. As soon as he enters the tranquil, sunny garden of the Loibergers' villa in the vacation resort Ischl, the news appears so unreal and grotesque to the narrator that he is tempted to turn back:

> Suddenly I felt that what I had before me for the next minutes was so grotesque, so unbearable, so unfeasible, that I felt myself severely tempted *to turn around* before anyone saw me, to simply run away. (IR 205, my italics)

> [Plötzlich empfand ich, was mir für die nächsten Minuten bevorstand, als so grotesk, so unerträglich, so undurchführbar, daß ich mich ernsthaft versucht fühlte, *umzukehren*, noch ehe mich jemand erblickt, ja einfach davonzulaufen. (EW 6:261, my italics)]

The cause of the duel—Loiberger's affair with his challenger's wife—doubtless makes it doubly difficult for Eissler to tell the news. The clash between the carefree holiday atmosphere of the villa and the extraordinary situation of death, with sexual intrigue lurking behind it, is highlighted by contrasting spaces. This is one of Schnitzler's standard devices. Here the bright daylight outside the villa, associated with the possibility of telling the news, stands in stark contrast with the dark interior, where Eissler's words will fail him utterly. As is usual in Schnitzler's stories, we are to imagine reality as seen through the main character's focus. Thus the contrast between light and dark is largely an apparent one, the difficulty one has in adjusting one's eyes when passing from bright sunlight into an unlit interior. It represents the difficulty Eissler feels in adjusting the news to the present setting.

This is the groundwork on which the plot of the story, a scandalous impropriety, is based. Once he has entered the inner sanctum of the house, Eissler not only fails to announce the news of Loiberger's death, but starts an affair with the dead man's wife. A double transgression, then: the hero not only shirks his unpleasant duty but is sucked into the spell of the place, which holds memories of a past flirtation, and makes love to Agathe after accepting her dinner invitation. The seduction takes place in Agathe's boudoir. Thus there are three places in the story: the place of the unreal and shocking death (outside), the place of placid everyday life (inside), and the place of the illicit love affair (boudoir).

In the boudoir episode the protagonist appears to have transgressed another boundary: he crosses another threshold, enters another room, goes from normal social interaction into an illicit sexual relationship. In fact, however, this act is both spatially and conceptually *between* the two previous realities. We are to imagine the boudoir as located between the inside and the outside. Whereas the inside is in "deep shadows," in the boudoir the window is open, curtains flutter, presumably causing light and shade to alternate as they do so, and "garden and air shimmered through with blurred colors" (IR 208). Eissler's actions are likewise uneasily situated between the inside and outside worlds. This story is dominated by the theme of repetition and seconding, a theme that begins with the title and the title figure, "the second." Here in the boudoir, although Eissler fails to introduce the events that took place outside into the interior by giving a verbal account of them, he reenacts or repeats them with his deeds. As Loiberger's second he "seconds" Loiberger in the sense of committing adultery (the reason for the duel) and thereby taking on a rival, at least in Agathe's affections, namely Loiberger himself. He also "seconds" Loiberger in the sense of making love to Loiberger's wife. Yet what he does is at the same time in a continuum with the "everyday" world of inside: he is alone with the mistress of the house, who had made tentative advances to him the summer before. Thus, whereas at first estimation Eissler's actions represent deepening transgression, on closer inspection they appear as an odd compounding of the repetition of recent events and the realization of unconscious or semiconscious desires, so that the entire boudoir scene presents itself as a curious mélange of elements from the two incompatible realities of inside and outside and thus as a form of mediation between them.

After making love to Agathe, Eissler falls asleep and dreams. Of all the dreams in Schnitzler's literary work, this is the one that most invites Freudian interpretation.[36] The plot is fantastic and disjointed. The dream overtly uses Freudian techniques: references to recent material (the duel and the seduction), the representation of external sensory stimuli (the fluttering curtains in the room reappear in disguised form), reversal (Loiberger kills the man who shot him), and even a dream within the dream (Eissler believes he is awake at one point, and is aware that his dream is a dream). Above all, the dream fulfills the dreamer's wishes: it reflects Eissler's desire to continue his affair with Agathe; his desire that she not find out the news of her husband's death; and his desire to go unpunished for having seduced her. If the boudoir scene represents a second transgression and at the same time mediates between the reality of the duel with its tragic denouement and the everyday reality of the holiday resort, the dream, proceeding to a yet more outrageous level of wish fulfillment, itself mediates between the yet more incompatible realities of Loiberger's death and Eissler's seduction of his wife.

One is tempted to say that Eissler's only way out of his dilemma at this point is to fall asleep and dream. As in Hofmannsthal, Beer-Hofmann, and Freud, the dream here functions as a boundary-crossing device, which momentarily effaces the barrier between two irreconcilable states. In its general drift the dream becomes increasingly nightmarish. Eissler's fear crystallizes in the figure of Loiberger, who represents a double threat because he is dead (Agathe must not find this out) and because he is alive (Eissler resurrects his rival for the purpose of self-punishment). Yet this nightmarish tendency is counterbalanced by a string of wish fulfillments. Eissler continues his affair with Agathe: the dream opens with him lying at her side on a meadow, taking the place he remembers her husband occupying at a recent party. The news of Loiberger's death literally pursues the couple in the form of a man with a telegram as they rush off in a train, but it does not catch them. When

Loiberger turns up in person, Eissler wishes himself out of the picture ("I am no longer there at all," IR 211).

Twice, the wish fulfillments take the form of reversals. Reversal is a Freudian technique that Schnitzler mentions specifically in his notes on psychoanalysis.[37] Freud writes of reversals ("Umkehrungen") that they express the idea, "If only it had been the other way round!"[38] In this dream, we hear that Loiberger shot the cavalry captain (in fact, the cavalry captain shot Loiberger). This reversal presumably appeals to Eissler because it brings Loiberger back to life (thereby solving the problem of telling Agathe her husband is dead) and because it lets the adulterer (with whom Eissler identifies) kill the offended husband. A second reversal fulfills Eissler's wish to go unpunished: in the further course of the dream it proves that Eissler killed Loiberger ("So you are having breakfast with the gentleman who shot me," says Loiberger to Agathe).[39]

The dream ends with Eissler's drowning, or, more exactly, his sinking repeatedly into the lake, having been pushed in by Loiberger, but repeatedly surfacing. Dreams of diving into the water are birth dreams, according to Freud. Schnitzler particularly disagreed with this Freudian interpretation, however.[40] The most obvious interpretation of the sinking and surfacing is that it represents waking up, or gradually passing from sleep to wakefulness. Yet Schnitzler may have wished to suggest the Freudian interpretation also. Disagreeing with an aspect of Freud's theory would not have prevented his using a widely known symbol to communicate with the reader. The episode is overtly about life and death, for which waking and sleeping often figure as a metaphor. An earlier version of the dream, which ends in a wish for death and with the protagonist's drowning together with Agathe, supports the interpretation that Schnitzler had the connotation of death and rebirth in mind.[41] Finally, the back-and-forth motion of going under and surfacing is a *mise en abîme* for the dream's own see-sawing mode of marrying harsh truth to wishful fantasy. It underscores the mediating function of the dream, the theme of the possibility of compromise and hence transition between two irreconcilable realities.

The interpretation of the dream as a Freudian dream with wish fulfillment and reversal suggests a new interpretation of the immediately preceding episode. If we look back on the boudoir scene from the perspective of the dream, that entire scene might be interpreted as a dream, albeit an undistorted dream, involving wish fulfillment and reversal. In the boudoir scene the semiconscious wishes of the hero are fulfilled (Eissler had felt an attraction to Agathe at past social events). Moreover,

Eissler's "seconding" in the boudoir fulfills the wish of a second, a young man repeatedly on the peripheries of other people's adventures, to assume the role of hero. He repeats the action of Loiberger, seducing another man's wife, and thereby does to Loiberger what Loiberger did to another man. But he reverses roles in such a way as to make himself ultimately the winner (his *dead* rival can take no revenge). The hero's reflection as he stands in Agathe's garden, unwilling to enter the villa, "Ich fühlte mich ernsthaft versucht, umzukehren" ("I felt myself severely tempted to turn around"), now takes on a new meaning.

It is as though, in this entire boudoir episode, the dream had invaded and taken over a part of the real plot. This portion of the narrative, which stands between waking reality and the dream proper, which contains the *unerhörte Begebenheit* or transgressive wish fulfillment, which on first reading appears as a continuation of waking reality and in retrospect as a dream, which is located in a third space *between* the sunlit outdoors and the dark interior of the house, might be seen as an intentionally indeterminate, undecidable segment of the narrative, a segment whose function it is to hesitate between two interpretations.

Schnitzler is extremely inventive and playful with the repetition effects in the story. The boudoir scene itself is dominated by a repeating motif that itself takes the form of repeated motion, the motif of the fluttering curtains. The back-and-forth motion of the curtains suggests sleepiness, indeed a trance. Their rhythmic swaying seems to exert a hypnotic effect on the hero. In conformity with the boudoir scene's "normal" appearance at the beginning, Eissler perceives the dreamily moving curtains, as they flutter lightly during his dinner with Agathe, as *not* dreamlike: "I perceived . . . the gentle fluttering of the curtains, the silent appearance and departure of the servant in no way as a dream [keineswegs als traumhaft]" (IR 209). But when he awakens from his dream, the first things he notices are the curtains, much as if they were a hypnotic object under whose spell he had fallen: "The curtains were blowing more in the summer breeze" (IR 212).

The curtains, or rather their back-and-forth motion, recur throughout the boudoir scene and the dream. Repetition is thus doubled over on itself in this motif. The curtains' movement is echoed by the activity of the servant who serves the meal: "The servant . . . came in and out" (IR 208). Flapping curtains twice reappear in the dream, and the dream's final episode, where Eissler repeatedly goes under and surfaces in the lake, repeats the same motion.

Just as the episode of drowning and surfacing in the dream symbolized the transition between incompatible realities, between sleep and waking, between life and death, the fluttering curtains may be regarded as a symbol for the undecided status of the boudoir scene as a whole and for the interest in transitions that is characteristic of this part of the narrative. The insistently repeated back-and-forth motif suggests suspended, dreamlike, nonlinear time, which complements the "between" spatiality of the place and contrasts sharply with the resumption of linear temporality signaled by the auditory motif of steps crunching on gravel (we imagine hearing them come closer and closer) after the narrator wakes up, when he has "too few seconds" to tell the news.

From the central nucleus of the boudoir scene the see-saw effect, which subtly but insistently poses the question of what is reality and what is dream, ripples out over the narrative as a whole. Schnitzler teases the reader by persistently questioning what is dream and what is life. Thus from the standpoint of the boudoir adventure the narrative frame—the story of duel and death—appears dreamlike to Eissler. When he awakens out of his dream, he recollects that the other second, Mülling, was to visit him in the hotel that afternoon, and he wonders, "Was this still a dream? All of it perhaps? Even the duel? And Loiberger's death? Was it perhaps morning and I was sleeping—in my room in the hotel?" (IR 212).

Agathe, in contrast, upon awakening twice refers to the sexual encounter as a "dream" (IR 213). Little wonder—it is in her interest to deny that it ever happened.[42] The final sentences of the story echo the theme, reminding us that the narrator's central adventure is of indeterminate status. The narrator meets Agathe again many years later. She seems to remember nothing. The distance of the years and Agathe's innocent look conspire to make the narrator wonder whether he did not dream the whole adventure:

No one who saw us speaking together could have suspected that a strange, deep, common experience joined us together. Did it really join us together? I myself could have considered that strange and yet so happy hour in the quiet of summer a dream which I had dreamed alone; her look merged into mine so purely, so forgetfully, so guiltlessly. (IR 216)

[Niemand, der uns miteinander sprechen sah, hätte ahnen können, daß ein seltsames, tiefes, gemeinsames Erlebnis uns verband. Verband es uns wirklich? Ich selbst aber hätte jene sommerstille, unheimliche, und doch so glückliche Stunde für einen Traum halten können, den ich allein geträumt hatte; so klar, so erinnerungslos, so unschuldsvoll tauchte ihr Blick in den meinen. (EW 6:272)]

Schnitzler's masterly formulation, where the narrator's growing sense of the unreality of his memory is itself undercut by the subjunctive verb, places a permanent stamp of doubt on the episode.

In sum, these reflections remind us that all reality is profoundly subjective. What happens is not so important as the constructions we place on events. What is "real," what "illusion"? We chose to remember and to believe what suits us. Agathe could have had no interest in remembering that she had had an affair with a passing acquaintance the day her husband died.

The collective import of these repeated questionings, of the indeterminateness that the narrative tries to establish in the boudoir scene, and of the back-and-forth motif in its various permutations is, most broadly, to suggest to the reader that there is no fundamental difference between dream and life. Life is a dream, a dream is life—this is an insight that Schnitzler gained from the popular literary dream motif of the 1890s. In his own contemporaneous version of the idea, in which one can see traces of Machian monism, Grillparzer's identification of the dream with desire, and his own fascination with hypnosis and somnambulism, both dreams and life are reducible to the subject's momentary perception of things and to the psychic laws that govern this perception. Hence Schnitzler's ultimate purpose behind the artful blurring of the boundary between dream and reality in "The Second" seems to have been to put the new Freudian theory of dreams, which had meanwhile gained wide credence, at the service of his old and tenaciously held insight that there is finally little difference between subjective reality and the subject's dreams. Both are shaped by the same desires, the same interests, the same psychological mechanisms.

Schnitzler may not have been the first writer to appropriate Freudian dream mechanisms for narrative. One can suspect Kafka of having had the same idea earlier. Kafka, writing in the period when the reception of Freudian ideas was beginning to become widespread, takes the same strategy of using dream techniques to construct narrative much further. "The Metamorphosis" (1915) and The Trial (1914) have dreamlike elements, while "A Country Doctor" (1917) in particular lends itself to interpretation through Freudian dream theory.[43]

There are three significant differences between Schnitzler's and Kafka's use of dreams. First, the distinction between dream and reality, the delight in playing with and transgressing this boundary, the aspect of paradox, the art of illusion—in short the turn-of-the-century concerns—prominent in Schnitzler, are entirely absent from Kafka. Kafka conflates dream and narrative wholly: He does not acknowledge his dream techniques as such and even denies them—"It was no dream," he writes in "The Metamorphosis." He thereby eschews all traditional dream connotations, including the life-is-a-dream idea.

Second, it is not at all clear that Kafka used Freudian techniques intentionally. Could it not be, rather, that the presence of dreamlike elements in his works testifies to his success in achieving his stated goal, the "portrayal of my dreamlike inner life"?[44] It is always a moot point, when Freudian elements appear in a post-Freudian work of literature, whether the writer borrowed from Freud, or whether a "textual unconscious," which Freudian analysis could illuminate, comes into play: that is, whether the text implements Freud's theories or tends rather to substantiate them.

In Schnitzler's case there is every reason to believe that he was consciously using a technique and not that the text is mysteriously revelatory of unconscious processes. For Schnitzler knew Freud's theories well. Before "The Second" he had written a number of literary Freudian dreams. "The Second" was hardly a spontaneous birth but, rather, went through a number of versions, which reveal a high level of conscious construction. Finally, Schnitzler uses very similar techniques in the two other novellas "Casanovas Heimfahrt" and *Traumnovelle*. The central section of the plot in "Casanovas Heimfahrt" is so close to "The Second" that the later novella seems like a recasting in a preexisting mold. Like Eissler, Casanova repeats the actions of his rival, but in reverse, with himself victorious. As in "The Second," this repetition with reversal ends with sex under false pretenses, and the seduction ebbs into an extensive, psychologically realistic dream.

Third and finally, unlike Kafka, Schnitzler is not primarily interested in dream distortion, in applying this aspect of Freud's theory to narrative. Kafka's texts are not only full of the implausible turns of event and illogical jumps characteristic of dreams, but they employ devices that approximate the particulars of Freudian dream work. Thus we find composite formations (for example, the court in *The Trial* is simultaneously a tenement), displacement of affect (e.g., Gregor reacts inappropriately to being turned into a bug), and symbolization (blooming, defloration, and decay are evoked by the servant girl Rosa and the sick boy's roselike wound in "A Country Doctor"). Many critics call attention to Kafka's literalization of metaphors, a device first identified by Günther Anders. Anders's examples include Gregor's transmogrification in "The Metamorphosis" as a literalization of the metaphor "dreckiger Käfer" (dirty bug); the penal machine in "In the Penal Colony" as a literalization of the phrase "am eignen Leibe etwas erfahren" (to experience something oneself, "on one's own body"); and K.'s move into a schoolhouse in *The Castle* as a literalization of "er muß zur Schule gehen" (he has to learn a lesson: he must "go to school").[45]

Schnitzler, in contrast, is attracted to two of the most basic principles of the Freudian dream, wish fulfillment and the repetition of material from recent lived experience. Schnitzler believed that these were the fundamental principles of dreams long before he read *The Interpretation of Dreams*, as one of his earliest dream texts, *Alkandi's Lied* (1889), in which he employs precisely these techniques, attests. Reversal is an arresting strategy that fuses wish fulfillment and repetition: what is repeated is turned around so that it is in accordance with one's wishes. Schnitzler had used reversal as a device before in narratives that were thematically not connected to the dream (e.g., *Der tapfere Kassian* [*The Gallant Cassian*]) or in a way that did not directly engage the dream (in "Casanovas Heimfahrt"). But here the closeness to a device he uses in the dream itself strongly suggests that he wished to experiment with Freud's "Umkehrung" as a strategy in narrative.

Not an uncritical devotee of Freud's theories, Schnitzler preferred precisely those features of the Freudian dream that allowed him to adapt Freudian theory to his own insights. In privileging wish fulfillment and repetition, Schnitzler reaffirms that the fundamental principles of the dream are the fundamental motivating forces behind human behavior generally. Dreams repeat, or rather reconstitute, the dreamer's lived experiences and at the same time fulfill wishes. When the eponymous hero of Peter Handke's 1968 play *Kaspar* stumbles on stage, still innocent of all acquired language, he can nevertheless utter the single sentence, "I want to be a person like somebody else once was."[46] Schnitzler likewise suggests in "The Second" that desire, and imitation or repetition, are at the basis of all human behavior.

Wolle die Wandlung. O sei für die Flamme begeistert,
drin sich ein Ding dir entzieht, das mit Verwandlungen prunkt;
jener entwerfende Geist, welcher das Irdische meistert,
liebt in dem Schwung der Figur nichts wie den wendenden Punkt.
—Rilke, Sonnet to Orpheus II/12

NOTHING IS AS IT APPEARS to be, and nothing is unchanging: the Baroque theme of *vanitas*, of the illusory nature of appearances and the mutability of earthly things, reemerges as a principal theme of the Austrian turn of the century.

Albeit in a wholly secular version: reality and permanence no longer figure as attributes of a transcendent realm, but vanish along with that realm. Preoccupied with changing times and convinced that the individual is not self-identical, the Austrian writers saw the traditional categorizations of fiction versus reality or truth versus lying, which imply a stable stratum ("reality," "truth"), as simplistic. At the end of a century during which a sense of the stability of the external world was undermined by the rapid changes of industrial society, "reality" was interiorized, attributed to the psychological subject. The Jung-Wien group, following Hermann Bahr's lead, oriented itself toward France, where the rise of the study of psychology and the advent of psychological fiction testified to the interest in private worlds. Where "reality" becomes a product of individual or collective belief rather than of objective fact, however, it is readily reducible to its opposite, illusion. Permanence is denied entirely, for what passes for real at a given moment is bound to change. Playing with the boundaries between reality and illusion and permanence and change is, in contrast to previous instances, ultimately aimed at disproving that they exist.

At precisely this point in the literature of the Austrian turn of the century we see a proximity to the philosophy of Ernst Mach. Much critical attention has been devoted to the influence of Mach on his literary contemporaries. Mach's monism, as expressed in his popular work *Beiträge zur Analyse der Empfindungen* (*Contributions to the Analysis of Sensations*) of 1886, included the ideas that individuals and things are only fictitious entities, expedients that help us orient ourselves in practical life; that the world in fact consists of sensations, or rather "elements"—a term that avoids any distinction between the psychic and the physical; and that behind these sensations or elements, there is nothing. Mach's work was probably not received in literary circles until close to or after the turn of the century.[1] Similar ideas were definitely present in the Viennese literature of the 1890s, however, particularly in Hermann Bahr's theoretical essays and in the literary works of Schnitzler and Hofmannsthal. Critics call attention to parallels between Mach's dictum that "the self is unsalvageable" and Hofmannsthal's debunking of the "I," and between Mach's skepticism about the distinction between truth and illusion and Schnitzler's breakdown of play or dream and reality.[2] What these critics fail to mention, however, is that these ideas have a much more probable source in the latest French psychological fiction. Bahr and his circle devoured such fiction from the late 1880s on.[3] Indeed, Bahr articulates such ideas as "sensations alone are truth . . . ; the self is always a construction" precisely in the context of a discussion of French psychological fiction, of Maurice Barrès, Edouard Rod, Huysmans, J. H. Rosny, in *Die Überwindung des Naturalismus* (1891; The overcoming of Naturalism).[4] Bahr cites Eduard von Hartmann as a philosophical source; another, who was an inescapable influence on the French novelists, might well have been Hippolyte Taine. In his major philosophical work *On Intelligence* (1870) Taine debunks the "I" for the same reasons and with just as much energy as Mach will in his *Beiträge zur Analyse der Empfindungen*:

> The Ego itself is but a verbal entity and a metaphysical phantom. . . .
> The one permanent substance, distinct from events, is seen to vanish and re-enter the region of words. All that remains of us are our events, sensations, images, recollections, ideas, resolutions: these are what constitute our being; and the analysis of our most elementary judgments shows, in fact, that our Self has no other elements. . . . Our successive events then are successive components of

ourselves. The Ego is in turn each of these events. At one moment, as was clearly seen by Condillac, it is nothing more than the sensation of taste, at a second moment, nothing more than suffering, at the third, nothing more than the recollection of the concert.[5]

Critics tend to discuss the similarity between Mach and a writer like Schnitzler in terms of the relocation of truth in subjectivity. Yet there is another similarity between these two writers that deserves mention: a consciousness of the role of convention in establishing meaning. We will see it in Schnitzler's *Green Cockatoo*, where the breakdown of the illusion/reality distinction coincides with the theme of historical change. In short, belief is not a purely subjective matter, but is dictated by convention (in Mach, the "self" is a convention, "objects" are conventions; in Schnitzler, the "truth" is a convention). Beliefs, and hence actions, are engendered by the assimilation of models. In the coincidence of the themes of fiction and reality and of change, consequently, we see the emergence, vis-à-vis a philosophy of depth, of a philosophy of coding, or the recognition of what Jean Baudrillard, writing in the 1970s, calls the generation of reality by models, found in a developed form in Musil's *Man without Qualities* and Wittgenstein's *Philosophical Investigations*.

Where phenomena are no longer perceived to be manifestations of underlying principles, but as replications of existing phenomena, we also see a new view of history: a decisive parting with the teleological Romantic view of history that persisted into the nineteenth century in favor of the belief, as Musil puts it in *The Man without Qualities*, that there is no reason in history. Historical events blindly follow patterns that arise through accident. Not surprisingly, insights about the fundamentally accidental nature of history became more intense and profuse when society entered a stage of obvious flux, that is, with World War I. The iron law of change became a theme of major writers in the wake of the world war, when the stability of the prewar "world of security," as Stefan Zweig called it in *Die Welt von Gestern* (1942), was shattered and swept away with that world itself. In the monumental *The Man without Qualities*, which he wrote from the early 1920s on, Musil dwells on the historical and contingent nature of distinctions conventionally regarded as hard and fast. What *seems* stable, what most people believe is "the way things are," is really an accident of history, an order that comes into being and coexists with other orders haphazardly and is always threatening to dissolve. Musil uniformly makes fun of human attempts to put chaos into order—into political, legal, and philosophical systems. Systems of philosophy, Musil writes, are "violence against the world."[6]

In a more constructive vein, the poets Rilke, Valéry, and Wallace Stevens envision artistic adequations for a constantly changing reality. Valéry's dancer symbolizes metamorphosis and unity in multiplicity; Rilke's Orpheus is a symbol of transformation and the unification of opposites; Stevens's poet figure the Canon Aspirin wills "the whole, the complicate, the amassing harmony" of abstract and concrete. These poets have their roots in symbolism. Their work extends the prewar ethos of art-for-art's sake and the cult of the artist, especially of the poet-visionary, into the postwar context. All entertained the notion of what Stevens called a "supreme fiction": a constructed, man-made world of the mind that approximates, comprehends, yet surpasses the real world.

Yet, even before World War I, the themes of the fragility of the real and of the necessity of changing with changing times were serious topics, particularly in Schnitzler's and Hofmannsthal's work. Schnitzler's work of the 1890s constantly shows how reality evaporates into fiction—and how fiction, on the other hand, blossoms into reality.[7] Transitoriness was Hofmannsthal's obsession: if in his poetry and lyrical dramas of the 1890s there is a theme, among all the brilliance and erudition of his allusions, that one could properly call his own, it is this one. An acute consciousness of change is a constant in his work. It is difficult to doubt that it was deeply and sincerely felt. Take this diary entry of November 1894: "Today there was snow in the barrack-square. Then it melted and was mud and a wind like in March. 'My spring,' I said to myself and was conscious almost to the point of tears of the transitoriness of life."[8] Not surprisingly for creative writers, the perception of the necessity for transformation is narcissistically bound up with a privileging of the figure of the artist as supreme master of transformations. In Schnitzler's dramas *The Green Cockatoo* and *Große Szene* the artist is represented by the actor, who incarnates transformative power, who can present fiction so persuasively that it appears real, and indeed *becomes* real by affecting the course of reality. In Hofmannsthal's *Der Rosenkavalier* and *Ariadne auf Naxos*, where the themes of change and of fiction versus reality intersect, Hofmannsthal too makes reference to the transformative power of the artist. My purpose in this chapter will be to examine in detail one example by each writer—Schnitzler's *Cockatoo* and Hofmannsthal's *Ariadne*—and then look at one postwar treatment of the theme, Kafka's.

Writing from the vantage point of a later time, Kafka bitterly constates that times change. But the transformative power of artists, their ability to suspend the boundary between reality and illusion and to make the imaginary real, their optimistic mastery of the situation as projected by Kafka's predecessors, is not affirmed, but parodied. Especially in the pair of stories "A Report to an Academy" and "A Hunger Artist," and also in the autobiographical document "Letter to His Father," art and the art of self-transformation appear as a mere strategy for survival, a testimony to the artist's dependencies.

Schnitzler's *The Green Cockatoo*

We find the theme of the disappearing boundary between fiction and reality principally in Schnitzler's works about artists, of which there are many. In his dramas and stories about actors, such as *Das Märchen* (1891), "Die kleine Komödie" (1893), "Komödiantinnen" (1893; Comediennes), *The Green Cockatoo* (1899), "Die Weissagung" (1902; "The Prophecy"), *Zum großen Wurstel* (1905), and *Große Szene* (1915), he tirelessly poses the question, Where does acting end and life begin? To take one example, in *Das Märchen* the actress Fanny, a "fallen woman," plays a fallen woman as her first stage role. People identify the actress with her role. But is she, as her detractors say, so successful at her role because she has had plenty of practice in life? Or does her brilliant success lead her more and more into the precarious life of an actress and hence toward becoming her role? Other stories probe, and attack, the boundary between other art forms and the real world. In "Mein Freund Ypsilon" (1887) we find a writer believing in his own fictions; in *Die Frau mit dem Dolche* (1902) a painting inspires a woman to change her life; in "Der letzte Brief eines Literaten" (1917) a writer seeks experiences merely to have something to write about.

It has been remarked that at the root of Schnitzler's work lies the intention of unmasking the belief in truth as an illusion.[9] As we have seen, Schnitzler's message whenever he employs the dream-versus-reality theme is that there is no difference between these so-called opposites; all is illusion; the only "reality" is the illusion in which we currently believe. The closely related art-versus-reality theme bears precisely the same message. Schnitzler would have us believe that the supposed imitativeness and hence secondariness of art is unfounded, for art exercises a power over the imagination of the beholder, and also over the artist, comparable to the force of actual circumstances. If life affects art, art also affects life. Schnitzler underscores the alliance of art and power, thereby giving the art-versus-reality theme a somewhat different slant from the dream-versus-reality theme. Perhaps the best example of this alliance is Konrad Herbot, the actor-hero of *Große Szene*. Herbot embodies to an exaggerated degree the personality of Henri, the star actor of the troupe of *The Green Cockatoo*, in his extraordinary gift for mixing fiction and reality. He also magnifies to the utmost Henri's power of persuading audiences of the reality of his fictions. Imaginative, mendacious, charismatic, a magician, he persuades his mistress's husband-to-be, his friend, of her innocence and simultaneously wins back his own alienated wife through the power of his words.

The Green Cockatoo is perhaps Schnitzler's most interesting exposition of the theme of the breakdown of the distinction between fiction and reality because, here, he juxtaposes it with the topic of historical change. The play is set against the background of the French Revolution. The play and the play within the play that we witness both take place on the evening of 14 July 1789, the day of the storming of the Bastille. Thus the key in which the events on stage are orchestrated is the truth that things change. To demonstrate how perishable social orders are, Schnitzler focuses on a turning point, the beginning of the revolution. The spectators of Schnitzler's drama, though not the aristocratic spectators of the play within the play, know from the start that the old, hierarchical society, with its strict boundaries between social classes, is about to be overthrown. The mob will rule as dictatorially over the aristocracy as the aristocracy ruled over it. Moreover, the aim of the revolution is to efface all differences. Thus the old order will be reversed, and at the same time, order itself will be demolished.

It is unthinkable that Schnitzler could have written a play like this without a knowledge of Romantic works that question the fiction/reality distinction, in particular Tieck's *Der gestiefelte Kater* (1797; *Puss in Boots*). *Der gestiefelte Kater* is in fact the probable model for Schnitzler's pyrotechnics in *The Green Cockatoo*, for both Tieck and Schnitzler employ the same device, the play within the play, in which the boundary between dramatic reality and the embedded fiction is constantly transgressed. In both works a naive fictive audience is the target of satire. Whereas the fin-de-siècle fiction-versus-reality theme differs from its Baroque model in an essential element—namely, the transcendent implications vanish—the differences between a play like *The Green Cock-*

atoo and a Romantic work like *Der gestiefelte Kater* are far less obvious. Yet there are two crucial shifts in emphasis.

The first is that in *Der gestiefelte Kater* the breaking of the illusion illustrates a poetological point, whereas in *The Green Cockatoo* the point is psychological. Tieck mocks the classic "poetic styles" and "the rules." The (low) fictive public is stupid precisely because it insists on them. In *The Green Cockatoo*, in contrast, Schnitzler mocks the group of decadent French aristocrats who comprise the fictive public because they insist in believing that the spectacle they are watching is an illusion. In fact, the "illusion" presented by the play within the play is not an illusion at all, for, as more than one critic has pointed out, the actors, who perform their play in revolutionary France, genuinely hate the aristocrats they feign to detest.[10]

The second shift is that the historical dimension of Schnitzler's work is completely absent from Tieck. Schnitzler questions all orderings as *historically* contingent, an idea not present in *Der gestiefelte Kater*.

The historical aspect of Schnitzler's play has not commanded much critical attention, and such commentary as exists is unsatisfactory.[11] In the dearth of extratextual evidence to explain why Schnitzler decided to write a play about the French Revolution, it seems likeliest that Schnitzler chose this setting for the same reason that he chose the fall of Bologna as a backdrop for *Der Schleier der Beatrice*, namely, to explore the question of the boundary line on a further, historical level.[12] The historical dimension widens the play's psychological focus and places Schnitzler's argument on a broader epistemological base. That is, Schnitzler appears to be proposing that perception is not just a function of individual subjectivity, but is also ruled by collective belief, or convention. By setting his play against the background of Bastille Day, Schnitzler calls our foreground/background perception into question. The "permanent" social order is not, as we are apt to think, the "background" for the drama of our lives. For social permanence, as the revolution shows, is only relative. Our perception of the social order as an immutable "background" is just a convention of thought. "Background" and "foreground" dissolve into conventions standing side by side. The final scene of *The Green Cockatoo* illustrates this point. The background, the revolution, telescopes into the foreground when a real act of revolutionary violence is performed on stage. Background becomes foreground, and the reverse.[13]

Against the "background" of a historical turning point, then, Schnitzler sets a theater, with the purpose of examining the boundary between play and reality. The play is set in a tavern, the "Green Cockatoo." Actors representing criminals stage skits amid aristocratic patrons so as to give their jaded spectators the momentary illusion that they are really in a den of robbers, murderers, and prostitutes. The aesthetic style of the performance, in keeping with the eighteenth-century setting, is *trompe l'oeil*: the audience derives pleasure from being fooled for a moment, from feeling "a delicious shivery sensation" (OAP 221), without, however, experiencing any substantial or lasting confusion over what is what. But in fact, and this is Schnitzler's point, the distinctions between the actors, the roles they play, and the audience are not at all clear-cut. Differences between play and reality, actors and audience, criminals and the nobility do exist, but the identities are not absolute; the boundaries can be crossed or subverted. Thus an actor who plays a pickpocket is arrested outside the theater for picking a pocket; a genuine criminal becomes an actor at the "Green Cockatoo"; a noblewoman is basically a whore, and so forth.

The most brilliant aspect of the play is the dramatic buildup. Schnitzler progressively collapses the distinctions between seemingly ever more absolute contraries by letting the distinction between fiction and reality blur in the vision of characters who represent ever-higher levels of sophistication. We can distinguish three stages. In the first Schnitzler satirizes the blindness of the aristocracy, which affects to know the difference between play and reality but does not realize that it is on the eve of its own destruction. As already indicated, a gap in awareness yawns between the fictional and the real audiences: the real audience has the temporal advantage of knowing that the Bastille will be stormed and that the revolution will take place. The satire unfolds gradually. We are introduced to a variety of characters, such as the naive young nobleman from the provinces, Albin Chevalier de la Tremouille, who cannot tell the difference between play and reality and thinks he is really in a dangerous underworld haunt (later this will prove to be the most sophisticated attitude); François Vicomte von Nogeant, who is absolutely sure what is play and what reality, but then mistakes reality for play; and the marquise Séverine, a complete decadent who cares only about excitement and finds that the best spectacle is taking place on the streets.

In the second stage, Prospère, the director of the show at the "Green Cockatoo," loses his ability to tell what is fiction and what reality. With him, so do we. The most astute character in Schnitzler's drama, the director occupies the same level of sophistication as the audience. His macabre allusions to his noble guests' imminent deaths show that he uncannily anticipates not just the revolution but the Terror. The moment when Prospère loses his ability to distinguish between fiction and reality is the moment when the ironic gap that separated his (and our) level of knowledge from that of the nobility vanishes, and when the audience's authority collapses. That moment comes near the end of the play, during the star actor Henri's stage performance. In this stage performance Henri creates a fiction that, as both Prospère and the audience know, bears all the marks of being a real story.

The moment at which Prospère mistakes Henri's fiction for reality is the moment of the triumph of art. Here Schnitzler demonstrates the artist's power to present fiction so persuasively that it appears real. Indeed, fiction in this play *is* real, in the sense that the actual crime of passion follows on the heels of its artistic representation.

The same kind of anticipation of reality fills the entire play in the play. Of the five different skits performed prior to Henri's entrance, only one does not involve crimes perpetrated by commoners against the aristocracy. The play thus transgresses a boundary that has not yet been transgressed in reality: it goes a bit further than historical reality, by anticipating the revolution.

Schnitzler thus questions the traditional, imitative relationship of art to life. Implicitly he does so in the name of a recognition of the indifferent origin of triggering events. Actions engender actions in a process that manifests little reason or order. It makes no difference whether the originating action is real or fictional. Schnitzler turns this insight to the advantage of art.

In the third stage, the boundary between fiction and reality breaks down not merely in the eyes of particular spectators, but in actuality. When Henri murders Cadignan in the tavern, and a revolutionary sympathizer responds by shouting, "He who kills a Duke is the friend of the people—hurrah for liberty!" (OAP 225), play and reality, inside and outside, the world of the stage and the revolution in the streets, collapse into one.

Hofmannsthal's *Ariadne auf Naxos*

Change is Hofmannsthal's most persistent and haunting theme. Yet it is a subject on which he remained truly divided. We have seen in the example of *Electra* how a commitment to remembrance and fidelity on the one hand, and a conviction that things must change on the other, pulled him with seemingly equal strength in two directions. Throughout his work he struggled to find an acceptable compromise between these two positions, or his own version of Goethe's "Dauer im Wechsel" ("permanence in change"). The formulation he finally arrived at in *Ad me ipsum* involves placing permanence and change in temporal sequence—thereby seemingly giving the edge to change—as "preexistence" and "existence," or, as he writes, "Varied basic theme: the self as being and the self as becoming."[14] "Preexistence" gives the illusion of eternity. The youth is lifted out of time; in his state of magical dominance over the universe, he *is*, in a sense, the universe. But "preexistence" must end so that "existence," or true human life, may begin. For to be human is to exist in time, to change. "Existence" involves making choices, accepting certain possibilities and relinquishing others, and recognizing one's own mortality. Stability enters this version of change, making it a compromise formulation in itself: recognizing one's mortality goes hand in hand with marriage and having children. This ethos of "existence" is articulated in particularly decided terms in the two operas Hofmannsthal wrote after beginning *Ad me ipsum*, *Die Frau ohne Schatten* (1919; *The Woman without a Shadow*) and *Die ägyptische Helena* (1923–26; *Helena in Egypt*). In *Die Frau ohne Schatten* the fairy empress faces the challenge of becoming human by becoming mortal, that is, a temporal being. In *Die ägyptische Helena* the sorceress Aithra gives Menelas a forgetfulness potion so that he can forget the Trojan War and love a rejuvenated Helena, but the repressed returns: Menelas starts to repeat the "forgotten" past. The moral is that to be human means to live one's life in time.

Play after play draws its strength from the tension between the opposites of permanence and change. From work to work, Hofmannsthal oscillated in according preference now to change, now to permanence. In *Der Rosenkavalier* the balance is weighted in favor of change: the Marschallin, the wisest and most appealing character in the opera, observes, "You have to be light: / with a light heart and light hands, / holding and taking, holding and leaving . . . / Life punishes those that are not so, and God takes no mercy on them."[15] Yet "no genuine life is possible without a belief in eternity"—this sentence from a note in *Ad me ipsum* shows that Hofmannsthal's real attachment was to stability and permanence.[16] In his works transitoriness is always regretted; in his later works it is regretted more and more; and the dictum "it must change" is increasingly weighted with poignance. At heart, Hofmannsthal was always the conservative he eventually became. Traditions were always important to him: a connoisseur of the past as a youth, he became a proponent of marriage and family as a man and of a conservative political order after the war, where he envisioned Catholic Austria playing a guiding role in cultural restoration.

One of Hofmannsthal's strongest visions of the artist involved the unification, in this single figure, of permanence and change. In his several poems on the deaths of actors, written from 1897 to 1910, he pays tribute to the actor's power of transformation.[17] Thus in "Zum Gedächtnis des Schauspielers Mitterwurzer" (1897; "To the Memory of the Actor Mitterwurzer"), Hofmannsthal calls Mitterwurzer "the magician" and asks rhetorically, "But who was he, and who was he not?" Hofmannsthal attributed to the poet the power of *mirroring* the world. In this eulogy, the same power is ascribed to Mitterwurzer: "In his eyes our dreams flew / Past, as if the mirror image in deep water / Of flocks of wild birds. . . . / Thus there was in him the voice of all of life: / He became vast." In "Auf den Tod des Schauspielers Hermann Müller" (1899; On the death of the actor Hermann Müller), Hofmannsthal similarly praises Müller for his powers of transformation: "His body was so gifted / In transforming itself that it seemed no net / Would be able to catch him! What a creature!" And finally, in "Verse zum Gedächtnis des Schauspielers Josef Kainz" (1910; Verses to the memory of the actor Josef Kainz), Hofmannsthal apostrophizes Kainz as "one untransformed in many transformations, / A never bewitched bewitcher."[18] We find exactly the same idea in Bahr's discussion of the actor in his *Dialog vom Tragischen* of 1904, a work that, as we saw in our discussion of *Electra* in chapter 2, contains several close parallels to Hofmannsthal's contemporaneous ideas. Bahr's discussion is interesting mainly because he fleshes out philosophically the idea of the actor as master of transformations, connecting it to Mach's dictum of "the unsalvageable self" and to Nietzsche's debunking of selfhood. According to Bahr, the actor's powers of transformation are fascinating because they epitomize the "mystery of transformation" that informs all human existence: "Not the poet, not his play moved me, but the immense riddle of human transformation. . . . Whoever was once struck by it can never, I think, really get over it. Actors seem like magicians to him; he is almost afraid of them and yet can't get away from them; he almost has a horror of people who can change and interchange themselves, and yet they magically attract him, because he has a presentiment that the same marvel rules deep within himself."[19]

In the opera *Der Rosenkavalier* Hofmannsthal returns to the idea of the transformative power of the artist. Here the boorish Baron Ochs auf Lerchenau insists that by marrying Sophie, the daughter of a recently ennobled bourgeois, *he* will not change at all: "Man"—by which he means "Mann"—"bleibt doch schließlich, was man ist!" ("After all, a man remains what he is!").[20] He pigheadedly refuses to recognize that the social order changes and that, for the financial reasons that already affect his own nuptial choice, marriages between the nobility and the bourgeoisie will become commonplace. Yet belying his insistence that he is always himself, a gap yawns between his narcissistically swollen seeming (to be of the nobility) and his being (a boor). The theme of stability versus transitoriness, the message that things are mutable, opens readily into the theme of being versus seeming and the idea that appearances are not necessarily reality. The baron with his pretensions and hypocrisy is finally vanquished through a play within a play. This masquerade presents a patent fiction and hence uses the baron's own weapon, false seeming, but consciously. It is performed at an inn to which the baron has invited the servant-girl Mariandl—in fact his bride's lover Octavian in disguise—in order to seduce her. The baron is dumbfounded by the appearance of another woman (an actress) claiming to be his wife. When a literalistic policeman arrives he tries to lie his way out of an awkward situation, only to get himself ever deeper into trouble.

The play in the play shows up the truth: that Ochs is a fool, a liar, a hypocrite, and a lecher. Appearances *are* deceptive, the play within the play shows us: Ochs loses his identity, and hence his baronial authority, with his wig, which mysteriously vanishes when the policeman enters, while the compromising circumstances in which Ochs finds himself speak for themselves. At the same time the play shows, on its own example, the power of appearances. Ochs is unmasked, dewigged, by the actors, who contrive a pretense that is more persuasive than his own. They even succeed in pinning bigamy on him, of which he is *not* guilty. Hence the play in the play mirrors the theme of the divergence of appearance and reality found in the main plot. At the same time it asserts its authority, as a conscious artifice, over the baron's hypocritical false seeming.

Ariadne auf Naxos, a work that Hofmannsthal called "my darling among the children,"[21] is a full-blown exposition of his favorite theme, being and becoming, and of its aporias, which Hofmannsthal eloquently summarizes in the famous "Ariadne Letter" of 1912: "Transformation is the life of life, the true mystery of generative nature; persistence is paralysis and death. Whoever wants to live must transcend himself, must transform himself: he must forget. And yet all human dignity is connected to persistence, to not forgetting, to fidelity. This is one of the unfathomable contradictions over which human existence is built up, like the Delphic temple over its bottomless crevasse."[22]

These aporias are given their perfect formal mirror in the double construction of *Ariadne*. Like *Der Rosenkavalier*, this libretto presents the fiction of a subordinate drama. We may call this subordinate drama a play within the play, bearing in mind that Hofmannsthal's text never returns to the world of fictional reality (the "prelude"), but ends with the conclusion of the play in the play (the "opera"). The "prelude" introduces us to the milieu in which the "opera" will be performed. The composer of "Ariadne," a serious, high-flown, eminently tedious work, is horrified to learn that the wealthy patron for whom he wrote the opera intends to have it performed after a banquet, and followed by an opera buffa staged by commedia dell'arte actors. The fickle patron then orders another last-minute change: the serious and comic operas are to be performed simultaneously, mixed together into a single piece. The star of the opera buffa, Zerbinetta, is enthusiastic. She always improvises with her cast, and she quickly translates the plot of Ariadne into comedy terms. The opera seria company, in particular the idealistic young composer and the haughty prima donna engaged to play Ariadne, are aghast, but they let themselves be persuaded. The opera then actually does mix, in the style of E. T. A. Hoffmann's *Kater Murr*, the serious with the comic opera. While Aridane laments Theseus, who deserted her, and gives herself over to death, Zerbinetta and her male companions try to cheer her up. As in *Der Rosenkavalier*, Hofmannsthal pairs a woman of the world (Zerbinetta) with a ingenue (Ariadne). Zerbinetta tries to have a woman-to-woman talk with Ariadne, pointing out, in Marschallin fashion, how transitory affairs of the heart are, but Ariadne persistently turns a deaf ear to her admonitions.

The fundamental message of the play in the play or opera is "it must change." This message is articulated in the Ariadne plot on a higher, and in the Zerbinetta plot on a lower, level. Zerbinetta is the incarnation of mutability. She freely admits that she has had and foresees having a succession of changing lovers, quite in keeping with her philosophy that feelings change, that one never fully understands one's own heart, and that time heals all wounds. Ariadne, however, also changes, as if to prove Zerbinetta's words, upon the arrival of a new lover, Bacchus. Yet we are not meant to understand her transformation as a validation of Zerbinetta's truisms but, rather, as a miracle fraught with deeper meaning. The composer hints at this meaning in the "prelude," and Hofmannsthal elaborates it in the "Ariadne Letter." The "Ariadne Letter" is a necessary complement to the play, for the sense of the composer's brief and enigmatic comments in the "prelude" tend to elude the spectator or reader. Hofmannsthal's deeper meaning is that transformation is the secret of life—"Das Geheimnis des Lebens," as the composer says.[23] Love is its privileged agent, or in Hofmannsthal's words, "If [love] seizes hold of a being with all its force, the latter looses itself from its paralysis down into its deepest depths: The world is restored to him."[24] The composer summarizes what happens when Ariadne meets Bacchus: "She gives herself over to death—is no longer there—wiped away—plunges into the mystery of transformation—is born anew—comes to life again in his arms! Thereby he becomes a god."[25] Bacchus is of course Dionysus, and Ariadne's presumptive death, which is in fact a rebirth, recalls the dionysian life-in-death figure in *Death and the Fool*. What of the other transformation, Bacchus's? Inasmuch as Ariadne is born anew in his arms, Bacchus becomes a god. Hofmannsthal hence designates the power to transform, the power to create anew, as godly.

It is not farfetched to see in Bacchus a figure of the artist. There are numerous connections between Bacchus's powers and Hofmannsthal's longstanding view of the artist. First, as we have seen, in his various poems on the deaths of actors Hofmannsthal lauds the actors for their powers of transformation. The poem on the death of Josef Kainz in particular contains lines ("One untransformed in many transformations, / A never bewitched bewitcher") that remind one of Bacchus, who transforms Ariadne yet himself remains untransformed by Circe.

Second, Bacchus recalls Hofmannsthal's evocation of poetic power in "Das Gespräch über Gedichte" (The conversation on poetry). There Hofmannsthal describes the power of the symbol as magical: it is capable of transforming us ("uns unaufhörlich zu verwandeln").[26] Karen Forsyth, on the basis of an investigation of the Bacchus figure in Hofmannsthal's progressive versions of *Ariadne auf Naxos*, believes that Bacchus in his final form represents "one of [Hofmannthal's] too numerous idealized self-portraits which, as Hermann Broch has suggested, recur in his works in the figure of the 'sehr schöner Knabe.'"[27] But there is a more direct parallel between Bacchus and another poet figure. It is well known that Hofmannsthal revered Goethe. In his poem "Prolog zu einer nachträglichen Gedächtnisfeier für Goethe am Burgtheater zu Wien, den 8. Oktober 1899" (Prologue to a subsequent celebration in memory of Goethe at the Burgtheater in Vienna, 8 October 1899), Hofmannsthal ascribes to Goethe precisely the power to transform us, indeed to bring us to life, that Bacchus exercises over Ariadne:

> Just as he created Faust and the valiant Götz
> And that townsman's child in the narrow house
> And around them the fresh German countryside:
> *Thus too he created, with no weaker a magical hand,*
> *On your heart's heart in a thousand nights . . .*
> . . .
> And the creatures from the loveliest star
> They come alive for us; *we come alive in them!*[28]

> [Wie er den Faust schuf und den wackern Götz
> Und jenes Bürgerkind im engen Haus
> Und rings um sie das frische deutsche Land:
> *So schuf er mit nicht schwächrer Zauberhand*
> *An eures Herzens Herz in tausend Nächten . . .*
> . . .
> Und die Geschöpfe von dem schönsten Sterne,
> Sie werden uns, *an ihnen wir* lebendig! (italics mine)]

When Hofmannsthal addresses the question "Who is Bacchus?" in the Ariadne letter, his associations move to Goethe, who in his eyes is similarly superhuman: "Bacchus is almost a child, yet a god and more than a man; just as the Goethe of the 'Marienbad Elegy' was an old man and yet ageless, and also superior as a lover to any man."[29]

The "prelude" mirrors the opera. Here too, transformation is the theme, and the message is "it must change." The wealthy patron's arbitrary demand that the two entertainments be mixed demonstrates the transformative power of money. The opera seria company insists that their piece cannot be changed (just as their piece itself is about fidelity); yet the play *can* be changed, and for the better: Zerbinetta's troupe enlivens Ariadne's austere lament. Moreover, and here we see the transformative power of art, the two commentaries on life and change magically harmonize, in contrast to the "prelude," where all was at odds.

Critics dwell on the tension between the commedia dell'arte and the heroic elements in *Ariadne*. They find it endlessly problematic that the libretto does not close clearly in favor of either Ariadne's or Zerbinetta's position. If Hofmannsthal had wanted to validate Ariadne's fidelity and/or the "higher" type of mutual transformation through love, why did he make Zerbinetta such an attractive character? If, on the other hand, Zerbinetta was meant to win, why did Hofmannsthal let Ariadne and Bacchus have the last word? Often the problem is named Richard Strauss. Karen Forsyth, who devotes an entire monograph to investigating why the opera is "torn apart," finds the reason in Strauss's predilection for Zerbinetta, in contrast to Hofmannsthal's preference for Ariadne. She writes, "As a result of the contrast and the method of working [Hofmannsthal] found himself in the false position of having to write a large part . . . for a character who did not greatly interest him—beyond her symbolic value as the antithesis of Ariadne, the real heroine of the 'lyric drama.'"[30] To Forsyth's mind, the necessity for compromise plagued the opera down to its final, 1916 version: "The finished work fell short of its ideal form."[31] She concludes, "To find any sort of unity in *Ariadne* is a task well beyond the poetic sensibility."[32]

There is no doubt that the genesis of the libretto involved massive revisions. The opera was originally intended as a short divertissement to follow a production of Molière's *Le bourgeois gentilhomme*. When this combined theatrical and operatic production met with an unenthusiastic response after its 1912 performance, Hofmannsthal set about revising the opera as an independent work. He added the "prelude," or rather, transformed the already existing "intermezzo" between Molière's play and the opera into the "prelude" as we know it in the 1916 opera. But to regard the 1916 version as "torn apart" or disunified is to disregard the fact that Hofmannsthal remained particularly partial to this opera and even many years later termed it his "favorite." Moreover, the device of ambiguous closure is Hofmannsthal's very signature. Throughout his entire career he preferred to end his works, which are often structured around a play with antitheses, on a note of ambiguity or paradox. In his early poetry, the enigmatic final line of "Terzinen III"; the antitheses gathered into the last lines of "Terzinen IV"; the negative-positive image, "wie schwerer Honig aus den hohlen Waben" ("like heavy honey out of the hollow combs"), that ends "Ballade des äußeren Lebens"

("Ballad of the Outer Life"); or the gradual insinuation of a second, opposite meaning in "The Emperor of China Speaks," all testify to this preference. It is no different in his lyrical dramas: *Death and the Fool* ends with the idea of life in death; in *Der weiße Fächer* (The white fan) images in Miranda's dream undermine the dream's overt significance. To take an example closer to *Ariadne auf Naxos* in time and genre, the last lines of *Der Rosenkavalier*, Sophie's speech, "It's a dream, it can't be real / that we two are together, / together for all time and eternity," admits of two readings.[33] Taken at face value, these lines express Sophie's blissful amazement that she and Octavian are finally united despite all difficulties. But there is an ironic undertone: if taken *literally*, to mean that it is as unreal as a dream that the young lovers' relationship will last, Sophie's words validate the Marschallin's view that affairs of the heart are transitory and that all things change, which is the main message of the play. Given Hofmannsthal's fondness for double meanings and for dissolves into paradox, is it not therefore credible that he preferred *Ariadne auf Naxos* to all his other operas because it realized such a structure in the most perfect and at the same time most complex way?

I have said that the formal construction of the play mirrors the aporias of the theme of transformation. The play-in-a-play device is crucial to this mirroring. Let us examine how it works.

The opera contains two plots, the Ariadne plot and the Zerbinetta plot. The addition of the "prelude" (which makes the opera a play in the play) doubles each of these plots by giving it its counterpart in dramatic reality. Hence the entire opera *Ariadne auf Naxos* has not just a twofold but a fourfold structure. We can imagine a rectangle divided by a horizontal line (into the Ariadne and Zerbinetta plots) and also by a vertical line (into "prelude" and opera).

Let us see what happens when the Ariadne and the Zerbinetta plots each cross the line into fiction, or move from prelude to opera.

Both Ariadne and the prima donna who plays her represent permanence. The prima donna resists changes in her play and her part—as indeed the entire opera seria company resists them—while Ariadne believes that her sorrow at losing Theseus is eternal. Of course, both characters change in the end: Ariadne is transformed by Bacchus, while the prima donna not only accepts changes in her part but also transforms herself by donning the role of Ariadne. This latter transformation is crucial. The prima donna, a narcissistic personality consumed by professional jealousy who is evidently carrying on an amorous intrigue with a count, is not at all an ingenue. In order to play the sublime "symbol of human loneliness" represented by Ariadne, she has to transform herself utterly.[34] The same dichotomous relationship obtains between the divine Bacchus and the thoroughly human tenor who plays him. Hence in this strand of the drama, a gap opens between fiction and reality: once the actors cross the boundary between backstage and stage, once they enter into fiction, they become entirely different personalities.

Zerbinetta, in contrast, who embodies change, is always the same. In the play she plays the same role as in real life: "She always plays only herself."[35] Fiction does not change her. Her frivolous troupe of lovers, likewise, consists of timeless Italian masks.

Thus if the Ariadne strand of the libretto represents the cause of permanence, and the Zerbinetta half represents mutability, then the second division of the rectangle, into prelude and opera or "reality" and "fiction," turns these affiliations on their head. In moving onstage, the opera seria company changes, while the opera buffa troupe remains the same!

Hence both roles and both positions, the position that embraces change and that which embraces permanence, end in paradox. Each incorporates a tendency that undermines its own basic premise. The figure representing change is immutable. The figures representing immutability change. Zerbinetta's continuous succession of changing fables, of ephemeral love stories, of self-delusions, is impervious to change. The prima donna puts on an act about lasting values and ultimate truths, but it is an act: fidelity and permanence are ideals, the stuff of fiction.

The mirroring, whereby each position eventually undermines itself and substantiates the opposing one, goes even further than this. It might seem that Hofmannsthal favors the Ariadne strand of the opera, because there transformation is enacted on a sublime and on an artistic level. But the fate of the idealistic young composer who wrote *Ariadne*, the principal figure in the "prelude," belies this conclusion. This student composer parallels his creation Ariadne by falling in love after resisting change.[36] Yet more interesting, at the end of the "prelude" this naive young man presents an inverted image of his own creation, Bacchus, at the end of the opera. Where Bacchus resists transformation by Circe and himself transforms Ariadne (bringing her to life and hence becoming a god), the composer succumbs to Zerbinetta's (= Circe's) seductions, after having cut his own piece![37] Is Hofmannsthal covertly contrasting the figure of the artist-genius with the impotent neophyte? Perhaps. Does this mean that Zerbinetta wins? No, because although she wins in the prelude, easily charming the man who opposes her performance, in the opera, she transforms nothing: she does not change the composer's planned end, which is about transformation on a level (as Hofmannsthal's Ariadne letter informs us) too high for her to comprehend.

Der Rosenkavalier left us with the following equation: change is real, permanence fiction. The play-in-the-play device in that opera aimed at underscoring this statement in an ornamental, theatrically entertaining way. By presenting a preposterous but momentarily plausible spoof, the play in the play illustrated the statement "the claim to reality is deceptive," which is a variation on the play's primary statement, "things change." In *Ariadne*, the message is similar, though more complex. The use of the fiction-versus-reality theme, or play-in-the-play device, is much more sophisticated: it is an integral part of making the statement. The opera is constructed like a figure 8. As we move from "prelude" to opera, we see (as in *Der Rosenkavalier*) that change is real, permanence fiction. But as we reflect back on the "prelude," where all is confusion and dissention, from the vantage point of the harmoniously balanced opera, we see why art, which involves transformation, can lay claim to permanence, while reality, supposedly stable, is bound to change.

Kafka's "A Report to an Academy"

"A Report to an Academy" is a polished and, by Kafka standards, relatively clear story, one neither brimming over with muddy details (like "A Country Doctor"), nor ambiguous in its very fiber (like *The Trial*). It has inspired mainly allegorical readings—understandably, for it is both easy and profitable to coax this animal fable into the pen of allegory. Here I wish to take a somewhat different approach, looking at the story's form before considering its meaning, localizing the "Report" as a response to one of Kafka's crucial insights as expressed in a major complex of texts. These texts include *The Trial* and the simpler, geometric restatement of its theme in "Before the Law"; "An Imperial Message"; and—to name texts written after "A Report to an Academy"—*The Castle* and "The Burrow." All of these texts are informed by the structure of the frustrated quest. Striving ostensibly to attain a goal, the hero soon runs up against an obscure, probably self-imposed, but all the more ineluctable barrier. The rest of the story then consists in an elaboration of the futility of the quest, of a *process* that follows the law of infinite regress. Kafka was fascinated by this strategy and tried it out in many variations. "Before the Law," "The Refusal," and "A Little Fable" go from a large, hopeful panorama to a small, negative answer; "An Imperial Message," "The Great Wall of China," and "The City Coat of Arms" dissipate from a positive, orderly state of affairs into disorder. In any case the more, the longer the hero strives, the farther from the goal he gets. The end of *The Trial* in particular reads like a parody of Goethe's hopeful dictum in *Faust*: "Wer immer strebend sich bemüht, den können wir erlösen" ("For him whose striving never ceases we can provide redemption").[38] Josef K.'s "youthful love," Fräulein Bürstner, miming "the eternal feminine," leads his way—to death. The very law of Josef K.'s existence seems to consist in two contrary imperatives: the life process itself, and the setting of a goal outside the life process that by definition this process cannot reach but that inexorably determines its direction. As Kafka writes in a diary entry of 19 October 1921, "Moses fails to enter Canaan not because his life is too short but because it is a human life."[39]

"A Report to an Academy" seems at first to move toward a realization of the same structure. Early in the ape Rotpeter's narrative he is captured and placed in a cage. He thus seemingly reaches the dead end familiar from Kafka's other stories. Just as in "Before the Law" the man from the country failed to enter the law, here, there seems to be no exit for the ape. Landing in the cage should be the end of the ape's story. Or rather, if the tale followed the model of the other "Before the Law"–type narratives, we might expect the ape to become diverted by something inside his cage, and so on ad infinitum. But the ape's life is no "human life." Rather, it is an "äffisches Vorleben" (ĸ 4:139; "ape's pre-life"). The laws that by Kafka's reckoning govern *human* life consequently do not hold. Searching desperately for an "Ausweg" ("way out"), the ape succeeds in finding one. He escapes his no-exit situation—by transforming himself (if one disregards his hairy exterior) into a man! He acquires human attributes, and finally even the definitive one of human speech.

Thus the frustrated-quest structure is parodied, and the usual impossibility of arriving at a goal is reversed. The ape's story is closed, that is, he lands in a cage. Then it is opened up again, in a peculiar way, in an odd kind of monkey business: the ape becomes no longer an ape. The existential fatality of "Before the Law" is turned on its head. Where the doorkeeper in the parable informed the man from the country, "This gate was made only for you," in "A Report to an Academy" the ape reckons that if the cage was meant for him, he will change his identity. He enacts an impossible transformation that is reminiscent of "The Metamorphosis," but one that goes in the opposite direction. In "The Metamorphosis" a man involuntarily turns into an insect and is, by consequence, trapped in his room. In "A Report to an Academy" an ape turns himself into a man by dint of an extraordinary conscious effort and thereby escapes his cage.[40] This tale, then, is not stretched by a movement from ends to means and yet smaller means in the quest for an unreachable goal. Rather, it is extended by a miraculous turn of events. The story has a clear beginning (apedom), a middle (the turning point), and an end (humanness). The narrator has a goal, which he achieves. In Kafka's world, this is a paradigm for the impossible.

The ape-into-man plot has primarily, and fruitfully, been interpreted allegorically: as a form of speeded-up evolution,[41] as the exchange for the freedom of the wild animal for a constrained human "freedom,"[42] as man's fall from Paradise,[43] as escape from the Jewish ghetto only through conversion to Christianity.[44] Here I would like to propose another allegorical reading (without trying to reduce the richness of the text by claiming that it is the only possible reading), regarding the ape's transformation as that of an ordinary mortal into a successful artist. Several critics have suggested that the ape might be interpreted as an artist—a reading that is, of course, directly suggested by the text, inasmuch as the narrating ape tells us that he is an artist on the variety stage—but even the critic who goes furthest with this line of interpretation, Klaus-Peter Philippi, does not, in my opinion, go far enough.[45]

The reading of the ape's story as the story of a successful artist has several advantages. First, it explains the parody of the frustrated-quest structure and of the metamorphosis theme. Indeed, this parody functions precisely to elucidate the role of the artist—the question of his identity, his motivations, and his mode of functioning—within the larger problematic of life. Second, it has the merit of accounting for the word play in the text that Lawrence O. Frye has in part drawn attention to.[46] Finally, it links the story to its obvious complement and companion piece, "A Hunger Artist."[47]

The "report" form of the "Report" is persiflage. The idea of a "report" to an "academy" evokes the notion of a sober, scientific presentation of facts about far-off exotic places and things, in Darwinian style, to a body of scholars. Here, an impossibility is put at the story's center. The event that will be related is so unheard of, so fantastical, as to defeat the credulity of the most gullible listener—if the very existence of the report (presuming the ape himself wrote it) did not itself validate the incredible fact he recounts. From the start, the ape's phrasing, his stagy presentation, his highly metaphorical language, undermine the notion of a "report." He begins with a "Bild" ("image")—one of himself not as a privileged eyewitness to simian life, but as an athlete running a race, or a performer: "Nearly five years separate me from apehood, a time which is perhaps short when measured by the calendar, but endlessly long to gallop through, as I did, accompanied for stretches by excellent people, advice, applause, and orchestral music, but basically alone, because all accompaniment, to stick to the image, kept well behind the barrier."[48] This metaphor is proleptic for the actual plot, for the captive ape contemplating trying to run or flee to freedom. The rest of the paragraph is a web of such anticipatory metaphors, consisting of an elaborate playing with the words "offen" ("open"), "geschlossen" ("closed"), "fest" ("tight," "fast"), and various expressions denoting openings.[49] All these expressions, which here are used metaphorically, point forward to the main events of the actual story, the captivity in the cage and the ape's miraculous self-liberation. In and of themselves, however, they serve the purpose of lending credibility to the idea that the ape is no longer an ape. For the ape does not do as asked; he does not write about his "äffisches Vorleben." Rather, he wishes to defend himself against apedom, to close what he refers to as the "hole in his past." The rest of the paragraph forms an elaborate apology for the ape's failure to write about the topic that he was invited to report on and at the same time strategically defends his status as a man.

The ape thus tells his fictive readers that he would have been unable to transcend his apehood "wenn ich eigensinnig hätte an meinem Ursprung . . . festhalten wollen" ("if I had stubbornly wished to hold tight to my origins"). Thus his ape memories "verschlossen sich . . . immer mehr" ("closed up more and more") as the ape felt "wohler und eingeschlossener in der Menschenwelt" ("more comfortable and enclosed in the human world"). "Das ganze Tor" ("the whole gate") that the heavens form over earth, scene of his apedom, has contracted into a "Loch in der Ferne" ("hole in the distance"). Further expressions, in particular plays on "offen" ("open") are used to give the ape's discourse the trappings of sincerity. The ape apes the dignified scholar, the learned authority, the unimpeachably honest historian. "Offen gesprochen" ("Stated openly"), he assures us, his apedom is far behind him. Thus he can report on his former life only "im eingeschränktesten Sinn" ("in the most limited sense"). This metaphorical openness testifies to his humanity. Frankness was the first quality he acquired (says he with devious purpose) upon overcoming his apedom: "Das erste, was ich lernte, war: den Handschlag geben; Handschlag bezeigt *Offenheit,* mag nun heute, wo ich auf dem Höhepunkt meiner Laufbahn stehe, zu jenem ersten Handschlag auch *das offene Wort* hinzukommen" ("The first thing I learned was to shake hands; shaking hands betokens *openness.* Today, when I stand at the peak of my career, I may add *the open word* to that first handshake") (my italics throughout).

All these turns of phrase reveal the ape-turned-artist, the actor, the imitator—and hence of course the ape. For the ape is not just humankind's evolutionary predecessor but also, in the metaphor of common speech, a follower, one who imitates. "Nachäffen" in German means "to ape." The ape's hairy exterior attests that he is not really a man, but at best a split being. In this part of his report the ape chooses to emphasize the positive side of this split. At the end of the paragraph he assures his listeners that he is not only *"festgesetzt"* (*"established"*) in the human world, but that his "Stellung auf allen grossen Varietébühnen der zivilisierten Welt sich . . . bis zur Unerschütterlichkeit *gefestigt* [hat]" ("position on all the great variety stages of the civilized world has become *secure* to the point of being unshakable"). He has transformed his pitiable situation in the cage, where, he says, he was *"festgerannt"* (*"run to a standstill"*) into something truly splendid: the brilliant career of a successful actor on the variety stage (my italics here, too).

In becoming an artist, the ape is more than just an ape exercising his imitative talent. The bravura display of metaphors and word play in the opening paragraph bears testimony to the ape's principal achievement, the act of imagination that led to his escape from his cage: sensing the metaphorical potential behind a concrete state of affairs. In the protracted process of observing his human captors, the ape must have realized that things can be transformed into what they are not. "Ein hohes Ziel dämmerte mir auf" ("A lofty goal dawned before me"): he stood a chance of becoming like the sailors on board ship. An awkward state of affairs—the state of being a caged ape—could potentially be transformed into something quite different. This remarkable ape plainly possessed the symbolic imagination necessary for learning human language, and learning language surely reinforced and deepened his mental agility. For to learn language is to learn that things can be deftly altered and rearranged through language, changed in value and even whisked out of existence.[50] By the time he delivers the report, the ape has thoroughly mastered the art of linguistic legerdemain. Specifically, he has permuted all the concrete terms of his old ape's existence into new, figurative senses. In the opening paragraph, as we have seen, he has displaced the idea of entrapment by "closing the door" on his apedom, so that now, instead of being trapped in the human world, he is "secure." As part of the bargain he has exchanged the open spaces he enjoyed as an ape for a personal "openness," for the human quality of sincerity.

In the narrative that follows, his description of the cage itself, that all-too-concrete obstruction to a wild animal's freedom, is curiously infiltrated by metaphor. The metaphors come from a specific semantic area. The ape describes his cage: "Es war kein vierwandiger Gitterkäfig; vielmehr waren nur drei Wände an einer Kiste festgemacht; die Kiste also bildete die vierte Wand" (K 4:141; "It was not a four-walled barred cage; instead, only three walls were fastened to a crate; the crate thus formed the fourth wall"). The "fourth wall" is theater terminology. In the theory of the Naturalist theater the stage is a room with the fourth wall removed. The audience that is privy to the scene replaces the fourth wall. In the cramped cage, the ape turns toward this "fourth wall": "Ich hockte . . . , da ich zunächst wahrscheinlich niemand sehen und immer nur im Dunkel sein wollte, zur Kiste gewendet" ("I squatted . . . , since at first I probably wanted to see no one and only to be in the dark, turned toward the crate"). He describes it thus: "Geradeaus vor mir war die Kiste, Brett fest an Brett gefügt. Zwar war zwischen den Brettern eine durchlaufende Lücke, die ich, als ich sie zuerst entdeckte, mit dem glückseligen Heulen des Unverstandes begrüßte, aber diese Lücke reichte bei weitem nicht einmal zum Durchstecken des Schwanzes aus und war mit aller Affenkraft nicht zu verbreitern" ("Straight ahead in front of me was the crate, board joined tightly to board. There was, to be sure, a gap between the boards that ran their whole length, which, when I first discovered it, I greeted with a blissful howl of incomprehension, but this gap was not nearly wide enough even to stick your tail through and couldn't be widened even with all of an ape's strength.") "Brett an Brett" ("board to board"), "die Bretter" ("the boards")—this is more terminology from the theater. Die Bretter is synonymous with the stage.

In the innocent ape or subject of the narration, this impenetrable crate wall initiated a chain of reflections (in the stomach, the narrating ape presumes) about having no "Ausweg," no way out. Truly, concretely, in the fullest and most literal sense, the ape in the cage, cramped, with his face pressed against a wall, is in an auswegslose Situation, a no-exit situation.

But the narrator's word choice reveals that in retrospect, the cage has for him the significance of his first stage, the launching of his career as an artist. The gap or opening in the boards, disappointing as it proves to the captured ape who hopes to squeeze through it bodily, becomes a symbol to the narrating ape. The escape route he so badly needs will lead through the stage. In its final metamorphosis, indeed, the word "open" reappears as "Öffentlichkeit" ("public"). The fourth wall of the cage, with its disappointingly tiny opening, will turn into the fourth wall of the stage, the public or "Öffentlichkeit." The exit to freedom through the small opening, the "Flucht" (K 4:143; "flight") that the caged ape contemplates, will become the open-ended progress of a career, the orderly "Fortschritte" (K 4:146; "progress") that the variety stage audience witnesses.

The idea that the ape's cage is his proto-stage invites us to reflect on what it meant, for Kafka, to be an artist. Here he appears to be suggesting that artistic creativity originates in entrapment. "Necessity is the mother of invention" (*Not macht erfinderisch*)—the further course of the text suggests that Kafka was not just writing a story around this commonplace, but exploring an existential problem pertaining to the motivation and exigencies of the artist, a problem of some depth and of great importance to himself. Let us look at the ape's reflections on his "way out" and freedom:

> I am afraid that people won't understand exactly what I mean by way out. I use the word in its most common and fullest sense. I purposely do not say freedom. I don't mean that great feeling of freedom in all directions. I perhaps knew it as an ape and I have met human beings who yearn for it. But as for me, I demanded freedom neither then nor today. By the way, among humans, people deceive themselves with freedom all too often. And just as freedom counts among the most sublime of feelings, the corresponding illusion [Täuschung] counts among the most sublime. Before my performance in the variety halls I have often seen some pair of artists busying themselves on trapezes up above at the ceiling. They swung, they rocked, they leaped, they glided into each other's arms, one carried the other by his hair with his teeth. "That too is human freedom," I thought, "self-controlled movement." What a mockery of holy Nature! No building would withstand the laughter of apedom at this sight. (K 4:142)

The message is clear: art is not freedom. If there is freedom, it lies in nature, not in the disciplined, practiced, imitative action of art. "What a mockery of holy Nature!" cries the ape. A trapeze artist is—says the ape, snidely enumerating the details—a man imitating the freedom of an ape! If the ape imitates men to get out of his cage, art is at base no more than nostalgia for lost freedom. To mistake art for freedom is, according to Rotpeter, a "Täuschung," a deception—though, he adds, one of the most sublime. Art, then, in the ape's definition, is the sublime illusion of freedom.

Practically speaking, art for Rotpeter is at most a way out. Rotpeter continues to expatiate on the subject of *Täuschung*. In his cage, he considered the possibility that his way out might be a "Täuschung": "Sollte der Ausweg auch nur eine Täuschung sein; die Forderung war klein, die Täuschung würde nicht größer sein" ("Even if the way out should only be an illusion, the demand was small, the illusion would not be greater"). It is unclear whether "Täuschung" means self-deception or an illusion prepared for others. In learning human speech, in becoming a successful actor, does the ape delude himself that he has found a way out, or does his way out consist in deceiving others? The sentence is no doubt intentionally ambiguous: it reminds one of the confusions connected to the theme of *Täuschung* in the "Before the Law" parable and the attendant discussion, where it is unclear whether the man from the country deludes himself about the nature of the law, whether he is deceived by the doorkeeper, whether the doorkeeper himself is deceived, and so on.

Becoming an actor, becoming an artist, of course involves pretense, and deception of the most conventional and legitimate sort. By convention, art presents the audience with an illusion. On a darker and less openly acknowledged level, however, art may deceive others about the true nature and motivations of the artist. Kafka suggests that the brilliant artist might be, at heart, a poor ape longing for freedom. On the other hand, this "way out" might prove a self-delusion for the ape. Rotpeter's objective in becoming an artist is to persuade his captors that he is worthy of liberation from his cage, that he is no longer a mere ape. This act of persuasion requires such self-discipline, such a transformation of the natural self that—although he succeeds in escaping from his cage—as a form of liberty his new state is a self-deception. The studied adoption of a role, forcing oneself through desperate necessity to change, does violence to original innocence. And in original innocence alone lies freedom.[51]

It is remarkable that this story, which is about deception and self-deception, is at once such a true expression of inner being, of an existential problem, and Kafka's consciousness of it.[52] At the heart of the story, after the ape's stagy, rhetorically devious opening, behind all the irony implicit in the metaphorical displacement and punning, lies the cruel problem of the necessity for adaptation to circumstances, a problem that must have affected a person like Kafka severely. "In Hagenbeck apes belong on the crate wall—well, so I would stop being an ape. A clear, fine train of thought" (k 4:142). If belonging to a certain category brings with it negative consequences in the eyes of those in power—change oneself so that one fits into a different category! This is the thought process not of the moralist, but of the disappointed innocent turned fledgling realist. For the change involves terrible self-flagellation and self-mutilation: "Ah, you learn if you have to; you learn if you want a way out; you learn relentlessly. You oversee yourself with the whip; you lacerate yourself at the slightest resistance" (k 4:146).

The ape's great achievement, then, is to change himself into a man—or at least into a being who outwardly mimics man. Here is Kafka's opportunity for satire: to the ape's naive, observant eye, the distinguishing features of humanity are spitting, smoking, and drinking alcohol! Throughout the text the ape's account of his achievements raises doubts as to whether they should be evaluated as progress or regression. The ape successfully completes his transformation into an artist when he drinks from the schnapps bottle:

> What a triumph then, after all, for . . . me, when one evening before a large circle of spectators I . . . seized a schnapps bottle that had accidentally been left standing there, uncorked it according to the rules while the company began to watch me with mounting attention, set it to my mouth, and without hesitating, without grimacing, as a professional drinker, with rolling eyes, throat splashing over, really and truly drank it empty; threw the bottle away no longer as a desperate creature, but as an artist. (k 4:145–46)

Kafka builds a pleasing symmetry into the story: the scene in which the ape transforms himself into an artist echoes that in which he is captured and caged. Both involve drinking, and both involve something that could be described as two successive similar noises. The ape's transition from freedom to captivity takes place while he is going to drink, "when I ran to the watering place in the evening in the midst of a pack" (k 4:140). He is shot—twice. After the ape successfully downs the contents of the schnapps bottle he calls out "Hallo!"; this is echoed (similar to the double

gunshot) by human cries ("Listen, he's talking!"), which he feels corpo-
really—not, of course, as pain, but as a "kiss."

Ambiguity, the possibility of a contradictory evaluation, pervades all
aspects of the ape's rise to stardom. On the positive side, the ape has
turned himself into an actor, his cage into a stage, his captors into the
public or "Öffentlichkeit." Unable to pursue the object of his desire,
freedom, he has, ingeniously, turned *himself* into an object of desire. As
Klaus-Peter Philippi writes, "He himself is an artist and an object of art,
a work of art, in one."[53] He is the idol of the public, the object of his
spectators' rapt gaze. (One is reminded that Kafka will speak to Max
Brod in a letter of 5 July 1922 of his writing as "a solar system of vanity.")[54] Now, instead of being shut in and exposed, the ape is exposed and
secure. Being put on display as one's self, as a naked ape, means insecu-
rity. Thus the ape initially turned his back to the barred part of his cage,
through which he could be seen. But a performer enjoys a mystique; he is
protected by an invisible wall that the idea of a performance erects between stage and audience. In the same measure, the ape's narrative, pur-
portedly an exposé, is in fact a defense—for the ape's security lies in convincing audiences that he has essentially become a man.[55] Exposure is a
central theme in the narrative, occurring most explicitly in the narrator's account of how he is in the habit of pulling down his pants to reveal
his gunshot wound to visitors. According to Rotpeter, displaying the scar
(a testimony to his "closed" past) is a gesture of sincerity, while being
able to pull his pants down in front of whomever he wants (he implies) is
freedom. This anecdote hints at how close together "sincerity" and vanity, freedom and security really lie.

On the negative side, the ape's stage might well be just another cage.
The artist has made a tremendous effort and accomplished the truly impossible. Yet in terms of solving basic problems of life it is only a dubious trick, a sleight of hand involving the deception of others and self-
delusion. He deceives others about his veritable nature and motivations,
and this deception brings with it a terrible loss of his own identity,
whence only natural freedom comes. He has become a split being, neither this nor that, half this and half that. The final images in the narrative, the ape's picture of himself at the present time, represent this dividedness. Rotpeter strings together "neither this nor that," "half this
and half that," and "now this, now that" constructions: "ich klage
weder, noch bin ich zufrieden" ("neither do I complain, nor am I satis-
fied"); "ich liege halb, halb sitze ich im Schaukelstuhl" ("I half lie, half

sit in the rocking chair": "Schaukelstuhl" in particular is a wonderful image, indicating comfort and ease in dividedness); "nachts erwartet mich eine kleine halb dressierte Schimpansin. . . . Bei Tag will ich sie nicht sehen" (к 4:147; "at night a little half-trained chimpanzee awaits me. . . . By day I don't want to see her"). Moreover, Rotpeter has exchanged one kind of fourth wall for another, for the public and an attendant dependence on its expectations. For a performer must constantly strive to please an audience: he derives his identity from convincing other people. The closing words of the story—"To you too, distinguished gentlemen of the Academy, I have only made a report"—which take the narrative back to its beginning and are surely meant to be read ironically, underscore this necessity. "Even if the way out should only be an illusion, the demand was small, the illusion would not be greater": while the idea that art is freedom is a *great* delusion, the ape's delusion in believing that art would be a way out was only small. By anyone's standards, he is a successful artist. Sitting in his rocking chair, the ape is not so deluded about the true state of affairs, nor has his art not been, in some sense, a way out.

In *Ariadne*, the artist, embodied by Bacchus, is the agent of triumphant transformation: Bacchus brings Ariadne back to life. Kafka's "Report" parodistically mimics this type of artistic triumph: the ape crosses an equally uncrossable boundary and becomes a man. But here the similarities between Hofmannsthal's and Kafka's views of the artist end. An essential element of Bacchus's power is that he himself remains untransformed. Hofmannsthal's artist figures generally have the power to transform reality for others while remaining untransformed themselves ("one untransformed in many transformations"). The same is true of Schnitzler's Herbot and Henri. Kafka's ape, in contrast, motivated by sheer necessity, transforms *himself*, and moreover, transforms (and hence deforms) himself *into an artist*. In Kafka's view art is not a miracle, not a magical act, but the consequence of bleak necessity. According to Kafka's story, art from its inception bears the deforming stamp of the other, on whom the artist-subject depends. Crossing the boundary is not triumphant transition, but dark transgression of a boundary that would better remain inviolate, the boundary of the integrity of the self.

We have seen in turn-of-the-century writers the tendency to privilege a mysterious "beyond" as a site of power—a beyond represented by a spectrum of involuntary psychic forces encompassing repressed desires, traumatic memories, and guilt, but also by the real stripped of domesticizing concepts. Concurrently, the pretensions of everyday reality to stability were unmasked. Such reality figured above all under its aspect of mutability and subjectivity. It was a climate in which the artist, like the hypnotist, stood to gain. In works by Schnitzler and Hofmannsthal, the artist, represented above all by the actor, breaks through the (already attenuated) barrier between fiction and reality, which would relegate fiction to a subsidiary and secondary status, and demonstrates the artist's power to transform the real world through fictions.

Kafka's ape appears to do likewise: by persuading his audience that the reality of his apehood is a fiction, he manages to transform the circumstances of his existence, to turn his cage into a stage. Yet this feat does not redound unequivocally to the glory of the artist. For Kafka shows that personal necessity, the need to escape dire circumstances, lies at the heart of such illusionism. The artist's sleights of hand do not testify to the malleability of the real; instead they are desperate responses to its obduracy. While the dark and mysterious beyond is voided of all definitive claim to reality in Kafka's stories, the real world appears all the more obdurate. In his stories of the frustrated quest Kafka is attentive to the force of circumstances. Characteristic of these stories is that the heroes, in the measure that they persist in striving toward a goal, become mired in circumstances, in the myriad impediments and contingencies that constitute everyday life. And although the ape-artist seems to reverse the outcome of the frustrated quest, miraculously escaping from the cage that threatened to end his story, he in fact confirms it: the place where he lands, the stage, is just as entrammeled in circumstances, just as devoid of the absolute, as his cage.

These considerations locate "A Report to an Academy" within Kafka's reflections about the nature of art, in particular within the thematic of art as freedom versus art as deception. For where Kafka envisages the possibility that art might mean existential freedom for the artist, he tends simultaneously to question this freedom as being intimately bound up with deception and self-deception. An early articulation of this self-questioning line of thought is found in the "Nature Theater of Oklahoma" chapter of *Amerika*. The angels blowing trumpets at the recruiting station suggest that this all-embracing theater, where everyone is welcome, is a utopian *theatrum mundi*, heaven on earth. Indeed, in this theater everyone gets to "play" the role one is suited to. Kafka's choice of a theater company as the framework for this utopia suggests that art might be the site of real being. But on renewed reflection, it also suggests the opposite, namely, that real being, utopian being, is merely pretense, an unattainable ideal.

The same problematic is found in a much more developed form in the vertiginous levels of argumentation of the "Letter to His Father," a text written seven years later. Kafka brilliantly and tortuously argues the case of himself versus his father from every angle and from both sides. He takes, in turn, the following positions: Does Kafka's writing represent a place free of his father, a place uniquely his, where he can breathe freely? Or has the shadow of his father's gigantic figure fallen on this part of the "map," too? "My writing was all about you," Kafka admits.[56] Is his writing hopelessly determined by his conflict with his father, so that the notion of freedom through writing is a self-delusion? Or, finally— and here, at the end of the letter, vanity mingles with desperation—has Franz Kafka, the writer, essentially *created* the relationship to his father that he describes, ascribing to his father views about himself that he himself invented single-handedly? This idea is contained in seminal form in the final paragraph of the letter, where Kafka rejoins to his father's final putative rejoinder: "My answer to this is that, after all, this whole rejoinder . . . does not come from you, but from me."[57] With this volte-face, he displaces the entire conflict back into himself, or more specifically into his artistic and writerly activity.

"A Report to an Academy" is a key piece in Kafka's reflections on art, deception, and freedom. The other one is "A Hunger Artist." For if the story of the escape-artist ape echoes and parodies earlier narratives, it itself is clearly the seminal text for "A Hunger Artist," a story in which Kafka takes up the same complex of questions using the same central image, the *Gitterkäfig* (barred cage). To judge from Kafka's conversations with Gustav Janouch, *Gitter* (bars) became a favorite metaphor of his around 1920. Janouch quotes Kafka as saying, "Every man lives behind bars, which he carries within him. That is why people write so much about animals now. It's an expression of longing for a free natural life. . . . But . . . men are afraid of freedom and responsibility. So they prefer to hide behind the prison bars [Gitter] which they build around themselves."[58] As an artist type, the hunger artist is the ape's opposite. He is a purist, an artist who is so totally true to himself that one could accuse his art of not being art: it is nature. Fasting is so easy for him that he can hardly bring himself to stop. Yet he is not free. With his art of self-denial he is the antithesis of the natural animal (figured by the voracious panther who is moved into his cage after his death). In contrast to the ape, he voluntarily lives in and practices his art in a cage. As becomes clear when he admits that he could never find the food that appealed to him, he is oriented entirely toward spiritual values, which remain elusive. The hunger artist's forty-day fasts remind one of Jesus' words during his forty-day fast in the desert: "Man shall not live by bread alone, but by every word that proceedeth out of the mouth of God" (Matthew 4:4).

The ape's success derives from his ability to go with the flow, to adapt strategically to changing circumstances. The hunger artist's art, in contrast, consists in fighting a (necessarily losing) battle against time. When pushed to its limit, this battle results in his death. Moreover, his failure to change with changing times, to accommodate public taste, loses him the only gratification his art affords him—public admiration. "I always wanted you to admire my fasting" (cs 277), says he. Where the ape assumes a manipulative attitude toward his audience, captivating his captors and hoodwinking the "distinguished gentlemen" about his humanity, the purism of the hunger artist's art directly conflicts with his dependence on an audience. The "barred cage" to which the hunger artist confines himself voluntarily, which represents enclosure yet openness, security yet exposure to the eyes of others, is an image for this dependence on his spectators' admiration.

It is a humble admission on Kafka's part that this purist should be so dependent on the recognition of others. For the hunger artist surely represents a truer and more complete aspect of Kafka's artistic personality than the ape. In an isolated comment of 1914 Kafka adopts the persona of the sleight-of-hand man:

> All these fine and very convincing passages always deal with the fact that someone is dying, that it is hard for him to do, that it seems unjust to him, or at least harsh, and the reader is moved by this, or at least he should be. But for me, who believe that I shall be able to lie contentedly on my deathbed, such scenes are secretly a game; indeed, in the death enacted I rejoice in my own death, hence calculatingly exploit the attention that the reader concentrates on death.[59]

In this diary entry Kafka connects artistic success with trickery; he wrote his best scenes, he says, when he himself remained detached and calculatedly pulled the audience's heartstrings. Certain parallels can also be drawn between Rotpeter's story and Kafka's own life.[60] But the vast majority of Kafka's statements about himself and his writing go in an opposite direction. His corpus is full of remarks that testify that he cannot seriously entertain the idea of being the blithe pretender. His self-perception is founded on the conviction that he is self-identical, even *fatally* himself (in hunger artist fashion). He sees himself as driven to write even though his writing eats him up, even though it deprives him of a life in the world and consigns him to a life of isolation that is nowhere grounded. In statements made through the summer of 1914, his own ambition for his art is that it be adequately expressive of his inner state, his dreamlike inner life. In statements made in 1917 and after, he hopes that his art will be redemptive of the world. Thus if in "A Report to an Academy" Kafka articulated the recognition that successful art involves faking and that—as he made painfully explicit in "A Hunger Artist"—the purist is doomed to failure, these ideas have the status of bitter constatations. In "A Report to an Academy" Kafka explores how art is motivated by an urge for freedom and how it is ultimately unfree, first for that reason and second because it is inextricably bound up with catering to an audience (the artist's captors) and hence with self-deformation. In "A Hunger Artist," he explores how the converse is *not* therefore true. There, art is nature, its practice an existential necessity for the artist—hence, we would be led to expect by "A Report," potentially synonymous with freedom, although it may in the process have lost its character as art. Yet nature masquerading as art by that very token makes a bid for others' admiration and is hence unfree. Personal freedom through art is thus entirely ruled out, for, as these two stories and virtually all Kafka's statements about his own writing attest, one becomes an artist through necessity of one kind or another, not choice. And "artistic freedom," artists' freedom to do as they please in their art, is questionable by the same reasoning, for a person whose productivity is bound up with material necessity ("A Report to an Academy"), psychological necessity ("Letter to His Father"), or metaphysical necessity ("A Hunger Artist") is hardly capable of creating freely.

Most people suffer from this mental weakness: they believe that because a word
is there, it has to be the word for Something. Because a word is there, it has to
correspond to something real. . . . As if lines scribbled accidentally by a fool
always had to be a solvable rebus!
—Fritz Mauthner, *Beiträge zu einer Kritik der Sprache*

Language Skepticism in Austria

KAFKA'S WORK IS NOT rich in topical pieces, but in his rewriting of
the biblical story of the Tower of Babel, to which Max Brod gave the title
"Das Stadtwappen" ("The City Coat of Arms"), it is difficult not to see a
thinly veiled reference to the language pluralism in the Austro-Hungarian
Empire and to the resulting contentions. This short parable, which shows
how high aspirations founder on the inescapable exigencies of practical
life and eventually degenerate into chaos, admits of a reading on two
levels: one reading regards the political and social realities of language
pluralism, and the other, less overt but closer to the poet's heart and correspondingly of greater interest to us here, bears on poetics and the philosophy of language.

Kafka takes the biblical motif of building a tower that will reach to
heaven as his point of departure: "People argued this way: the essential
thing in the whole undertaking is the idea of building a tower that will
reach to heaven."[1] But thereafter, Kafka's parable revises its biblical
model in two notable respects.

First, where Genesis 11 cites divine wrath to account for the origin of
the plurality of languages on earth, in Kafka's rewriting, language plurality is no longer a punishment but, rather, an original working condition.
In the biblical story, God, angered at men's presumptuousness in wishing to build a tower to heaven, obstructed their enterprise by making

them speak different tongues so that they could no longer communicate, and hence they failed to complete the tower. The first sentence of "The City Coat of Arms" begins, "At first all the arrangements for building the Tower of Babel were in reasonable order; indeed, there was perhaps too much order, people gave too much thought to guides, *interpreters*" (italics mine). In Kafka's text, the men who came together to build the tower did not originally speak one language, for they needed *interpreters*.

In this first revision, then, Kafka whisks away the biblical account of the origin of many languages and replaces it with a tongue-in-cheek account of the origin of a political and social hodgepodge of different language groups, such as the milieu he grew up in in Prague. But this first part of the parable may be interpreted more profoundly as a poetological, rather than as political, commentary. For Kafka constructs an edifice—the tower—that in its vertical reaching for the ineffable functions as a poetological paradigm, one based on a particular philosophy of language.

In altering the initial premise of the biblical story, that one language was succeeded by many, Kafka implicitly rejects the notion of an original Adamic language spoken by all peoples. The dominant interpretation attached to the notion of the Adamic language since the Renaissance was that, since Adam was in a state of almost divine knowledge when he named the animals, words and things existed in a natural and harmonious relationship, and not an accidental or arbitrary one. By making language pluralism the preexisting condition for building the tower, Kafka discards all of this antiquated lore about language. And this is not surprising: for linguistic theory of his day recognized the plural origin of language families and the arbitrariness of the sign. Yet in the most famous turn-of-the-century Austrian language crisis text, Hofmannsthal's "Letter of Lord Chandos" ("Ein Brief," 1902), the fictive author of the letter describes his early euphoria about writing in terms that recall the theory of the Adamic language. Chandos's crisis sets in when he loses the sense that language is in harmonious unity with the rest of the world. We know from Max Brod how impressed Kafka was by "The Letter of Lord Chandos" when he was a university student.[2] Might we see in this text, written eighteen years later and in sober postwar circumstances, an ironic commentary on the language skepticism of Hofmannsthal and his contemporaries, a skepticism behind which lay a desire for a perfectly referential, perfectly expressive language?[3]

Moreover, in a context of preexisting language pluralism, building the tower takes on a new significance. Most obviously, the plan to construct the tower may be seen as nostalgia for a mythical transcendence, the kind of nostalgia for ulterior meaning that motivates all of Kafka's narratives modeled on the pattern of the frustrated quest. But since building so often doubles for writing in Kafka's work, this motivating nostalgia, the project of constructing this tower in the middle of language pluralism, might also represent his precedessors' obsession with the insufficiencies of ordinary language, coupled with their desire to attain by poetic means what they determinedly called *das Unaussprechliche*, "the inexpressible."[4] The irony that attaches to the enterprise of building the tower—Kafka writes, "the second or third generation had already recognized the senselessness of building a tower that reached to heaven, but by that time people were too deeply involved with each other to leave the city"—fits Kafka's attitude toward his predecessors' language doubts, for in time he became quite critical of complaints about the inadequacy of language to express feeling.[5]

Second, Kafka's parable departs from the biblical model by changing the focus. Necessarily no longer about the origin of the plurality of languages, Kafka's piece shows us how the city came into being. The tower, which is never even begun, dwindles to a mere *idea*, a pretext for the construction of the workmen's city at its base: "They troubled less about the tower than the construction of the workers' city." The vertical relation in the biblical text, the verticality of a tower reaching to heaven, of the relation of secular to transcendent and also of signifier to signified, hence becomes purely mythical, and is replaced by the *actuality* of a horizontally sprawling city.

In this image of urban sprawl, where the nationalities' conflicting interests perpetuate constant quarrel, it is easy to recognize an oblique reference to the Austro-Hungarian Empire or indeed, more specifically, to that capital of linguistic discord, Prague. Kafka writes, "Every nationality wanted the finest quarter for itself, and this gave rise to disputes, which intensified into bloody conflicts." Conflict emerges not as a result of divine punishment, as in the Bible, but as a natural result of the conglomeration of nationalities. In a similar inversion, the myth of origin in the biblical story (the origin of the plurality of languages) is replaced in Kafka's version by a myth of the end, by apocalyptic longing. "Everything in the way of legends and songs that came into being in that city is filled with longing for a prophesied day when the city will be destroyed by five blows in rapid succession from a gigantic fist. It is for that reason too that the city has a fist on its coat of arms." This vision of destruction by "five blows" may contain another veiled reference to the Austro-Hungarian Empire, this time to the specific manner of its dissolution after World War I. Kafka wrote "Das Stadtwappen" in September 1920. A year previously, on 10 September 1919, the Austro-Hungarian Empire was liquidated by the Treaty of St. Germain into five new nations: Poland, Austria, Czechoslovakia, Hungary, and Yugoslavia. The city coat of arms with the fist may have been inspired by the city coat of arms of Prague, which bears two towers and a sword with a fist.

If we pursue the connection between building and language use, Kafka's replacement of an intentional vertical quest by an accidental horizontal sprawl appears to confront two different theories of language with one another, a theory that considers language as reference (the vertical) and one that considers language as a medium of social intercourse, as usage (the horizontal). By unmasking the quest for meaning as a mere "idea" and validating the pragmatic view of language as a social and historical entity and a means of communication (however inadequate it may be), Kafka seems intuitively to anticipate Wittgenstein's revocation of his referential theory of language in the *Tractatus*, where he aimed at replacing confusing ordinary language with a formalized logical language, in favor of the theory advanced in the *Philosophical Investigations*, which views language as usage, as an evolving and constantly changing set of games played among speakers. In the later work Wittgenstein will use a similar metaphor of building: "Our language can be seen as an ancient city: a maze of little streets and squares, of old and new houses, and of houses with additions from various periods; and this surrounded by a multitude of new boroughs with straight regular streets and uniform houses" (para 18).

The much-publicized language skepticism of Kafka's predecessors around the turn of the century—of Mach and Mauthner, of Hofmannsthal and Musil—concerned reference: it took the form of finding language inadequate to express experience.[6] The ideas that fueled the so-called language crisis in the Austro-Hungarian Empire were not born there. Indeed, it is more correct to say, in view of Wittgenstein's turnabout and Kafka's skeptical parable, that after a long and abundant final flowering, these ideas, and in particular the intense concern over reference, died there. We already find a questioning of the referential adequacy of language in John Locke: language does not serve knowledge, since it creates entities that correspond to nothing in reality; these concepts are derived metaphorically from words designating sensible things;

the linguistic sign is arbitrary. The documentable source of language-critical ideas for the two Austro-Hungarian authors most affected by skepticism, Mauthner and Hofmannsthal, is Nietzsche. Nietzsche's works abound in remarks that view the constructions of language with suspicion. In the early (though unpublished) essay "On Truth and Lie in the Extramoral Sense" (1873) he dismisses words as a moving army of metaphors, metonymies, and anthropomorphisms that have no referential value but that have acquired a deceptive literalness in the course of time. In the influential *On the Advantage and Disadvantage of History for Life* he transposes a central idea of the earlier, unpublished essay into the context of a polemic against the current mode of education of German youth and lashes out against concepts, "covered bowls which may well be empty" and that obstruct the "unmediated perception of life" ("unmittelbare Anschauung des Lebens") of which German youth might be capable if their heads were not packed with concepts (AD 63, 60). Mauthner, in his autobiography *Prager Jugendjahre*, cites *On the Advantage and Disadvantage of History for Life* as an influence on the language skepticism that came over him in 1873.[7] Hofmannsthal's earliest language-critical poem "Gedankenspuk" (1890), in which he criticizes the "inadequacy" of the artist's "handicraft," is indebted to precisely the same source: it bears an epigram from the same work by Nietzsche.[8] Finally, the ideas behind turn-of-the-century Austrian language skepticism were by no means restricted to Austria but flourished elsewhere in Europe at the same time. Thus Oscar Wilde writes in 1891 that "language . . . is the parent, and not the child of thought";[9] Stéphane Mallarmé, in the celebrated essay "Crise des vers" (1895) writes of "the insufficiency of languages";[10] Valéry writes in his notes on language in 1898, "What obscures nearly everything is language—because it obliges you to fix things and generalizes without your wanting it to." [11]

Yet there is no question that language skepticism infected writers of the Austro-Hungarian Empire with particular virulence. Mauthner's doubts blossomed by 1901 into a massive three-volume critique of language, *Beiträge zu einer Kritik der Sprache*. The principal message of this rambling work is that language is useless for knowledge. Language consists basically of metaphors that have been degraded into literal meaning; in particular, concepts are monsters that designate nothing; language is a closed system, telling us nothing about the world; moreover, it controls and obstructs our perception. We have words for things that do not exist, and no words for things that do exist.[12]

Hofmannsthal compresses similar ideas into the brief fictional letter of Lord Chandos. This piece recapitulates so well in the crisis of the fictive narrator the main stages of European thought about language from the sixteenth century to Hofmannsthal's own day that it warrants a brief discussion here, even though it has already elicited an enormous quantity of commentary, some of it very good.[13] For the Chandos letter, whatever its relevance may have been to Hofmannsthal's own feelings about language, is a highly contrived artifact.[14] It is meticulously placed in the historical context appropriate to the crisis that Chandos documents. Chandos addresses his letter to Francis Bacon and dates the year of composition 1603, the year of James I's accession to the throne and hence the beginning of the Jacobean era.

Chandos eloquently describes the three successive stages of consciousness about the world and language that he has experienced: initial euphoria, crisis, and his present state. Initially, life appeared to Chandos as a great unity. The world stretched out, his experiences succeeded each other, without essential difference. To him everything was equally part of nature: he made no distinctions between intellect and matter, solitude and society, appearances and reality, self and world. He claims that he read books as he drank milk, not distinguishing the one from the other. His experience consisted of successiveness without breaks, of horizontality without boundaries: "And thus it prevailed through the whole expanse of life in all directions" (SP 132). If there is a semiotics of this world of relatedness, it consists in the interchangeability of signified and signifier. Chandos writes, "I divined that all was allegory [Gleichnis] and that each creature was a key to all the others." It is a state that closely resembles the world view of the Renaissance as described by Michel Foucault in *The Order of Things*:

> Up to the end of the sixteenth century, resemblance played a constructive role in the knowledge of Western culture. It was resemblance that largely guided exegesis and the interpretation of texts; it was resemblance that organized the play of symbols, made possible knowledge of things visible and invisible, and controlled the art of representing them. The universe was folded in upon itself: the earth echoing the sky, faces seeing themselves reflected in the stars, and plants holding within their stems the secrets that were of use to man.[15]

In short, as Foucault writes, "The relation of languages to the world is one of analogy rather than of signification."[16] Language was viewed as originally God-given, and languages, though no longer transparent, were still not seen to be separate from the world.

Chandos's crisis consists in the sensation that thought, and with it language, has come undone from things. Suddenly, the old, friendly world where all was *Gleichnis*, similitude, has vanished, and in Chandos's vision a new, dual world has constituted itself: a world where the realm of the signifier (language, consciousness, cognition) is distinct and separate from that of the signified (world, feeling, intuition). The function of the signifier is to *represent* the signified. A dual, vertical relation has replaced the old horizontal one.

This crisis coincides with the profound epistemological change which, according to Foucault, took place around the beginning of the seventeenth century. "What has become important is no longer resemblances but identities and differences."[17] The sign came to be looked on as arbitrary and man-made, the relation to signifier to referent as one of representation.[18]

With this new *épistémè* is born the realization that language represents the world badly, inadequately, even deceptively. Chandos at first feels queasy about abstract concepts. "The abstract terms . . . crumbled in my mouth like mouldy fungi" (SP 133–34). Then moral judgments (good, bad, etc.) appear suspect. Suddenly Chandos begins to see everything from close up ("My mind compelled me to view all things occurring in such conversations from an uncanny closeness"). His malaise finally blossoms into a general crisis of language as a medium of representation, which marks the destruction of "the world as a great unity": "For me everything disintegrated into parts, those parts again into parts; no longer would anything let itself be encompassed by one idea. Single words floated round me; they congealed into eyes which stared at me and into which I was forced to stare back—whirlpools which gave me vertigo and, reeling incessantly, led into the void" (SP 134–35). Philosophies strike him as a mere closed play of concepts, without reference to the world: "These ideas [Begriffe], I understood them well: I saw their wonderful interplay rise before me like magnificent fountains upon which played golden balls. I could hover around them and watch how they played, one with the other; but they were concerned only with each other, and the most profound, most personal quality of my thinking remained excluded from this magic circle" (SP 135). Thus here in Chandos's second state we find the same ideas as in Mauthner, the first volume of whose *Beiträge zu einer Kritik der*

Sprache Hofmannsthal acknowledged having read soon after it appeared.[19]

After his crisis Chandos pursues a placid, unintellectual existence. Yet it is characterized by certain "gay and stimulating moments" (SP 135). In these moments Chandos, who again has the sensation of a "harmony transcending me and the entire world" (SP 138), seems to have regained the euphoria of his original state. Yet there are several significant differences. First, in the new state his joy is condensed into rare and precious moments and is not, as before, the continuous fabric of his days. These moments stand in sharp contrast with the "incredible emptiness" of the rest of his existence. Second, the moments are epiphanies that reveal to him something that is higher than and excluded from everyday life ("filling like a vessel any casual object of my daily surroundings with an overflowing flood of higher life," SP 135). Thus the dual, vertical orientation of his state of crisis persists. Next, the epiphanies are inexpressible in language ("words desert me," SP 135). That is, language continues to be conceived as representation. The fourth difference is that the most humble objects now serve as vehicles for the transcendent. "A pitcher, a harrow abandoned in a field, a dog in the sun, a neglected cemetery, a cripple, a peasant's hut—all these can become the vessel of my revelation" (SP 135–36); "This combination of trifles sent through me . . . a shudder at the presence of the Infinite" (SP 137). Thus the moments live precisely on the sort of contrast between the spiritual and the mundane that Chandos did not perceive in his first state. The humble objects that bring on a sense of the sublime and infinite are symbols, in Charles Baudelaire's sense. To recall some of Baudelaire's formulations: "All forms of beauty, like all possible phenomena, have within them something eternal and something transitory—an absolute and a particular element"; "In certain almost supernatural states of the soul, the profundity of life is entirely revealed in any scene, however ordinary, that presents itself before me. The scene becomes its symbol."[20] In the same vein, the most moving experiences may occur in the *absence* of the actual object or scene, says Chandos. "Even the distinct image of an absent object, in fact, can acquire the mysterious function of being filled to the brim with this silent but suddenly rising flood of divine sensation" (SP 136). This is an essentially modern—Romantic and post-Romantic—conception. One is reminded of Wordsworth's "spots of time," moments of abrupt illumination "when the light of sense goes out in flashes that have shown to us the invisible world" (*Prelude* 6.534–36, 1805 edition), moments of an access of the imagination that are essentially different, for Wordsworth as in the Chandos letter, from the steadiness and continuity imputed to nature. Proust would take the idea of presence in absence—the absence of the material object as a condition of its spiritual presence for the subject—to new extremes. The key to these new experiences of Chandos's, then, is contrast: the experience of presence in absence, a sense of infinity in the face of the most humble object. It is precisely contrast, difference, that was lacking in Chandos's first state. Finally, whereas his first state was solipsistic and childlike—he was at the center, everything mirrored him—the second is mystical, and involves self-dissolution. Chandos thinks that he can *flow* into things: "Among the objects playing against one another there is not one into which I cannot flow" (SP 138). In the first stage, he is "intoxicated"; he has a sense of himself opening the secrets of the universe as if with keys. In the final state, he himself becomes the intoxicating beverage: "It is then that I feel as though I myself were about to ferment, to effervesce, to foam and to sparkle" (SP 140).

In assessing the Austrian language crisis, we stand before three questions: What gave rise to the language-critical ideas to begin with? Why were they particularly widespread in Europe toward the end of the nineteenth century? Why did they occur in a particularly intense and visible form in the Austro-Hungarian Empire? Let us look at some answers that have been given.

As an answer to the first question, to the question of the emergence of language-critical ideas since Locke, the explanation proffered by two nineteenth-century thinkers, Taine and Nietzsche—for both give the same—is as good as any that has been named since.[21] Taine in *On Intelligence* (1870) ascribes the demystification of purely "verbal entities" to the progress of science during the last three centuries. He speaks of "that army of verbal entities which formerly invaded all the provinces of nature, and which during the last three hundred years, the progress of the sciences has one by one upset. There are only two left at present, the Ego and matter; but at that time, during the avowed or dissembled empire of the scholastic philosophy, men imagined that, underlying events, were a number of chimerical beings."[22] Nietzsche advances much the same opinion in *Human, All Too Human* (1[1878]: para 11 ["Language as an alleged science"]): "The importance of language for the development of culture lies in the fact that, in language, man juxtaposed to the one world another world of his own, a place which he thought so sturdy that from it he could move the rest of the world from its foundations and make himself lord over it. . . . He really did believe that in language he had knowledge of the world. The shaper of language was not so modest as to think that he was only giving things labels; rather, he imagined that he was expressing the highest knowledge of things with words; and in fact, language is the first stage of scientific effort. Here, too, it is *the belief in found truth* from which the mightiest sources of strength have flowed. Very belatedly (only now) is it dawning on men that in their belief in language they have propagated a monstrous error."[23]

As an answer to the second question, that of the prevalence of language-critical ideas in Europe toward the end of the nineteenth century, the dissolution of religious belief, especially in Catholic Austria, is surely important. Doubts about religion can only have exacerbated the conviction that meaningless expressions were rampant, while true reality, which had been vacated by God, lacked words. The rise and subsequent impasses of contemporary linguistic science are also often cited as a reason for the loss of faith in words. Gérard Genette tells us in *Mimologiques* that the discovery of Sanskrit and the birth of the comparative grammar of Indo-European languages bred disappointed Cratylists, who would no longer point with conviction to the astonishing parallels between different languages as proof that verbal sounds were mimetic of things.[24] Faith in the new science itself then suffered a blow in the 1860s when linguistic scholars—Michel Bréal, William Dwight Whitney—expressed skepticism in the idea that language is ruled by laws and that the study of language is therefore comparable to a natural science. In 1872 Johannes Schmidt then showed that the idea of an Indo-European original language was a fiction. These developments left their mark on the realm of letters: to the philosophical and poetic eye, the new science seemed not to live up to its promise and to be failing before the important questions, notably the question of the origin of language. Thus Mauthner reminisces that Nietzsche's debunking of laws in history led to a suspicion that there were no laws in linguistics either; linguistics was not a science comparable to the natural sciences; the "original Indo-European language was a dream that had been dreamed to its end."[25]

To turn to the third question, the multilinguistic situation in the Austro-Hungarian Empire surely fostered an increased conciousness of language, and with it language skepticism. For these languages did not live at peace with each other. As the furor following the Badeni ordinances of 1897, which mandated a knowledge of Czech as well as German for civil servants in Bohemia and Moravia, epitomized most dramatically, language was a perpetual political issue. Fritz Mauthner, the outstanding example of turn-of-the-century Austro-Hungarian language skepticism, cites in his autobiography the trilingual context of his youth in Prague as the probable source of his questioning attitude toward language.[26] Merely *knowing* several languages encourages a questioning attitude; hence language skepticism was a probable byproduct of Hofmannsthal's extensive humanistic education. Musil's scientific education can, for different reasons, be held accountable.

But I would like to suggest that language skepticism with an Austrian accent found such a ready foothold because it presented itself as a further permutation of an entrenched dualistic mode of thought. Nietzsche's attack on concepts is one of the complaints that turn-of-the-century Austrian critics of language reiterate most often.[27] But Nietzsche's vitalistic obverse is an even more broadly unifying characteristic of the turn-of-the-century Austrian criticism of language. The rather different views on language found in such classic language-crisis texts as Hofmannsthal's "The Letter of Lord Chandos" and Musil's *Törless* have a central idea in common, and one they share, moreover, with Wittgenstein's *Tractatus*: the idea that some precious and important experience is accessible to us, although it is wholly beyond the grasp of our language and our reason. Thus Hofmannsthal's Lord Chandos speaks of epiphanies in which "something entirely unnamed, even barely nameable" announces itself to him by filling some ordinary object of his everyday life "with an overflowing flood of higher life" (sp 135); in *Törless* Musil speaks of experiences that were "so distinct that he was pierced through by their intensity," but that they "escaped him the moment he sought for words to grasp them with" (yt 67); Wittgenstein affirms at the end of the *Tractatus*, "There are, indeed, things that cannot be put into words." Bahr speaks of the "inadequacy of language, which cannot express anything one feels."[28]

Thus we have not only a distrust of language, but a positive celebration of a realm beyond language. The duality language/the inexpressible is a logical extension of the duality reason/the irrational. For it was a philosophical commonplace of long standing that language is allied to reason and thought. It was a commonplace of Wagnerian opera that language is incapable of expressing *feeling*. As Richard Wagner put it in *Oper und Drama* (1850–51), "In modern prose we speak a language we do not understand with our feeling. . . . We cannot, in a certain sense, participate in this language according to our innermost sentiment . . . ; in it, we can communicate our sentiments only to the intellect, but not to the confidently understanding feeling; and therefore, quite consequentially, in our modern development feeling has sought to flee the absolute language of the intellect for the absolute language of sound, for our contemporary music."[29]

Wagner, following Schopenhauer, who had declared music the only art form directly expressive of the Will, claimed for music a power he emphatically denied to language, the power to express emotion. It remained for the poets to except their art from the muddy flow of everyday discourse and make similarly ambitious claims for poetic language. For the obverse of language skepticism, which narrowed language's purview to an imperfect referentiality in the service of a blind rationality, was a promotion of art to the mouthpiece of all that ordinary language was too coarse, clumsy, or debased to express. Language skepticism did not impoverish the poet. Rather, it invited one to claim a vast terrain that lay open by default and that with a certain dexterity one could call one's own. Language experiment is born of the same spirit as language skepticism: language becomes a medium to work with, rather than a respected edifice to find one's way into. Language is no longer seen to express preexisting thoughts, but to generate thoughts, while language distortion may express "inexpressible" thoughts.[30] Given language skepticism, declaring new poetic subjects and refashioning poetic language became a particular challenge. Mallarmé and Valéry are the best-known theoreticians of the new poetics. Mallarmé envisioned a poetic language that would redeem the mimetic inadequacy and arbitrariness of "the language of the tribe." For Valéry, the highest arts were those that were not referential, music and architecture. Poetry, hampered by its unfortunate dependence on a medium that was already attached to meanings, could nevertheless strive to emulate the necessity we associate with the constructions of music and architecture by deriving, in similar fashion, its laws from the properties of its medium, language. That is, poetry should aspire to unite sound and sense. The successful poem, according to Valéry, affects its reader like a magic formula or charm.

Of the Austrian poets, it was principally Hofmannsthal who occupied himself with theory. "Das Gespräch über Gedichte" is the centerpiece of his affirmative statements about poetry. There Hofmannsthal voices his belief in the magical power of poetry to conjure forth the thing in its elemental fascination. A quotation suffices to show that Hofmannsthal emphatically excepts poetry from language in crisis: "It is precisely poetry which strives feverishly to posit the thing itself, with a completely different energy from dull everyday language, with a completely different magical power from the feeble terminology of science. . . . [Poetry] speaks words for the sake of the words; that is its magic. For the sake of the magic power which words have to touch our bodies, and incessantly to transform us."[31]

Other writers, notably Rilke, Schnitzler, and Musil, took up the challenge of devising poetic means to express what was on the borderlines of the knowable—that is, their own particular, special insights into the world—and beyond the reach of the sayable in ordinary terms.[32] Rilke is the outstanding example: he pursued the quest for new forms of expression more persistently and hence more successfully than most of his contemporaries. For Rilke, not the sanctified art of his generation, music, but rather sculpture, notably Auguste Rodin's, served as model. As he wrote in the celebrated letter to Lou Andreas-Salomé of 10 August 1903, "Somehow I too must manage to make things; written, not plastic things,—realities that proceed from handwork. Somehow I too must discover the smallest basic element, the cell of *my* art, the tangible medium of presentation for everything, irrespective of subject matter."[33] Rilke's *Neue Gedichte* (*New Poems*) and *Neue Gedichte anderer Teil* (*New Poems: The Other Part*), the first fruits of that resolve, are monuments to his attempts to make "Kunstdinge," art objects that are more real than their natural counterparts. To judge from the poems, Rilke discovered the "smallest basic element" of his art in metaphor. The poet's power to recreate the world in language lies precisely in the poet's ability to juxtapose far-flung subjects, thereby alienating the poetic object from its habitual context and letting it appear in a new light. In Rilke's hands the art of metaphor attained new heights. In particular his technique of the narrative metaphor, which is the structural principle in such poems as "Spanische Tänzerin" ("Spanish Dancer"), "Die Fensterrose" ("The Rose Window") and "Die Flamingos," deserves mention. Rilke compares the subject of the poem to one or two other objects, about whom quasi-independent stories are told. Frequently the subject recedes behind the other, foregrounded narrative strands. For example, in "Dame vor dem Spiegel" ("Lady at a Mirror") the subject, a woman dressing before a mirror, recedes behind the secondary subject, the story of a woman mixing and drinking a magic potion. The effect is to conjure forth the titular subject, which is barely delineated, as if by magic: by pulling the strings, as it were, of an explicit or implicit comparison. Rilke's achievement in such poems is to circumvent naming. In fact, naming as a condition for reference is a limit that Rilke constantly tries to transcend in the poetic experiments in these volumes. Metaphor is a first step, for as practiced by Rilke, it achieves reference without description. In other poems Rilke uses yet more drastic techniques. "Der Panther," for example, operates with the technique of the implied negative. This poem, which is about a caged panther, lives off the implied contrast with a wild panther stalking its prey in its natural habitat. In "Der Stifter" ("The Donor") Rilke attempts to figure the transcendent by leaving a blank spot in the logic of an image. The image is one of the hunt; the blank spot, to be filled by the reader, is that of the hunter's prey, a timid wild animal.

Schnitzler's single most significant achievement as a writer lies in his attempts to portray consciousness. He carried out these experiments with brilliant success and without theoretical ado. Besides his many sympathetic and apt portrayals of the female psyche, three stories in particular deserve mention: "Leutnant Gustl" and "Fräulein Else," where he used interior monologue, a new narrative technique adapted from Edouard Dujardin, to capture the psychology of a young officer and a nineteen-year-old girl; and "Flucht in die Finsternis," where he rendered the mental habits of an obsessional neurotic in free indirect style. Choosing the right technique to render the psychological processes of a particular character type was Schnitzler's forte. Both Gustl and Else are immature, distractible, reactive personalities whose conscious processes are largely given over to free-ranging daydreaming. Under their false consciousness lie deep, undiscovered unconscious conflicts. In both cases a traumatic shock brings out the latent conflict. Schnitzler captures this type of psyche with particular skill and wit by using the highly manipulable interior monologue. In "Flucht in die Finsternis," in contrast, free indirect style with its pseudo-objectivity is the ideal vehicle for rendering the thought processes of a neurotic who is intensely preoccupied with one idea, remains relatively unaffected by outside events though he persistently misinterprets them, and is strictly logical in his relentless pursuit of his delusion.

Musil's stories in *Unions* are also experiments in portraying consciousness, or rather the interplay of conscious and unconscious impulses that result in a processual fluctuation and ultimately an alteration in perception. Musil described these experiments in later years as the "way of the smallest steps," the "principle of the heaviest loading of the smallest step," and the "way of the most gradual, most imperceptible transition."[34] Musil's obsession, evident already in *Törless*, was the flicker in consciousness when our perception of something suddenly changes, or to borrow an image from Wittgenstein, the duck-rabbit effect. The narrative "The Perfecting of a Love," the story of a woman's infidelity, consists of a procession of such moments. Musil reinforces them with inverted images, where foreground becomes background and vice versa: thus whereas Claudine and her husband initially look out from their brightly lit living room into the darkness, when Claudine later approaches the moment of infidelity she supposes herself standing outside in the darkness and watching her husband inside a lit room. Musil deploys other spatial leitmotifs to figure Claudine's change in sensibility: island, sphere, enclosure, frozen place, and a hall of mirrors first characterize the emotional stability and protection her marriage affords, but later describe the city that will be the scene of her infidelity. It is typical of Musil to resolve seeming antithesis not into unity, but into one final, grand, irresolvable opposition. Thus a counternote to these increasingly like-seeming opposites, these superficial places of abode, are the spaces between and around them and the depth below them: the water surrounding the island, the snow surrounding the room, the depth into which roots grow, and the darkness, distance, and emptiness of space. With these images Musil figures his heroine's fundamental selfhood. In the other story, "The Temptation of Quiet Veronica," Musil immediately confronts the reader with the premise of the inexpressibility of feeling. Both main characters labor inarticulately to express powerful but elusive sensations: "That I might say: You are God" (FW 179); "All I've said still isn't it at all" (FW 185). Musil's own task then becomes the communication of this "incomprehensible other thing" (FW 179), this "indefinable thing" (FW 180) through the language of his text. In his depiction of his heroine's spiritual rebirth (to choose a relatively clear example), where Veronica experiences an afflatus or sensation of unification with things, Musil exploits the device of reversal, of a giving and taking back of images, a shuttling between and hence undermining of opposites. Two examples of the interplay of theme and countertheme in this episode (marked by A and B) will suffice:

A [The objects were] curving and bulging, arching high, with something emanating from them that was a kind of excess—until the sense of the moment rose like a hollow cube around Veronica B and she herself became a silent room full of flickering candles, herself a room enclosing everything. (FW 209)

[A So wölbten und bogen sie [die Dinge] sich in die Höhe, und unaufhörlich strömte dieses Übermäßige von ihnen aus und das Gefühl des Augenblicks hob und höhlte sich um Veronika, B wie wenn sie selbst plötzlich wie ein Raum mit schweigend flackernden Kerzen um alles stünde. (M 6:214)]

A . . . nowhere herself; and B yet she felt nothing but herself, and wherever she went A she both was and B was not. (FW 215)

[A . . . . nirgends sie und B doch fühlte sie nichts als sich und wo sie ging, A war sie und B war nicht. (M 6:218)]

Freud and Language

While critics have industriously documented and scrutinized the turn-of-the-century Austrian language crisis as it affects literary writers, Sigmund Freud's views on language have received little attention, and his relationship to language precisely within the context of that skepticism, none. Since Freud is an, even *the*, outstanding example of the dualistic habits of thought that run through the work of his contemporaries; since their language-critical ideas may be regarded as part of this same tendency; and since, finally, language plays a central role not only in psychoanalytic practice but also in Freud's metapsychological theory, I shall devote the rest of this chapter to investigating Freud's assumptions about language and his use of it within the framework of his theoretical constructs.

At first glance, Sigmund Freud does not appear to share his contemporaries' critical views on language. On the contrary, the practice of psychoanalysis would seem to be founded on an unbounded confidence in language as a medium of therapy, while Freud's theoretical writings affirm at every turn the inexhaustible richness of language as an analytic resource. Freud and Breuer's early "cathartic method" is predicated on the notion that language is adequately referential. Freud's enterprise is interpretation, and he therefore has a vested interest in continuity, in the possibility of transformation and translation from one medium to another, from body to psyche, from hidden desires to oneiric images. He freely draws on language as a medium that helps him make these transitions. The impurity, the constantly changing nature of language that drove Mauthner, for one, to despair is precisely Freud's capital.

My thesis is, however, that there *is* a language crisis in Freud's work, in the sense that problems relating to language create a conflict between the hermeneutic and the metapsychological aspects of his work. The crisis comes to a head in the course of the tortured sentences and drifting argument of chapter 7 of *The Interpretation of Dreams* and centers on the concept of the unconscious. In an effort to resolve the problem Freud will turn what appears as a language crisis in some of his contemporaries into a psychic crisis—into a dualistic psyche, in which an area that uses language is sharply distinguished from another, more mystical region that is beyond the grasp of language. Freud also creates, in order to achieve access to that inexpressible beyond, what can be regarded as a new literary form.

It is remarkable that, although language played an enormously important role in both Freud's thought and his clinical practice, Freud never devoted an entire essay to expounding his views on the subject. The critic must therefore try to reconstruct these views out of statements that are scattered throughout his works or, yet more precariously, by reading between Freud's lines. It is symptomatic of the problems involved that two previous critics, both of them careful readers of Freud's texts, have come up with readings that are diametrically opposed. Interestingly, for both critics the crucial question is the relation of language to the unconscious. To be sure, the critics come from different ideological camps, and they base their reconstructions on different texts by Freud. Jacques Lacan's writings are guided by a desire to "bring . . . the psychoanalytic experience back to speech and language."[35] To this end he applies Saussurian linguistics to Freud's theories and eventually finds that they are inscribed there already: "What the psychoanalytic experience discovers in the unconscious," he writes, "is the whole structure of language."[36] Hans Martin Gauger, in pointed disagreement with Lacan, believes that the subject of language is greatly overestimated today in all disciplines, and he proposes that linguistics has something to learn from Freud, rather than the reverse. He stresses that the Freudian unconscious is wordless. But, he says, the unconscious does contain its own archaic, wordless mode of expression, which we could perhaps consider as the remote historical progenitor of our present-day language.[37]

The stakes in this discussion are high. Both parties want to substantiate theories about the role of language in psychic life by appropriating the authority of Freud. Lacan, by inscribing language in the unconscious, asserts that its structures are fundamental to and formative for the human psyche. Gauger, by insisting that the unconscious is wordless, argues for a historically based, evolutionary conception of psychic development, whereby the oldest and most fundamental part of our psyche, the unconscious, predates language as we know it today.

Odd though this may seem, both Lacan's and Gauger's readings—that the unconscious contains the whole structure of language and that the unconscious is wordless—are not only possible but actually correct, given the different texts on which each author bases his interpretation. The reason is that Lacan draws his arguments from Freud's early works, in particular his hermeneutic texts (*Studies on Hysteria*, chapter 6 of *The Interpretation of Dreams*, *The Psychpathology of Everyday Life*, *Jokes and their Relation to the Unconscious*), by performing a subtle though synthetic reading, while Gauger focuses on Freud's later and metapsychological texts (he starts with Freud's metapsychological essays of 1915) and bases his conclusions on passages in which Freud states his views clearly.[38] I would first like to stress, in contrast principally to Gauger, that it is an open question whether Freud even *had* a unified theory of language. The critic who approaches his texts with the assumption that Freud's views are consistent and can be synthesized into a coherent whole has already jumped to an unwarranted conclusion. We can safely assume that Freud was systematically interested in language from the beginnings of his psychological career, and even before those beginnings, with his work on aphasia published in 1891.[39] His early biological and metapsychological interest in language persisted throughout his career; moreover, there are ample indications that it was paralleled by an interest in linguistic theory, specifically in the history of language, which, to judge from Freud's remarks in the *Introductory Lectures*, blossomed into a fairly intensive study in the first decade and a half of the century. If he did not write an essay on language it is probably because— and here again I disagree with Gauger—the topic posed a problem for him; he had invested too much in being able to operate with language in different and not always compatible ways. It is surely no accident that he speaks in *The Psychopathology of Everyday Life* of a book catalog he misplaced because he regarded as a rival the author of one of the titles listed in it. His repression and distortion of the subject persists into his account of the incident. "I could remember the names of both book and author," Freud asserts. But he does not tell us the author's name, and the title he gives for it, "Über die Sprache," is almost certainly incorrect or abridged (SE 6:139–40).

I should preface my own reading of Freud on language by saying that I read his texts only for their own intrinsic logic, as a literary critic. My reading hence departs from different premises than, and consequently will be different from, Freudian readings such as Lacan's or Gauger's. What is common to Lacan's and Gauger's readings is a belief in the existence of the unconscious. Both authors take the unconscious as that psychic fundament on which further arguments, concerning the role of language in psychic life, can be grounded. Lacan and Gauger disagree merely in their interpretation of the Freudian unconscious. A literary critic who approaches Freud's work as text (and hence, it must be conceded, perhaps unfairly disregards the dimension of clinical experience that may have inspired, validated, or subsequently disproved his theories), and without a Freudian bias, is inclined to approach the notion of the unconscious with an attitude of skepticism. As was discussed in detail in chapter 1, the unconscious as it is presented in *The Interpretation of Dreams* seems less a discovery than a construct.[40] In this optic, a reading of Freud on language changes entirely: language appears as a *means* that Freud exploited to arrive at interpretations of puzzling psychic phenomena (hysterical symptoms, dreams), as well as a theoretical object in itself, and the unconscious, in that context, figures as a battleground where Freud's hermeneutic enterprise and his temporal and energetic conception of the psyche coexist in uneasy deadlock.

It must first be stated that Freud shows extraordinary consistency throughout his writings when it is a question of assigning language a metapsychological place. From the "Preliminary Communication" in *Studies on Hysteria* to *The Ego and the Id*, his thinking is all of a piece: he connects language with rational thought. This is of course precisely the connection Musil makes in *Törless*, and it is evident that both Freud and Musil are reiterating a notion that, while not universally accepted by theoreticians of language, was nevertheless of both long and firm standing. Traditionally credited to Johann Gottfried von Herder, the idea of the interdependence of language and reason has more recently been traced to Etienne Bonnot de Condillac.[41] Schopenhauer postulated it in *On the Fourfold Root of the Principle of Sufficient Reason* (para 26). "Without speech no reason, without reason no speech": this idea was a cornerstone of the theories of Max Müller.[42] Current, Darwinistic thought (as represented for example by George Romanes, whose work Freud read carefully), modifying Müller's absolute stance, considered that reason and language evolved simultaneously and dialectically and that the process is recapitulated in the development of the individual child.[43] In the *Project* Freud elaborates the idea in some detail. Our "speech associations" are "quality signs" that allow our psychic apparatus to bring memories to consciousness. These speech signs are "signs of the reality of thought" and are thus at the service of the secondary process, in contrast to the primary process, which confines itself to the hallucinatory revival of desired objects. Indeed, Freud asserts that thought that cathects the speech signs systematically is "the highest and most certain form of cognitive thought," for it is least contaminated by the wishful, purposive mode of the primary process.[44] When Freud introduces the preconscious in a letter to Fliess of 6 December 1896, he defines it as a "thought consciousness," whose transcription of memories is "bound to verbal images [Wortvorstellungen]."[45] In the essay "The Unconscious" of 1915, Freud adds a statement about the contents of the unconscious to his earlier conclusions. He writes that the unconscious contains representations of things (*Sachvorstellungen*) only, whereas the preconscious contains the representations of things plus the verbal representations (*Wortvorstellungen*) belonging to them. Thus the unconscious is preverbal, the preconscious verbal (SE 14:201).

My discussion of language in the context of Freud's hermeneutics will center on *Studies on Hysteria* and *The Interpretation of Dreams* and will focus in particular on two passages. As is well known, Freud's first hermeneutic object was the hysterical symptom, which he comprehends as a motivated sign for a psychic referent—a *motivated* sign, of course, because he intends to interpret it. One of the major tasks Freud and Breuer set for themselves in *Studies on Hysteria* is to explain how the sign is motivated, or in other words, the patient's choice of symptom. Why does one patient smell burned pudding, while another has pains in her leg? The solution the authors propose in the "Preliminary Communication" is that the symptom is determined by a precipitating trauma. In the course of the case studies, as Freud comes to view the conflicting affect generated by the psyche itself as the cause of hysteria, he attaches less and less importance to the trauma. He retains the trauma mainly as a way of explaining the symptom. The symptom is determined by the trauma in one or more different ways: it can reproduce some element of the traumatic situation, like the smell of burned pudding; it can revive a preexisting somatic condition that the patient associates with the trauma, like pains in the leg; or it can symbolize an emotion the patient felt at the traumatic moment.

What is this symbolism? Freud and Breuer at first equate it with a standard association between a feeling and a physical reaction, like vomiting upon a feeling of moral disgust. But Freud soon becomes more daring; he designates as a symbol any symptom that realizes a verbal expression, specifically, metaphors of the body for psychic states. Thus Freud asserts toward the end of his final case study on Elisabeth von R. that facial neuralgia can symbolize the idea of a "slap in the face"; a violent pain in the heel can symbolize the idea of "not being on the right footing" with someone; a stabbing sensation in the region of the heart can symbolize "it stabbed me to the heart." In short, what Breuer resistingly calls "some ridiculous play on words" becomes a sufficient motivation for the symptom. The hermeneutic gain is obvious. When one considers how many verbal expressions for bodily pains are metaphors for psychic states, one understands to what degree Freud relieved himself of the responsibility of searching his patients' biographies for symptom-motivating traumas by interposing linguistic usage between the somatic symptom and its psychic referent. The field of language, of linguistic ambiguity and metaphor, is plainly far more fertile than the field of the patient's lived experience.

With his symbolic hypothesis Freud performs a strange reversal on the theory of language implicit in the cathartic method that he and his colleague formulated in the "Preliminary Communication," according to which language represents the trauma and speech expulses it. In Freud's new conception, language becomes a referent (for the somatic symptom) as well as a metaphoric sign (for the hidden affect). In the final paragraph of the case study of Elisabeth von R., he tries to modify the unconventional notion that language can be a referent. Let us look at this paragraph (the division into three parts is mine):

[1] In taking a verbal expression literally and in feeling a "stab in the heart" or the "slap in the face" after some slighting remark as a real event, the hysteric is not taking liberties with words, but is simply reviving once more the sensations to which the verbal expression owes its justification. How has it come about that we speak of someone who has been slighted as being "stabbed to the heart" unless the slight had in fact been accompanied by a precordial sensation which could suitably be described in that phrase and unless it was identifiable by that sensation? What could be more probable than that the figure of speech "swallowing something," which we use in talking

of an insult to which no rejoinder has been made, did in fact originate from the innervatory sensations which arise in the pharynx
when we refrain from speaking and prevent ourselves from reacting
to the insult? All these sensations and innervations belong to the
field of "The Expression of the Emotions," which, as Darwin has
taught us, consists of actions which originally had a meaning and
served a purpose. (2) These may now for the most part have become
so much weakened that the expression of them in words seems to us
only to be a figurative picture [bildliche Übertragung] of them,
whereas in all probability the description was once meant literally;
and hysteria is right in restoring the original meaning of the words
in depicting its unusually strong innervations. (3) Indeed, it is perhaps wrong to say that hysteria creates these sensations by symbolization. It may be that it does not take linguistic usage as its model
at all, but that both hysteria and linguistic usage alike draw their
material from a common source. (SE 2:181)

Freud begins (1) by suggesting that the verbal expression is not a
metaphor for the psychic state at all, but rather an indirectly motivated
metonymy, because originally, the emotion, the sense of being slighted,
was accompanied by the precordial sensation that the verbal phrase designates literally. Second (2), he points out that since the hysterical symptom is nothing more than an exact replica of this precordial sensation,
the hysteric in fact only restores the original meaning to the words. At
this point in the discussion the relation between the symptom and the
verbal expression becomes thoroughly unclear; the two seem to revolve
around each other, vying for the positions of signifier and signified.
Freud also alludes to the notion that will become abundantly familiar as
"regression" in his later writings, here in the limited sense of etymological regression. The idea that words originally had concrete and sensory
reference and became increasingly metaphorical and abstract in the
course of their history is a commonplace that Freud could have drawn
from any number of contemporary or older sources.[46] In *The Interpretation of Dreams* etymological regession will become a major hermeneutic
resource; Freud will use it to support his claim that pictorial dream images are a translation of verbal dream thoughts. The dream literalizes the
thought, regressing along the path established by linguistic theory. Thus
for example the dream work turns the notion of self-limitation, "sich
einschränken," into the image of a closet or "Schrank." Here he calls on

the idea merely to naturalize the hysteric's use of words in the formation of the symptom.

In the last two sentences (3) Freud draws the logical inference: hysteria does not take linguistic usage as its model at all but, rather, hysteria and linguistic usage draw their material from a common source. This conclusion would seem to have several evident advantages. It would restore the verbal expression to its conventional status as sign and oust it from its dubious position as a referent; it would introduce a more perfect determination into the motivation of the symptom, for the symptom would be directly mimetic of its referent and no longer rely on an arbitrary verbal sign; and most important, it would economically bypass a seemingly unnecessary stepping-stone in the motivation of the symptom. But Freud does not affirm his hypothesis; instead, he breaks off abruptly. It is plain that he hesitates to remove the linguistic intermediary definitively from his theory of symbolic symptom formation. Why? Let us imagine for a moment that he did remove it. He would then, as an interpreter, be faced with the task of compiling a dictionary of equivalences between psychic states and bodily sensations. He would have to answer such questions as, Does every psychic state have its bodily "translation"? Does each psychic state have its consistent bodily expression? Is the system reversible, so that specific bodily sensations always bring on specific psychic states? These propositions are unlikely, but more telling, the questions are unanswerable, and the project of compiling the psychic-somatic dictionary is unfeasible, because if Freud were to survey a pool of patients in order to determine "symptom usage," these patients would not be able to identify the mental states corresponding to their symptoms except by speaking. Clearly, only by using the intermediary of language can we compile a usable table of correspondences between mental states and bodily sensations. Moreover, only conventional linguistic usage gives the interpreter an intersubjectively plausible criterion for connecting a non-verbal phenomenon to a hidden psychic referent.

In *Studies on Hysteria*, language with its conventional meanings becomes a referent for a nonlinguistic sign, and the sign is motivated by the slipping nature of the meaning of the linguistic expression itself, so that the associative possibilities of language become a hermeneutic resource. In *The Interpretation of Dreams* Freud extends his premises and expands on his technique. Like the symptom, the dream is a sign, and the referent—in this case we could speak of the meaning—is the latent dream thoughts, whose nonconformity with the dream is attributed to censorship. Particularly in the chapter on the dream work, chapter 6, Freud becomes extremely confident about the procedure of linking the sign to its meaning through language that he still affirmed hesitatingly in *Studies on Hysteria*. He extends the range of linguistic motivations to include not only the use of literal and concrete expressions for abstract ideas, but also homophony and puns. Thus a kiss in a car signifies auto-eroticism, an elephant's trunk, "vous me trompez," and so on. Contrasting his methods with the "arbitrary" symbol-coining of previous interpreters, he asserts that interpretation through double-meaning expressions and etymology is sufficient to show that a given dream can be traced to certain specific dream thoughts. He writes, "In the case of symbolic dream-interpretation the key to the symbolization is arbitrarily chosen by the interpreter; whereas in our cases of verbal disguise the keys are generally known and laid down by firmly established linguistic usage" (SE 5:341–42). In short, according to Freud his own determinations of meaning are not arbitrary because the transformations he ascribes to the dream work are already inscribed in the intersubjective medium of language.

Freud not only explains dreams through linguistic ambiguities; as such critics as Lacan and Benveniste have pointed out, the transformations performed by the dream work, condensation and displacement, resemble those performed by rhetorical figures.[47] Freud does not say that the dream work performs these transformations on language, but rather on thought, on the latent dream thoughts. But we can understand the latent dream thoughts as being in language; not only does Freud once say, in a kind of inadvertent but essentially correct shorthand, that the dream thoughts are in words (SE 5:418), but it becomes amply evident that these thoughts, described by Freud as "correct" (my translation of "korrekt"; SE 5:506 gives "rational"), "immediately comprehensible" (SE 4:277), and in "a completely logical sequence" (SE 5:592; "vollkommen logisch gefügt"), have the same structure as the sentences we use in prose. For Freud, rational thought is homologous with language.

In chapters 2 through 6 Freud introduces us to a dualistic structure that is essentially derived from his hermeneutic theory. The actual dream, the manifest content, is separated from the latent content by the censor, that is, by distortion, as well as by its pictorial medium. The interpreter's task is to outwit the censor, to penetrate its distortions, and thus to arrive at the real meaning of the dream. This hidden meaning consists of the dream thoughts, and also of a wish: particularly in chapters 2–5 Freud associates the repressed wish with the verbally expressible dream thoughts as part of the latent content.[48]

When we begin to read the first metapsychological section of chapter 7, therefore, the section on regression where Freud presents us with the first version of the topography, it is with this hermeneutic duality of manifest content versus hidden meaning in mind. We expect that Freud will superimpose this hermeneutic duality onto his topography, the more so since his metapsychology is evidently intended to ground his interpretative assumptions in a generalization about the human mind. Indeed, Freud places the censor at the frontier between the unconscious and the preconscious. The reader thus readily assumes that Freud will place the wish and the latent dream thoughts, and with them the potential of being expressed in language, in what he designates as the Ucs.

Let us look at the only passage in this section where Freud makes an oblique reference to language, and in particular, at its last two sentences:

> Experience shows us that this path leading through the preconscious to consciousness is barred to the dream-thoughts during the daytime by the censorship imposed by resistance. During the night they are able to obtain access to consciousness; but the question arises as to how they do so and thanks to what modification. *If what enabled the dream-thoughts to achieve this were the fact that at night there is a lowering of the resistance which guards the frontier between the unconscious and the preconscious, we should have dreams which were in the nature of ideas* and which were without the hallucinatory quality in which we are at the moment interested. *Thus the lowering of the censorship between the two systems Ucs. and Pcs. can only explain dreams formed like "Autodidasker"* and not dreams like that of the burning child which we took as the starting-point of our investigations. (SE 5:542, my italics)

> [*Würde dies den Traumgedanken dadurch ermöglicht, daß nachts der Widerstand absinkt, der an der Grenze zwischen Unbewußtem und Vorbewußtem wacht, so bekämen wir Träume in dem Material unserer Vorstellungen*, die nicht den halluzinatorischen Character zeigen, der uns jetzt interessiert.
>
> *Das Absinken der Zensur zwischen den beiden Systemen Ubw und Vbw kann uns also nur solche Traumbildungen erklären wie Autodidasker*, aber nicht Träume wie den vom brennenden Kinde,

den wir uns als Problem an den Eingang dieser Untersuchungen gestellt haben. (*Studienausgabe*, 2:518, my italics)]

The "Autodidasker" dream is a purely verbal dream involving a condensation of the expressions "Autor," "Autodidakt," and "Lasker" (the name of a politician). The dream of the burning child is a hallucinatory dream that involves no distortion. How is the "Autodidasker" dream formed? The obvious reading of the two final sentences, the reading based on our assumptions up to this point in the text, would be that an improper thought (or "idea"), expressed in ordinary language, comes from the unconscious; this thought is allowed to go through the diminished censorship and attract the attention of consciousness at the price of distortion, that is, through displacement and condensation respectively; the final dream, "Autodidasker," is thus in distorted words. But the more one looks at the passage the more its sense seems to change. Above all, the expression "das Material unserer Vorstellungen" is teasing. Is it an elegant circumlocution for "words"? Another reading suggests itself: the unconscious product is an improper thought, on which the censorship imposes as the price of entry into the preconscious the "Material unserer Vorstellungen," or a verbal form. And if one takes the sentences out of their context, yet a third possible reading emerges from them: the unconscious product is improper in the sense of being improperly formulated, and the "lowering of the censorship" means that its gobbledegook, namely "Autodidasker," is able to penetrate to the preconscious.

If the hermeneutic is grounded in the topography, then the topography is in turn grounded in the actual biological and social development of the individual, and accordingly, in the following sections of chapter 7, those entitled "Wish-Fulfilment" and "Arousal by Dreams—The Function of Dreams—Anxiety Dreams," Freud develops the temporal and dynamic aspects of the metapsychology. The unconscious is defined in temporal terms as the first psychic place. As such it is the source of the first psychic function, desire, whose dynamic equivalent, energy, sets the psychic mechanism in motion. The dream wish, which Freud defines as an *infantile* wish, comes from the unconscious and provides energy for the dream formation.

What is said in the course of this discussion about language? Our assumption, formed by the hermeneutic chapters, that there is language in the unconscious, proves to conflict with the notion of the infantile unconscious, for infants are by definition without speech. And thus we feel only slightly seasick, but not wholly surprised, when Freud clearly and explicitly places language in the preconscious in his revised version of the topography in the section called "The Function of Dreams." Using the terminology of the *Project* and the letter to Fliess, Freud writes, "The Pcs. system needed to have qualities of its own which could attract consciousness; and it seems highly probable that it obtained them by linking the preconscious processes with the mnemic system of linguistic symbols [Sprachzeichen], a system which was not without quality" (SE 5:574). Suddenly, when we look back at the passage in the section on regression, the second of the three interpretations seems to be the correct one.

In the immediately following section called "The Primary and Secondary Processes," where Freud revises the topography for a second time and modifies it to accommodate the dynamic function, he makes a sharp distinction, which he had hinted at previously, between the dream thoughts and the wish. The dream thoughts, like all thought, belong to the preconscious, while the unconscious is the source only of the wish. In consequence, the hermeneutic object is removed from the unconscious and placed in the preconscious, while the unconscious is voided of everything except wishes. In what medium, we may ask, is the unconscious wish? Mere energy? If so, we are left with an unconscious that for hermeneutic purposes is empty, and Freud's hermeneutic endeavor is imperiled through trivialization. If we look back over the preceding sections for *nouns* Freud uses to designate the contents of the unconscious in other than wishful or dynamic terms, we find few, and these few are vague: "thought structure" (SE 5:542; "Gedankenbildung") and "path of thoughts" (SE 5:578; "Gedankenweg"—Freud evidently hesitates to say "thoughts," "Gedanken"); "idea" (SE 5:562; "Vorstellung"—this reminds us of the "Material unserer Vorstellungen"); "ideational content" (SE 5:582; "Vorstellungsinhalt"); in the unconscious memory traces there are "scenes," "phantasies" (SE 5:574, 576), and these memories form the basis for the "release of affect" brought about by the unconscious wish (SE 5:604). However, being prelinguistic, these memories also seem preinterpretative.

At this point, Freud undertakes to resolve the disparities left by the preceding sections, to close the immense gap that has opened between the expectations aroused by the hermeneutics and the constraints that the temporal aspect imposed on the metapsychology, this time through a dynamic reading of the psychic systems. At the same time he miraculously rescues the unconscious from the emptiness to which it had begun to seem condemned and restores to it all the power and fascination that the hermeneutics promised. We learn, namely, that the unbound energy of the unconscious *has access to* preconscious thoughts—or, topographically speaking, the unconscious can draw preconscious thoughts into itself, where its energy transforms them. This ability of the Ucs. to "draw in" preconscious thoughts is presumably what Freud has in mind when, on rare occasions, he ascribes or implicitly ascribes "thoughts" to the Ucs. (SE 5:542). Moreover, Freud sets this disposition of unconscious energy, which he calls the primary process, equivalent to the dream work—not just to the hallucinatory cathexis of desired objects, as in the *Project*, but mysteriously and remarkably, to "the activity which leads to dreams and to hysterical symptoms" (SE 5:603; "die zum Traume und zu den hysterischen Symptomen führende Arbeit"), to the distortions that Lacan and Benveniste compare to rhetorical figures. It is not clear why Freud makes this ascription, unless to give body to the unconscious, which was on the verge of being reduced to bleakly energetic terms or, as a hermeneutic object, being crossed out. It is, however, clear where Lacan got his conclusion that what we find in the unconscious is "the whole structure of language." For language is accessible to the unconscious, though not in it, and the processes of rhetorical figuration are its own. The ascription of the dream work to the Ucs. will become particularly definite in *Jokes and Their Relation to the Unconscious;* Freud speaks of "the dream work proper in the unconscious" (SE 8:165; "die eigentliche Traumarbeit im Unbewußten"). By the same measure, the third reading of the chameleon passage in the section on regression now seems the correct one.

From the hermeneutic standpoint, Freud's ascription of the dream work to the unconscious is felicitous at least in one regard: the unconscious is turned into a kind of poet! To be sure, in the process our sense of what is latent and what is manifest, of surface and depth, is severely deranged. For what was manifest in the hermeneutics—the incoherent and garbled dream itself—is now located in the unconscious: the dream becomes a direct manifestation of the primary process. And what of the latent? What was latent in the hermeneutics, the linguistically expressible dream thoughts, has been ascribed to a more manifest region, the preconscious.

We can draw several conclusions from the structure of Freud's argument in chapter 7. First, the topography, for which Freud adopts the surface/depth dichotomy of the hermeneutics, is a device intended to connect the hermeneutics with the metapsychology and for that reason occupies its key position at the beginning of the metapsychological sections. The magical term "regression" links the dynamic or hallucinatory wish fulfillment of the *Project* with the temporal notion of an infantile unconscious and with the etymological regression that Freud described in chapter 6. But this overdetermined word masks the fact that topic regression, which supposed the hallucinatory revival of a past fulfillment, is not entirely compatible with temporal regression, which implies a return to the unfulfilled desires of childhood;[49] and that moreover, neither topic nor temporal regression can be made to fit linguistic regression, which has no basis in the psychic and experiential history of the individual, but rather introduces a mythology of the origin and development of languages by the back door. Formal regression could be linked to topic and temporal regression only by arguing that ontogenesis recapitulates phylogenesis. Freud will not hesitate to make this argument in his later writings.[50]

In the second place, for the hermeneutics it is essential that the latent content, the meaning of the dream, be expressible in language, but for the temporal version of the metapsychology, it is essential that the Ucs. be free of rational discourse. Language, the erstwhile hero of the hermeneutics, has no role in the "anderer Schauplatz" of the Ucs. Freud is thus obliged to create two types of unconscious, one for his hermeneutics and one for his metapsychology. Freud clearly created the preconscious in order to accommodate language and rational thought.

Third, Freud plainly wants to ground his hermeneutics in his metapsychology, and not the reverse, and thus he makes the hermeneutic unconscious, the preconscious, secondary. But in fact the primary process cannot be comprehended as other than dependent on the prior existence of the secondary process.[51] When Freud ascribes the dream work to the primary process he writes the hermeneutics (the ploys he devised to achieve intersubjectively plausible interpretations) into the metapsychology; he posits of the object studied, the psyche, the means he used to study it. Just as Freud could not have asserted that the dream is a motivated sign that is derived from the dream thoughts by certain specific modes of transformation without presupposing ordinary language, there can be no dream work, no primary process, without a prior "correct" order of things, a secondary process that formulates verbalizable thoughts. The literal precedes the figure: this idea is basic to

Freud's theory of regression. Here the hermeneutics holds out a trap for the metapsychology and ensnares it.

Finally, despite Freud's efforts to reconcile the metapsychological and the hermeneutic through the dynamic, it remains unclear why the primary process, which in dynamic terms consists in the release of "uninhibited energy" on preconscious material, should perform on this material the relatively regular and systematic types of distortion that Freud described as the dream work, distortions that, we recall, resemble rhetorical figures.[52] In his later writings Freud will consistently affirm that the dream work takes place in the unconscious, but he will never clarify the connection between freely moving energy and verbal figuration; it is something we must take on faith.

Freud's views on the unconscious changed over the course of time. A tendency exuberantly to affirm the verbal reaches its height in *Jokes and Their Relation to the Unconscious* and gives us a picture of a clever, verbally talented, poetic unconscious. In the next decade Freud adopts a much more cautious, strictly dynamic view of the unconscious; in the "Metapsychological Supplement to the Theory of Dreams" of 1917 he goes so far as to ascribe the dream wish to the *preconscious*, no doubt in order to validate the wish as a hermeneutic object.[53] But whatever its vicissitudes, the unconscious shows a tendency to take on body, to become fuller and more definite. Freud achieves this objective of filling out the unconscious by emphasizing its temporal, infantile aspect.[54] In the essay "The Unconscious" of 1915 he compares its contents to an "aboriginal population";[55] it is filled with inherited instincts and the discarded material of childhood. Since we can picture the life of the mind of a child, the unconscious waxes fat. In the *Introductory Lectures* he announces that "the unconscious is a particular realm of the mind with its own wishful impulses, its own mode of expression and its peculiar mental mechanisms."[56] Where the unconscious is now a "realm," Freud will try harder and harder to draw an analogy between its mode of expression and a primitive language.[57] This tendency has its precedent in *The Interpretation of Dreams*, where Freud compares dream interpretation to the decipherment of hieroglyphics. But in the *Introductory Lectures* Freud, who has been pursuing linguistic studies and has even informed himself about Chinese in the hope of finding an analogy to the mode of expression of dreams, begins to insist on the parallels between dreams and "primitive" languages and between the interpretation of dreams and the deciphering of an ancient language.[58] It now becomes clear how Gauger comes to his conclusion that the unconscious mode of expression is the ancestor of our own language, for Freud comes close to saying the same thing himself. But as such writers as Wittgenstein and Benveniste have pointed out, dreams are far from being a language. As Benveniste says, language is a system; its work is not random; its categories are consistent.[59] Freud cannot demonstrate any such regularities in dreams. The only rules they manifest are those by which they derive from the "dream thoughts" or ordinary language. Correspondingly, one cannot read dreams as texts in their own right, as one could read hieroglyphic inscriptions or works in Chinese; one can only translate them. Wittgenstein remarks aptly in his *Lectures and Conversations on Aesthetics, Psychology, and Religious Belief,* "Suppose you look on a dream as a kind of language. . . . But then the translation ought to be possible both ways. It ought to be possible by employing the same technique to translate ordinary thoughts into dream language. As Freud recognizes, this never is done and cannot be done."[60]

Benveniste says that dreams can be compared not with a language but with a style. We come back to the idea of the unconscious as a poet. Indeed, some of the more striking mannerisms of this stylist or poet have their parallels in devices used by Freud's literary contemporaries. We have seen in chapter 5 how Kafka uses the literalization of figures of speech in his stories. Oskar Kokoschka uses the literalization of figures of speech as a central device in his plays *Sphinx und Strohmann* (*Sphinx and Strawman*) and *Hiob* (*Job*). Rilke uses metaphors of the body for psychological states and concrete images for abstract ideas in *Die Aufzeichnungen des Malte Laurids Brigge* (*The Notebooks of Malte Laurids Brigge*) (e.g., the idea of being chased by the heart; the woman without a face) and puns and homophony based on etymological association in his later poetry. Finally, Hofmannsthal, Schnitzler, and Musil, among others, use literary dreams much as Freud uses real dreams, as a nexus of associations and a way of linking disparate realms. Thus Freud ascribes to the unconscious an original mode of expression, an oneiric literary form with which it can outwit the literalistic censor and reveal its own truths. For Freud, it is only an advantage that the interpreter can decipher this new mode of expression and, above all, paraphrase it in rational, everyday language.

AFTERWORD

A BRIEF RECAPITULATION of my argument using conventional historical terms instead of the structural terms employed in the chapters is
perhaps in order. This study began with the observation that there existed across disciplines in the last decades of the nineteenth and the beginning of the twentieth century an intense interest in a space that,
since Nietzsche, had been vacated by God. This space, which remained
vested with the attributes of importance, value, and power, was antithe-
sized with respect to the everyday, known, social world, its conventions,
and its conventional language. These chapters have attempted to trace,
principally on the example of writers of the Austro-Hungarian Empire,
some of the results of this fascination: the various reidentifications and
reevaluations of that space, the permutations of its interactions with the
known, and the conditions proposed for its access.

In the wake of Schopenhauer, Nietzsche, and Wagner, and of French
psychopathological research (Binet, Charcot, Janet, Max Dessoir), this
"dark area" was psychologized; it became the irrational within. The notion that the irrational within ourselves was a powerful force which
eluded conscious control, scrutiny, or even identification inverted an
assignation of power familiar from Kleist's "Marionettentheater" essay
and other Romantic texts and reinforced by the plots of countless novels
especially in the second half of the nineteenth century: the idea that
precisely consciousness is a powerful force, something we can suffer
from in excess, something that can turn against us in the form of self-
consciousness and vitiate the naive, vital, "animal" part of our being
that controls our capacity for volition and action. The notion of the powerful irrational within signaled the exit of the thematics of self-consciousness: despite exceptions such as Gottfried Benn, self-consciousness dwindled as a literary theme in the early twentieth century. From
Dostoevskij's Underground Man to Musil's Törless, from Arne Garborg's

Gabriel Gram to Rilke's Malte, the accent fell on a different syllable: no longer on pernicious self-consciousness, but on mysterious and compelling inner experiences that consciousness cannot touch and language can barely express.

With increased attention to the idea of an irrational force within ourselves, the stage was set for the emergence of conflict psychology. Prior to conflict psychology—whose major theorist was Freud—health was identified with the idea of a removal of the conflict, that is, with wholeness and harmoniousness. This essentially Romantic ideal figured as a cultural prescription that transcended the bounds of individual psychology in Nietzsche's *On the Advantage and Disadvantage of History for Life;* as an ethical prescription, or recipe for "life," in Hofmannsthal's *Death and the Fool;* and as a psychological prescription in Breuer and Freud's *Studies on Hysteria.* These works are only examples of what was in fact a standard, clichéd valorization of harmoniousness, of the image of the circle applied to the self, ubiquitous in pre-Freudian literature, that attempted to resist the challenge of its newest modish rewriting, the inverted Romantic ideal of decadence, the idea of installing oneself in an artificial enclosure designed to shut the world out. In particular one finds the ideal of harmoniousness persistently applied to the feminine. For example in Lou Andreas-Salomé's 1899 feminist essay "Der Mensch als Weib," woman figures as essentially whole, round, complete, harmonious, and at peace with herself, hence quiescent, while these circular, perfect qualities elude the (admittedly more interesting) man, who is represented as restless, discontented, striving, active, linear.

Interesting and genuinely new was the moment when conflict was no longer lamented, but embraced. Principally Freud, but also the psychologically interested Schnitzler, capitalized on the notion that the other within is not only powerful but unexcisable. The idea had strong explanatory potential. Why are human actions not lucid and rational? How can inexplicable psychic manifestations be explained? In answering these questions, the proposition of a dynamic originating in a powerful, antithetical, yet wholly implicated dark area or irrational within proved extraordinarily useful. Freud capitalized on conflict as the key to interpretation, positing that the illegible dream is a compromise formation resulting from the inevitable clash between irreconcilable psychic agencies, the unconscious and the preconscious. Schnitzler exploited the idea of psychological conflict in constructing his plots and chose narrative techniques that expose such conflict: unreliable narration, interior monologue. An interest in the mechanisms of transitions and interference sprang up, notably in Freud's elaboration of the dream work and Musil's inquiry into precisely what takes place when consciousness tries to grasp the irrational.

The modernist legitimation of art, where art figures as a new religion, played into the same dualistic structure that came to inform psychology. Underlying this transposition is modernist artists' deeply ambivalent sense of the worth of their enterprise—of aesthetic creation and the aesthetic sensibility, which was viewed as existing in opposition to a hostile empirical world. On the one hand, the artists expressed their self-doubt by tracing the art work and the creative afflatus that engenders it to psychological sources—desire, memory, association. These sources produce things that are beautiful but fragile and transitory, illusions verging on constructs of narcissism, which are capable only temporarily of transforming an obdurate real. As we have seen, the traditional devices of the mirror and dream are reevaluated, for example by Hugo von Hofmannsthal, as means to temporarily sublate a profound and ineluctable duality. On the other hand, the art work is insistently affirmed. The sacred space vacated by God is posited as accessible only to the artist-initiate, where art compensates for the failings of a referentially inadequate everyday language. In this gesture of self-affirmation, the obdurate other is devalued, scorned as mere convention, inauthenticity, illusory negativity. Art crosses the boundary to the authentic, stripping off its veils.

This fascination with the hidden winds down into parody in the work of Franz Kafka. Kafka's work is dominated by the theme of a quest for a mysterious and elusive other. But particularly his writings of 1917 and after, by focusing on the mechanisms by which the subject fails to arrive at a goal rather than the goal itself, pose the question of whether the logic of the other, antithetical area conceived as a goal, including its elusiveness, is not just a reflection of a psychological mechanism of the subject, of the subject's desire. The subject, invested in questing, manufactures the unattainability of its object, compulsively throwing a dark and heavy barrier across his path. We see the negative of this pattern in "The Burrow": there, the psychic mechanism that keeps the other at a distance is driven by fear, and the other is seen as an enemy who must be kept at bay. This psychological reading is proved by its exceptions: To pass the barrier that rises up before one, one must do what in Kafka's texts is generally impossible—change one's mind set, as does the party guest in "Unmasking a Confidence Trickster," or even change oneself, as the ape does in "A Report to an Academy."

The dualistic model, the impetus to give an account in terms of something hidden, was eventually jettisoned in favor of a new model that privileged convention as an explanatory key. A clear and pointed refutation of the turn-of-the-century *épistémè* as something merely conventional is found in Wittgenstein's late work *Philosophical Investigations*. In sections of this work composed in the mid-1930s in which Wittgenstein subjects his earlier work *Tractatus logico-philosophicus* to a sharp critique, he polemicizes against the concepts of depth, the hidden, essence, and the prior—phantoms which, he argues, caused philosophical logic to appear as something particularly sublime. But in fact, logic is not the royal road to what is deep, hidden, essential, and prior; it is not, as a metalanguage, a superior instrument that is capable of showing us what our everyday language obscures. Rather, it blindly pursues what are merely figures that our everyday language suggests and in which we therefore believe. Questing for the "real artichoke," we pull off its leaves (para 164). Here, convention is not discredited through an appeal to an all-important hidden which it is incapable of grasping, but the hidden is discredited as the product of conventional language.

NOTES

Introduction

1   Roland Barthes, *S/Z*, trans. Richard Miller (New York: Hill and Wang, 1974), p. 27.

2   Ralph Waldo Emerson, *Selections*, ed. Stephen E. Whicher (Boston: Houghton Mifflin, 1960), p. 55.

3   Studies that attempt to establish interdisciplinary connections within turn-of-the-century Austrian culture include the following. Allan Janik and Stephen Toulmin, *Wittgenstein's Vienna* (New York: Simon and Schuster, 1973), identify structural patterns in a variety of cultural phenomena. They focus on Wittgenstein's *Tractatus*, maintaining that both the picture theory and the final propositions on the sense of the world, ethics, and aesthetics reflect concerns with the inadequacy of existing modes of representation, the correct use of media, and the limits of language and expression which are traceable in all spheres of Austrian cultural life. They emphasize Karl Kraus's purism, Adolph Loos's polemics against ornament, Arnold Schönberg's concern with the authenticity of musical discourse, Mauthner's language skepticism, and Hofmannsthal's language crisis, and they stress an all-pervasive belief in a realm of authentic values that lies beyond representation. The result, they find, is a strict separation of the effable, which is the area of interest, from the ineffable. The structural pattern they perceive is not wholly dissimilar to that which I have described in terms of light and dark, but their conclusions are predicated on a one-sided, insufficiently representative selection of material. If these authors overemphasize the quest for clarity, simplicity, and correct representation, it is because they give only cursory attention to turn-of-the-century Austrian literature and all but bypass Freud. Carl E. Schorske, *Fin-de-Siècle Vienna*, is primarily interested in relating high culture to politics; he traces the "hothouse development" of turn-of-the-century Austrian culture to the decomposition of Austrian liberalism. He pointedly avoids a synthetic approach to the cultural phenomena themselves, but inasmuch as he generalizes at all, he finds common to the work of Hofmannsthal, Freud, Gustav Klimt, Leopold Andrian, and Schönberg precisely the opposite

of what Janik and Toulmin describe, namely a blurring of traditional lines of division, a sense of the dissolution of boundaries between such categories as self and world, or body and psyche. Another work of intellectual history, J. McGrath, *Dionysian Art and Populist Politics in Austria* (New Haven: Yale University Press, 1974), foregrounds the interest in the irrational in the intellectual climate of the Austrian fin de siècle and studies its impact on the demise of liberalism and sudden rise of mass political parties in Austria. McGrath traces the reception of early Nietzsche, Schopenhauer, and Richard Wagner and the attendant interest in the emotional, irrational, or "dionysian" in the Pernerstorfer Circle as of 1875, and by extension, the impact of this new style of thinking on modern Austria's three great mass parties. A work with a predominantly literary emphasis is Manfred Diersch, *Empiriokritizismus und Impressionismus*. Drawing support from Hermann Bahr's enthusiastic heralding of Ernst Mach as the "philosopher of the era," Diersch attempts a synthesis of Viennese cultural phenomena on the basis of their resemblance to Mach's philosophy. Diersch and other critics, including Wunberg, *Der frühe Hofmannsthal*, Fritsche, *Dekadenz*, and Magris, "Der Zeichen Rost," draw attention to the parallels between Mach's and Hofmannsthal's debunking of the "I," between Mach's dissolution of the world into "sensations" and the interior monologue as practiced by Schnitzler, and between Mach's and Schnitzler's refusal of any distinction between reality and illusion. The trouble with these studies is that with the exception of Richard Beer-Hofmann, who read Mach in 1898, and the possible exception of Hofmannsthal, who is said to have heard lectures by Mach in 1897, there is no evidence of reception. The parallels occur primarily in the literature of the 1890s, whereas reception of Mach probably took place, if at all, after 1900, when his ideas became known outside of scientific circles. Moreover, Viennese literature is precisely its most "Machian" when it is at its most French. French symbolist and decadent literature is a documented influence on it in the 1890s and provides in abundance—and in a more attractive form for literary writers—precisely the ideas in which Mach's "Analyse der Empfindungen" and Viennese literature of the 1890s overlap. Judith Ryan, *The Vanishing Subject*, gives a more comprehensive account of the impact of empiricist philosophy, including Mach's philosophy, on literature at the turn of the century. Emphasizing the representation of consciousness as the overarching characteristic of modernist literature in the German-speaking countries, England, and France, she argues convincingly that this tendency is traceable to the empiricist philosophies of Franz Brentano, Mach, and William James, which, focusing on sense impressions, overthrew the traditional conceptualization of the self and postulated that the only reality was that of consciousness. In Ryan's account, individual writers engaged with this sea-change with varying degrees of enthusiasm or apprehensiveness, Rilke being an example who, in

Malte, desperately tried to save the "vanishing subject." Concerning writers of the Austro-Hungarian Empire, her account of Franz Kafka's reception of Brentano, to which she traces Kafka's pervasive narrative technique of restricted third-person perspective, is useful and interesting (pp. 100, 227). She notes that the Austrian writers were "more divided" than the followers of William James, like Henry James and Gertrude Stein; they were caught in a "rivalry between empiricist and Freudian psychologies" (p. 227), an assertion with which I concur. Worbs, *Nervenkunst,* gives a scrupulously detailed, broadly based account of the interrelations between the Freud circle and the Viennese literary circles, focusing on Bahr, Kraus, Schnitzler, and Hofmannsthal. This literary history not only fills an important gap in studying the relationship between psychoanalysis and literature at the turn of the century, but it places both developments within the context of later nineteenth-century European culture as a whole, recognizing sources and parallels in England, Scandinavia, and above all France.

4   Wittgenstein, *Tractatus logico-philosophicus,* p. 3.

5   Nietzsche, *Sämtliche Werke* 7:24, my translation.

6   Mach, *Knowledge and Error,* p. 6.

7   See Michael Worbs, "Wissenschaft und Literatur im Fin de siècle," *Sprache im technischen Zeitalter* 68 (1978):302–16.

8   Young Vienna's interest in Maeterlinck is demonstrated by their staging of his play *L'Intruse* in 1892 under the leadership of Hermann Bahr, as Rieckmann, *Aufbruch in die Moderne,* pp. 63–65, shows.

9   Nike Wagner, *Geist und Geschlecht: Karl Kraus und die Erotik der Wiener Moderne* (Frankfurt a.M.: Suhrkamp, 1982), pp. 153–65.

10 Sigmund Freud, "Briefe an Arthur Schnitzler," *Die Neue Rundschau* 66 (1955): 1, 3, my translation.

11 In 1921 Kenneth Burke, "Modifying the Eighteenth Century" (review of "Casanova's Homecoming") *The Dial* 71 (1921): 707, commented aptly on Schnitzler's method: "There is one species of poet who, if he quarrels with his mistress in the morning—supposing that poets still possess such lovely baggage—writes a poem that day on quarreling with his mistress; whereas, if he had been awakened by piano playing next door, he would have composed some Variations on Being Awakened by a Piano. In a much broader way, Schnitzler's procedure has about it something analogous to this."

12 A useful exploration of Schnitzler's techniques is found in Richard Plant, "Notes on Arthur Schnitzler's Literary Technique," *Germanic Review* 25 (1950): 13–25. He finds that "Umbruch" or sudden reversal (under which he subsumes changes in mood, reversals of fortune, and reversals from reality to fiction) is Schnitzler's fundamental technique.

13 Critics persistently fight, with little consensus to date, over an understanding of why the poet suddenly changed his course at the turn of the century

and over an evaluation of the two phases. This debate is perpetuated by the lack of a complete edition of Hofmannsthal's letters and diaries. Between the two major stages of Hofmannsthal's career falls the famous "Letter of Lord Chandos" of 1902, which has been elevated to the *locus classicus* of the European language crisis. This prose piece, which seemingly provides a key to Hofmannsthal's about-face, has provoked an extraordinary amount of commentary. The other "key" document in Hofmannsthal's writing is his own autobiographical statement and self-interpretation *Ad me ipsum*, begun in 1916 and left a fragment, in which he himself offers terms in which his two-phase career can be understood. Yet there is much controversy over whether *Ad me ipsum* can be taken at face value, whether its terms "preexistence" and "existence" can be applied to explain Hofmannsthal's own "turn" sixteen years earlier or whether one runs amiss to follow Hofmannsthal in impressing these categories retrospectively onto his earlier, less explicit, less easily interpretable work.

14 Manfred Hoppe argues convincingly that Hofmannsthal's main ideas and seemingly profoundest convictions in the 1890–91 period were merely assimilated literature, reflecting the ideas of Nietzsche, Schopenhauer, Paul Bourget, and others, and that Hofmannsthal had little or no contact with life; "Hofmannsthals Welterfahrung . . . stammt fast ausschließlich aus der Literatur" (*Literatentum, Magie und Mystik im Frühwerk Hugo von Hofmannsthals* [Berlin: W. de Gruyter, 1968], p. 56). But this conclusion cannot properly be extended to the 1894–96 years, when Hofmannsthal's lyric gifts were at their height and when his accounts of his experiences in his diaries echo the major themes of his poetry: the experience of mystic unity, an obsession with transitoriness, afflatus ("erhöhter Zustand") and a sense of magic ("Verhältnisse mit Zauberblick zu ergreifen"). It is probably more correct to evaluate Hofmannsthal's preference for adaptation not in terms of an estrangement from human experience but, with Kesting, p. 148, as a "weakness of imagination."

15 Hermann Broch, *Hofmannsthal und seine Zeit* (Frankfurt a.M.: Suhrkamp, 1974), p. 138, my translation.

16 Hofmannsthal, *Reden und Aufsätze III*, p. 464, my translation.

17 Robert Musil, "Toward a New Aesthetic: Observations on a Dramaturgy of Film," in *Precision and Soul: Essays and Addresses*, ed. and trans. Burton Pike and David S. Luft (Chicago: University of Chicago Press, 1990), pp. 198–99.

18 Wagenbach, *Franz Kafka*, pp. 80–83.

19 Thus Mark Spilka, *Dickens and Kafka: A Mutual Interpretation* (Bloomington: Indiana University Press, 1963), p. 39, writes, "Kafka was not a technical innovator, as so often held, but a great synthetic writer; he built his works on frames supplied by other authors, and was original only in the best sense, in

his development of the latent tendencies in older forms." See also Marthe Robert, *As Lonely as Franz Kafka*, trans. Ralph Mannheim (New York: Schocken, 1986), pp. 163–64.

20 Exceptions include Gerhard Kurz, "Einleitung: Der junge Kafka im Kontext," in *Der junge Kafka*, ed. Gerhard Kurz (Frankfurt a.m: Suhrkamp, 1984), pp. 7–39, who discusses Kafka's reception of Hofmannsthal; Mark M. Anderson, *Kafka's Clothes: Ornament and Aestheticism in the Hapsburg Fin de Siècle* (Oxford: Clarendon Press, 1992), who places Kafka in the context of aestheticism, decadence, Jugendstil, and the battle against ornament; and Andrew Barker, "Franz Kafka and Peter Altenberg," in *Turn-of-the-Century Vienna and Its Legacy, Essays in Honor of Donald G. Daviau*, ed. Jeffrey B. Berlin, Jorun B. Johns, and Richard H. Lawson (n.p.: Edition Atelier, 1993), pp. 221–38, who notes parallels between Kafka and Altenberg.

21 Franz Kafka, *Briefe 1902–1924*, ed. Max Brod (Frankfurt a.M.: Fischer, 1975), p. 495; Wagenbach, *Franz Kafka*, p. 102.

22 Max Brod, *Über Franz Kafka* (Frankfurt a.M: Fischer, 1966), p. 276 (note); Brod, *Franz Kafka als wegweisende Gestalt*, pp. 14–15; Wagenbach, *Franz Kafka*, pp. 103, 121, 217.

23 Kafka's diary entry of 10 July 1912, in *Tagebücher*. Hartmut Binder, *Motiv und Gestaltung bei Franz Kafka* (Bonn: Bouvier, 1966), pp. 92–114, documents Kafka's relationship with psychoanalysis extensively.

24 Kafka, *Tagebücher*, my translation; Kafka, *Letters to Friends*, p. 401.

25 For exceptions within the third-person works, see Roy Pascal, *Kafka's Narrators* (Cambridge: Cambridge University Press, 1982).

26 Walter H. Sokel, "Freud and the Magic of Kafka's Writing," *The World of Franz Kafka*, ed. J. P. Stern (New York: Holt, Rinehart, and Winston, 1980), pp. 145–58, gives an interesting account, with many examples, of Kafka's use of techniques resembling Freudian repression and projection.

27 Anders, *Kafka: Pro und Contra*, pp. 39–44.

28 Kate Flores, "The Judgment," in *Explain to Me Some Stories of Kafka*, ed. Angel Flores (New York: Gordian Press, 1983 [originally pub. 1947]), pp. 34–53. For an extensive and interesting account of self-division as a pervasive characteristic of Kafka's fiction, see Clayton Koelb, *Kafka's Rhetoric: The Passion of Reading* (Ithaca: Cornell University Press, 1989), pp. 28–31 and 182–207.

29 With this assertion my reading of Kafka differs from a prevalent critical tendency to assume that both terms of Kafka's dualities are full and to name them. Thus Ritchie Robertson, *Kafka*, posits that Kafka "assumes that there is an irreconcilable antithesis between two aspects of reality," which Robertson labels "being" and "consciousness" (p. x). "Being" in Robertson's reading in fact turns out to comprise a number of other concepts, such as "unconscious guilt" in "The Judgment" (p. 33) and "das Unzerstörbare" in *The Cas-*

tle (p. 240). While I fully agree with Robertson that one of Kafka's terms can be labeled "consciousness," I doubt whether the other term can be identified at all, even with a concept as general as "being," beyond the label given to it in each individual text, for example, the law ("Before the Law"), the message ("An Imperial Message"), the castle (*The Castle*), the enemy ("The Burrow"), the source of food ("Investigations of a Dog"). Moreover, what is important is not the specific content of the second term, but the universal mechanism of the frustrated quest of which it forms the object. Thus we repeatedly see in Kafka's texts someone wanting to but failing to attain *something*. What is important is the invariant structure (which, given the very lack of definition of the "something," appears more likely to express a law of the subject than a law of the universe), not the identity of the "something." A reading which, like Robertson's, sees Kafka's work as structured by irreconcilable dualities of which both terms are real and can be named implicitly puts Kafka into an entirely different relation with his Austrian predecessors. According to this reading his position would be consonant with theirs; it would not go beyond it. Kafka's use of dualities would thus be identical to Freud's or to Musil's. I believe, however, that the shift of emphasis in Kafka away from the object of the quest onto the mechanisms of nonarrival, including the infinite regress technique, speaks against such an assimilation and for a reading of his stories as an ironic psychological restatement of their serious belief in a mysterious and powerful ulterior reality.

30   This reading is widely acknowledged by critics, starting with Max Brod, κ 5:260. Subsequent critics, who identify the details, disagree in their interpretation of the meaning of the phenomenon. Compare John Winkelmann, "Kafka's 'Forschungen eines Hundes,'" *Monatshefte* 59 (1967): 204–16; Horst Steinmetz, *Suspensive Interpretation am Beispiel Franz Kafkas* (Göttingen: Vandenhoeck & Ruprecht, 1977), pp. 120–45; and Ritchie Robertson, *Kafka*, pp. 275–79.

31   See Ingeborg Henel's illuminating comments on the "Gegenordnung" (counterorder) as a projection of the hero in "Die Deutbarkeit von Kafkas Werken," pp. 256–57, 259–60. Henel's view that the "Gegenordnung" is called into being in *The Trial* by the hero's guilt and in *The Castle* by the hero's lying and that its double aspect accordingly mirrors the hero's sense of guilt and his self-certainty works for these novels but cannot be applied universally to Kafka's work. Many of his stories posit a "Gegenordnung" without overt moral failure on the part of the hero.

32   That Kafka's texts thematize the impossibility of understanding is the thesis of Theo Elm, "Problematisierte Hermeneutik: Zur 'Uneigentlichkeit' in Kafkas kleiner Prosa," *Deutsche Vierteljahrsschrift* 50 (1976): 477–510. Stephen D. Dowden's reading of *The Trial* (*Sympathy for the Abyss* [Tübingen: Niemeyer, 1986], pp. 94–134), as a novel that thematizes even as it enacts the aporia of representation, goes in the same direction.

1 Figures of Duality

1 Mauthner, *Prager Jugendjahre*, p. 209, my translation.

2 Nietzsche, *Sämtliche Werke*, 7:285.

3 Philippe Lacoue-Labarthe, "History and Mimesis," in *Looking after Nietzsche*, ed. Laurence A. Rickels (Albany: State University of New York Press, 1990), p. 217.

4 Hofmannsthal, *Gedichte, Dramen I*, p. 287, my translation.

5 It requires more tolerance on the part of the reader to accept that the three ghosts at the end of the play should make similarly self-conscious autobiographical statements, since the very fact that they do so undermines their status as counterexamples. See the discussion by Benjamin Bennett, *Hugo von Hofmannsthal: The Theatres of Consciousness* (Cambridge: Cambridge University Press, 1988), pp. 52–56.

6 Niels Axel Grossert, "Eine Analyse von Hugo von Hofmannsthals 'Der Tor und der Tod,' " *Text und Kontext* 7, no. 2 (1979): 10, shows that this passage cites Ecclesiastes 9.11: "Ich wandte mich und sah, wie es unter der Sonne zugeht, daß zu laufen nicht hilft schnell sein, zum Streit hilft nicht stark sein—Sondern alles liegt es an der Zeit und Glück." But Hofmannsthal rephrases his source interestingly, inserting the word "life," substituting nominal forms ("Schnellsein," "Tapfersein"), and adding a phrase in order to heighten the contrast between concepts and life.

7 Wallace Stevens, "Sunday Morning," *The Palm at the End of the Mind* (New York: Knopf, 1971), p. 7.

8 In his excellent interpretation of *Death and the Fool*, "Der Tod des Ästheten" in *Über Hugo von Hofmannsthal*, p. 75, Richard Alewyn remarks aptly that in the dionysian Death figure the heathen mystery of Dionysus and Christian mysticism meet: in both, a symbolic death becomes the key to true life.

9 Adolf Grünbaum, *The Foundations of Psychoanalysis*, shows that Freud based his claim for the scientific status of his clinical theory on his therapeutic achievements (p. 93, cf. pp. 167, 182). Thus Freud substantiates the concept of repression (inadequately, in Grünbaum's opinion) through the success of therapy. I concur with Grünbaum, who views Freud's "theory of parapraxes and of dreams as *misextrapolations* of the generic repression etiology of neurotic symptoms, which had at least had prima facie therapeutic support" (p. 194).

10 "The Unconscious," SE 14:186–89; *The Ego and the Id*, SE 19:20. Freud would supply further grounding in the child's social development when he formulated the relation of the metapsychology to the Oedipus complex in *The Ego and the Id*. In the Oedipus complex, which succeeds the stage of early infancy, the young boy hates his father as a rival for his mother's affections. The Oedipus complex is resolved when the boy identifies with his father; this identification constitutes the superego.

11   Ricoeur, *Freud and Philosophy*, pp. 95, 106–7.

12   Stan Draenos, *Freud's Odyssey* (New Haven: Yale University Press, 1982), over-simplifies the situation in *The Interpretation of Dreams* when he asserts that in his "grounding operation," which establishes the priority of the Ucs., Freud makes the body, specifically the sexual instincts, the ground of the mind. In fact the "grounding operation" of the discovery of the Ucs. involves positing some much more tenuous entity than the body: an entity concocted to fit the requirements of unacceptability, hiddenness, and immortality—that is, infantile sexual desires, and ones moreover that are fixated on certain persons.

13   Carl E. Schorske, *Fin-de-Siècle Vienna*, pp. 181–207.

14   In *The Genealogy of Morals*, in attempting to explain why the strong did not win out in human history, Nietzsche shows how the will to power turned dramatically against the self. The aggressive instincts were interiorized and the bad conscience born. Later, priests put the bad conscience at the service of the ascetic ideal in order to demonstrate that the root of suffering lay in sinfulness. They thus denied all that was vital in man and attacked the health of Europe. But Nietzsche shows how, at each juncture in this development, an aspect of the will to power is really at work. Finally, by giving man an explanation for his suffering, indeed by ascribing it to him, the ascetic ideal in fact *saved* man's will. Even where the will wants nothingness, says Nietzsche, it is nevertheless still a will.

2   The Uses and Abuses of Memory

1   For example, E. M. Butler, "Hoffmannsthal's [sic] 'Elektra': A Graeco-Freudian Myth," pp. 164–75; Liselotte Dieckmann, "The Dancing Elektra," *Texas Studies in Literature and Language* 2 (1960): 3–16; Gerhart Baumann, "Hugo von Hofmannsthal: 'Elektra' "; Michael Hamburger, *Hofmannsthal: Three Essays* (Princeton: Princeton University Press, 1972—the essay "Plays and Libretti" was first published in 1963). Hamburger believes that "Freud, at most, was one of Hofmannsthal's many diverse guides" to depth psychology (p. 86). The longest studies to date are Heinz Politzer's "Hugo von Hofmannsthal's 'Elektra': Geburt der Tragödie aus dem Geiste der Psychopathologie," pp. 95–119; Worbs, *Nervenkunst*, pp. 259–95; and Ritchie Robertson, " 'Ich habe ihm das Beil nicht geben können': The Heroine's Failure in Hofmannsthal's *Elektra*," *Orbis Litterarum* 41 (1986): 312–31, who sees the influence of Freud's interpretation of *Hamlet* as well as of *Studies on Hysteria* and Erwin Rohde's *Psyche* on the play. Worbs's study stands out for presenting a wealth of interesting new material on Hofmannsthal's relationship to Freud, including the Freud circle's reaction to *Electra* and other works by Hofmannsthal. Hofmannsthal's interest in psychological questions and the findings of psychological research was particularly intense during the period 1900–1907 and coincides with his

exploration of the Greek myths. It expresses itself in the dramas *Electra* and *Ödipus und die Sphinx*, in various mythological fragments, in the heavily psychologized Calderón adaptation *Das Leben ein Traum* (Life is a dream), which is the earliest version of *Der Turm* (*The Tower*), and in the first drafts of *Andreas*. While we know that Hofmannsthal read Freud and assimilated certain Freudian ideas into certain literary works, however, there can be no question that Freud exerted a central or even a privileged influence over Hofmannsthal's thinking. There is no evidence, as there is in Schnitzler's case, that Hofmannsthal made a point of trying to come to terms with Freud's ideas, nor that he tried to adapt any of Freud's theories to his literary production, as Schnitzler did with Freud's dream theory. Hofmannsthal was immensely widely read and borrowed from everywhere; Freud was, as Worbs (pp. 298–303) shows, only one source among many authors on psychological topics.

2   Michael Hamburger, "Hofmannsthals Bibliothek," *Euphorion* 55 (1955): 27.

3   BII 142. Hofmannsthal goes on to say that he wants to consult the work in connection with *Das Leben ein Traum*. The editors of *Briefe* II place the undated letter in the period November 1903–May 1904, but both Alewyn, *Über Hugo von Hofmannsthal*, p. 190, note 45, and Urban, *Hofmannsthal, Freud*, pp. 30, 141, note 183, assume that it was written a year earlier. Urban, p. 17, believes that Hofmannsthal read *Studies on Hysteria* about seven years after it was first published.

4   Worbs's assumption, *Nervenkunst*, p. 140, that Bahr's "Auseinandersetzung mit der Psychoanalyse" started in 1903 is therefore incorrect. Bahr's "Notizbuch" entry for 13 April 1902 contains a list of psychiatric titles, including works by Hippolyte Bernheim, Charcot, and Janet. This "Merkbuch" and "Notizbuch" and all other unpublished Bahr materials that I cite are found in the Theatersammlung of the Österreichische Nationalbibliothek, Vienna. The translations are mine.

5   Hofmannsthal, *Reden und Aufsätze III*, p. 452, my translation.

6   See the chapter "Andreas und die 'Wunderbare Freundin': Zur Fortsetzung von Hofmannsthals Roman-Fragment und ihrer psychiatrischen Quelle," in Alewyn, *Über Hugo von Hofmannsthal*.

7   In Electra herself Politzer sees, above all, repressed eroticism and incestuous wishes as evidence of hysteria (he is thinking of Carl Gustav Jung's "Electra complex," and he ingeniously finds evidence of it in Hofmannsthal's play). He also finds that Electra's behavior manifests Charcot's four phases of the hysterical attack as Breuer and Freud list them in *Studies on Hysteria*. Urban, p. 37, gives a reasonable critique of Politzer's interpretation, pointing out how Electra diverges from a hysteric as well as conforms to one. According to Politzer, Clytemnestra's hysteria is bound up with her suffering from a "repressed deed" (p. 108). Politzer's diagnosis of hysteria in Chrysothemis appears not so well founded.

8   Worbs, *Nervenkunst*, pp. 280–87.

9   "Das Gespräch über Gedichte" (The conversation on poetry), *Erzählungen*,
    p. 497. This is perhaps the sense in which we can understand his later com-
    mentaries on *Electra* in which he persistently stresses that the play ques-
    tions the concept of the individual. These include a diary entry of 1905,
    where Hofmannsthal writes that in *Electra* the individual is "blasted to bits
    from the inside," by the "contents of its life" (*Reden und Aufsätze III*, p.
    461), and in "Aufzeichnungen zu Reden in Skandinavien" (1916), where he
    observes that he "put into question the concept of personality" (*Reden und
    Aufsätze II*, p. 31).

10 Bahr, *Dialog vom Tragischen*, pp. 59–61, 68–75.

11 For example, Walter Jens, *Hofmannsthal und die Griechen* (Tübingen: Max
    Niemeyer Verlag, 1955), pp. 61, 57–58, 65–66; Baumann, "Hugo von Hof-
    mannsthals 'Elektra,' " pp. 285–87, 277, 293–94; William H. Rey, *Wel-
    tentzweiung und Weltversöhnung in Hofmannsthals griechischen Dramen*
    (Philadelphia: University of Pennsylvania Press, 1962), pp. 68–73, 91–95.
    Hans-Joachim Newiger, "Hofmannsthals *Elektra* und die griechische
    Tragödie," *Arcadia* 4 (1969), tries to break down these hard-and-fast opposi-
    tions, pp. 153–57.

12 Hofmannsthal, *Dramen II*, p. 206, my translation.

13 For example, Jens, *Hofmannsthal und die Griechen*, p. 57; Baumann, "Hugo
    von Hofmannsthals 'Elektra,' " p. 276; Wolfgang Nehring, *Die Tat bei Hof-
    mannsthal* (Stuttgart: Metzler, 1966), pp. 37, 52, 75–76, 93.

14 Butler, "Hoffmannsthals 'Elektra,' " p. 169.

15 Hofmannsthal, *Reden und Aufsätze III*, p. 603.

16 Hofmannsthal, *Dramen II*, p. 195, my translation.

17 Hofmannsthal himself did not subscribe to Nietzsche's view that memory
    and too great a respect for the past were responsible for the deficiencies of
    present-day culture. He writes in a diary entry of 29 June 1902: "On some ad-
    vantages of reading older books. A terrible consequence of the lack of mem-
    ory that pervades the present: lack of judgment about achievements, indeed
    about qualities" (*Reden und Aufsätze III*, p. 436, my translation).

18 David H. Miles, *Hofmannsthal's Novel* Andreas: *Memory and Self* (Prince-
    ton: Princeton University Press, 1972), p. 67.

19 EW 1:227, my translation.

20 M 7:957, my translation.

21 Musil, *Tagebücher*, 1:347, my translation.

22 Corino, *Robert Musils "Vereinigungen,"* p. 222. In his excellent article on
    the language of *Unions*, Jürgen Schröder, "Am Grenzwert der Sprache: Zu
    Robert Musils 'Vereinigungen,' " *Euphorion* 60 (1966): 311–34, writes of
    Musil that "his sign and his fate" is the boundary (p. 316), and he goes on to
    show in considerable detail how Musil's use of particles in *Unions* mirrors

his preoccupation with borders and transitions. Gerhart Baumann, "Robert Musil: Dichter der *Vereinigungen*" (originally pub. 1976), in Baumann, *Vereinigungen* (München: Fink, 1972), p. 199, also remarks on Musil's plays with oppositions.

23 Much critical attention has been devoted to Musil's relationship to psychoanalytic theory. His knowledge of Freud's theories in the early years of his career as a writer, and thus the possibility of Freudian influence on his first novel *Young Törless*, is disputed. His later involvement with psychoanalysis and his ambivalent, frequently negative attitude toward it is well documented, especially by Johannes Cremerius, "Robert Musil: Das Dilemma eines Schriftstellers vom Typus 'poeta doctus' *nach* Freud," *Psyche* 33 (1979): 761. As is frequently the case when a critic investigates Freud's influence on a writer, this essay is written from a psychoanalytic point of view: thus Musil's negative comments on psychoanalysis and his "forgetting" of psychoanalytic texts are judged by Cremerius as "repression" (p. 759). On the question of Musil's putative knowledge of psychoanalysis in his early years, Cremerius argues that a writer who began to write after 1900, who spent several hours daily in Viennese cafés until 1903, and who frequented Berlin literary cafés from 1903 to 1910, could not have avoided hearing about psychoanalysis (p. 743). As far as *Studies on Hysteria* goes, it is documented that Musil had read it by 1913 (Karl Corino, "Ödipus oder Orest?," p. 177, note 94). But textual evidence from "The Temptation of Quiet Veronica" indicates that he had almost certainly read it by 1910 at the latest, while other, less clinching textual evidence points at a reception before 1908, even by 1905–6. Its influence is plain on the diary version of "Veronica" (1910) and also on the earlier "Veronica" fragment, as my argument will show. Karl Corino, *Robert Musils "Vereinigungen,"* p. 126, believes that this fragment was written in 1908. He declares that "all signs" point to the fact that Musil read works by Freud (and Breuer) by 1905–6 at the latest (p. 128), but he cites as proof a not very convincing instance of their influence on a letter Musil wrote in 1905. Cremerius, p. 744, note 8, points out that Musil, who wrote his dissertation on Ernst Mach, read Mach's *Prinzipien der Wärmelehre* in 1902, where Breuer's and Freud's results are mentioned; Musil also knew Weininger's *Geschlecht und Charakter* (1903), which contains a similar reference. Musil refers in his diary to Hermann Bahr's *Dialog vom Tragischen* (1904), where Breuer and Freud's theories of hysteria figure prominently (*Tagebücher*, 1:37–38).

24 Remarkably, no critic so much as noticed the parallels between "The Temptation of Quiet Veronica" and *Studies on Hysteria* before Karl Corino's "Ödipus oder Orest?" (1973). It has been primarily Corino, followed by Peter Henninger, who has pursued this line of investigation. Especially in his book *Robert Musils "Vereinigungen,"* Corino discusses the parallels between the novella and Breuer and Freud's work in some detail. But his perception of

them as well as the conclusions he draws are largely different from mine. Henninger, *Der Buchstabe und der Geist*, p. 186, gives significant insights on the "cryptoquotations" from *Studies on Hysteria* in "The Temptation of Quiet Veronica," but he is interested primarily in echoings of vocabulary in the novella's final version while I am interested in the evolution of a single theme from version to version.

25 Most critics of "The Temptation of Quiet Veronica" discuss the double significance of animals for Veronica, whereby Johannes personifies the impersonal animal and Demeter the aggressive one. See, for example, Hans Geulen, "Robert Musils 'Die Versuchung der stillen Veronika,' " *Wirkendes Wort* 15 (1965): 175, 177; F. H. Langmann and E. A. Langmann, "A Tale of Robert Musil's," *Critical Review* (Melbourne, Sydney) 11 (1968): 95–96; Frederick G. Peters, *Robert Musil: Master of the Hovering Life* (New York: Columbia University Press, 1979), p. 81; and Dietmar Goltschnigg, "Liebe, Moral und Psychotherapie in Robert Musils Erzählung 'Die Versuchung der stillen Veronika,' " *Erzählung und Erzählforschung im 20. Jahrhundert*, ed. Rolf Kloepfer and Gisela Janetzke-Dillner (Stuttgart: Kohlhammer, 1981), pp. 149–60.

26 Corino, *Vereinigungen*, p. 180, my translation, my italics.

27 Ibid., pp. 175, 177, my translation.

28 Ibid., p. 195, my translation.

29 An interesting and persuasive interpretation of Musil's hesitation is found in Susan J. Erickson, "Writer's Block: Robert Musil and the Mother," *SubStance* 41 (1983): 78–90.

30 Annie Reniers-Servranckx, *Robert Musil*, p. 127, my translation. On the same subject, see also Corino, *Vereinigungen*, pp. 235–39.

31 Compare Reniers-Servranckz, *Robert Musil*, p. 135, who asserts that in the definitive version the difference between words and actions on the one hand, and what they "mean" on the other, is stressed. She discusses examples and the implications of this new metaphorical style.

32 Henninger, *Der Buchstabe und der Geist*, in an excellent analysis, shows how Musil's borrowings from Breuer and Freud are essentially poetic rather than conceptual (pp. 183–89).

3 Processes, Middles, and Barriers

1 In similarily structured works like E. T. A. Hoffmann's "Der Sandmann" (1815), Edgar Allan Poe's "The Black Cat" (1843), Guy de Maupassant's "Le Horla" (1887), and Henry James's *The Turn of the Screw* (1898), the appearance of mysterious phenomena raises primarily the question of *the nature of their source*: is the character who sees a bizarre apparition or senses its presence deranged, or is the apparition genuinely of demonic origin? In Schnitz-

ler's stories, in contrast, the third thing always has a commonsense explanation. The question becomes one of its effect: why does its appearance have such a devastating effect on the character's psychic life, and what does this effect consist of?

2   Schnitzler himself describes the evolution of the idea in "Zur Physiologie des Schaffens," *Neue Freie Presse* (Wien, 25 December 1931). He also turned the pantomime into a seventeen-page film script in October 1911, according to Walter Fritz, "Arthur Schnitzler und der Film," *Journal of the International Arthur Schnitzler Research Association* 5, no. 4 (1966): 12.

3   Ricoeur, *Freud and Philosophy*, finds that this type of displacement is a fundamental gesture of interpretation: "To interpret is to displace the origin of meaning to another region" (p. 91); see also p. 54.

4   Ibid., p. 93. Samuel Weber, "The Divaricator: Remarks on Freud's Witz," *Glyph* 1 (1977): 1–27, also notes the hermeneutic circularity of Freud's thinking, his belief in the power of psychoanalytic thought to fathom the entire psychic system of which it itself is merely a part.

5   Harry Goldgar, "The Square Root of Minus One: Freud and Robert Musil's *Törleß*," *Comparative Literature* 17 (1965): 117–32; Annie Reniers, " 'Törleß': Freudsche Verwirrungen?" in *Robert Musil: Studien zu seinem Werk*, ed. Karl Dinklage et al. (Reinbek bei Hamburg: Rowohlt, 1970), pp. 26–39; Karl Corino, "Ödipus oder Orest?" Since the present chapter first appeared as an article, however, Andrew Webber, "Sense and Sensuality in Musil's Törleß," *German Life and Letters* 41 (1988): 106–30, discusses parallels between *Törless* and Freud extensively and perceptively, from a point of view that is well informed psychoanalytically as well as based on a close textual reading. Although Webber focuses mainly on *Three Essays on the Theory of Sexuality*, he also refers to *The Interpretation of Dreams*. One of Webber's points is that sense and sensuality are correlated in *Törless* in their quest for a perpetually deferred goal, which operates according to the logic of desire's relation to its object.

6   In Ludwig Wittgenstein, *Philosophische Untersuchungen* (Suhrkamp: Frankfurt a.M., 1971), p. 309.

7   The idea is also present in the motto from Maeterlinck, according to which stones and objects look different, depending on whether they are seen under water or not.

8   Dorrit Cohn, "Castles and Anti-Castles, or Kafka and Robbe-Grillet," *Novel* 5 (1971–72): 19–31, shows that the space in Kafka's stories is often an expression of psychic processes, "determined by the drives of the self, improvised as the psyche traverses it" (p. 24).

9   These conclusions are similar to those reached by Franz Kuna in "Rage for Verfication: Kafka and Einstein," in *On Kafka: Semi-Centenary Perspectives*, ed. Franz Kuna (New York: Harper & Row, 1976), pp. 83–111. Kuna as-

serts that Kafka is "at pains to demonstrate the total division between the seen and an assumed unseen reality" (p. 100). He finds that Kafka's narrative structures imply a radical critique of metaphysics; Kafka stubbornly upholds a "Kantian dualism" (p. 110) in which "mystical states are no more than partial eclipses of human consciousness" (p. 111).

4   Mirrors and Mirroring

1   Herbert Grabes, *Speculum, Mirror und Looking-Glass* (Tübingen: Niemeyer, 1973), p. 127.

2   Meyer Abrams, *The Mirror and the Lamp* (London: Oxford University Press, 1953), and Richard Rorty, *Philosophy and the Mirror of Nature* (Princeton: Princeton University Press, 1979), provide extensive discussions of the use of the mirror in the history of aesthetic theory and the Cartesian philosophical tradition, respectively; Abrams goes on to discuss expressive theories of art.

3   The mirror at Mme Basile's in Rousseau's *Confessions* has been interpreted in this way by Jean Starobinski, *L'Oeil vivant* (Paris: Gallimard, 1961); cf. also Jacques Derrida, *Of Grammatology*, trans. Gayatri Chakravorty Spivak (Baltimore: Johns Hopkins University Press, 1974), p. 141. Rilke uses the mirror similarly in the famous costume scene in *Die Aufzeichnungen des Malte Laurids Brigge* (*The Notebooks of Malte Laurids Brigge*); so does Margaret Atwood in *Surfacing* (Toronto: McClelland and Stewart, 1972).

4   The concern with dualities, with overcoming boundaries and recovering losses, is not peculiar to Austrian writers of the period alone; Marcel Proust would be an obvious example of a writer from a different milieu who shared similar interests. Yet Proust's devices, his "composite images," his oxymora and metaphors, are designed to abolish rather than to abolish-and-insist-on the bar between two disparate terms and are thus somewhat different from the devices I consider here. It could be said that Proust actively searches for devices that establish or create presence, rather than affirm the idea of absence/presence.

5   Heinrich von Kleist, "About the Marionette Theatre," trans. Cherna Murray, *Life and Letters Today* 16, no. 8 (1937): 103.

6   John Brenkman's interpretation in "Narcissus in the Text," *Georgia Review* 30, no. 2 (1976): 293–27, is interesting in this context. He likewise finds that the aspect of desire is preeminent in Ovid's Narcissus story: "Both before and after his demystification there is an excess of desire over knowledge and over the possibility of satisfaction" (p. 323). But it is the moment of knowledge that interests him, the "Kleistian" aspect of the story. He asserts that the moment at which Narcissus recognizes that the image is indeed not another but himself takes on a key function in what he calls Narcissus's "drama of the self." The spatially removed image, in Brenkman's view, represents the

other (p. 322). Inasmuch as it affects the self instead of responding to it, it can be seen to be anterior to the self. Drawing a parallel between the image and Derrida's conception of the "trace," Brenkmann concludes that the Narcissus fable compromises the notion of the self-presence or purity of the self by showing that the self is primordially entangled with the other.

7   *Le Séminaire de Jacques Lacan*, Texte établi par Jacques-Alain Miller, 27 annual series, 1953–80 (Paris: Seuil, 1975), 1:161, 180.

8   In "Leben, Traum und Tod" (Life, dream, and death), "Brief (an Richard Dehmel)" (Letter [to Richard Dehmel]), and "Besitz" (Possession), all 1893, in *Gedichte, Dramen I*, pp. 149, 152, 157, Hofmannsthal makes his conception of the dream clear. It is a "third thing," neither life nor death; it represents the possibility of having all in one: "All in one, kernel and shell / This happiness belongs to the dream . . . / To comprehend deeply and to possess! / Has this a place anywhere in life?" (p. 157, my translation).

9   "Ein Knabe" ("A Boy") of 1986 and "Der Jüngling und die Spinne" (The youth and the spider) of 1897. Earlier, in a diary entry of May 1895, *Reden und Aufsätze III*, p. 398, Hofmannsthal mentions Narcissus in connection with Leopold von Andrian's *Der Garten der Erkenntnis*.

10 *Reden und Aufsätze III*, p. 599, my translation. Critics persistently misinterpret the significance of the mirror in Hofmannsthal's writings. For example, Pestalozzi, *Sprachskepsis und Sprachmagie*, consistently imposes on Hofmannsthal's mirror imagery the pejorative Romantic connotation of the mirror as a symbol of pernicious reflection (e.g., pp. 22–23, 75).

11 Hofmannsthal, *Gedichte, Dramen I*, p. 163, my translation.

12 Compare Hofmannsthal's complaint in a diary entry of 1912: "The gradual circumscription. Wish to see the whole world, to give up nothing, and belief in this . . . ," *Reden und Aufsätze III*, p. 513, my translation.

13 Hofmannsthal writes in *Ad me Ipsum*, "The magical mastery over the word the image the sign may not be taken out of preexistence over into existence." *Reden und Aufsätze III*, p. 601, my translation.

14 Hofmannsthal, "Verse auf ein kleines Kind" ("Verses on a Small Child") of 1897, *Gedichte, Dramen I*, p. 47.

15 Compare *Ad me Ipsum*: "Fear and longing to leave this condition: by what path?" *Reden und Aufsätze III*, p. 600, my translation.

16 Hofmannsthal, *Gedichte, Dramen I*, pp. 50–51, my translation.

17 Compare "Ein Traum von großer Magie" ("A Dream of Great Magic") of 1895, where the dream and its magician abolish walls, recover past time, and put the dreamer in sympathetic unity with all humankind. A remark in "Buch der Freunde" (Book of friends) of 1922 can be applied to explain the emperor's love of mirror images of himself: "A certain finer transcendental vanity is an element which we cannot live without. Like a curved mirror it paints for us a universe whose animating midpoint we ourselves are; without

it we feel we would plunge away from ourselves into the darkness, the non-world." *Reden und Aufsätze III*, p. 242, my translation.

18 Compare Ingeborg Henel, "Die Deutbarkeit von Kafkas Werken," pp. 258, 262, and Hermann J. Weigand, "Franz Kafka's 'The Burrow' ('Der Bau'): An Analytical Essay," *PMLA* 87 (1972): 152–66. Weigand writes, "The burrow comes to assume the status of the self objectified, bearing the same relation to its designer as body and soul in ordinary parlance. The master-builder and his burrow are one" (p. 153). In the wake of interpretations that draw analogies between the construction of the burrow and textual production—Henry Sussman, "The All-Embracing Metaphor," and Winfried Kudszus, "Verschüttungen in Kafkas 'Der Bau,' " in *Probleme der Moderne: Studien zur deutschen Literatur von Nietzsche bis Brecht*, ed. Benjamin Bennett et al. (Tübingen: Niemeyer, 1983), pp. 307–17—Gerhard Richter, "Difficile Dwellings: Kafka's 'The Burrow,' " in *The Poetics of Reading*, ed. Eitel Timm and Kenneth Mendoza (Columbia SC: Camden House, 1993), pp. 1–18, argues that the story is an allegory of the subject's struggle to constitute itself through writing.

19 In "An Imperial Message," the vision of the emperor who has a message for the subject living on the outskirts of the city takes place in a dream; in *The Castle* K. falls asleep at the very moment when a breakthrough to the Castle finally seems possible, during the visit of the official Bürgel.

20 Critics generally agree that the hissing sound comes from the animal himself; see Heinrich Henel in "Kafka's 'Der Bau,' or 'How to Escape from a Maze,' " in *The Discontinuous Tradition: Studies in German Literature in Honour of Ernest Ludwig Stahl*, ed. P. F. Ganz (Oxford: Clarendon Press, 1971), pp. 224–46. Henry Sussman's argument in "The All-Embracing Metaphor," pp. 111–19, that the enemy is a figment of the animal's imagination, a product of his desire to ground himself outside of himself, is similar to mine.

21 The emphasis in "The Burrow" switches from space to time. In the first half of the story the emphasis is on space: the animal describes the layout of the burrow and its environs as though he were giving a guided tour, in a durative-iterative present tense suggesting timelessness. Then, when the hissing noise that makes the animal suspect the actual presence of an enemy begins, the illusion of a timeless situation is abandoned; the narrative mode switches to interior monologue. The reader is suddenly confronted with an ongoing process in the present tense. In addition, on account of the temporal phenomenon of the noise, which has no apparent spatial source, the animal becomes spatially disoriented; he thinks less about architecture and more about the temporal process of life. For a discussion of the switch from the durative-iterative present tense to interior monologue, see Dorrit Cohn, *Transparent Minds* (Princeton: Princeton University Press, 1978), pp. 195–98, and Heinrich Henel, "Das Ende von Kafka's *Der Bau*," *Germanisch-Romanische Monatsschrift* 22 (1972): 3–23, as well as the detailed critique in J. M. Coet-

zee, "Time, Tense, and Aspect in Kafka's 'The Burrow,' " *Modern Language Notes* 96 (1981): 556–79. Many critics, including Cohn and Henel, interpret the interior monologue section in the light of the last sentence of "The Burrow" ("But all remained unchanged") as neurotic worrying that is endless and infinitely repeatable. Since a first-person narrator cannot narrate his or her own end or death, however, and since it remains unclear whether "The Burrow" is a fragment or not, the lack of such a conclusion does not form a certain basis for interpretation.

22   These two episodes involving mirrors, which Freud marginalizes rather than exploits, tend to support Lacan's rewriting of Freud as I discuss it at the end of this chapter. In *Beyond the Pleasure Principle* the eighteen-month-old child who makes himself disappear and then reappear before the mirror in a version of the *fort/da* game appears to be in Lacan's "mirror stage," for he recognizes his image in the mirror, although, to be sure, the child is not lost in narcissistic self-admiration at all but is rather intent on his peekaboo game (SE 18:15). In "The Uncanny" Freud describes how he himself *misrecognized* himself in the mirror on the washroom door in a train compartment (SE 17:248). He believed that he saw "an elderly gentleman in a dressing gown and a travelling cap," and "thoroughly disliked his appearance." Freud's own rather hapless interpretation of the incident—he hazards that a vestige of the archaic sense of the uncanny at the sight of the double may be found even in an unsuperstitious man of science like himself—is significant because it itself produces a self-image. Both the episode and the interpretation show what Lacan will posit, namely that our self-image is an idealized construct, a product of our desire. This self-image, at a later stage in our lives, of course does not coincide with the disappointing image we see of ourselves in the mirror.

23   Rank, *Der Doppelgänger* (Leipzig: Internationaler Psychoanalytischer Verlag, 1925 (originally pub. *Imago* 3 [1914]), presents an extensive survey of the double in literature and mythology and also treats the shadow and the mirror image, which he asserts are variations on the same idea. He concludes that the significance of the double changed in the course of its history. Originally, in primitive culture, the double represented the spirit or immortal part of a person and thus functioned as a guarantee for the immortality of the self. Later, the double came to represent a part of the self that the self wished to defend itself against. As the sinful part of the self, its approach can betoken death. The double also frequently functions as a rival in love.

24   For the abundance of further problems created by the narcissism essay, see the critical anthology *Freud's "On Narcissism: An Introduction,"* ed. Joseph Sandler et al. (New Haven: Yale University Press, 1991), and especially the article by Willy Baranger, "Narcissism in Freud," pp. 108–30.

25   In a footnote Freud qualifies that it would perhaps be more cautious to say that the child identifies with *the parents*, since the child does not estimate

father and mother differently before it is sure of the difference between the sexes, that is, the lack or possession of a penis. The implication seems to be that identification is based, in a child of either sex, in admiration, not in the observation of its resemblance to the parent of the same sex.

26   Laplanche and Pontalis, *The Language of Psycho-Analysis*, p. 251.

27   Ibid., p. 251.

28   Lacan, "The Mirror Stage as Formative of the Function of the I," *Ecrits*, p. 2.

29   Lacan, "On a Question Preliminary to Any Possible Treatment of Psychosis," *Ecrits*, p. 198.

30   Lacan, "The Mirror Stage," p. 2.

31   Ibid, p. 1.

5   The Literary Dream

1   Hofmannsthal, *Gedichte, Dramen I*, p. 22, my translation.

2   This phrase, "der Zauberkreis der Kindheit," is found in "Studie über die Entwickelung des Dichters Victor Hugo" (1901), *Reden und Aufsätze I*, p. 254, and in "Das Gespräch über Gedichte" (1903), *Erzählungen*, p. 499.

3   Hofmannsthal, *Gedichte, Dramen I*, pp. 47, 46, my translations.

4   Steven P. Sondrup, "Terzinen," in *Seltene Augenblicke: Interpretations of Poems by Hugo von Hofmannsthal*, ed. Margit Resch (Columbia, SC: Camden House, 1989), p. 196, traces the image of the cherry trees (in the context of children, moon, and heavenly body), to two frequently anthologized poems by Berthold Heinrich Brockes.

5   William Shakespeare, *The Tempest*, 4.1.152–56.

6   Theodor Reik, *Richard Beer-Hofmann* (Leipzig: Rudolf Eichler, 1912), p. 14, my translation. Fischer, "Richard Beer-Hofmann," pp. 219–23, gives an extensive rhetorical analysis of the style.

7   Fischer, "Richard Beer-Hofmann," p. 216.

8   Even Freud's theory of the dream as the expression of an unconscious wish—in his view, the most significant part of his discovery—cannot have seemed outlandish to readers of Grillparzer, or for that matter to readers of Schopenhauer, among whom Hofmannsthal can certainly be numbered. In the essay "Transcendent Speculation on the Apparent Deliberateness in the Fate of the Individual," Schopenhauer's account of how dreams originate in the "will," far from consciousness, sounds like Freud's account of the genesis of dreams in the unconscious: "Life generally bears a resemblance [to the dream] that has long been recognized and often expressed. . . . In the dream, circumstances by pure chance coincide and there become the motives of our actions, circumstances that are external to and independent of us and indeed often abhorrent. But yet there is between them a mysterious and appropriate connection since a hidden power that is obeyed by all the incidents in the

dream controls and arranges even these circumstances and indeed solely with reference to us. *But the strangest thing of all is that this power can ultimately be none other than our own will, yet from a point of view that does not enter our dreaming consciousness.* And so it happens that the events in a dream often turn out quite contrary to our wishes therein, cause us astonishment, annoyance, and even mortal terror" (italics mine). Arthur Schopenhauer, *Parerga und Paralipomena*, 2 vols., trans. E. F. J. Payne (Oxford: Clarendon Press, 1974), 1:216–17.

9   An excellent account of Schnitzler's and Freud's relations, including a useful documentation of Schnitzler's reception of Freud, is found in Worbs, *Nervenkunst*, part 3, ch. 3, esp. pp. 203–24. Hofmannsthal's reception of *The Interpretation of Dreams* is much less certain. While his library contained the first edition and he claimed in 1908 to have read "all of Freud's works," the year in which he read *The Interpretation of Dreams* is a matter of conjecture, based on how critics interpret his works. Urban, *Hofmannsthal, Freud und die Psychoanalyse*, pp. 39, 53–62, and Worbs, pp. 303–20, concur that *Ödipus und die Sphinx* (1906) shows the influence of *The Interpretation of Dreams* in its treatment of the Oedipal myth. I find that the fragmentary drama *Das Leben ein Traum* (1904), which Hofmannsthal adapted from Calderón and which he would eventually rework as *Der Turm*, also warrants consideration as a piece that reflects knowledge of Freud's dream theory. Act 3 of this fragment presents Sigismund's day as a king. In this episode, which is later explained away as a dream, the hitherto imprisoned prince sets about fulfilling his repressed desires in a series of extravagant libidinal outbursts. Although act 3 itself barely differs from the J. D. Gries translation of *La vida es sueño* (*Das Leben ein Traum* [Berlin: Nicolaische Verlagsbuchhandlung, 1868]) that Hofmannsthal used as his source, the previous acts, which Hofmannsthal freely revised, recast Calderón's Segismundo as a psychological character who has been driven half mad by confinement and sexual deprivation. Thus in act 3 itself, where his repressed passions break forth in arrogant language and acts of violence such as attempted rape, we seem not only to witness a "dream" in Calderón's sense, but to peek into the "seething cauldron" of Sigismund's unconscious. Hofmannsthal's published notes show that he was preoccupied with psychological theory when he was writing the play, but they do not point specifically to Freud. Worbs, pp. 295–98, however, persuasively establishes a connection between *Das Leben ein Traum* and *Studies on Hysteria*, evident in the hypnotist/psychoanalyst figure Clotald.

10 Michaela L. Perlmann, *Der Traum in der literarischen Moderne*, a study of Schnitzler's literary dreams exemplary for its thoroughness, draws the same conclusions (pp. 75, 209–10).

11 Perlmann, *Der Traum*, pp. 70–74, extensively discusses the parallels between the two plays.

12   Franz Grillparzer, *Der Traum ein Leben* (Stuttgart: Reclam, 1982), p. 92, my translation.

13   Perlmann, *Der Traum*, p. 83.

14   See for example Frederick J. Beharriell, "Schnitzler's Anticipation of Freud's Dream Theory." More moderate discussions of the parallels between Schnitzler's works and Freud's theories are given by Herbert I. Kupper and Hilda S. Rollman-Branch, "Freud and Schnitzler—(Doppelgänger)," *Journal of the American Psychoanalytic Association* 7 (1959): 109–26, who show parallels between Schnitzler's dramatic form and Freud's concept of psychic conflict, and Bernd Urban, "Aus den Anfängen des 'Doppelgängers.' Zur Differenzierung dichterischer Intuition und Umgebung der frühen Hysterieforschung," *Germanisch-Romanische Monatsschrift* N.F. 24 (1974): 193–223. Wolfgang Nehring, "Schnitzler, Freud's Alter Ego?" *Modern Austrian Literature* 10 (1977): 179–94, who warns against identifying Schnitzler too closely with Freud, discusses parallels and differences, as does Friedrich Hacker, "Im falschen Leben gibt es kein richtiges," *Literatur und Kritik* 163–64 (1982): 36–42. Worbs, *Nervenkunst*, who treats Schnitzler's relationship with Freud exhaustively, finds Beharriell's conclusions, that Schnitzler anticipated Freud's theories of the sexual etiology of the neuroses and of the childhood trauma, exaggerated (pp. 232, 236), but cites *Beatrice* to support Schnitzler's own statement in a 1930 interview with George Sylvester Viereck, "I anticipated the Freudian theory of the dream in my plays" (p. 211). Worbs also notes that the motif of the dream as a wish is already found in Grillparzer's *Der Traum ein Leben* (p. 211).

15   The question of influence is not definitively settled, however, for we know from Ernest Jones's biography that Freud's main thesis was not unknown before he published *The Interpretation of Dreams*. Freud lectured on the topic of the interpretation of dreams to Jewish groups in May 1896 and 1897 (Ernest Jones, *The Life and Work of Sigmund Freud*, 3 vols. [New York: Basic Books, 1965, originally pub. 1953], 1:355). Yet if we look for a source for Schnitzler's lines, Grillparzer seems the more probable choice.

16   Arthur Schnitzler, "Zur Physiologie des Schaffens," *Neue Freie Presse* (Wien, 25 December 1931), my translation.

17   Diary entry of 1 November 1897. (Schnitzler's diaries are in the process of publication: most of what I cite here may be consulted in the Schnitzler-Tagebuch-Stelle of the Österreichische Akademie der Wissenschaften in Vienna.)

18   Diary entry of 12 December 1902, my translation. Schnitzler adds in parentheses, "that's why I hurried up so much to get on with it."

19   Fritsche, *Dekadenz im Werk Arthur Schnitzlers*, makes the same point: "Schnitzlers 'Der Schleier der Beatrice' . . . verrät . . . wie kaum ein anderes seiner Stücke die Nähe des jungen Hofmannsthal" (p. 99).

20   Hofmannsthal, *Gedichte, Dramen I*, p. 46, my translation.

21   This and all other citations from *Der Schleier der Beatrice* variants are from the Schnitzler archive Box 82, University Library at Cambridge, England. The translations are mine.

22   It seems probable that the wild dreams he had in the wake of Mizi Reinhardt's death spurred his interest in a work that offered a key to the meaning of dreams.

23   In later years discussions about dream interpretation stimulate his dreaming: "Very vivid dreams, as I have already sometimes had after pursuits and conversations that have to do with the interpretation of dreams" (diary entry of 6 July 1912, my translation). A plan to visit Freud has a similar effect: "The especial liveliness of the dream could also be due to my intention to visit Freud. (Just as I dreamed unusually much when I read his *Interpretation of Dreams* in 1900.)" (Diary entry of 18 November 1924, my translation.) For statistics on how much Schnitzler dreamed and why, see Perlmann, *Der Traum*, pp. 25, 63, 212.

24   For example, in dreams of 6 July 1912, 9 April 1913, 18 August 1915, 21 October 1922.

25   Reik, *Arthur Schnitzler als Psycholog* (Minden [Westfalen]: J. C. C. Bruns, 1913).

26   Diary entry of 17 September 1912.

27   Kenneth Segar, "Determinism and Character: Arthur Schnitzler's *Traumnovelle* and His Unpublished Critique of Psychoanalysis," *Oxford German Studies* 8 (1973): 118–21; Worbs, *Nervenkunst*, pp. 215, 252–58. Perlmann, *Der Traum*, discusses the differences exhaustively, pp. 36–61 and in most of her interpretations of the fictional dreams.

28   Arthur Schnitzler, "Über Psychoanalyse," ed. Reinhard Urbach, *Protokolle* 2 (1976): 281, my translation.

29   Beharriell, "Schnitzler's Anticipation of Freud's Dream Theory," calls the early, unpublished sketch "Frühlingsnacht im Seziersaal" (Spring night in the dissecting room) of 1880 a work that "demands [psychoanalytic] interpretation and is capable of no other," p. 84, and Worbs, *Nervenkunst*, p. 257, has echoed his conclusion that the dream in this piece is a correctly formed Freudian dream. Beharriell succeeds in showing that the dream *may* be interpreted in Freudian terms; but he certainly does not prove that Schnitzler anticipated Freud's dream theory with this slight early piece. The dream in "Frühlingsnacht im Seziersaal" is different in style from the literary dreams Schnitzler wrote after having read *The Interpretation of Dreams*. It is not a dream that is distorted in the same fashion but, rather, a dream that starts as a semiplausible extension of waking reality (as in *Alkandi's Lied*, Schnitzler does not mark its beginning) and gradually becomes more fantastic, just like the dream in Grillparzer's *Das Leben ein Traum*. It has a Romantic rather than a Freudian flavor, reminding the reader of E. T. A. Hoffmann's fantastic

narratives. By not marking the dream's beginning, Schnitzler plainly intended to tease the reader with the question: What is dream, what reality? Lantin, "Traum und Wirklichkeit," supports this interpretation (p. 141). Ekfelt, "The Narration of Dreams," p. 115, note 3, likewise writes that this dream is "too coherent . . . to be plausible as a real dream." Perlmann, *Der Traum*, pp. 68–69, strongly opposes the psychoanalytic reading, noting that the dream is based on the pre-Freudian theory that dreams arise on account of sensory stimuli. Jandl, *Die Novellen Arthur Schnitzlers*, already goes as far as is necessary in attributing "Freudian" insights to Schnitzler in this early story, asserting that the dream contains, for the dreamer, a recognition of latent love and jealousy, which then influence his life after he wakes up (p. 40).

30   Lantin, "Traum und Wirklichkeit," writing without access to Schnitzler's diaries, dream catalog, or criticisms of Freud, concludes, principally on the basis of textual interpretation, that Schnitzler's literary dreams are formed according to psychoanalytic insights. See pp. 48–76.

31   Perlmann, *Der Traum*, pp. 99–108, lists elements of Freud's dream work that appear in "Frau Berta Garlan." She contends that here as in Schnitzler's other distorted—that is, Freudian dreams—one also sees a strong influence of the pre-Freudian sensory stimulus dream theory.

32   Compare Perlmann, *Der Traum*, p. 31.

33   Jandl, *Die Novellen Arthur Schnitzlers*, pp. 141–42 considers them a dream; Lantin considers them reality. For Lantin, "Traum und Wirklichkeit," they are nonetheless dreamlike: on the basis of an analysis of *Traumnovelle*, pp. 14–24, he concludes that dream and reality in the work overlap inasmuch as both are chaotic (p. 47). Ekfelt, "The Narration of Dreams," believes that Fridolin's adventures are not clearly real, in contrast to his wife's dream, but lie between dream and reality (p. 172). He supports this conclusion with a statistical analysis, which shows that the adventures resemble Schnitzler's dream narration in their high frequency of sensory adjectives and their low ratio of abstract to concrete nouns, and nondream narration in containing high percentages of internal report and dialogue. He concludes that the "dreamlike world" is meant to symbolize "moral chaos" (p. 170). Dorrit Cohn, "A Triad of Dream-Narratives," believes that Schnitzler paired a "psychologically realistic dream and a dream-like fictional reality" (p. 69).

34   Cohn, "A Triad of Dream-Narratives," p. 67.

35   Ill at the time, he could not work up much enthusiasm for the project. In a letter to Suzanne Clauser of 9 September 1931 he wrote: "Work on 'The Second' goes unspeakably slowly; the truth is that I lack all desire to work" (Arthur Schnitzler, *Briefe 1913–1931*, ed. Peter Michael Braunwarth, Richard Miklin, Susanne Pertlik, and Heinrich Schnitzler [Frankfurt a.M.: Fischer, 1984], my translation). On 5 September 1931 Schnitzler had actually begun

rewriting "The Second" as a third-person narrative (there is a draft in the Schnitzler archive in Cambridge, Box 26). He never finished this last version.

36 For such an interpretation, see Lantin, "Traum und Wirklichkeit," who finds explanations for such details as the casino and the Indian (pp. 143–46).

37 Contained in the Schnitzler archive, Box 1–7.

38 *The Interpretation of Dreams*, SE 4:327.

39 An earlier sketch of the dream, dated 23 July 1928, adds here, "I know without any astonishment that I was his opponent in the duel" (Schnitzler archive, Box 26, my translation).

40 *The Interpretation of Dreams*, SE 5:400. Schnitzler had many water dreams himself; after dreams of this type he wrote in a diary entry of 7 November 1922, "Lots of dreams of an erotic nature, with memories of childhood—according to Freud (water . . . *Bad*gasse!) even birth memories, which I consider wrong." In a separate note, he goes into more detail: "Definitely a mistaken doctrine, that water dreams are to be interpreted as birth dreams. Only the events that have entered into our consciousness (and everything that is in our subconscious was once in our actual consciousness; there is no other way into the subconscious; innate subconscious things don't exist; even horror etc. has to be learned) can be used for dream interpretation. When we were still sleeping in the womb we had no consciousness; consequently, it is impossible for us to remember this time. You could just as well—and more logically—interpret such water dreams as the memory of childhood bed-wetting" (my translations).

41 This version reads: "Let's sleep on, sleep into death. —Oh no, that is not granted to us, but something else, down to the lake. We row far out. I let the oars drift, she surrenders herself to me, I press her to me. The canoe turns on its side and we sink into the flood . . ." (Schnitzler archive, Box 26, my translation).

42 Perlmann's reading of "The Second" emphasizes the use of the dream, on the part of both Eissler and Agathe, as a euphemism covering their sexual encounter (*Der Traum*, pp. 204, 207).

43 Many critics have remarked that Kafka's texts are structured like dreams. Thus Theodor W. Adorno, "Notes on Kafka," *Prisms*, trans. Samuel and Shierry Weber (London: N. Spearman, 1967), observes that "Kafka takes dreams *à la lettre*" (p. 248). The analogousness of Kafka's style to the structure of dreams is one of the cornerstones of Walter H. Sokel's reading of Kafka. See Sokel, *Franz Kafka: Tragik und Ironie*, pp. 9–12, also pp. 109–10, 166, 168, 205, 289, 295–96, and Sokel, *Franz Kafka* (New York: Columbia University Press, 1966), esp. pp. 4–9. Other critics who pursue this line of interpretation include in particular Eric Marson and Keith Leopold, "Kafka, Freud, and 'Ein Landarzt,' " *German Quarterly* 37 (1964): 146–60; V. Murrill and W. S. Marks III, "Kafka's 'The Judgment' and *The Interpretation of*

Dreams," Germanic Review 48 (1973): 212–28; Katherine Stockholder, "Franz Kafka, *A Country Doctor:* The Narrator as Dreamer," *American Imago* 35 (1978): 331–46; and Edward Timms, "Kafka's Expanded Metaphors: A Freudian Approach to *Ein Landarzt,*" in *Paths and Labyrinths,* ed. J. P. Stern and J. J. White (London: Institute of Germanic Studies, 1985), p. 67.

44 Franz Kafka, *Tagebücher,* p. 300, my translation.

45 Günther Anders, *Kafka: Pro und Contra,* pp. 39–44.

46 See Peter Handke, *Kaspar* (Frankfurt a.m.: Suhrkamp, 1969), p. 13. For English translation, see Peter Handke, *Kaspar and Other Plays,* trans. Michael Roloff (New York: Farrar, Straus and Giroux, 1969), p. 65.

6   The Transformative Power of Art

1 The principal work that documents this reception is Bahr's *Dialog vom Tragischen* (1904). Wunberg, *Der frühe Hofmannsthal,* p. 25, gives 1899–1900 as the date of Bahr's reception of Mach; Diersch, *Empiriokritizismus und Impressionismus,* p. 69, gives 1903–4; Monti, "Mach und die österreichische Literatur," gives 1902–3. Rainer Hank, *Mortifikation und Beschwörung* (Frankfurt a.M.: Lang, 1984), p. 202, shows, however, that Beer-Hofmann was reading Mach's *Populärwissenschaftliche Vorlesungen* in the summer of 1898, and Wunberg, p. 39, asserts that Hofmannsthal registered for one of Mach's lecture courses in the summer semester of 1897.

2 Wunberg, *Der frühe Hofmannsthal,* p. 31, draws the parallel between Mach's and Hofmannsthal's debunking of the self. Claudio Magris, "Der Zeichen Rost," p. 64, agrees. Judith Ryan, *The Vanishing Subject,* pp. 115–17, sees empiricist influences principally in Hofmannsthal's work of the early 1890s; she finds that he later, in an effort to salvage the notion of self, relegated the permeability of self and world to the psychological phase of preexistence. But Wolfgang Nehring, "Hofmannsthal und der österreichische Impressionismus," *Hofmannsthal-Forschungen* [Freiburg] 2 (1974): 68–69, 193, energetically denies that Hofmannsthal's rejection of the idea of a coherent self, which appears in his work as early as 1890–91, derives from Mach. Claudio Magris and Anton Reininger, "Jung Wien," *Deutsche Literatur: Eine Sozialgeschichte,* vol. 8: *Jahrhundertwende: Vom Naturalismus zum Expressionismus, 1880–1918,* ed. Frank Trommler (Reinbek bei Hamburg: Rowohlt, 1982), p. 232, also see parallels between Mach's debunking of concepts and the Chandos letter. Fritsche, *Dekadenz im Werk Arthur Schnitzlers,* p. 215, compares Mach's philosophy with Schnitzler's skepticism, while Ryan, pp. 128–31, points to Schnitzler's empiricist, presumably Machian, representations of consciousness and the discontinuous self. Diersch, *Empirokritizismus und Impressionismus,* pp. 46–82, passim, gives an account of Bahr's re-

ception of Mach and draws parallels to Schnitzler (e.g., the use of the interior monologue) and Hofmannsthal (e.g., the theme of transitoriness) as well. Monti, "Mach und die österreichische Literatur," p. 268, echoes Diersch in drawing parallels between Mach and Bahr's aesthetic theories in *Die Überwindung des Naturalismus* (1891) and *Studien zur Kritik der Moderne* (1894).

3   On Bahr's 1888–89 trip to Paris, which revolutionized his literary taste, see Rieckmann, *Aufbruch in die Moderne*, pp. 25–26.

4   Hermann Bahr, *Die Überwindung des Naturalismus*, p. 149, my translation.

5   Taine, *On Intelligence*, 1:208.

6   M 1:253, my translation.

7   Critics, echoing Schnitzler himself, call it his "Grundmotiv"; see Singer, "Arthur Schnitzler: 'Der grüne Kakadu,' " pp. 62–63, and Melchinger, *Illusion und Wirklichkeit*, p. 17.

8   Hofmannsthal, *Reden und Aufsätze III*, p. 388, my translation.

9   Melchinger, *Illusion und Wirklichkeit*, p. 17.

10 As Melchinger, ibid., p. 118, puts it succinctly, "Die Schauspieler der Truppe Prospères 'meinen' vielmehr jedes Wort, das sie an ihr Publikum richten, wörtlich. Ihr Spiel ist eine Tarnung, ihre Masken sind Masken, ihre Rollen Rollen, die Täuschung ist Täuschung."

11 Critics have advanced varying arguments. One is that the last days of French absolutism represent the last days of the Austro-Hungarian Empire, where the Viennese, like the French aristocrats in the drama, are dancing on the edge of a volcano (Alfred Doppler, *Wirklichkeit im Spiegel der Sprache* [Wien: Europa-Verlag, 1975], pp. 23–24). Another is that Schnitzler wished to criticize the French Revolution, and revolutions generally, from a conservative point of view (Amy-Diana Colin, "Arthur Schnitzlers 'Der grüne Kakadu,' " *Literatur und Kritik* 124 [1978]: 224–27). Finally, Marianna Squercina, "History and Fiction in a Drama on Revolution: Arthur Schnitzler's *Der grüne Kakadu*," *New German Review* 5–6 (1989–90): 98–108, sees Schnitzler along with Mach and Nietzsche as a "deconstructionist of the fin de siècle" (p. 99), who wished to demonstrate that history dissolves into interpretations.

12 Fritsche, *Dekadenz im Werk Arthur Schnitzlers*, p. 191, offers an interpretation similar to mine.

13 Many critics interpret the end in terms of the world-as-a-stage metaphor, a reading that is compatible with mine. As Hunter G. Hannum, " 'Merely Players': The Theatrical Worlds of Arthur Schnitzler and Jean Genet," in *Festschrift für Bernhard Blume* (Göttingen: Vandenhoeck & Ruprecht, 1967), p. 376, puts it, "History is simply a broader stage than the one to be found in the theater." Melchinger, *Illusion und Wirklichkeit*, p. 124, and Singer, "Arthur Schnitzler: 'Der grüne Kakadu,' " pp. 75–76, interpret the end of the *The Green Cockatoo* in this way: the play will go on, but in the larger

theater of the streets. Gerhart Baumann, "Arthur Schnitzler: Spiel-Figur und Gesellschafts-Spiel," in *Vereinigungen* (München: Fink, 1972), p. 170, also discusses the world-as-a-theater concept in Schnitzler.

14   Hofmannsthal, *Reden und Aufsätze III*, p. 602, my translation.

15   Hofmannsthal, *Dramen V*, p. 41, my translation.

16   Hofmannsthal, *Reden und Aufsätze III*, p. 613, my translation.

17   See Michael Hamburger, "Art as Second Nature," *Romantic Mythologies*, ed. Ian Fletcher (London: Routledge & Kegan Paul, 1967), pp. 226–32, for a discussion of these poems. A further example is found in Hofmannsthal's undated note to a fictitious dialogue, cited by Stern, "Der Briefwechsel Hofmannsthal-Fritz Mauthner," p. 23: "The actor is κατ' ἐξοχήν the self in flux, the always changing exposition" (my translation).

18   Hofmannsthal, *Gedichte, Dramen I*, pp. 72, 74, 79, my translations.

19   Bahr, *Dialog vom Tragischen*, pp. 65,67, my translation.

20   Hofmannsthal, *Dramen V*, p. 21, my translation.

21   Letter to Strauss of 14 February 1924, Richard Strauss, Hugo von Hofmannsthal, *Briefwechsel* (Zürich: Atlantis, 1964), p. 513, my translation.

22   Hofmannsthal, *Dramen V*, p. 297, my translation.

23   Ibid., p. 190, my translation.

24   Ibid., p. 298, my translation.

25   Ibid., p. 197, my translation.

26   Hofmannsthal, *Erzählungen*, p. 503. Robert Mühlher, "Hugo von Hofmannsthals 'Ariadne auf Naxos," *Interpretationen zur österreichischen Literatur des 19. und 20. Jahrhunderts*, ed. Institut für Österreichkunde (Wien: Hirt, 1971), p. 76, draws attention to the parallel between this line from "Das Gespräch über Gedichte" and Bacchus.

27   Karen Forsyth, *Ariadne auf Naxos*, p. 88.

28   Hofmannsthal, *Gedichte, Dramen I*, pp. 76–78, my translation, my italics.

29   Hofmannsthal, *Dramen V*, p. 299, my translation.

30   Forsyth, *Ariadne auf Naxos*, p. 141.

31   Ibid., p. 263.

32   Ibid., p. 262.

33   Hofmannsthal, *Dramen V*, p. 104, my translation.

34   Daviau, "Hugo von Hofmannsthal's *Ariadne auf Naxos*," pp. 54–55, draws attention to the dissimilarity between the prima donna and Ariadne, whereas Zerbinetta, in contrast, always remains the same.

35   Hofmannsthal, *Dramen V*, p. 195, my translation.

36   The parallels between the composer and Ariadne are pointed out by Daviau, "Hugo von Hofmannsthal's *Ariadne auf Naxos*," p. 62, and Forsyth, *Ariadne auf Naxos*, p. 237.

37   Daviau, "Hugo von Hofmannsthals *Ariadne auf Naxos*," pp. 52, 63, notes the similarity between the composer's seduction by Zerbinetta and the Bac-

chus and Circe encounter, but interprets them as parallel (inasmuch as the composer also escapes seduction) rather than as opposite.

38 Johann Wolfgang von Goethe, *Faust I and II*, trans. Stuart Atkins (Boston: Suhrkamp, 1984), p. 301.

39 Kafka, *Diaries 1914–1923*, p. 196.

40 In his excellent chapter on "A Report to an Academy" in *Franz Kafka: Tragik und Ironie*, Sokel contrasts the metamorphosis of Gregor Samsa and Rotpeter at some length, pp. 369–70.

41 For example, Wöllner, *E. T. A. Hoffmann und Franz Kafka*, p. 137; Ralf R. Nicolai, "Nietzschean Thought in Kafka's 'A Report to an Academy,' " *Literary Review* 26 (1983): 553.

42 For example, Klaus-Peter Philippi, *Reflexion und Wirklichkeit*, p. 460, interprets the story as being about the essential difference between animal and man. Such an interpretation of course dislocates the story from the tradition of animal fables, according to which it would be a tale about man (in animal guise), and asserts instead that it is actually a tale about an ape. Kafka's allusions to Darwin's theory of evolution legitimate such a reading.

43 For example, G. Schulz-Behrend, "Kafka's 'Ein Bericht für eine Akademie': An Interpretation," *Monatshefte* 55 (1963): 5; Patrick Bridgwater, "Rotpeters Ahnherren, oder: Der gelehrte Affe in der deutschen Dichtung," *Deutsche Vierteljahrsschrift* 56 (1982): 460.

44 William C. Rubinstein, "Franz Kafka's 'A Report to an Academy,' " *Modern Language Quarterly* 13 (1952): 372–76. Robert Kauf, "Once Again: Kafka's Report to an Academy," *Modern Language Quarterly* 15 (1954): 359–66 believes that the story is about the assimilated (rather than the converted) Jew, as does Robertson, *Kafka*, pp. 164–71.

45 Sokel, pp. 389–90, suggests it briefly. He attaches significance to the fact that the ape is a variety actor: in his view, the ape becomes *merely* an entertainer and hence not a full-fledged human being. Karl-Heinz Fingerhut, *Die Funktion der Tierfiguren im Werke Franz Kafkas: Offene Erzählgerüste und Figurspiele* (Bonn: Bouvier, 1969), pp. 251–53, proposes that the caged ape is a Kafka-type artist, an outsider, who seeks contact with human society (wishes to cease being an ape). Fingerhut, too, stresses the negative connotations of the variety stage. The ape fails to integrate himself into society, for attaining the variety stage only marginalizes him. Wöllner, *E. T. A. Hoffmann und Franz Kafka*, p. 134, also stresses the degrading nature of the variety stage. Philippi, *Reflexion und Wirklichkeit*, pp. 139–47, finally, who develops the topic at much greater length and comes closer to the reading I shall propose, sees no problem in letting "variety stage artist" stand for "artist," as I do not. Philippi believes that the ape's transformation is the transformation into an artist; the ape becomes an artist through existential necessity; and as such he remains on the boundary of the human world, by

definition incapable of overcoming the split between being and consciousness.

46   Frye, "Word Play," pp. 457–75.

47   "A Report to an Academy" and "A Hunger Artist" have been compared sensibly by Sokel, *Franz Kafka: Tragik und Ironie*, pp. 373, 395–98, who sees the protagonists as contrasting artist-types, and by A. P. Foulkes, "Kafka's Cage Image," *Modern Language Notes* 82 (1967): 468–71.

48   K 4:139. My translation of "Ein Bericht für eine Akademie" here and throughout; also my italics.

49   The reader is referred to Lawrence O. Frye's valuable article "Word Play" with its extensive discussion of the word play in this story. Frye focuses on plays on "open-closed" and "large-small." He gives the narrative a chronological reading aimed at explaining the narrator's psychology, which he wishes to account for in terms of psychic mechanisms, development, change, and so on. He explains the function of this word play using Kierkegaard's concept of irony and Freud's ideas of suppression and compensation. Thus in Frye's view, the ape uses word play in order to compensate for his unhappiness at his restriction, at the human life that has been imposed on him. The ape thereby makes the concrete abstract and also pits expressions connoting largeness and openness against ones connoting smallness and enclosure. Frye's interpretation is interesting and convincing, although his contention that the key words move from a concrete to a more abstract level of reference in the course of the story is, I think, not borne out by the text.

50   Compare Stanley Corngold's extensive discussion of Kafka's metaphors in *Franz Kafka: The Necessity of Form* (Ithaca: Cornell University Press, 1988). Corngold's statement that "Kafka perceives that the apparent harmlessness of metaphors in common usage conceals the struggle of wills to make words mean one thing rather than another" (p. 95) is particularly relevant to "A Report to an Academy."

51   Klaus-Peter Philippi, *Reflexion und Wirklichkeit*, presents, as the main thesis of his essay on "A Report to an Academy," a generalized version of this insight. For him, freedom is not something that can be lost by human beings, for it was never part of the human condition to start with. In becoming a man—specifically, in acquiring consciousness—the ape loses his freedom. This reading has the advantage of putting "A Report to an Academy" in a line of descent from the Romantics (one thinks especially of Kleist's "Marionette Theatre" essay, which is certainly subliminally present in the ape's commentary on the trapeze artists) and Nietzsche. The only objection I have to it is that it moves the impetus for the story's central problematic from a personal to an academic level. Everything about the story suggests that at its core is a complaint about being forced to transform oneself into an alien creature, to learn self-deforming tricks in order to survive—as Kafka was forced to spend

his days working for a living when he would rather have been writing, or to compromise with his publisher, for example—a complaint that, to be sure, is surrounded by ironic distancing. Losing one's freedom through consciousness—this is a philosophical abstraction, not a painful personal experience.

52 Gerhard Neumann, " 'Ein Bericht für eine Akademie': Erwägungen zum Mimesis-Charakter Kafkascher Texte," *Deutsche Vierteljahrsschrift* 49 (1975): 166–83, points out that the story is basically about coming to terms with reality and interestingly theorizes the tensions that arise when the ideal of personal effort is put to the service of slavish imitation.

53 Philippi, *Reflexion und Wirklichkeit*, p. 140, my translation.

54 Franz Kafka, *Letters to Friends, Family, and Editors*, p. 334.

55 Philippi, too, stresses the point that the ape's self-assurance is founded on others' acknowledgment of him (*Reflexion und Wirklichkeit*, pp. 134–35).

56 Kafka, *Letter to His Father*, p. 87.

57 Ibid., p. 125.

58 Gustav Janouch, *Conversations with Kafka*, trans. Goronwy Rees (New York: New Directions, 1971), pp. 22–23.

59 Kafka, *Diaries 1914–1923*, p. 102.

60 Thus Frye writes, "Based on the probable date of conception for the *Bericht* (1917), the Kafka year [i.e., the year corresponding to Rotpeter's capture] would be 1912. This was also a year of crisis, with unsuccessful flight and suppression, for Kafka according to his diary for 25 December 1915" ("Word Play," p. 475n). The year 1912 is also an acknowledged turning point in Kafka's literary productivity, the year in which he wrote most of *Amerika*, "Das Urteil," and "The Metamorphosis."

7 Language Crisis and Literary Form

1 K 5:70; my translations here and throughout.

2 Brod, *Franz Kafka als wegweisende Gestalt*, pp. 14–15.

3 This text may also be an ironic commentary on Kafka's own earlier views. Walter H. Sokel, "Kafka's Poetics of the Inner Self," *Modern Austrian Literature* 11, no. 3/4 (1978): 37–58, shows to what extent the early Kafka subscribed to the widespread *Sprachskepsis* of his day. Walter H. Sokel, "Language and Truth in the Two Worlds of Franz Kafka," *German Quarterly* 52 (1979): 364–84, discusses the importance of the idea of a shared communal language for Kafka.

4 The best-known theories of compensatory poetry are those of Mallarmé and his disciple Valéry. But Hofmannsthal articulates the same combination of skepticism in the referential power of language and belief in the expressive power of poetic language in a letter to Edgar Karg von Bebenburg of 18 June 1895 (in Hugo von Hofmannsthal and Edgar Karg von Bebenburg, *Briefwech-*

sel, ed. Mary E. Gilbert [Frankfurt a. M.: Fischer, 1966]]; a more public document on the power of poetry, and the height of his claims for poetry, is "Das Gespräch über Gedichte" (1903).

5   Steven Dowden, "Robinson Crusoe's Banner: Quixotic Nihilism and Moral Imagination in Franz Kafka," *Southern Humanities Review* 24 (1990), writes, "Kafka was not the extreme language critic he is sometimes made out to be. It is true that he frequently grouses about the perfidies of language and the exigencies of writing, but his skepticism, as he explained in a letter to Felice, has limits" (p. 21). Kafka writes in *Letters to Felice*, ed. Erich Heller and Jürgen Born, trans. James Stern and Elisabeth Duckworth (New York: Schocken, 1973), p. 198, "I am not of the opinion that one can ever lack the power to express perfectly what one wants to write or say. Observations on the weakness of language, and comparisons between the limitations of words and the infinity of feelings, are quite fallacious. The infinite feeling continues to be as infinite in words as it was in the heart."

6   In an exceptionally perspicacious article, entitled " 'Words Are Also Deeds' ": Some Observations on Austrian Language Consciousness," *New Literary History* 12 (1981): 509–25, J. P. Stern justifiably attacks, as no Germanist writing on *Sprachskepsis* hitherto has done, the distinction between language and reality that fuels most of the language-conscious thinking of the turn of the century. In Stern's interpretation, Karl Kraus's views are precisely a corrective to this kind of distinction: "From a certain point onward Kraus's work becomes an explicit refutation of the spurious distinction." For Kraus, "a piece of information is not . . . a set of words but an event; a speech is not just a speech but a piece of life" (p. 523). Stern sees two basic lines in Austrian language consciousness. One includes Mauthner and his literary descendants (Hofmannsthal's Chandos letter, Wittgenstein's *Tractatus*; see pp. 519–20). The other leads from Kraus to Wittgenstein of the *Philosophical Investigations*, which "marks the end of an exclusively referential view of language" (p. 525).

7   Mauthner, *Prager Jugendjahre*, pp. 208–15.

8   Many other works by Nietzsche, such as *Human, All Too Human* and *Beyond Good and Evil*, contain language-critical ideas. Paul Requadt, "Sprachverleugnung und Mantelsymbolik im Werke Hofmannsthals," *Deutsche Vierteljahrsschrift* 29 (1955): 255–62, argues persuasively, in one of the best articles on the Chandos letter, that Hofmannsthal's language-critical ideas come from Nietzsche, and Nietzsche's from Georg Christoph Lichtenberg. Schopenhauer, however, should not be overlooked as another source for Nietzsche. Thus in Arthur Schopenhauer, *The World as Will and Representation*, 2 vols., trans. E. F. J. Payne (New York: Dover, 1966), 1:57, we read, "Concepts, with their rigidity and sharp delineation . . . are always incapable of reaching the fine modifications of perception."

9   Oscar Wilde, "The Critic as Artist," in *The Artist as Critic: Critical Writings of Oscar Wilde*, ed. Richard Ellmann (New York: Random House, 1968), p. 359.

10 Mallarmé, "Crise des vers," in *Oeuvres complètes* (Paris: Gallimard, 1945), p. 364, my translation. See the interpretation of the passage in Genette, *Mimologiques*, pp. 271–74.

11 Paul Valéry, *Cahiers*, 2 vols., ed. Judith Robinson (Paris: Gallimard, 1973), 1:382, my translation. Valéry's notebooks are full of such statements, for example, "A mesure que l'on s'approche du réel, on perd la *parole*" (1902?, 1:386), or "Il n'y a ni concepts, ni catégories, ni universaux, ni rien de ce genre" (1902–3; 1:388).

12 Fritz Mauthner, *Beiträge zu einer Kritik der Sprache*, 3 vols. (Stuttgart: Cotta, 1901), 1:49, 107, 46, 10, 41, 84, 149, 180.

13 The interpretation closest to mine in its approach is Kuna, "The Expense of Silence," pp. 69–94.

14 The chief controversy over the Chandos letter, which has attracted an immense amount of commentary, concerns its status: Is it an autobiographical testimony, or a purely literary work? While earlier readings, such as Alewyn's 1949 essay "Hofmannsthals Wandlung," in *Über Hugo von Hofmannsthal*; Paul Kluckhohn, "Die Wende vom 19. zum 20. Jahrhundert in der deutschen Dichtung," *Deutsche Vierteljahrsschrift* 29 (1955): 7–9; Richard Brinkmann, "Hofmannsthal und die Sprache," *Deutsche Vierteljahrsschrift* 35 (1961): 80; Benjamin Bennett, "Werther and Chandos," *Modern Language Notes* 91 (1976): 552–58; and Benjamin Bennett, "Hofmannsthal's Return," in *Germanic Review* 51 (1976): 37–38, consider the work reflective of a language crisis in Hofmannsthal's own life, later ones, such as H. Stefan Schultz, "Hofmannsthal and Bacon: The Sources of the Chandos Letter, *Comparative Literature* 13 (1961): 1–15; Rolf Tarot, *Hugo von Hofmannsthal* (Tübingen: Niemeyer, 1970); Kuna, "The Expense of Silence"; Franz M. Kuna, "Von Barres' Philippe bis zu Philipp Lord Chandos: Die Entwicklung einer Form," in *Peripherie und Zentrum: Studien zur österreichischen Literatur*, ed. Gerlinde Weiss und Klaus Zelewitz (Salzburg: Das Bergland Buch, 1971), pp. 121–35; Joachim Kühn, *Gescheiterte Sprachkritik: Fritz Mauthners Leben und Werk* (Berlin: de Gruyter, 1975), pp. 20–29; Hans Steffen, " 'Wahre Sprachliebe ist nicht möglich ohne Sprachverleugnung': Die Kunstform des Chandos-Briefs," *Germanisch-romanische Monatsschrift*, N.F. 24 (1974): 430–45, emphasize the literariness of the Chandos letter. Stern, "Der Briefwechsel Hofmannsthal—Fritz Mauthner," p. 31, note 5, gives an assessment of the situation that is probably closest to the truth, namely, the letter is both literary and autobiographical.
    About Hofmannsthal's views on language, the following can be said. First, Hofmannsthal repeatedly articulated that language was an inadequate system of reference, which exerts a dangerous influence over thought, from

1891 on. His diary entry of 21 March 1891 contains an extensive comment in that regard. Pestalozzi, *Sprachskepsis und Sprachmagie*, pp. 43–54, documents language skepticism in Hofmannsthal's early poetry. A particularly significant document is the essay "Eine Monographie" of 1895, where Hofmannsthal writes, "Words have placed themselves before things. Hearsay has swallowed the world. . . . We are in possession of a horrible procedure for suffocating thought totally under concepts. . . . When people have become weak and words very strong, the ghostly connections of words triumph over people's naive power of speech." *Reden und Aufsätze I*, pp. 479–80, my translation. Second, in about 1893–94, beginning with the diary entry "2 holy works: the dissolution and the formation of concepts," Hofmannsthal begins to express optimism about poetic language. Particularly in the letter to Edgar Karg von Bebenburg of 18 June 1895, Hofmannsthal tempers his skepticism over the insufficient referential power of language with the opinion that there must be correspondences between the way appearances affect our soul, and combinations of words. This optimism finds further, more radical expression in the "Gespräch über Gedichte" of 1903, where Hofmannsthal affirms the magical power of poetic language. Finally, in the period 1900–1902, by his own account, Hofmannsthal experienced a creative crisis. In a letter to R. A. Schröder of 14 February 1902, he writes of "the terrifying paralysis of my productive powers, which has lasted almost for two years now, with certain deceptive interruptions" (my translation). Before this period Hofmannsthal had achieved his fame primarily as a lyric poet. After it, he decisively changed genres and devoted his energy to drama. Hence it seems probable that the productive crisis in fact marked a drying up of his poetic vein, of the magical sense of language that had motivated his poetry particularly in its greatest period, 1894–97. Hofmannsthal composed the Chandos letter soon after his unproductive period, in August 1902. Thus it seems plausible to conclude, with Requadt, pp. 262–63, and Bert Nagel, "Die Sprachkrise eines Dichters: Zum Chandos-Brief Hugo von Hofmannsthals," in *Antiquitates Indogermanicae*, Gedenkschrift für Hermann Güntert, ed. Manfred Mayrhofer et al. (Innsbruck: Institut für Sprachwissenschaft, 1974), pp. 488–89, that the letter is a stylized form of an immediately preceding crisis in productivity.

15   Foucault, *The Order of Things*, p. 17.

16   Ibid., p. 37.

17   Ibid., p. 50.

18   Aarsleff, *From Locke to Saussure*, p. 22, criticizes Foucault's dating of the new *épistémè* as too early by nearly a century, but he concedes that Bacon offers a critique of resemblance with his theory of "idols" early in his century. Aarsleff also criticizes Foucault's terms "resemblance" (he finds Adamicism a more fundamental quality) and "representation."

19   See Stern, "Der Briefwechsel Hofmannsthal–Fritz Mauthner," p. 33.

20 "The Salon of 1846," in Charles Baudelaire, *Selected Writings on Art and Artists*, trans. P. E. Charvet (Cambridge: Cambridge University Press, 1972), p. 104; "Rockets," in Charles Baudelaire, *My Heart Laid Bare and Other Prose Writings*, ed. Peter Quennell, trans. Norman Cameron (New York: Haskell House, 1975), p. 165.

21 Some explanations proffered by recent critics include the following: Richard Sheppard, "The Crisis of Language," *Modernism*, ed. Malcolm Bradbury and James McFarlane (Harmondsworth: Penguin, 1976), pp. 324–25, asserts that "this overwhelming sense of the imminence of linguistic aridity and imaginative death is an aspect of a much wider socio-cultural problem: the supersession of an aristocratic, semi-feudal, humanistic and agrarian order by one middle-class, democratic, mechanistic and urban." The Chandos letter is cited as an example. C. A. M. Noble, *Sprachskepsis: Über Dichtung der Moderne* (München: text & kritik, 1978), pp. 10–11, asserts that language has not kept pace with quickly changing reality, so that there is a gap between our complex reality and inadequate language. Hartmut Scheible, *Literarischer Jugendstil in Wien* (München: Artemis, 1984), p. 26, believes that the discrepancies between the phraseology of liberalism and political reality were responsible for the language crisis in Austria specifically.

22 Taine, *On Intelligence*, 1:211.

23 Friedrich Nietzsche, *Human, All Too Human*, trans. Marion Faber, with Stephen Lehmann (Lincoln: University of Nebraska Press, 1984), pp. 18–19.

24 Genette, *Mimologiques*, ch. 10.

25 Mauthner, *Prager Jugendjahre*, p. 212, my translation.

26 Ibid., pp. 197–98.

27 Even Schnitzler, who expresses little or no language skepticism before or around the turn of the century, playfully uses the idea that concepts are imprecise and not congruent with reality in *Anatol* (1893), when Anatol expresses reluctance to ask the hypnotized Cora if she is faithful ("this question . . . is not precise enough"), albeit to poke fun at Anatol, who hides his fear of a straightforward negative answer behind sophistical philosophizing (DW 1:36, my translation). For commentary on Schnitzler's language-critical remarks in his later career, see Lantin, *Traum und Wirklichkeit*, p. 42, and Ernst L. Offermanns, *Arthur Schnitzler: Das Komödienwerk als Kritik des Impressionismus* (München: Fink, 1973), pp. 85–90.

28 Hermann Bahr, *Briefwechsel mit seinem Vater*, ed. Adalbert Schmidt (Wien: Bauer-Verlag, 1971), p. 239, my translation. On Bahr's *Sprachskepsis* from 1890 on see Jens Rieckmann, "Hermann Bahr: Sprachskepsis und neue Erzählformen," *Orbis Litterarum* 40 (1985): 80–82.

29 Richard Wagner, *Dichtungen und Schriften*, 10 vols. (Frankfurt a.M.: Insel, 1983), 7:225–26, my translation.

30 Katherine M. Arens, "Linguistic Skepticism: Towards a Productive Defini-

tion," *Monatshefte* 74 (1982): 145–55, likewise finds that language skepticism and language experimentation have the same roots; she finds the reason in the replacement of the Romantic interest in developmental aspects of language by an interest in formal aspects.

31   Hofmannsthal, *Erzählungen*, pp. 498–99, 503, my translation. Marianne Kesting, "Hofmannsthals Krise," in Kesting, *Entdeckung und Destruktion*, pp. 149–50, notes quite rightly that despite his language criticism, Hofmannsthal, essentially because of a weakness of the imagination, uses traditional language and avoids the language revolution—unlike Mallarmé or Rimbaud.

32   Richard T. Gray, "Suggestive Metaphor: Kafka's Aphorisms and the Crisis of Communication," *Deutsche Vierteljahrsschrift* 58 (1984): 465–66, argues that Kafka in his aphoristic texts used "open" metaphors or pure pictures to the same end.

33   Rilke, *Letters 1892–1910*, pp. 124–25.

34   Musil, M 7:972 and *Tagebücher*, 1:934, my translations.

35   Lacan, *Ecrits*, p. 77.

36   Ibid., p. 147.

37   Gauger, "Le Language chez Freud," pp. 189–90, 197, 201, 206.

38   Gauger derives Freud's theories on dreams primarily from the *Introductory Lectures*, shying away, remarkably, from *The Interpretation of Dreams*.

39   For example, in the letters to Wilhelm Fliess (in *Aus den Aufängen der Psychoanalyse*) he considered explaining the problematic choice of neurosis through whether the traumatic sexual scene preceded or followed a child's acquisition of language.

40   The Freudian unconscious has also been subjected to this critique from within the field of psychiatry. Donald P. Spence, *The Freudian Metaphor* (New York: Norton, 1987), argues that the substantive unconscious is a "metaphor" without "evidence of convergent effect or cross-validation" (p. 19), hence an "empty construct" (p. 23) which is "significantly unfalsifiable" (p. 36). In his view it has, as yet, "little hard evidence for its support": "Countless applications of a wrong-headed theory—in the absence of accumulated evidence—add nothing to its validity" (pp. 17, 19). Philosophers of science have consistently been critical of Freud's ideas, including the unconscious. Adolf Grünbaum, *Foundations*, gives an extensive discussion. Grünbaum himself attacks not Freud's metapsychology, which is avowedly "speculative," but rather his clinical theory, which claims scientific status. He shows in particular that the concept of repression—the "cornerstone" of Freud's edifice—is poorly substantiated.

41   Aarsleff, *From Locke to Saussure*, in the chapter "The Tradition of Condillac," pp. 146–209.

42   Max Müller, *Lectures on the Science of Language*, 2 vols. (New York: Scribners, 1865), 2:79.

43 George Romanes, *Mental Evolution in Man: Origin of Human Faculty* (London: Kegan, Paul, Trench, 1888), e.g., p. 73. See also Wilhelm Wundt, *Völkerpsychologie,* (Leipzig: Wilhelm Engelmann, 1900), I (*Die Sprache*), 2. Teil, in the section entitled "Allgemeine Ergebnisse der psychologischen Untersuchung."

44 Freud, *Aus den Anfängen der Psychoanlyse,* p. 453 (my translation).

45 Ibid., p. 186, my translation.

46 The idea was believed (e.g., by Max Müller) to have originated in Locke. In fact, Aarsleff, *From Locke to Saussure,* pp. 66–67, 82, documents that two of Locke's predecessors, Johann Clauberg, *Ars Etymologica Teutonum* (1663) and Pierre Besnier, *Reunion des Langues* (1674), had already argued that words for the operations of the intellect originally referred to sensible things. After Locke, the idea spread. We find it (for example) in Charles De Brosses, in Jean Paul, in Ernest Renan, in Max Müller, in Heymann Steinthal, in Wagner, and in Nietzsche. Finally, it appears in sources that Freud himself cites in his later works or is known to have read: in the Darwin student Romanes; in Rudolf Kleinpaul, *Das Leben der Sprache und ihre Weltstellung.* Bd. I: *Sprache ohne Worte* (Leipzig: Wilhelm Friedrich, 1893); and in Wundt's *Völkerpsychologie.*

47 Lacan's 1953 essay "Function and Field in Speech and Language," in *Ecrits,* p. 58, lists as syntactical displacements ellipsis, pleonasm, hyperbaton, syllepsis, regression, repetition, apposition; and as semantic condensations, metaphor, catachresis, autonomasis, allegory, metonymy, synecdoche. Emile Benveniste's 1956 essay "Remarks on the Function of Language in Freudian Theory," in Benveniste, *Problems in General Linguistics,* p. 75, lists euphemism, allusion, antiphrasis, preterition, litotes, metaphor, symbols, metonymy, synechdoche, ellipsis. Lionel Trilling, in the 1940 essay "Freud and Literature," already declared that "Freudian psychology . . . makes poetry indigenous to the very constitution of the mind," and that "psychoanalysis is . . . a science of tropes, of metaphor and its variants, synecdoche and metonymy." Reprinted in *Freud: A Collection of Critical Essays,* ed. Perry Meisel (Englewood Cliffs NJ: Prentice-Hall, 1981), pp. 107, 108.

48 For example, SE 4:244, 266.

49 Ricoeur, *Freud and Philosophy,* p. 96, points out this discrepancy.

50 For example, in *Introductory Lectures,* SE 15:199, or the paragraph added in 1919 to the section on "Regression" in *The Interpretation of Dreams,* SE 5:548–49. In the 1900 edition of *The Interpretation of Dreams* the idea is possibly implied in Freud's remark that "the dream-work is doing nothing original in making substitutions [of pictorial expressions for abstract ones] of this kind. In order to gain its ends—in this case the possibility of a representation unhampered by censorship—it merely follows the paths which it finds already laid down in the unconscious [im unbewußten Denken]" (SE 5:345–46).

51   Samuel Weber, *The Legend of Freud* (Minneapolis: University of Minnesota Press, 1982, originally pub. 1979), p. 38, argues the same point in terms of the dynamic itself: "For there is another aspect of the primary process that renders its primacy highly questionable: for any cathexis whatsoever to be formed, even the highly mobile cathexes of the primary process, energy must be *bound* to representations so as to insure a minimal reproducibility of those representations, for instance as 'perceptual indentities.' "

52   Freud describes the dream work as "something that is much more bound" ("etwas weit mehr Gebundenes"); SE 5:592 translates this as "with a much narrower connotation."

53   He writes, "The preconscious dream-wish is formed, which gives expression to the unconscious impulse in the material of the preconscious day's residues," and speaks again of "this wishful impulse, which in its essence represents an unconscious instinctual demand and which has been formed in the Pcs. as a dream-wish (a wish-fulfilling phantasy)" (SE 14:226).

54   SE 15:210–11, 225.

55   SE 14:195.

56   SE 15:212.

57   For example, SE 15:172, 179–80, 199, 229–32.

58   Thus in "Remarks on Dream-Interpretation" (1923), Freud writes, "It is as though one had before one a chapter from some work in a foreign language— by Livy, for instance" (SE 19:112).

59   Benveniste, *Problems*, p. 71.

60   Ludwig Wittgenstein, *Lectures and Conversations on Aesthetics, Psychology, and Religious Belief* (Berkeley: University of California Press, n.d.), p. 48.

The bibliography lists only those works that are referred to more than once in the notes.

Primary Texts

Bahr, Hermann. *Dialog vom Tragischen.* Berlin: Fischer, 1904.
———. *Die Überwindung des Naturalismus.* Dresden: C. Pierson, 1981.
Beer-Hofmann, Richard. *Der Tod Georgs.* Stuttgart: Reclam, 1980.
Freud, Sigmund. *Aus den Anfängen der Psychoanalyse.* London: Imago, 1950.
———. *Standard Edition of the Complete Psychological Works of Sigmund Freud.* Translated by James Strachey. 24 vols. London: Hogarth Press, 1953–74.
———. *Studienausgabe.* Edited by Alexander Mitscherlich, Angela Richards, and James Strachey. 10 vols. and Supplement. Frankfurt a.M.: Fischer, 1974–78.
Hofmannsthal, Hugo von. *Briefe 1890–1901.* Berlin: S. Fischer, 1935.
———. *Briefe 1900–1909.* Wien: Bermann Fischer Verlag, 1937.
———. *Gesammelte Werke in zehn Einzelbänden* (Frankfurt a.M.: Fischer): *Gedichte, Dramen I* (1979); *Dramen II* (1979); *Dramen V. Operndichtungen* (1979); *Erzählungen, Erfundene Gespräche und Briefe, Reisen* (1979); *Reden und Aufsätze II* (1979); *Reden und Aufsätze III, Aufzeichnungen* (1980).
———. *Plays and Libretti.* Edited by Michael Hamburger. New York: Pantheon, 1963.
———. *Poems and Verse Plays.* Edited by Michael Hamburger. London: Routledge & Kegan Paul, 1961.
———. *Selected Prose.* Translated by Mary Hottinger, Tania Stern, and James Stern. New York: Pantheon, 1952.
Kafka, Franz. *The Complete Stories.* Edited by Nahum N. Glatzer. New York: Schocken Books, 1976.
———. *The Diaries of Franz Kafka 1914–1923.* Edited by Max Brod. New York: Schocken, 1949.

———. *Gesammelte Werke.* Taschenbuchausgabe in 7 Bänden. Frankfurt a.M.: Fischer, 1976.

———. *Letters to Friends, Family, and Editors.* Translated by Richard and Clara Winston. New York: Schocken, 1978.

———. *Letter to His Father. Brief an den Vater.* Translated by Ernst Kaiser and Eithne Wilkins. New York: Schocken, 1966.

———. *Tagebücher.* N.p: Fischer, 1967.

Mach, Ernst. *Knowledge and Error.* Translated by Thomas J. McCormack. Dordrecht, The Netherlands: D. Reidel, 1976.

Mauthner, Fritz. *Beiträge zu einer Kritik der Sprache.* 3 vols. Stuttgart: Cotta, 1901–2.

———. *Prager Jugendjahre: Erinnerungen.* Frankfurt a.M.: Fischer, 1969.

Musil, Robert. *Five Women.* Translated by Eithne Wilkins and Ernst Kaiser. New York: Delacorte, 1966.

———. *Gesammelte Werke in neun Bänden.* Edited by Adolf Frisé. Reinbek bei Hamburg: Rowohlt, 1978.

———. *The Man without Qualities.* Translated by Eithne Wilkins and Ernst Kaiser. 3 vols. London: Pan Books, 1988.

———. *Tagebücher.* Edited by Adolf Frisé. 2 vols. Reinbek bei Hamburg: Rowohlt, 1983.

———. *Young Törless.* New York: Pocket Books, 1978.

Nietzsche, Friedrich. *On the Advantage and Disadvantage of History for Life.* Translated by Peter Preuss. Indianapolis: Hackett, 1980.

———. *Sämtliche Werke in zwölf Bänden.* Stuttgart: Kroner, 1964.

Rilke, Rainer Maria. *Letters of Rainer Maria Rilke 1892–1910.* Translated by Jane Ballard Greene and M. D. Herter Norton. New York: Norton, 1969.

———. *Sämtliche Werke.* 12 vols. Frankfurt a.M.: Insel, 1976.

Schnitzler, Arthur. *Anatol: Living Hours; The Green Cockatoo.* Translated by Grace Isabel Colbron. Great Neck NY: Core Collection Books, 1977.

———. *Gesammelte Werke in Einzelausgaben* (Frankfurt a.M.: Fischer, 1977–79. *Das erzählerische Werk* (7 vols.); *Das dramatische Werk* (8 vols.).

———. *Illusion and Reality. Plays and Stories of Arthur Schnitzler.* Translated by Paul F. Dvorak. New York: Lang, 1986.

———. "Über Psychoanalyse." Edited by Reinhard Urbach. *Protokolle* 2 (1976): 277–84.

Taine, Hippolyte. *On Intelligence.* Edited by Daniel N. Robinson. Translated by T. D. Haye. 2 vols. Washington DC: University Publications of America, 1977.

Wittgenstein, Ludwig. *Tractatus logico-philosophicus.* Translated by D. F. Pears and B. F. McGuinness. London: Routledge & Kegan Paul, 1961.

Secondary Literature

Aarsleff, Hans. *From Locke to Saussure.* Minneapolis: University of Minnesota Press, 1982.

Alewyn, Richard. *Über Hugo von Hofmannsthal.* Göttingen: Vandenhoeck und Ruprecht, 1958.

Anders, Günther. *Kafka: Pro und Contra.* München: C. H. Beck, 1951.

Baumann, Gerhart. "Hugo von Hofmannsthal: 'Elektra.' " In *Hugo von Hofmannsthal. Wege der Forschung* vol. 183, edited by Sibylle Bauer, pp. 274–310. Darmstadt: Wissenschaftliche Buchgesellschaft, 1968. First published in *Germanisch-Romanische Monatsschrift* N.F. 9 (1959): 157–82.

Beharriell, Frederick J. "Schnitzler's Anticipation of Freud's Dream Theory." *Monatshefte* 45 (1953): 81–89.

Benveniste, Emile. *Problems in General Linguistics.* Coral Gables: University of Miami Press, 1971.

Brod, Max. *Franz Kafka als wegweisende Gestalt.* St. Gallen: Tschudy, 1951.

Butler, E. M. "Hoffmannsthal's [sic] 'Elektra': A Graeco-Freudian Myth." *Journal of the Warburg Institute* 2 (1938–39): 164–75.

Cohn, Dorrit. "A Triad of Dream-Narratives: *Der Tod Georgs, Das Märchen der 672. Nacht, Traumnovelle.*" In *Focus on Vienna 1900,* edited by Erika Nielsen, pp. 58–71. München: Fink, 1982.

Corino, Karl. "Ödipus oder Orest? Robert Musil und die Psychoanalyse." In *Vom "Törleß" zum "Mann ohne Eigenschaften."* Edited by Uwe Baur and Dietmar Goltschnigg, pp. 123–235. München: Fink, 1973.

———. *Robert Musils "Vereinigungen."* München: Fink, 1974.

Daviau, Donald G. "Hugo von Hofmannsthal's *Ariadne auf Naxos:* An Analysis and Interpretation of the 'Vorspiel.' " *Modern Austrian Literature* 6, nos. 1 & 2 (1973): 41–71.

Diersch, Manfred. *Empiriokritizismus und Impressionismus.* Berlin: Rütten & Loening, 1973.

Ekfelt, Nils. "The Narration of Dreams in the Prose Works of Thomas Mann and Arthur Schnitzler: A Stylistic Study." Ph.D. diss., Indiana University, 1973.

Fischer, Jens Malte. "Richard Beer-Hofmann: 'Der Tod Georgs.' " *Sprachkunst* 2 (1971): 211–27.

Forsyth, Karen. *Ariadne auf Naxos by Hugo von Hofmannsthal and Richard Strauss: Its Genesis and Meaning.* Oxford: Oxford University Press, 1982.

Foucault, Michel. *The Order of Things.* New York: Random House, 1970.

Frye, Lawrence O. "Word Play: Irony's Way to Freedom in Kafka's 'Ein Bericht für eine Akademie.' " *Deutsche Vierteljahrsschrift* 55 (1981): 457–75.

Fritsche, Alfred. *Dekadenz im Werk Arthur Schnitzlers*. Bern: Lang, 1974.

Gauger, Hans Martin. "Le Langage chez Freud." *Confrontations psychiatriques* 19 (1981): 189–213.

Genette, Gérard. *Mimologiques*. Paris: Seuil, 1976.

Grünbaum, Adolf. *The Foundations of Psychoanalysis: A Philosophical Critique*. Berkeley: University of California Press, 1984.

Henninger, Peter. *Der Buchstabe und der Geist*. Frankfurt a.M.: Lang, 1980.

Jandl, Ernst. "Die Novellen Arthur Schnitzlers." Ph.D. diss., Wien, 1950.

Jens, Walter. *Hofmannsthal und die Griechen*. Tübingen: Max Niemeyer Verlag, 1955.

Kesting, Marianne. *Entdeckung und Destruktion*. München: Fink, 1970.

Kuna, Franz. "The Expense of Silence. Sincerity and Strategy in Hofmannsthal's 'Chandos Letter.' " *Publications of the English Goethe Society* N.S., 40 (1970): 69–94.

Lacan, Jacques. *Ecrits: A Selection*. Translated by Alan Sheridan. New York: Norton, 1977.

Lantin, Rudolf. "Traum und Wirklichkeit in der Prosadichtung Arthur Schnitzlers." Ph.D. diss., Köln, 1958.

Laplanche, L., and J.-B. Pontalis. *The Language of Psycho-Analysis*. Translated by Donald Nicholson-Smith. New York: Norton, 1973.

Magris, Claudio. "Der Zeichen Rost." *Sprachkunst* 6 (1975): 53–74.

Melchinger, Christa. *Illusion und Wirklichkeit im dramatischen Werk Arthur Schnitzlers*. Heidelberg: Carl Winter, 1968.

Monti, Claudia. "Mach und die österreichische Literatur: Bahr, Hofmannsthal, Musil." *Akten des Internationalen Symposiums "Arthur Schnitzler und seine Zeit,"* pp. 263–83. Bern: Lang, 1985.

Perlmann, Michaela L. *Der Traum in der literarischen Moderne. Untersuchungen zum Werk Arthur Schnitzlers*. München: Fink, 1987.

Pestalozzi, Karl. *Sprachskepsis und Sprachmagie im Werk des jungen Hofmannsthal*. Zürich: Atlantis, 1958.

Philippi, Klaus-Peter. *Reflexion und Wirklichkeit. Untersuchungen zu Kafkas Roman "Das Schloß."* Tübingen: Niemeyer, 1966.

Politzer, Heinz. "Hugo von Hofmannsthal's 'Elektra': Geburt der Tragödie aus dem Geiste der Psychopathologie." *Deutsche Vierteljahrsschrift* 47 (1973): 95–119.

Reniers-Servranckx, Annie. *Robert Musil: Konstanz und Entwicklung von Themen, Motiven und Strukturen in den Dichtungen*. Bonn: Bouvier, 1972.

Ricoeur, Paul. *Freud and Philosophy*. Translated by Denis Sauvage. New Haven: Yale University Press, 1970.

Rieckmann, Jens. *Aufbruch in die Moderne*. Königstein: Athenäum, 1985.

Robertson, Ritchie. *Kafka: Judaism, Politics, and Literature*. Oxford: Clarendon Press, 1985.

Ryan, Judith. *The Vanishing Subject: Early Psychology and Literary Modernism.* Chicago: University of Chicago Press, 1991.

Schorske, Carl E. *Fin-de-Siècle Vienna.* New York: Knopf, 1980.

Singer, Herbert. "Arthur Schnitzler: 'Der grüne Kakadu.' " In *Das deutsche Lustspiel* II, edited by Hans Steffen, pp. 61–78. Göttingen: Vandenhoeck & Ruprecht, 1969.

Sokel, Walter H. *Franz Kafka: Tragik und Ironie.* Frankfurt a.M.: Fischer, 1976. First published by Albert Langen Georg Muller Verlag, München, 1964.

Stern, Martin. "Der Briefwechsel Hofmannsthal—Fritz Mauthner." *Hofmannsthal Blätter* 19/20 (1978): 509–25.

Sussman, Henry. "The All-Embracing Metaphor: Reflections on Kafka's 'The Burrow.' " *Glyph* I (1977): 100–131.

Urban, Bernd. *Hofmannsthal, Freud und die Psychoanalyse.* Frankfurt a.M.: Lang, 1978.

Wagenbach, Klaus. *Franz Kafka, Eine Biographie seiner Jugend, 1883–1912.* Bern: Francke, 1958.

Wöllner, Günter. *E. T. A. Hoffmann und Franz Kafka: Von der "fortgeführten Metapher" zum "sinnlichen Paradox."* Bern: Paul Haupt, 1971.

Worbs, Michael. *Nervenkunst.* Frankfurt a.M.: Europäische Verlagsanstalt, 1983.

Wunberg, Gotthart. *Der frühe Hofmannsthal: Schizophrenie als dichterische Struktur.* Stuttgart: Kohlhammer, 1965.

INDEX